BITTER WAR
OF MEMORY

———— ————

BITTER WAR OF MEMORY

The Babyn Yar Massacre, Aftermath, and Commemoration

Victoria Khiterer

Purdue University Press • West Lafayette, Indiana

Copyright 2025 by Victoria Khiterer. All rights reserved.
Printed in the United States of America.

Cataloging-in-Publication Data is available from the Library of Congress.
978-1-62671-112-9 (hardback)
978-1-62671-113-6 (paperback)
978-1-62671-114-3 (epub)
978-1-62671-115-0 (epdf)

Cover: *Menorah* monument at Babyn Yar memorial complex, place of massacres carried out by German forces during World War II. (Sckrepka / iStock Editorial via Getty Images Plus)

To the Memory of Yevgeny Yevtushenko

CONTENTS

	List of Maps and Illustrations	*ix*
	Acknowledgments	*xi*
	Maps	*xv*
	Introduction	1
1.	Kyivan Jews in the Interwar Period	9
2.	The Babyn Yar Massacre: The Holocaust of Jews in Kyiv	39
3.	Other Victims of the Nazi Regime in Kyiv	67
4.	Jewish Life and Anti-Semitism in Postwar Kyiv	97
5.	Aftermath of the Babyn Yar Massacre	123
6.	Broken Silence over Babyn Yar	152
7.	Babyn Yar Commemoration in Independent Ukraine	202
	Conclusion	221
	Notes	*227*
	Bibliography	*271*
	Index	*291*
	About the Author	*305*

ILLUSTRATIONS

MAPS

Map 1. Eastern Europe 1933, Kyiv indicated.	xv
Map 2. Einsatzgruppen massacres in Eastern Europe, Babyn Yar indicated.	xv
Map 3. Kyiv environs.	xvi
Map 4. Babyn Yar massacre in Kyiv, 1941.	xvi

FIGURES

Figure 1.1. Khreshchatyk Street, Kyiv, 1941.	10
Figure 2.1. Babyn Yar before World War II.	41
Figure 2.2. Portrait of three-year-old Anna Glinberg, a Jewish child who was killed at Babyn Yar.	50
Figure 2.3. Portrait of four-year-old Malvina Babat and three-year-old Polina Babat, who were killed at Babyn Yar.	50
Figure 3.1. Soviet prisoners of war covering the bodies of Jews killed at Babyn Yar.	75
Figure 4.1. Liberation of Kyiv, Khreshchatyk Street, November 1943.	98
Figure 4.2. Kharkiv Ukrainian Theater poster for *Tevye the Dairyman*, Kyiv, 1947.	99
Figure 5.1. A press party being taken through the Babyn Yar site after the liberation of Kyiv.	127
Figure 5.2. In liberated Kyiv, Jewish prisoners of war who escaped from Babyn Yar: Efim Vilkis, Leonid Ostrovsky, and Vladimir Davydov, 1943.	129
Figure 5.3. W. H. Lawrence's article "Little Evidence Supports Story of Nazi Atrocity" published in the *Buffalo Courier-Express* on November 29, 1943.	130
Figure 5.4. Dina Pronicheva, a Jewish survivor of the Babyn Yar massacre, testifies about her experiences during a war crimes trial in Kyiv.	132
Figure 5.5. Defendant Paul Blobel is sentenced to death by hanging at the Einsatzgruppen trial.	135
Figure 5.6. Vasily Ovchinnikov, *September 29*.	148

Figure 5.7. Vasily Ovchinnikov, *Road of the Doomed*. 148
Figure 6.1. *Babyn Yar Monument* model by Kyiv city architect A. Vlasov and sculptor E. Kruglov, 1945. 155
Figure 6.2. *Babyn Yar Monument* model detail, 1945. 156
Figure 6.3. Babyn Yar in 1959. 159
Figure 6.4. Mud flood from Babyn Yar into Kyiv, March 1961. 162
Figure 6.5. Book cover: Yevgeny Yevtushenko, *The Most Famous Symphony of the 20th Century. Dmitri Shostakovich Symphony #13*. 164
Figure 6.6. Anatoly Kuznetsov, author of *Babi Yar: A Document in the Form of a Novel*, 1966. 166
Figure 6.7. *Babyn Yar Monument* model by Iosif Karakis from the 1965 competition. 168
Figure 6.8. *Babyn Yar Monument* model by Avraam Miletskii, Ada Rybachuk, and Vladimir Mel'nychenko from the 1965 competition. 168
Figure 6.9. Victor Nekrasov at an unsanctioned meeting at Babyn Yar on September 24, 1966. 170
Figure 6.10. Unsanctioned meeting at Babyn Yar on September 29, 1966. 172
Figure 6.11. Official ceremony at the Babyn Yar Massacre stone marker, late 1960s–early 1970s. 174
Figure 6.12. 1976 Babyn Yar monument detail. 189
Figure 6.13. 1976 Babyn Yar monument detail. 191
Figure 6.14. 1976 Babyn Yar monument detail. 195
Figure 6.15. Dedication of Soviet monument at Babyn Yar, July 2, 1976. 196
Figure 6.16. Dedication of Soviet monument at Babyn Yar, July 2, 1976. 197
Figure 7.1. Memorial *Menorah*, 1991. 203
Figure 7.2. Memorial to the children killed at Babyn Yar, 2001. 204
Figure 7.3. *The Roma Wagon* monument, opened September 23, 2016. 204
Figure 7.4. The *Mirror Field* memorial at Babyn Yar, opened September 29, 2020. 212
Figure 7.5. The 80th anniversary commemoration of the Babyn Yar massacre. 214
Figure 7.6. Russian attack on Babyn Yar, March 1, 2022. 216

ACKNOWLEDGMENTS

I BEGAN TO WORK ON MY BOOK DURING THE COVID-19 PANDEMIC AND COMpleted it during the Russian war against Ukraine and the Hamas-Israeli war. Unfortunately, the world did not become a better place during those years. I felt distracted many times by the horrible news, and I continuously worried about my relatives and friends who are living in Ukraine and Israel. But I felt that it is my duty to complete this monograph as a tribute to all Kyivans who perished at Babyn Yar, and as a tribute for those who struggle to preserve the memory of the Holocaust of Jews in Kyiv.

I really appreciate the support of my colleagues in my work. I am very grateful to Professor Antony Polonsky, who read the draft of my monograph and suggested excellent improvements. I received lots of valuable information on the debates and publications about the commemoration of the Babyn Yar massacre from my colleagues at the Babyn Yar Holocaust Memorial Center (BYHMC) in Kyiv and from Professor Wolf Moskovich. I really appreciate their help. I am very grateful to the deputy CEO of the BYHMC, Anna Furman, who provided copies of archival materials and sent me new books about the Holocaust published by the BYHMC.

I joined the BYHMC as a founding member of the Academic Council and worked on the historical narrative for the future Babyn Yar Holocaust Memorial Museum with my colleagues Dr. Karel Berkhoff, Dr. Martin Dean, Dr. Vladyslav Hrynevych, Dr. Aleksandr Kruglov, and Mr. Mikhail Kalnitsky. Our meetings and discussions about the Babyn Yar massacre and its commemoration gave me lots of valuable information for my book. I am also grateful to my colleagues at the Center for the Studies of History and Culture of East European Jewry and its director, Leonid Finberg, for providing their archival materials for my research.

In 2021, Ruslan Kavatsiuk, then the deputy director-general of the BYHMC, invited me to participate in the official commemoration ceremony devoted to the eightieth anniversary of the Babyn Yar massacre and the international conference "The Mass Shooting During the Holocaust as a Criminal Process." I really appreciate this opportunity. My meetings and discussions of my work with my colleagues gave me many new ideas for this monograph. I incorporated in my work my eyewitness experience of the very impressive commemoration ceremony devoted to the eightieth anniversary of the Babyn Yar massacre.

I am grateful to Dr. Ieva Zake, dean of the College of Arts, Humanities and Social Sciences, Millersville University, who allowed me to travel to Kyiv in the middle of the semester to attend the commemoration ceremony. Millersville University provided several travel grants for me to conduct my research in Ukrainian, Israeli, and US archives. I first presented my monograph as a work-in-progress at Millersville University. I am grateful to my colleagues Dr. Katarzyna Jakubiak and Dr. Justin Mando for organizing my presentation and their feedback on my talk.

I researched documents for this monograph in four Ukrainian archives in Kyiv: the Sectoral State Archive of the Security Services of Ukraine (HDA SBU), the Central State Archives of Public Organizations of Ukraine (TsDAHO U), the Central State Archive of the Supreme Bodies of Power and Government of Ukraine (TsDAVO U), and the Central State CinePhotoPhono Archives of Ukraine (TsDKFFA U). I also researched documents in the Yad Vashem Archive and the Central Archives for the History of the Jewish People (CAHJP) in Israel and at the United States Holocaust Memorial Museum Archive in Washington, DC. I would like to express my gratitude to the archival workers, who helped me to find and copy the documents necessary for my monograph.

Unfortunately, Russian state archives have become inaccessible for Western researchers due to the political situation. I used a few documents from the Russian state archives that are available online. I really appreciate the help of the first vice president of the Federation of Jewish Organizations and Communities—VAAD of Russia, Natasha Schmidt, who provided documents from the Archive of VAAD about Babyn Yar commemorations.

I was fortunate to meet with the renowned Russian poet Yevgeny Yevtushenko and talk about the creation of his poem "Babi Yar." He was the keynote speaker at the Millersville University Conference on the Holocaust and Genocide in 2010, which I helped organize as a Conference Committee member. Yevtushenko's story about the creation of the poem "Babi Yar" and his presentation of this and other poems at the conference made a great impression. I grew up in the Soviet Union in the 1970s–80s, and I remember the poisonous anti-Semitic atmosphere. Only courageous people challenged state and popular anti-Semitism, and publicly expressed their compassion for Jews. Everyone who did this risked their careers and were harassed by anti-Semites as Jew-supporters and national traitors. Yevtushenko wrote his poem "Babi Yar" because he despised chauvinists and anti-Semites, and he wanted to focus the attention of society on the absence of a monument at the largest Holocaust site in the Soviet Union. I devote my book to the memory of Yevgeny Yevtushenko.

I am grateful to Kyiv Jewish activist Emanuel Diamant, who shared with me his memories about the organization of two unauthorized commemoration meetings at Babyn Yar in 1966, devoted to the twenty-fifth anniversary of the massacre. He was a key person in organizing these events. Diamant gathered a valuable collection of materials about the commemoration of the Babyn Yar massacre and donated this collection to the Central Archives for the History of the Jewish People in Jerusalem. These materials, Diamant's memories, and his memoirs became important sources for my work.

In 2021, I conducted twelve interviews with Kyivans-Holocaust survivors for the BYHMC. They shared with me their memories about their escape from Kyiv to the Soviet interior, life in evacuation, and return to Kyiv after the war. I learned a lot from their unique experiences and incorporated this information into my book. My parents, Mikhail Khiterer and Ludmila Brovarnik, were among those whom I interviewed. I am very grateful indeed to everybody who shared their memories with me.

I also used in my book the memories of my late grandparents about their evacuation and return to Kyiv. The memories of my maternal grandmother, Evgenia (Gitel) Brovarnik, about her escape with my two-year-old mother from Kyiv in August 1941, when the Nazis were already on the outskirts of the city, made me aware of the Babyn Yar tragedy from my childhood.

I am grateful to my husband, James E. Danaher, who was the first reader of my monograph, for his corrections and edits. I really appreciate his moral support and encouragement during my work on this book.

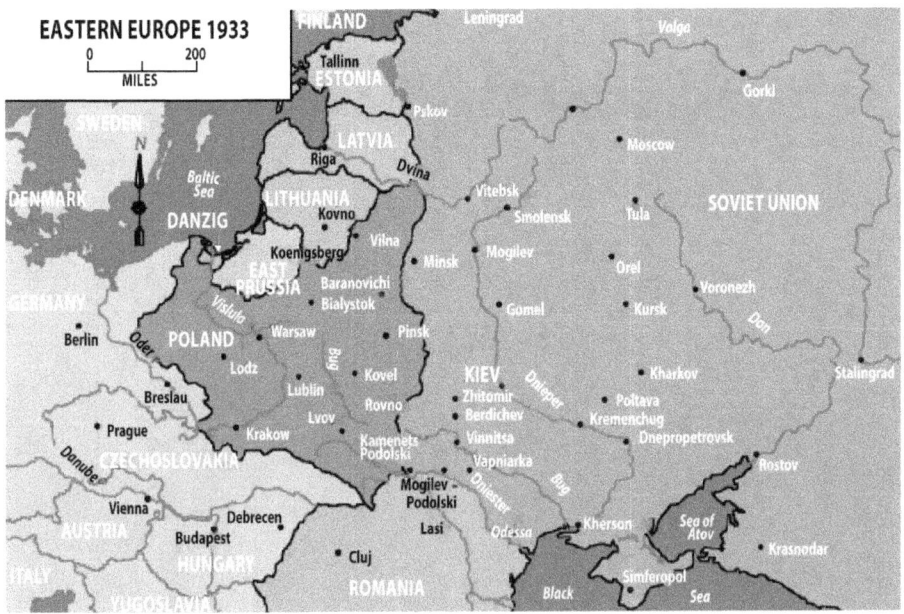

Map 1 Eastern Europe 1933, Kiev (Kyiv) indicated. (Courtesy of the United States Holocaust Memorial Museum.)

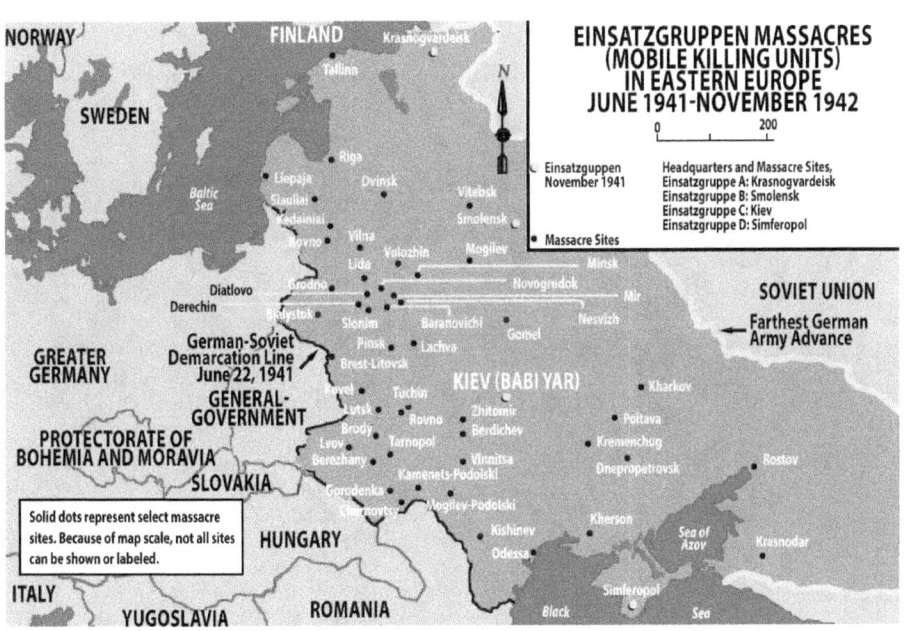

Map 2 Einsatzgruppen massacres in Eastern Europe, Babi Yar (Babyn Yar) indicated. (Courtesy of the United States Holocaust Memorial Museum.)

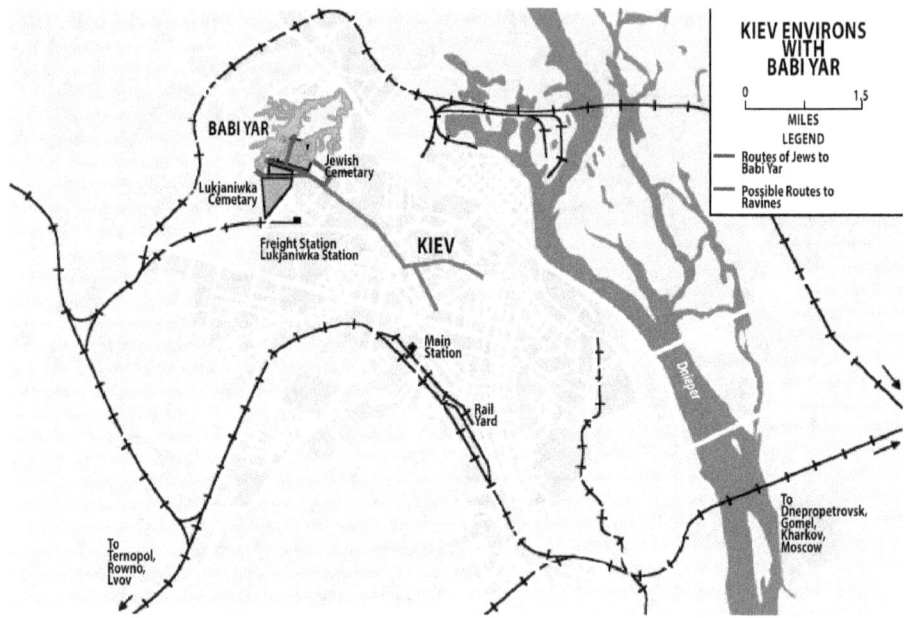

Map 3 Kiev (Kyiv) environs. (Courtesy of the United States Holocaust Memorial Museum.)

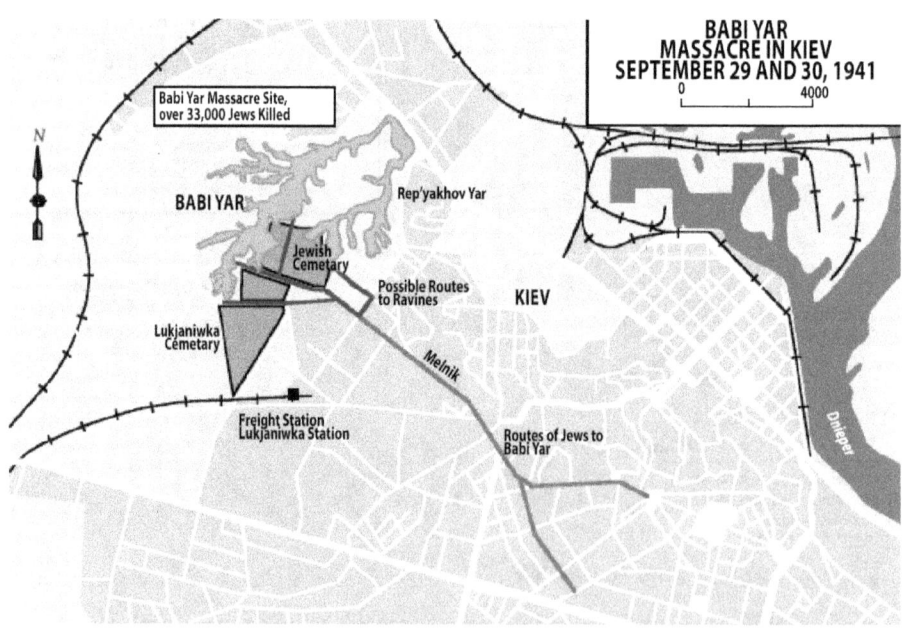

Map 4 Babi Yar (Babyn Yar) massacre in Kyiv, 1941. (Courtesy of the United States Holocaust Memorial Museum.)

INTRODUCTION

I WAS BORN AND GREW UP IN KYIV IN A JEWISH FAMILY AND THE SHADOW OF Babyn Yar has loomed large in my life. In my childhood, I heard many times my grandmother's story about how she, with my then two-year-old mother, escaped from Kyiv on the last train to evacuation when the Nazis were already on the outskirts of the city. She told me about her family members, relatives, and friends who perished at Babyn Yar. Thus, Babyn Yar always was for me a place of the greatest tragedy of Kyivan Jews.

I was astonished and shocked by my childhood friend's Babyn Yar story. Her high school teacher took her senior class to Babyn Yar to commemorate the "victims of fascism" in 1985. As soon as the class arrived at the Soviet Babyn Yar monument to "over one hundred thousand Kyivans and prisoners of war killed in 1941–43 by German fascists," some of her classmates played cheerful music and began to dance. Certainly, sixteen- and seventeen-year-old youth knew full well about the Babyn Yar massacre, and that most of its victims were Jews. Thus, they understood that they were dancing on a mass grave, and this was a public demonstration of their attitude toward the Holocaust of Jews in Kyiv. Unfortunately, this was not an unusual scene at Babyn Yar in Soviet times. The Russian-Jewish poet and playwright Alexander Galich wrote in 1969 in his poem "Zasypaia i prosypaias'" (Falling asleep and waking up) that "laughter and music sounds over Babyn Yar."[1]

Soviet propaganda since World War II emphasized that Babyn Yar is a site of the universal tragedy of the Soviet people and that the Nazis killed thousands of prisoners of war and peaceful Soviet citizens there. But all the efforts of Soviet propaganda to obscure the fact that most victims at Babyn Yar were Jews never succeeded. The truth was known by all Kyivans, including the high school students, and by many people in the Soviet Union and abroad. However, attitudes toward the massacre of Jews at Babyn Yar varied: deep grief of those who lost their relatives and friends, compassion of other Jews and liberal gentile intelligentsia, and expressions of satisfaction by anti-Semites. For many years after the war, Kyivan anti-Semites harassed Jews by telling them that Babyn Yar would be the most appropriate place for all of them. I heard this several times in my childhood and youth: "Too bad the Nazis didn't kill all Jews at Babyn Yar."

My monograph explains why the largest massacre of Jews in the Soviet Union occurred in Kyiv. It shows how long-lasting anti-Semitic traditions in the city prepared the appropriate grounds for the massacre. My book reveals why most Jews who remained in Kyiv during the Nazi occupation perished at Babyn Yar and only a very few escaped. It analyzes the justifications for the murder of Jews of the Nazi perpetrators and their local collaborators, as well as the attitude of the local gentile population toward the massacre.

This work explores postwar state-sponsored and popular anti-Semitism in Kyiv, and Holocaust denial. This is key for understanding why the Soviet authorities for many years after the war refused to admit that most of the victims at Babyn Yar were Jews and refused to build a monument at Babyn Yar. When the Soviet monument was finally built at Babyn Yar in 1976, it was distorted by censorship to fit the Soviet concept of the Babyn Yar massacre as the universal suffering of "Soviet people" during World War II. My monograph shows the struggle of Jews and gentile liberal intelligentsia for commemoration and memorialization of the Babyn Yar tragedy, which became a symbol of the Holocaust for the entire Soviet Union.

The book also explores the commemoration and memorialization of the Babyn Yar massacre in independent Ukraine. The work describes the new monuments that have been built at the site after the collapse of communism. It analyzes the heated debates and different approaches to memorialization of the Babyn Yar massacre in modern Ukraine. My book shows the impact of the Russian-Ukrainian war on Babyn Yar commemoration and explores the prospects for future memorialization of the Babyn Yar massacre.

HISTORIOGRAPHY AND SOURCES

The Babyn Yar massacre and the commemoration and memorialization of the Holocaust of Jews in Kyiv deserve more attention in historical literature than they have received. The modest amount of scholarly literature on the topic can be explained by the Soviet policy of state anti-Semitism and Holocaust denial from the late 1940s until the late 1980s. Research on the Holocaust and Jewish history was forbidden in the

Soviet Union in those years, and Jewish collections in archives were classified. After the collapse of communism, most documents on the Holocaust and Jewish history were opened for researchers.

There are several books, articles, and collections of documents published by Ukrainian, American, and Russian historians, journalists, and writers on the Holocaust of Jews at Babyn Yar. The first monograph on the topic was written by Alexander Shlaien in 1985 but was not published until a decade later in 1995 because Soviet censorship did not allow any publications on the Holocaust. The strong point of Shlaien's work is that during its preparation some Babyn Yar survivors and witnesses were still alive, and Shlaien interviewed them and incorporated their memories into his book. But at the same time, his work includes many Soviet stereotypes and concepts.[2]

The monograph by Sergiy Karamash, *Babyn yar—u tragichnykh podiiakh 1941–1943 rokiv. Istoria i Suchasnist' (istoriko-arkhivne doslidzhennia)* (Babyn Yar in the tragic events of 1941–1943: History and present [historical-archival research]), is based on documents from Kyivan archives.[3] Karamash describes the victims of Babyn Yar: Jews, Roma, Soviet prisoners of war, Ukrainian nationalists, and mentally ill people. There is valuable information, especially the testimony of eyewitnesses. However, Karamash believes that Jews comprised less than half of all victims at Babyn Yar. Using the number of victims that the Soviets provided for the Nuremberg trials, 100,000 victims, Karamash wrote that 39,000 to 40,000 Jews were killed in Babyn Yar and 50,000 to 60,000 people of other nationalities. He did not provide any reference for these statistics.

Historian Feliks Levitas used memoirs and his family recollections in his book *Babi Yar: Sud'by i pamiat'* (Babyn Yar: Fates and memory).[4] Although the author used some historical documents, this work does not present a comprehensive history of the Holocaust of Jews in Kyiv.

The Harvard Ukrainian Research Institute published a collection of poetry, *Babyn Yar: Ukrainian Poets Respond*, edited by Ostap Kin, dedicated to the eightieth anniversary of the Babyn Yar massacre.[5] The book includes poems about the Babyn Yar massacre written in 1941–2018 by more than twenty Ukrainian poets.

Russian philologist Pavel Polian compiled an anthology of world literature about Babyn Yar, *Babi Yar: Refleksiia* (Babyn Yar: Reflection).[6] Polian included his essays about the representation of the Babyn Yar massacre in music, paintings, film, architecture, and sculpture.

Martin C. Dean wrote the first monograph in English about the Babyn Yar massacre, *Investigating Babyn Yar: Shadows from the Valley of Death*.[7] Dean focuses on the Holocaust of Jews in Kyiv. Using many testimonies "by perpetrators, survivors, and other witnesses, as well as ground photographs, aerial photographs, maps," Dean provides a detailed description of the Babyn Yar massacre on September 29–30, 1941.[8] He also discusses the war crimes investigations and trials of the massacre perpetrators.

Il'ia Levitas, who was not a professional historian but a Jewish public figure, created the Memory of Babyn Yar Foundation of the Jewish Council of Ukraine. The foundation collected information about Jews who perished at Babyn Yar, Holocaust survivors of the Babyn Yar massacre, and gentiles who rescued Jews in Kyiv. The foundation collected information about 431 gentiles who helped Jews survive in Kyiv. Based on this information, Levitas published his book *Pravedniki Bab'ego Yara* (The righteous of Babyn Yar). Levitas described the personal stories of Holocaust survivors in Kyiv and their gentile rescuers.[9]

Proceedings of the international scholarly conference *Babyn Yar: Masove ubuvstvo i pam'iat' pro n'ogo* (Babyn Yar: Mass murder and its memory) (Kyiv, October 24–25, 2011) and the collection of articles *Babyn Yar: History and Memory* analyze different aspects of the Babyn Yar massacre and its representation in film, literature, and arts.[10]

Several scholarly publications are devoted to the commemoration and memorialization of the Holocaust in Kyiv. Lucy S. Dawidowicz in her article "Babi Yar's Legacy," published in *The New York Times* on September 27, 1981, discussed the problems with commemorations of the Babyn Yar massacre in the Soviet Union and the persecution of Jewish activists who organized unsanctioned commemoration ceremonies at the ravine.[11] Jessica Rapson, in her monograph *Topographies of Suffering: Buchenwald, Babi Yar, Lidice*, discusses the representation of the Babyn Yar massacre in literature and its memorialization in the Soviet Union, Ukraine, and the United States at the Babi Yar Memorial Park in Denver, Colorado.[12]

Several recent publications discuss the resistance of Soviet authorities toward construction of a monument to the victims of the Holocaust at Babyn Yar.[13] These publications focus on state anti-Semitism in the Soviet Union and the public protest of Jews and liberal gentile intelligentsia against the absence of a memorial to Holocaust victims at Babyn Yar. None of these publications discuss the influence of the Cold War, détente, and popular anti-Semitism on the decisions of the Soviet authorities. I show how the Cold War, détente, and the policy of state anti-Semitism affected the commemoration and memorialization of the Holocaust in Kyiv.

John-Paul Himka's, Aleksandr Burakovsky's, and Georgii Kasianov's articles discuss perceptions of the Babyn Yar massacre in independent Ukraine. They recount the heated public debates about Babyn Yar commemoration and memorialization. The articles emphasize that part of Ukrainian society refused to recognize Babyn Yar as a Holocaust site and consider it as a place of "universal suffering."[14] Vladimir Khanin's articles and field reports analyze the ongoing conflict between Jewish organizations in Ukraine regarding construction of the Jewish Heritage Center at Babyn Yar, and attitudes toward this project in different strata of Ukrainian society.[15]

I discuss in my work contested concepts for creation of a Babyn Yar Museum in Kyiv. In the early 2000s, Jewish activists proposed building the Babyn Yar Holocaust

Memorial Museum in Kyiv, but the project was not funded. In 2016 several wealthy Jewish donors provided funds for creation of the Babyn Yar Holocaust Memorial Museum in Kyiv. The Babyn Yar Holocaust Memorial Center (BYHMC) was established that same year and began preparations for building the museum. However, controversy about the concept of the Babyn Yar museum continues today. Some Ukrainian historians and politicians have contested memorializing Babyn Yar as a primarily Jewish place of memory.

PRIMARY SOURCES AND MEMOIR LITERATURE

Survivor and eyewitness testimony, along with memoir literature, play a significant role in understanding the Babyn Yar tragedy. Important eyewitness testimony and recollections of Holocaust survivors about the Babyn Yar massacre were published in *The Black Book*.[16] *The Black Book* was compiled under the editorship of Ilya Ehrenburg and Vasily Grossman. Work on *The Black Book* began during World War II. In 1943, Ilya Ehrenburg initiated the collection "of letters, diaries, memoirs, testimonies of victims and witnesses" of the Holocaust in the Soviet Union.[17] *The Black Book* was ready for publication in 1947; however, due to the changing Soviet policy and the rise of state anti-Semitism, publication was halted when the manuscript was already at the printing house.[18] *The Black Book* was ultimately published in Israel in 1980, and then republished in Russia and Ukraine after the collapse of communism in the early 1990s.

For *The Black Book*, the Department of Jewish Culture of the Ukrainian Academy of Sciences gathered testimony from witnesses and survivors of the Holocaust across various regions of Ukraine. Scholars who worked at the department organized meetings with Jewish partisans, recorded Yiddish songs about the Holocaust, and contacted state and public organizations with requests to collect and send to them materials about the Holocaust in Ukraine. Department members used some of the collected materials for their own articles, which they published in the Soviet press. Most of these materials were sent to Moscow for inclusion in *The Black Book*. The department's collection of materials about the Holocaust in Ukraine was very efficient; they sent many essays and documents to the Jewish Anti-Fascist Committee (JAC) in the beginning of 1945. These materials were collected by scholars, Jewish writers, and volunteers throughout Ukraine.[19] The chair of the Department of Jewish Culture, Elie Spivak, wrote in a letter to Ilya Ehrenburg sent with the prepared Holocaust documents:

> Our aim is to deliver the material to you as soon as possible, so we did not provide any literary editing of them. Furthermore, part of the materials are eyewitness

testimonies of the terrible events, and we consider it inappropriate to make any changes to them.[20]

Several writers edited and prepared eyewitness testimony and other materials received from Kyiv for publication in *The Black Book*. The chapter "Kyiv: Babyn Yar" was prepared for publication in *The Black Book* by the Russian-Jewish poet Lev Ozerov (pen name of Lev Goldberg, 1914–96). Ozerov was born and grew up in Kyiv. He moved to Moscow in the mid-1930s for his studies at the Moscow Institute of Philosophy, Literature and History (MIFLI) and for work. The Babyn Yar tragedy was taken very personally by the poet because he knew many Jews who perished there. Simultaneously with his work on the chapter for *The Black Book*, Ozerov wrote his poem "Babi Yar," which was published in the April–May 1946 issue of the literary journal *Oktiabr'* (October).[21]

Following the collapse of communism in the Soviet Union, most archival documents pertaining to the Holocaust and Jewish history were declassified. Based on these documents and materials from the Yad Vashem Archive, Ilya Altman and Joshua Rubenstein prepared *The Unknown Black Book*. This book contains eyewitness testimony about the Babyn Yar massacre, life in Nazi-occupied Kyiv, and Holocaust survivors' recollections.[22]

The first memoir about the Babyn Yar tragedy, *Babi Yar: A Document in the Form of a Novel*, was published by A. Anatoli (Anatoly Kuznetsov).[23] Kuznetsov was an eyewitness of the Babyn Yar massacre as a precocious twelve-year-old. He lived with his mother and grandparents in Kyiv during the Nazi occupation and described in his book the brutality of the Nazi regime. Kuznetsov's text is a valuable historical source about the Babyn Yar massacre and the Nazi occupation of Kyiv. Despite the book's title, it is not fiction, but rather a popular history written by a nonprofessional historian. Kuznetsov's book combines his personal memories with the eyewitness accounts of Babyn Yar survivors Dina Pronicheva and Vladimir Davydov. Kuznetsov also included in his book a chapter of Nazi documents.

Kuznetsov wrote in the introduction:

I am writing this book now without bothering about any literary rules....

I am writing it as though I were giving evidence under oath in the very highest court and I am ready to answer for every single word. This book records only the truth AS IT REALLY HAPPENED.[24]

The book was originally published in the Soviet Union in a censored form in 1966 in the journal *Iunost'* (Youth).[25] The uncensored text was published in the United States in 1970, after Kuznetsov defected to the United Kingdom in 1969.[26] Kuznetsov's work remains the most complete personal account of the Nazi occupation of Kyiv.

David Budnik and Yakov Kaper, prisoners of the Nazi concentration camp Syrets in Kyiv, participated in the uprising on September 29, 1943, and escaped from Babyn Yar. Of the 327 prisoners who attempted to escape, Budnik and Kaper were among the few who survived, as all the others were shot down while fleeing.[27] Their memoirs were published in 1993 in *Nothing Is Forgotten: Jewish Fates in Kiev*.[28]

The Nazis used prisoners of the Syrets concentration camp to eliminate evidence of the Babyn Yar massacre. Budnik and Kaper described how they were forced to build furnaces and burn the corpses of Babyn Yar victims in August–September 1943. Budnik stated that about sixty furnaces were built "and in each one over two thousand people were burnt."[29] So, by Budnik's estimation, the Nazis killed roughly 120,000 people at Babyn Yar.[30]

Tatiana Evstaf'eva and Vitalii Nachmanovich published 163 documents about the Babyn Yar massacre and its commemoration in Soviet times until 1971, with their introduction and comments. Their book was described as the first of five volumes of documents about Babyn Yar and its commemoration. But, after publication of the first volume in 2004, the other four volumes have not been published.[31]

Boris Zabarko, who was a child-prisoner of the Shargorod ghetto (Vinnytsia region, Ukraine), edited and published two volumes of the testimony of Holocaust survivors in Ukraine. Both volumes include the testimony of Jews from Kyiv who escaped from Babyn Yar and were hidden by their gentile neighbors.[32]

I used in my book documentary materials that I found in my visits to Kyiv's archives: the Sectoral State Archive of the Security Services of Ukraine (HDA SBU), the Central State Archives of the Supreme Bodies of Power and Government of Ukraine (TsDAVO U), the Central State Archive of Public Organizations of Ukraine (TsDAHO U), and the Central State CinePhotoPhono Archives of Ukraine (TsDKFFA U). I also used the rich collections of the United States Holocaust Memorial Museum Archive, the Yad Vashem Archives, and the Central Archives for the History of the Jewish People (CAHJP) in Jerusalem. I found there, and incorporated in this work, many unpublished documents on the life of Jews in Kyiv on the eve of World War II, the Babyn Yar massacre, postwar state and popular anti-Semitism in Kyiv, public attempts to commemorate the Holocaust in Kyiv in Soviet times, and about the commemoration and memorialization of the Babyn Yar tragedy in independent Ukraine.

MASS MEDIA

Due to the policy of state anti-Semitism, publications about Babyn Yar in the Soviet press were quite rare from the late 1940s until 1991. Those publications that appeared carefully avoided the term Holocaust and talked about Soviet citizens or Kyivan victims of the "fascist occupation" of the city.

In modern Ukraine, this situation is utterly transformed: The Babyn Yar tragedy and its commemoration have become focal points of Ukrainian mass media. Several articles on the topic are published by the Ukrainian press every month. Since the beginning of the Russian invasion, the focus of attention of society moved to the current war, but publications about Babyn Yar have appeared periodically in the Ukrainian and world press. These articles describe the heated debates in Ukrainian society about the Babyn Yar massacre and the forms and methods of its commemoration and memorialization. I analyze the most important of these publications in my work. Several ethnic groups and political factions have contested Babyn Yar as their memorial site. A bitter war of memory over the Babyn Yar site is continuing into the present day.

I

KYIVAN JEWS IN THE INTERWAR PERIOD

OUT OF THE GHETTO

At the beginning of the twentieth century, the Kyiv Jewish community was one of the wealthiest in the Russian Empire and had a high percentage of intelligentsia.[1] This concentration of wealthy and well-educated Jews was created by imperial laws that kept the city outside the Pale of Settlement. The presence of wealth and higher education opened the gates of the city for selected Jews. The same legislation limited and slowed the growth of the overall Jewish population in Kyiv. Despite the legal limitations, the size of the Kyiv Jewish community was quite large: In 1913, according to the census, 81,256 Jews lived in the city. After the February 1917 Revolution, the Provisional Government abolished all national and religious restrictions, and the Kyiv Jewish population began to grow rapidly on account of Jews who moved there from the nearby provincial cities and shtetls.

Kyiv had one of the largest urban Jewish populations in the Soviet Union. In 1926, the Kyiv Jewish population was 140,256 out of a total of 513,637 (27 percent); in 1939, 224,236 Jews lived in Kyiv out of 847,000 inhabitants (26.5 percent).[2] So, by the size of its Jewish population, Kyiv became the second city in the Soviet Union after Moscow.

Jewish-gentile relations were quite complicated in Kyiv in the interwar period. Kyivan Jewry changed rapidly in Soviet times. Before the February 1917 Revolution, most Kyivan Jews were only allowed to live in three outlying districts of the city: Podil, Ploskyi, and Lybedskyi. Only Jewish merchants of the first guild were allowed to settle anywhere in Kyiv. After the revolution, when national restrictions were abolished by the Provisional Government, Jews settled in all Kyiv districts. The rapidly increasing Jewish population and the presence of Jews in city districts where they were not allowed to live before the revolution greatly irritated anti-Semites. Russian nationalist Vasilii

Shul'gin surreptitiously visited his native Kyiv in December 1925.³ He reported: "On Kreshchatik [Khreshchatyk, the main street of Kyiv] it is possible to find at least a partial solution to the riddle of where the Jews from Podol [Podil] had disappeared. They are here ... on Kreshchatik the multitude of Jewish faces are very visible."⁴ He tried to measure the proportion of Jews versus gentiles on Khreshchatyk and estimated that there were "ten Russians for every forty Jews."⁵

Perhaps Shul'gin's calculation was an exaggeration, but it is obvious that many Jews moved from poorer outer districts of the city to downtown Kyiv during the New Economic Policy (NEP) period in 1921–28 when the Soviet government allowed small private businesses and trade. In downtown Kyiv there were good possibilities for business and trade, which made it even more attractive for Jews. According to the memoirs of Victor Nekrasov, there was a Jewish theater on Khreshchatyk Street in the 1930s.⁶ There were many schools, universities, theaters, and businesses in downtown Kyiv, and so it is not surprising that many Jews preferred to live there rather than in the remote districts of the former Jewish ghetto (figure 1.1).

However, the poorest Kyivan Jews remained in Podil. Poor Jewish artisans with large families could not afford to move to better districts of the city. Anatoly Kuznetsov vividly described the poverty and misery of prewar Podil in his novel *Babi Yar*:

> What a place that Podol was! (It was the most poverty-stricken part of Kiev, and you could recognize it simply by the smell—a mixture of things rotting, cheap

Figure 1.1 Khreshchatyk Street, Kyiv, 1941. (Unidentified photographer.)

fat and washing hung out to dry. Here from time immemorial had lived the poor of the Jewish community, the poorest of the poor—the shoemakers, tailors, the coal-merchants, the tinsmiths, porters, harness-makers, confidence tricksters and thieves.... The courtyards were devoid of grass or greenery, with evil-smelling rubbish tips, tumble-down sheds swarming with great fat rats, lavatories which were just holes in the ground, clouds of flies, miserable streets which were either dusty or muddy, houses in a state of collapse and damp cellars—that was Podol, noisy, overcrowded and utterly dreary.)[7]

As the poorest district of the city, Podil had a bad criminal reputation before and after the Second World War. The main character of the popular interwar period underworld-themed song "Zhil—byl na Podole Gop so smykom" was a cheerful burglar who lives in Podil. The central character says he does not fear death and is sure that all thieves go directly to heaven, where he will continue his "job." This song presents a fusion of Russian, Ukrainian, and Jewish folklore. The lyrics, in Russian, included Ukrainian and Yiddish phrases and underworld slang. According to the Russian folklorist Vladimir Bakhtin, the first variant of this song was recorded in Kyiv in 1926.[8] The star Soviet singer Leonid Utesov included this song in his repertoire, and it became a big hit in the Soviet Union.[9]

Despite the misery and poverty of Podil, Kyivans understood that this district, with its Jewish population, was as much a part of the city image as the Jewish district Moldavanka was part of the image of Odesa. Podil was a source of local Jewish folklore, and it gave the city a special charm and character. The popular song "Without Podol Kiev Is Impossible" was written after World War II and has the refrain:

> But without Podol Kiev is as impossible
> As St. Vladimir without a cross!
> It is a piece of Odessa,
> This is news for the press
> And memorial places.[10]

KYIV AS A CENTER OF SOVIET JEWISH CULTURE IN THE 1920S–30S

Kyiv was one of the two largest centers of Yiddish culture in the Soviet Union (the other was Minsk). Several factors of the history of Jews in Kyiv supported the creation of Soviet Yiddish cultural and research institutions and organizations in the city.

At the beginning of the twentieth century, the Kyiv Jewish community was one of the wealthiest in the Russian Empire. The percentage of Jewish intelligentsia (i.e., lawyers, medical doctors, writers, journalists, etc.) in the city was very high, comprising 13 percent of the Jewish population at the turn of the twentieth century.[11]

Several Jewish cultural and scholarly institutions that functioned in Kyiv in the 1920s were established during the revolution and civil war in Ukraine (1917–20). Historical literature usually describes this period as years of total devastation for the Jewish population. However, despite the recurring bloody pogroms, there were some very significant innovations in Jewish cultural life. On January 9, 1918, the Central Rada (the Ukrainian Parliament) passed a law entitled "Personal-National Autonomy of National Minorities of the Ukrainian Republic," which guaranteed national and cultural autonomy for minorities.[12] This law opened opportunities for cultural development for Ukrainian Jews that they had never had in the Russian Empire.

After the Bolsheviks took power in Russia in October 1917, the social and cultural conditions of life became more favorable for Jews in Ukraine than in Russia. Simon Dubnov wrote about this time: "It appeared then that with its 2 million Jews Ukraine was to realize the great legacy of the February Revolution and of the 'third emancipation.' Many members of Petersburg and Moscow Jewish society sought refuge in Kiev."[13] In 1917–21, several Yiddish poets, writers, and literary critics lived in Kyiv including David Bergelson (1884–1952), David Hofshtein (1889–1952), Itzik Fefer (1900–1952), Yeheskel Dobrushin (1883–1953), Der Nister (pseudonym of Pinkhas Kaganovich, 1884–1950), and others. These poets and writers became known in the history of Yiddish literature as the Kyiv Group.[14] Many of them wrote their works in symbolist and expressionist styles. In the beginning of the 1920s, most of the members of the Kyiv Group settled abroad due to the very difficult conditions of life in the Soviet Ukraine, but many of them returned to Kyiv or to other Soviet cities in the second half of the 1920s to the beginning of the 1930s.

Jewish intellectuals, together with leaders of the Bund, Paoley Tsion, Farainigte, and Folkspartey political parties, established in Kyiv the Jewish secular cultural-enlightenment organization Kultur-Lige (Cultural League) in January 1918. This organization became a source of many innovations in Jewish cultural life in Kyiv and Ukraine. The goal of Kultur-Lige was the promotion of Jewish secular culture. "It had sections for literature, music, theater, painting and sculpture, people's school, preschool education, and adult education."[15] Kultur-Lige opened secular Yiddish schools and kindergartens in various Ukrainian cities, and the Jewish University in Kyiv. The organization had its own printing house, library, club, music school, theater, and art studios. Several of these institutions were located in Kyiv, which became the center of activity of Kultur-Lige and the location of its Central Committee. Kultur-Lige organized concerts, exhibitions of Jewish artists, and literary evenings. Historian Zvi Gitelman wrote:

> The Lige was very active in publishing and worked through existing cultural organizations so that its influence was felt in every sphere of Jewish secular culture. By the

end of 1918 the Lige had 120 branches in the Ukraine, and similar groups had sprung up in Russia, Bessarabia, the Crimea, Lithuania, and even Siberia.[16]

Unfortunately, the civil war, anti-Jewish pogroms, and widespread anarchy in Ukraine overwhelmed many of these positive initiatives soon thereafter. For example, the Jewish University in Kyiv disintegrated during the civil war due to pogroms and the devastating economic situation.[17]

After the Soviets consolidated their power in Kyiv in 1920, the authorities took over all these Jewish institutions. They closed several of them but allowed others to function under Soviet censorship and control. Kultur-Lige continued its work under Bolshevik rule; however, its activities were restricted by the Soviets. Under pressure from the Communist regime, many prominent Kultur-Lige members left the country. Most of the board members of the first convocation moved to Warsaw, the artists Isaac Rabinovich and Alexander Tyshler went to Moscow, the poets Kvitko and Markish temporarily moved to Germany, and the poet David Hofstein left for Palestine.[18]

"Following a December 17, 1920 decree of the Kiev Gubrevcom (Kiev Province Revolutionary Committee)" the Central Committee of Kultur-Lige "was liquidated and replaced by an Orcom (Organizational Committee) the overwhelming majority of whose members were communists or representatives of Jewish socialist parties who were ready to collaborate with communists."[19]

In 1924 all Kultur-Lige educational institutions were subordinated to the People's Commissariat of Education of Ukraine, and most of its other institutions were dissolved. Only the Kultur-Lige publishing house, which was the largest Yiddish publishing house in the Soviet Union in the 1920s, continued to work in Kyiv until 1930.[20]

The processes of *proletarianization* occurred in all aspects of Soviet and Jewish cultural life at the end of the 1920s and beginning of the 1930s. In the 1920s, many different literary groups and styles existed in multicultural Soviet literature. However, in the 1930s, the authorities allowed only one literary style, "socialist realism," and one Union of Soviet Writers with its national departments. At the same time, the Soviets used the "carrot and stick" approach toward the "new intelligentsia." The regime badly needed obedient and faithful authors who would panegyrize it. Thus, the Soviets provided exclusive living conditions for the new Soviet elite, while enforcing strict censorship and repression for freethinkers. David Shneer highlighted in his monograph the process of the creation of "new proletarian" Jewish writers. Specifically, he wrote about David Hofshtein that after his return from Palestine to Kyiv in 1927

> he quickly understood that the proletarian writers group was the rising source of literary power. In 1928, he became a member of the Jewish section of the All-Ukrainian Proletarian Writers Organization (VUSP) and was a founding editor of the proletarian Yiddish journal, *Prolit*. He wrote to [another Yiddish writer, Daniel] Charny

in August: "I am now the jack of all trades at *Prolit*.... I am secretary and publisher of the journal.... I have an assistant, an office, a telephone and more."²¹

According to Shneer, "many important figures of Eastern European Yiddish culture were involved in building the Soviet state's Yiddish Cultural apparatus."²² Some of them even chose closer cooperation with the Soviet authorities and became, as did Yiddish poet Itzik Fefer, secret informers for the NKVD (People's Commissariat of Interior Affairs, the organization that was the predecessor of the KGB).

In the first years of Soviet rule, this cooperation can be explained by the political naïveté of some of the Jewish intelligentsia. Later, their praise of Stalin's regime cannot be justified. By the beginning of the 1930s, the brutal features of the Communist regime became so obvious that they were impossible to ignore: The victims of the Holodomor were dying on the streets of Kyiv, and many Kyivans became victims of repression.

However, the Soviet Yiddish authors, like most other Soviet authors, continued to publish their buoyant works and praise the "wise" Soviet government and Communist Party. Fear of repression kept most of the Soviet intelligentsia away from any form of political protest. The small minority who dared show their dissatisfaction with Soviet policy were executed in the 1930s or disappeared for many years into prisons and concentration camps. However, the Stalin regime even killed many of its own most faithful servants. Some Yiddish writers and literary critics became victims of repression in the Soviet Union in the 1930s. Many other Yiddish writers were arrested during the anticosmopolitan campaign in the late 1940s and early 1950s. Several Yiddish writers and poets were arrested and then executed on August 12, 1952, during the "Affair of the Jewish Anti-Fascist Committee." Among them were David Hofshtein, Itzik Fefer, Leib Kvitko, Perets Markish, and David Bergelson, who during various periods of their lives lived in Kyiv.²³ All these writers were generously gifted, but they devoted their talents to the Soviet system, which they helped to create and praised in their works, and which ultimately killed them.

Jewish theaters in the Soviet Union developed under similar restrictions as other areas of Jewish culture. In the 1920s and 1930s, several Jewish theaters held performances in Kyiv. The Ukrainian State Jewish Theater of Sholom Aleichem originally opened in the then-capital of Soviet Ukraine, Kharkiv, in 1925. But when the capital of Ukraine was moved to Kyiv in 1934, the Ukrainian State Jewish Theater also moved there. This was the largest and most prominent Jewish theater in Ukraine. The theater performed Jewish and world classic plays and the plays of Soviet Yiddish writers. All performances were in Yiddish. Among the productions were William Shakespeare's *The Merchant of Venice*, plays by Eugene O'Neill, and plays by Yiddish writers Itzik Fefer, Perets Markish, Lipe Reznik, and others.

In 1930–37, Boris Vershilov (a student of the prominent Russian theater directors Constantin Stanislavsky and Evgeniy Vakhtangov) was a director of the Ukrainian

State Jewish Theater. On October 10, 1937, the Kyiv Jewish newspaper *Der Shtern* (The Star) published an article under the title "Take Away the Mask from 'the Director' Vershilov." Six days later, a second article, "Vershilovshchina," was published by the same newspaper. By that time two actors of this theater, Libert and Dinor, had already been arrested, and the newspaper articles claimed that Vershilov was directly connected with these "enemies of the people."[24] This was an open denunciation and encouragement to arrest Vershilov. His pregnant wife, the actress Esther Bongrad, went to Moscow to Stanislavsky and begged him to save her husband. Stanislavsky sent a request to the Ukrainian Committee of Art Affairs to release his talented student Vershilov from his position in Kyiv, because "he is absolutely necessary to the [Moscow] Opera Theater" that was named after Stanislavsky during his lifetime. Moisei Loev wrote in his monograph *Ukradennaia Muza* (The stolen muse) about the role of Stanislavsky in this case:

> It is difficult to say if the great theater director's appeal to the authorities helped Vershilov, perhaps it was so. However, Esther, after her return from Moscow, decided not to wait for the possible arrest of her husband. The Vershilov family took only a few of their most necessary belongings and secretly at night left Kyiv.[25]

Later Boris Vershilov worked at the Moscow Opera Theater.

In 1929, two new Jewish theaters were opened in Kyiv: the Kyiv Jewish Theater of the Working Youth (Russian abbreviation TRAM) and the Jewish State Children's Theater.

TRAM did not have professional actors; all the people who performed there were workers, genuine Jewish proletarians. The repertory of the theater was completely in accordance with its name. The themes of the theatrical performances were listed in the report of the theater's work in 1931:

1. The heroic struggle of the working people for fulfillment of the industrial plan
2. Militarization of the working youth
3. Anti-religious theme and questions of the Cultural Revolution[26]

The Jewish State Children's Theater performed plays by Jewish authors Sholom Aleichem, Lipe Reznik, Jewish folklore stories about Hershele Ostropoler, and others. The theater was successful; however, before 1935 it did not have a permanent stage and gave performances at various clubs.[27] After the Second World War, all Jewish theaters in the Soviet Union were closed and many of their actors arrested for "Jewish nationalism."

In the 1920s and the first half of the 1930s, several Yiddish schools and Yiddish colleges were established in Kyiv. The Soviet authorities encouraged Jewish parents to send their children to Jewish schools because they considered the Soviet Yiddish schools as the "only strong antidote against the clerical influence of heder and Zionism."[28] However, when the Soviets suppressed Judaism and the Zionist movement, and liquidated the Jewish religious schools in the mid-1930s, they decided that Jewish secular schools were not necessary anymore and began the process of their liquidation. The other factor that became crucial for the fate of the Jewish schools was their unpopularity among Soviet Jews. Many Jewish parents desired that their children receive an education in Russian and Ukrainian schools, which opened better prospects for higher education and careers. Thus, in the 1924–25 academic year, only 19 percent of Jewish children of school age studied at Yiddish schools in Ukraine.[29] This percentage of students in Yiddish schools decreased with time.

The reorganization of the national schools was discussed at the Fourteenth Congress of the Communist Party of Ukraine in June 1938. The First Secretary of the Central Committee of the Communist Party of Ukraine, Nikita Khrushchev, said:

> Polish-German agents, bourgeois nationalists implanted so called national schools. ... There are 70 Jewish schools in the Vinnytsky district. There are a number of schools without first and second grades, because the parents don't want to send their children to Jewish schools. The enemies dragged by force Jews to Jewish schools. They did this to make the people angry, and on the other hand to create nests of enemies.[30]

Most Jewish cultural organizations and institutions were closed in Kyiv and all over the Soviet Union in the second half of the 1930s. The administration and members of these organizations were accused of bourgeois nationalism, and many of them were imprisoned or executed as "enemies of the people." Soviet Jewish culture never recovered from this blow, and Soviet policy soon thereafter acquired its clear anti-Semitic character.

JEWISH SCHOLARLY INSTITUTIONS IN KYIV

Several Jewish state scholarly institutions were established and functioned in Kyiv: the Jewish Historical-Archaeographical Commission (1919–29), the Institute of Jewish Proletarian Culture (1929–36), and the Department of Jewish Language, Literature, and Folklore of the Ukrainian Academy of Sciences (1936–49).

THE JEWISH HISTORICAL-ARCHAEOGRAPHICAL COMMISSION

The first Jewish scholarly organization in Kyiv, the Jewish Historical-Archaeographical Commission of the All-Ukrainian Academy of Sciences, was established during the civil war in Ukraine in 1919. Four Jewish historians were on the first staff of the commission: Ben-Zion Dinaburg (Dinur, later a well-known Israeli historian and politician),

Yakov Izraelson, Avraam Kagan (Abraham Kahana, biblical scholar and historian), and Ilia Galant. Ben-Zion Dinaburg and Yakov Izraelson prepared a detailed program of the commission's work. The goal of the commission was to gather, research, and publish documentary sources of Jewish history in Ukraine. Perhaps the Jewish Historical-Ethnographical Society, founded by Dubnov in St. Petersburg in 1908, was used as the model for the commission's activities. However, in 1918 Ukraine declared its independence, and Jewish historians who lived in Kyiv argued in their proposal for the establishment of the commission about the need for a local scholarly institution that would research the history of Ukrainian Jews. The work of the commission was interrupted from its beginning by the civil war, and three of the four members, Dinaburg, Izraelson, and Kagan, left the country.[31] It was impossible to replace them, because there were no other specialists in Jewish history in Kyiv. But the commission formally continued to function. Thus, Ilia Galant continued his work alone with archival sources on Jewish history.

Galant began his research of Jewish history when he settled in Kyiv in the early 1890s. He explored Jewish documents in the Kyiv Central Archive at St. Vladimir University. Because many of these documents were on the history of Jews in Ukraine, Galant devoted several of his works to this theme: "Arendovali li evrei tserkvi na Ukraine?" (Did Jews rent churches in Ukraine? [Kyiv, 1914]); "K istorii poseleniia evreev v Pol'she i Rusi voobshche i v Podolii v chastnosti" (On the history of the settlement of Jews in Poland and Russia in general and in Podolia in particular [Nezhin, 1898]). Galant prepared a manuscript on the history of Jews in Kyiv, but it was stolen together with his other belongings during the robbery of his apartment on December 8, 1924. Galant also often published his articles in local and Russian-Jewish periodicals *Kievskaia starina* (*Kyiv Antiquities*), *Voskhod* (*Sunrise*), and *Budushchnost'* (*The Future*).[32]

So, Galant was the moving force behind the Jewish Historical-Archaeographical Commission. In 1924, the commission was reestablished with a new staff. The chair of the commission was the famous academic orientalist, the secretary of the Ukrainian Academy of Sciences, Agafangel Krymsky (1871–1942). Krymsky did not participate actively in the work of the commission, but his well-known name gave the commission a higher status. The real head of the commission was Galant; the historians David Brodsky and David Vainshtein, Hebraist Victor Ivanitsky, and philologist Valery Rybinsky worked there. The members of the commission worked without a salary for a long time and only in the last two years of its existence in 1928–29 did two members of the commission receive any remuneration. Nevertheless, the commission was quite productive. The members of the commission researched and described a significant number of sources in Jewish history in Kyiv archives and gathered Jewish materials from private collections. The members of the commission also copied the most interesting documents in Jewish history from different archives and gathered them in the Collection of the Jewish Historical-Archaeographical Commission of the All-Ukrainian

Academy of Sciences, which is now located at the Central State Historical Archive of Ukraine in City Kyiv.[33]

The commission also published two volumes of its proceedings in 1928 and 1929, which consisted of articles about the history of Jews in Ukraine and many interesting documents on various aspects of this topic. The articles in the proceedings were published in Ukrainian, while the documents were published in their original language, Russian, even with the old Russian orthography, which was abolished by the Bolsheviks in 1918. The first volume of the proceedings has the title *Zbirnyk prats' Zhydivs'koi istorychno-archeografichnoi komisii* (Proceedings of the Jewish Historical-Archaeographical Commission, with the word *Zhydivs'koi* used for Jewish), while the second volume has the title *Zbirnyk prats' Ievreiskoi istorychno-archeografichnoi komisii* (the same title as the first volume, but with the word *Ievreiskoi* used for Jewish). Galant complained to Jewish historian Saul Borovoi that "some adherents of the Ukrainian language claim that the word *ievrei* [Jew in Russian and Ukrainian], does not exist in the Ukrainian language, only *zhyd* [Jew in Polish that is considered an insult in Russian]," which presumably does not contain any insulting meaning in Ukrainian, and the "foreign" word *ievrei* could spoil the Ukrainian language.[34] So, the commission was forced to use the word *zhyd* instead of *ievrei* in the first volume. Debates about which word should be used in the Ukrainian language, *zhyd* or *ievrei*, had continued in Ukrainian and Jewish literary circles since the 1860s. But perhaps the reaction to the publication of the first volume of proceedings with the word *zhyd* was very negative in Jewish circles, because Jews consider this word to be an insult. Probably, this reaction compelled the adherents of the word *zhyd* to give up the argument, and the second volume of the proceedings was published using the word *ievrei*.

Both volumes of proceedings contain articles and documents on the social status of Jews in the Russian Empire, anti-Semitism, "ritual processes," pogroms, and the economic and religious history of Jews in Ukraine, particularly Hasidism (about the Tversky Hasidic dynasty). There were also articles and documents published about Jewish agricultural settlements, expulsions of Jews in the Russian Empire, and Jewish education.

Despite the important work done by the commission, its members were all fired in 1929 from the Ukrainian Academy of Sciences "as hangers-on of the bourgeoisie and White Guards," and the local press published articles denouncing the commission.[35] The proximate cause of this accusation was that Ilia Galant reportedly published one of his articles in the emigrant press. (The title of the publication as well as where it was published was not mentioned in the disparaging articles.) But the real reason for the closure of the commission was a new course of Soviet politics leading to the suppression of the "old bourgeoisie" specialists. The Jewish Historical-Archaeographical Commission of the Ukrainian Academy of Sciences and the "old" Jewish scholarly organizations, which had functioned since prerevolutionary times in St. Petersburg—Petrograd—Leningrad: the Jewish Historical-Ethnographical Society and the Society for Spreading Enlightenment Among Jews in Russia (OPE), were closed almost simultaneously in 1929–30. Evsektsiia (the Jewish section of the Communist Party) and the Soviet press accused the latter two institutions of being "bourgeoisie organizations."[36] In all these cases, Jewish activists from Evsektsiia and the Communist Party initiated the campaigns against the "old bourgeoisie" Jewish organizations. Soviet authorities encouraged and directed these campaigns against "old bourgeoisie institutions and specialists" in general and against Jewish old bourgeoisie specialists in particular.

Soviet authorities were concerned about Ukrainian nationalism and cooperation between Ukrainian and Jewish intellectuals, who collaborated in their work on the commission. In the 1920s and the early 1930s, Soviet government policy required that the culture of national minorities should be developed in their national language, so Jewish culture was supposed to develop in Yiddish. The Jewish Historical-Archaeographical Commission, which published its proceedings in Ukrainian, also did not satisfy this requirement of Soviet nationalities policy.

After the liquidation of the Jewish Historical-Archaeographical Commission, all its members were fired from the All-Ukrainian Academy of Sciences. What happened to them later and whether they avoided Stalin's repression is unknown. In 1939, the Social Security Administration of Ukraine requested that the Academy of Sciences of the Ukrainian Soviet Socialist Republic (as the academy had been renamed) send them information about Galant's work. This information was needed to calculate Galant's pension. The chair of the Department of Jewish Culture, Elie Spivak, wrote the following description of Galant's work:

1. Before the revolution, Galant was a teacher of Jewish religious law (something like Jewish religious history) in one of Kyiv's commercial schools. People say that he was also a secretary of the capitalist Brodsky.[37]
2. His scholarly work as a "historian-archeologist"[38] in the proceedings of the so called "Zhydiskoi Commission" was class-hostile and did not have any connection to Soviet scholarship, particularly to Soviet Jewish scholarship.[39]

Spivak's characterization of Galant's work is more reminiscent of a denunciation. Certainly, with such a characterization of his work, Galant was not eligible for any pension and perhaps could even be arrested. The vice president of the Ukrainian Academy of Sciences, Aleksandr Vladimirovich Palladin, behaved in a much more noble manner toward Galant. He did not send Spivak's description of Galant's work to the Social Security Administration of Ukraine. Instead, Palladin wrote: "The Presidium of the Academy of Sciences Ukrainian SSR informs you that Galant I.V. has not worked in the Academy of Sciences for a long time. Therefore, the Presidium cannot provide a characterization of Galant's work."[40]

Why did Spivak and other Jewish proletariat scholars hate Galant and the other old bourgeoisie specialists so much? Perhaps it was true class hatred of the poor shtetl Jews toward the wealthy Kyivan Jews, who had spent most of their life in comfort. According to Jewish historian Saul Borovoi:

> Ilya Vladimirovich [Galant] was full of self-respect. He did not walk, but carried himself like a full wineglass which should not spill. The old Kyivans said that in pre-revolutionary years he sauntered along the Khreshchatyk every day in a top hat, finishing his walk in the cafe Samodeni, where he would drink a cup of coffee and where his admirers waited for him and to whom he would tell his ideas and political prognoses.[41]

Borovoi wrote that he did not know how Galant died, but he guessed that Galant might have perished at Babyn Yar.[42]

THE KYIV INSTITUTE FOR JEWISH PROLETARIAN CULTURE

As alternatives to the old Jewish scholarly organizations, "new proletarian" Jewish organizations were created. Thus, the Department of Jewish Culture of the Ukrainian Academy of Sciences was established in 1926 but was not officially opened until 1928. Yiddish linguist and philologist Nokhem (Naum) Shtif was appointed as the acting department chair. He was well known in Yiddish literary circles, because he had published articles on Yiddish philology since prerevolutionary times. In October 1920, Shtif emigrated, but in 1926 he returned to Kyiv, lured by the development of Jewish culture and scholarship in the Soviet Union. In 1924, Shtif proposed creating an academic Yiddish institute and library. This proposal was realized by other scholars, who established the Yiddish Scientific Institute, YIVO, in 1925 in Vilna (Vilnus).[43]

Shtif continued his scholarly career in the Department of Jewish Culture in Kyiv. He was soon replaced as chair of the department by Joseph Liberberg. Shtif became the head of the philological section of the department and later led this section at the Institute of Jewish Proletarian Culture in Kyiv.[44]

The new chair of the Department of Jewish Culture, Joseph Liberberg, did not have a scholarly reputation like Shtif. Liberberg defended his dissertation on the French Revolution in 1925 and taught Western European history in various Kyiv universities before he began to work at the Department of Jewish Culture. The authorities considered Liberberg a better candidate for the position of department chair than

Shtif, because Liberberg had been a member of the Communist Party since 1919 and served as a Red Army political agitator in 1918–24. From the moment of his appointment as department chair, Liberberg faithfully implemented the government policy regarding Jewish scholarship. He organized the public campaign against the Jewish Historical-Archaeographical Commission.[45]

Ukrnauka (Ukraine Department of Science) appointed to the Department of Jewish Culture communists recommended by the Evsektsiia of the Communist Party of Ukraine, ignoring whether these people had any scholarly background whatsoever. The All-Ukrainian Academy of Sciences resisted recognizing the department as a part of the academy. The scholarly secretary of the academy, Academic Krymsky, wrote to Ukrnauka and the Ministry of People's Education:

> The general convention of VUAN [of the All-Ukrainian Academy of Sciences] unanimously decreed that the Jewish Department, with its leaders, whom Ukrnauka appointed against the wish of the Academy of Sciences, absolutely do not satisfy the scholarly needs of the Academy, and therefore cannot be part of the Academy under any circumstances.[46]

However, the authorities ignored the opinion of the All-Ukrainian Academy of Sciences and forced the academy to accept the Jewish Department. The creation of this institution also foreordained the destiny of the Jewish Historical-Archaeographical Commission, as the academy claimed that it certainly did not need two Jewish scholarly organizations with similar goals.[47]

The Jewish Department of the Ukrainian Academy of Sciences was transformed into the Institute for Jewish Proletarian Culture in 1929. The staff of this organization was less academic than the Jewish Historical-Archaeographical Commission and the similar Institute for Jewish Culture, which opened in Minsk.[48] The main goal of the institute in Kyiv, according to its director, Joseph Liberberg, was "the struggle against the scholarship of the Jewish bourgeoisie."[49] Historian Saul Borovoi collaborated on several projects with the Kyiv Institute for Jewish Culture and knew many scholars there. He thus characterized the institute and its administration in his memoirs:

> The administration of Jewish academic institutions was not overly burdened by knowledge and rejected the scholarly-cultural tradition, and consequently took extreme left (*levatskie*) positions. The Institute for Jewish Culture of the Academy of Sciences of Ukraine was renamed into the Institute for Jewish Proletarian Culture. However, it remained unclear what this institute is supposed to do and what does the term "proletarian culture" mean. The philologists gave the answer to this question. It turned out that Jewish literature began not from the Bible and not even from Mendele [Moykher-Sforim],[50] but from Govsher and Winchevsky, i.e., little-known

self-educated workers, who published their works in the U.S. in workers' (sometimes with an anarchist shade) newspapers.[51]

The academic library at the Institute for Jewish Proletarian Culture was named after the socialist Yiddish poet and writer Morris Winchevsky (pseudonym of Benzion Novakhovich, 1856–1932). The library was created based on the library collection of the closed Society for Spreading Enlightenment Among Jews in Russia (OPE), some local Jewish libraries, and private collections. In the 1930s, the library held over 60,000 volumes. After the closure of the Institute for Jewish Proletarian Culture, the Winchevsky Library was purged by the NKVD and many books were confiscated and destroyed. The remainder of the library collection was inherited by the Department of Jewish Culture. After the liquidation of the Department of Jewish Culture, the library was also closed and for many years its collection was kept in one of the closed churches in Kyiv and, since the 1960s, in the *spetskhran* (special holdings) department of the Vernadsky Library of the Academy of Sciences of Ukraine, which was closed to researchers. In the late 1980s to the early 1990s, the books were moved to the newly created Jewish Department of the Vernadsky Library.[52]

Due to the great energy of Liberberg and his even greater ambitions, Kyiv became a center of Soviet Jewish scholarly life in the first half of the 1930s. Between the Kyiv and Minsk Institutes of Jewish Culture, there was competition for dominance in Jewish scholarship.[53] Liberberg had strong connections with the communist nomenclature, and this resulted in the victory of the Kyiv Institute for Jewish Culture. The Minsk Institute began to decline from the early 1930s, while the Kyiv Institute was at its zenith.[54] Seventy-six to seventy-eight scholars worked in the Kyiv Institute in the mid-1930s.[55] The institute originally had six sections: Jewish literature, philology, history, ethnography, social-economic, and pedagogical. Later, with the creation of the Birobidzhan project, the institute also created the Section for the Study of Birobidzhan.[56] The institute published the journal *Di Yiddishe Shprakh* (The Yiddish language, from 1931 called *Afn shprakhfront* [On the language front]). The Kyiv Institute opened a branch in Odesa in December 1928, but for unknown reasons the Odesa branch did not last long, and it was not mentioned in documents after June 1929.[57]

Liberberg prepared a project for the organization in Kyiv of the All-Ukrainian State Jewish Historical Archive.[58] But this project was never realized. The Jewish section of the Kyiv Central Historical Archive, which was led by institute presidium member Iona Khinchin, was closed in 1932.[59] The official explanation was that the Jewish section was closed due to lack of a suitable place for it. The Historical Section of the Kyiv Institute for Jewish Proletarian Culture was led by the historian Asher Margolis. According to Abraham Greenbaum, the work of the Historical Section was not very productive. The historians published only a few journal articles. In 1935, the Historical Section reported that "it had expended much energy 'getting rid of its bad inheritance' and had blocked the publication of four books for political reasons."[60] Greenbaum wrote that the work of the Kyiv Institute for Jewish Proletarian Culture in general was much less productive than expected.[61]

From the early 1930s, Liberberg actively supported the creation of Jewish autonomy in Birobidzhan. Gennady Estraikh wrote that Liberberg "convened and presided over the most representative forum in the history of Soviet Yiddish-language planning: the Kyiv Yiddish Language Conference."[62] On the opening day of the conference, May 7, 1934, "the Soviet government declared that the Birobidzhan Jewish National District had been upgraded to the status of a Jewish National Region."[63] In fall 1934, Liberberg was appointed as the head of the organizational committee of the Birobidzhan Jewish National Region and moved to Birobidzhan. In December of the same year, Liberberg was elected as the first chair of the Jewish Region's Soviet (Council) of People's Deputies. Liberberg planned to create in Birobidzhan the all-Soviet Jewish cultural and academic center and move to Birobidzhan the Kyiv Institute for Jewish Proletarian Culture as well as other Jewish scholarly and cultural institutions. However, he did not realize his plan, because the Kyiv Institute for Jewish Proletarian Culture was closed in May 1936 and Liberberg was arrested on August 20, 1936.[64]

The arrest of the scholars at the Kyiv Institute for Jewish Proletarian Culture began in November 1935 with the arrest of Chaim-Boris Iosif Lekhtman, who, under torture, admitted to belonging to a counterrevolutionary terrorist organization. Lekhtman gave evidence against four other scholars who worked at the institute: Mikhl Levitan (1881–1937?), Maks Erik (pseudonym of Solomon Lazarevich Merkin, 1898–1937), Isaak Izraelivich Bliashov (1886–?) and Iona Meerovich Khinchin (1892–1940). They were accused of Trotskyism, terrorism, and counterrevolutionary activities. These four scholars received five-year terms in concentration camps, but three of the four scholars did not survive their imprisonment.[65] Efim Melamed wrote that in the second half of the 1930s, twenty scholars who worked at the Kyiv Institute for Jewish Proletarian Culture became victims of repression and eight of them were executed.[66]

Liberberg had lived and worked in Birobidzhan since fall 1934, but this did not save him from accusation and arrest. He was accused of creating a "Trotskyist-terrorist organization at the Ukrainian Academy of Sciences."[67] Perhaps some lazy NKVDist did not want to take the long train ride to Birobidzhan to arrest Liberberg, or they felt uncomfortable arresting a political leader of the Jewish Autonomous Region in Birobidzhan. So, Liberberg was invited to come to Moscow to report about the development of the Birobidzhan Jewish Autonomous Region and to deliver his written autobiography.

On August 20, 1936, Liberberg arrived in Moscow. A car sent by the authorities met him at the train station and took him to one of the best hotels in the city, Metropol. Later that night, an NKVDist knocked on the door of his hotel room and showed the order for his arrest. Liberberg denied all his alleged crimes until October 15, 1936, but then under the "special methods" of Soviet interrogation (i.e., torture, sleep deprivation, etc.), he admitted his participation in the Trotskyist-terrorist organization and other alleged crimes.[68] Liberberg's trial took only ten minutes: it began at 7:20 p.m. and ended at 7:30 p.m. on March 9, 1937. Liberberg was sentenced to death by the Military Collegium of the Supreme Court of the USSR and executed that same evening.[69]

Liberberg and other members of the Kyiv Institute of Jewish Proletarian Culture became victims due to the changed course of Soviet nationalities policy. In the second half of the 1930s, the Soviet government changed its policy from the encouragement of national minorities cultures to their suppression. The Birobidzhan project failed: Significantly fewer Jews moved to the Jewish Autonomous Region than the Soviet government had anticipated. So Liberberg, with his great ambitions and plans for the development of the Jewish Autonomous Region, became unnecessary, as did the Kyiv Institute for Jewish Proletarian Culture, which he created.

The Minsk Institute for Jewish Proletarian Culture and the Kyiv Institute for Polish Culture were closed in 1935 (a year before the Kyiv Institute for Jewish Proletarian Culture was liquidated). People's Commissar of Education of Ukraine Volodymyr Zatonsky reported to the Plenum of the Central Committee of the Communist Party (Bolsheviks) of Ukraine in November 1933:

> All workers of the Institute for Polish Culture from its director to the dishwasher were specifically selected. Some of them were the members of the Communist Party, some were not, but all of them were members of a counter-revolutionary organization.[70]

Thus, the fate of the Kyiv Institute for Jewish Proletarian Culture was not unique. The liquidation of national minorities' institutions was a general policy in the mid-1930s. In other national minorities' institutions, repression began even earlier than in the Kyiv Institute for Jewish Proletarian Culture. One of the scholars of the Minsk Institute, Israel Sosis (1878–1967), who was branded in the early 1930s as an "un-Marxist historian" and his works as "nationalist and Bundist," fled from Minsk to Kyiv and continued his work at the Kyiv Institute for Jewish Proletarian Culture until its liquidation. Elissa Bemporad wrote:

> Expelled from the party and publicly vilified in Minsk for his "idealization of the Bund and manifestations of Jewish chauvinism," in late 1931 Sosis relocated to Kiev where he worked in the local Jewish academic institutions at least until the mid-1930s. Sosis was Marxist enough for Jewish scholarship in Kiev, but not for Minsk.[71]

When the Kyiv Institute for Jewish Proletarian Culture was closed, Sosis was arrested, but he survived the concentration camps and become a member of the Historical

Commission of the Jewish Antifascist Committee (JAC) in 1946. In the 1960s, Sosis worked on "The History of Jews in Russia," which has remained unpublished.[72]

THE DEPARTMENT OF JEWISH LANGUAGE, LITERATURE, AND FOLKLORE

At the end of 1936, the Department of Jewish Language, Literature, and Folklore of the Ukrainian Academy of Sciences (brief title: the Department of Jewish Culture) was opened in Kyiv as result of the "reorganization" of the Kyiv Institute for Jewish Proletarian Culture.[73] Elie Spivak was appointed as director of the Department of Jewish Culture. He was head of the philological section of the Kyiv Institute for Jewish Culture and editor of its periodical *Afn shprakhfront* after the death of Nokhem Shtif in 1933. Spivak was reportedly the author of fifty Yiddish textbooks, some of which he wrote with his friend David Hofshtein, a Yiddish poet. Spivak also published several monographs on the Yiddish language. His work *Di shprakh in di teg fun der foterlendisher milkhome* (The language in the time of the patriotic war, 1946) was the last Yiddish linguistic publication during Stalin's rule.[74]

The Department of Jewish Culture had three sections: philological, literature, and folklore. The latter section was led by Jewish folklorist Moisei Beregovsky. The department remained the only Jewish scholarly institution in the Soviet Union, and many thought that it would not last long due to changes in the nationalities policy and ongoing repression. So, in the late 1930s, the members of the department preferred to keep a low profile and focus on some local projects without the previous grand ambitions of Liberberg for making Kyiv the center of Jewish culture for the entire Soviet Union. The department was also much smaller than the institute. Only eleven to twelve scholars worked there in 1936–49.

SUPPRESSION OF JEWISH POLITICAL AND RELIGIOUS LIFE IN KYIV

From the first days of their rule, the Soviet authorities began to eliminate Jewish political parties and organizations and Jewish communal and religious institutions. The Bolsheviks were especially hostile toward Zionist organizations and had already begun to attack them during the civil war in Ukraine. In 1919 the Bolsheviks banned the use of Hebrew, calling it a "counter-revolutionary language." They, with the support of Jewish pro-Communist organizations, also dissolved Jewish communal institutions. Thus SETMAS (Union of Jewish Working People) "made the first attack on the *kehilla*

[Jewish community] in Kyiv, literally smashing and wrecking its offices, and it was the Ukrainian Kombund which destroyed the Society to Aid Pogrom Victims in May 1919."[75] By the mid-1920s, only one legal Jewish party, the Jewish Communist Workers' Party, Po'alei-Zion, was left in Soviet Ukraine; it was eliminated in 1928.

Starting in the early 1920s, Soviet authorities closed many religious institutions in Ukraine: churches, mosques, and synagogues. To avoid the accusation of anti-Semitism, the Bolsheviks entrusted the liquidation of Jewish institutions and organizations and the requisitioning of their property to Jewish sections of the Ukrainian Communist Party. The annual report of the Jewish sections of the Kyiv Province Department of the Commissariat of Education stated that in 1921 these sections, together with the Jewish sections of the Kyiv Committee of the Communist Party, organized a campaign against clericalism, heder, Zionism, and religion, featuring lectures and show trials.[76] Zvi Gitelman wrote about one of these trials:

> On *Rosh Hashonoh*, 1921, the *Evsektsiia* [Jewish section of the Ukrainian Communist Party] in Kiev "tried" the Jewish religion, ironically, in the same auditorium where the Beilis trial had been held [in the building of the Kiev District Court]. [An actor dressed as a] "rabbi" testified that he taught religion in order to keep the masses ignorant and servile. When someone in the audience accused him of being a "lying ignoramus," "stormy applause" broke out, according to the stenographic report. The interpellator in the audience was immediately arrested. After further testimony by a corpulent "bourgeois," bedecked with glittering gold and diamond rings, the Evsektsiia "prosecutor" summarized the "case against the Jewish religion" and asked for a "sentence of death for the Jewish religion." Moshe Rosenblatt, a Kiev Hebrew teacher, rose to defend Judaism and the sympathies of the crowd were clearly with him. He was arrested immediately after completing his speech. The "judges" retired to their chambers and returned with a verdict of death to the Jewish religion.[77]

The closure of synagogues in Ukraine was protested by believers, who were sometimes violently suppressed. However, in the beginning and mid-1920s, the authorities still considered the mood of religious people; thus, before 1928, only 10 percent of synagogues were closed in Soviet Ukraine. But, starting in the second half of the 1920s, the Soviet rulers declared total war on religion. They closed and used for other purposes or destroyed most of the houses of worship in Ukraine. The Soviet authorities always liked to show that they were fulfilling the will of the working people. So, they organized collective letters signed by working-class Jews with requests to close synagogues and Jewish prayer houses. Jews signed these letters because they were afraid of losing their jobs and falling under the suspicion of the NKVD as a "counter-revolutionary religious element." In this way, most synagogues in Kyiv were closed. For example, in 1924, the Kyiv Convention of Jewish Working People discussed a question about the closure of the Kyiv Choral Synagogue and passed the following resolution:

> We need a cultural center that can satisfy our cultural needs and rebuild our everyday life, and reeducate us, our wives and children.
>
> The only building that has the size and location to satisfy these needs is the Brodsky Choral synagogue.
>
> During many decades this synagogue spread religious poison among Jewish working people and took their attention away from the struggle against exploitation. [The synagogue was built in 1898 by sugar industry tycoon and Jewish communal leader Lazar Brodsky.]
>
> This synagogue, which was named after one of the largest Russian capitalists and bankers, is the best evidence of the existence of the tight connection between religion and capital.
>
> Our revolutionary consciousness cannot tolerate that a building located in the center of the city that satisfies the religious needs of a few tens of nepmen (i.e., bourgeoisie), while 12,000 Kyiv Jewish workers desperately need the facility for a club.[78]

This attack on the Brodsky synagogue was quite sensitive for Kyiv religious Jews because the synagogue served as the focal point of the city's varied Jewish activities. In 1926, the Brodsky synagogue was closed and transformed into the Central Club of Jewish Handicraftsmen "Der Shtern" ("The star").[79] The Borishpol'sky synagogue in Kyiv had been closed a year earlier, in February 1925. In 1929, the last Kyiv synagogue in Podil was closed. The buildings of these two synagogues were also transformed into clubs of Jewish handicraftsmen and workers. However, by 1940 all Jewish clubs in Kyiv were shut down and the buildings of the former synagogues were used by the city administration for other "city needs" that were not at all related to Jewish cultural life.[80] In 1930–31, the building of the former Galitsky synagogue was transformed into a dining hall for workers of a local plant, the Merchant synagogue was made into a gym, and the Jewish prayer house Tal'ner was demolished. All the pleas of religious Jews and their requests to return the synagogues and prayer houses were ignored.[81]

In the end of the 1920s and beginning of the 1930s, by the order of Soviet authorities, there were requisitions of the silver ritual objects from both the working and closed synagogues and the Torah scrolls from the closed synagogues. Later, many of the Jewish silver ritual objects were melted down and the Torah scrolls were sent to various Ukrainian archives. However, archive workers resisted these donations and explained to the authorities that Torah scrolls were not proper archival documents. They sought permission to sell the Torah scrolls to Gostorg (the State Trade Organization), and some of them that were written on parchment were handed over to the Young Pioneers (the Communist youth organization) for the manufacture of drums.[82]

The policies of the Ukrainian Communist Party and the Ukrainian government toward national minorities were completely subordinated to the policies of the Soviet leaders. Among the leaders of the Ukrainian Communist Party and the Ukrainian government, there were some Jews in the 1920s and 1930s. The most odious figure among them was Lazar Kaganovich (1893–1991), the general secretary of the Ukrainian Communist Party in 1925–28.

THE HOLODOMOR AND JEWS IN KYIV

The Holodomor (death by famine) affected the entire population of Ukraine in 1932–33. Although the peasants suffered the most from the Holodomor, the urban population of Ukraine was also starving and dying during this tragic period. The moral impact of the Holodomor on the population was tremendous: People got used to seeing starving and dying people on the streets. The Holodomor and repression brutalized society and, in this way, prepared the ground for the Babyn Yar massacre.

The Holodomor changed the structure of the population of Kyiv. It accelerated the flood of migrants to Kyiv from surrounding towns and rural areas. Naum Korzhavin, a Russian poet of Jewish origins, recalled in his memoirs: "Kyiv, and our yard in particular, was literally flooded by the wave of migrants from the province. They occupied all basements in the city."[83] He wrote that among the migrants there were not only peasants, but also shtetl Jews, because the famine was in the shtetls as well as the villages. There was also a severe shortage of food in Kyiv and other large cities of Ukraine in 1932–33, but the situation in the villages and small towns was even worse. The authorities attempted to stop the newcomers: They directed the OGPU (Joint State Political Directorate) to organize roadblocks in Ukraine, North Caucasus, and in some regions of Russia.

However, despite all the obstacles and barriers, some peasants and town inhabitants found their way to Kyiv and other large cities. Russian writer Vasily Grossman, who visited Kyiv for three days in 1933 and was an eyewitness of the Holodomor, wrote:

> All the stations were surrounded by guards. All the trains were searched. Everywhere along the roads were roadblocks—troops, NKVD.[84] Yet despite all this the peasants made their way into Kiev. They would crawl through the fields, through empty lots, through the swamps, through the woods—anywhere to bypass the roadblocks set up for them. They were unable to walk; all they could do was crawl.[85]

Based on eyewitnesses' memories, historian Andrei Zubov gives an account similar to Grossman's:

> Kyivans recalled how crowds of peasants swollen from starvation filled the city streets, where they hoped to find a job and receive ration cards. Only a few succeeded in this. The rest were dying by the hundreds. They were lying down under the open sky. The special police units caught the peasants. They threw them in trucks and took them outside the city.[86]

THE INDIFFERENCE OF KYIVANS TO STARVING AND DYING PEOPLE

Grossman described the Kyivans' indifference to the suffering of the starving newcomers:

> People hurried about on their affairs, some going to work, some to the movies, and streetcars were running—and there were the starving children, old men, girls, crawling about among them on all fours. They were like mangy dogs and cats of some kind.[87]

The indifference of Kyivans toward the starving and dying people on the street was also observed by an American journalist, a correspondent of the New York Yiddish daily *Forverts* (Forward), Harry Lang.[88] He visited Kyiv in fall 1933 during the Jewish high holidays. He wrote:

> The main street of the city, the famous Krestchatik [Khreshchatyk], told a harrowing tale of famine at the first glance. It was early in the morning. The sidewalks were crowded, thousands marching to work carrying their rations of coarse black bread. It was their breakfast—at which they nibbled on their way....
>
> Suddenly I saw a woman, still young, drop to the ground. She had an empty basket in her hands, and the basket rolled down the sidewalk. Her arms were convulsed for a moment, then they stretched out. Her eyes opened wide once or twice, then they closed. Her head shook fitfully, then it hit the stone pavement, and relax[ed] into stillness.
>
> The passersby kept marching. Not one of them turned around. My first thought was that the woman had slipped and fallen by accident. I made a move to help her rise. With me was a man from my hotel. He quickly stopped me:
>
> "Don't! Under no circumstances should you go! It is not fitting for you, a visitor, a foreigner, to intervene."[89]

RATIONS AND THE "COMMERCIAL" STORES

There were several reasons why Kyivans showed such indifference toward the starving people on the streets. The main reason was that the majority of Kyivans had barely enough food for themselves and had nothing to share with the newcomers. Robert Conquest wrote:

> As early as the summer of 1932 office workers' rations in Kiev were cut from one pound to half a pound of bread a day, industrial workers from two to one-and-a-half pounds. Students at the Kiev Institute of Animal Husbandry got a ration of 200 grammes of ersatz bread a day, plus a plate of fish broth, sauerkraut, two spoonfuls of kasha or cabbage, and fifty grammes of horsemeat.[90]

In Kyiv, so-called commercial stores were opened that began to sell unrationed bread at high prices. "The lines were half a kilometer in length the night before the stores even opened."[91] People who stood in these lines

> held onto the belts of those ahead and clung for dear life. If one person stumbled, the whole line would shake and quaver as if the wave had passed along it.... Now and then, some young hoodlums would break into the line. They would look for the places where the links in the chain were weakest. And when the hoodlums came near, everyone would start to howl again with the fear.... They were city people standing there in line for unrationed "commercial" bread—deprived people, non-Party people, craftsmen—or else people from the suburbs. Many of them were people who had been refused ration cards.... The greatest number of corpses were near the unrationed "commercial" bread stores. A swollen, starving person would eat a crust and it would finish him off.[92]

Many newcomers arrived in Kyiv in such a horrible condition that nobody could help them. Grossman wrote: "They lay starving on the ground, and they sputtered and begged but were unable to eat. A crust might lie right next to them, but they couldn't see it, and they lay dying."[93]

Naum Korzhavin describes that one day in their yard a woman lay down swollen from famine. Korzhavin's uncle asked Naum's father to tell the woman that she should leave their yard, because the police strictly prosecuted the inhabitants if they allowed the homeless to stay in their yards. Somebody suggested that woman was Jewish and did not understand Russian, so Korzhavin's father tried to talk to her in Yiddish. But it was too late; the woman died within a few minutes.[94]

THE HOLODOMOR AND THE CRIMINAL SITUATION IN KYIV

The hunger created a new kind of crime. People stole food to survive. Lang was an eyewitness to one such case in Kyiv:

> Basin [Basseinaia] st. was the headquarters of these "bandits." It also was the stomping ground of veterans of the Red Army, a ghastly collection of cripples and invalids pursuing unsavory affairs. The two parties were in alliance. The cripples acted as spotters, the street wolves carried out the open robberies.
>
> I saw a woman carrying away food from the "open market" in Basin st. The street wolves prefer to attack women. One of them swooped down upon her and bit her arm. She dropped her food and shrieked. The "bandit" snatched his loot and fled. A crowd formed quickly, but no one even tried to catch the thief. The policeman who came up to comfort the woman remarked:
>
> "It's the hunger that's driving them on."[95]

Hunger changed the people's morals, and they would do anything to survive. Some prisoners behaved similarly in the Nazi concentration camps. There were many hunger-embittered people in Kyiv. They felt that a human life was worth nothing in the Soviet Union, and that they could only help themselves.

There were also some open sadists who exercised their power over the starving newcomers. Grossman testified that he saw how a janitor kicked a young girl, "and she slid into the street. She didn't even look back. She just kept crawling along swiftly, trying to find the strength to go on."[96] Perhaps it was not the first time that the girl had been kicked on the street, and she had gotten used to such brutality.

THE HOLODOMOR DEATH RATE

The famine in the Soviet Union had begun in fall 1932 and continued at least until fall 1933. According to recent demographic research, Holodomor losses are "estimated at 4.5 million, with 3.9 million excess deaths and 0.6 million lost births. Rural and urban excess deaths are equivalent to 16.5 and 4.0 per cent of respective 1933 populations."[97] There are no statistics available on the Holodomor losses by nationality. So, it is unknown how many Jews perished during the Holodomor in Kyiv and Ukraine. According to official reports, in February 1933 in the streets of Kyiv, 918 corpses of Jews who had died from the famine were picked up.[98] The total number of Jewish famine victims in Kyiv was certainly much higher than 918 people. Grossman wrote:

> In the morning horses pulled flattop carts through the city, and the corpses of those who had died in the night were collected. I saw one of such flattop cart with children lying on it. They were just as I have described them, thin, elongated faces, like those of dead birds, with sharp beaks. These tiny birds had flown into Kiev and what good had it done them? Some of them were still muttering, and their heads were still turning. I asked the driver about them, and he just waved his hands and said: "By the time they get where they are being taken, they will be silent too."[99]

Grossman wrote that on the same day when he saw the carts with dead and dying children, he purchased a Moscow newspaper in which an article was published

> by Maxim Gorky in which he said that children needed cultural toys. Are we to suppose that Maxim Gorky did not know about those children being hauled off on a flattop cart drawn by dray horses? What kind of toys did they need? But perhaps he did know, too, for that matter. And perhaps he, too, kept silent, like all the rest.[100]

Certainly, it was naïve to anticipate truthful publications about the famine in the Soviet press. Censorship would never allow it.

Harry Lang's eyewitness accounts suggested that the Holodomor took many Jewish lives in Kyiv and was a real calamity for the Jewish community. Lang wrote:

> It was the season of the Jewish new year. I visited the central synagogue. It was crowded with the thousands of worshippers, despite the threats of persecution by the Communist godless society.
>
> There is a special Jewish prayer which enumerates all the known forms of death. Its text contains a reference to death from famine. While I was in the synagogue, the man officiating at the services recited that prayer. When he came to the words, "And he that dies from hunger," he repeated the last word three times with burning anguish. Thousands of Jews sobbed and cried after him:
>
> "Hunger, hunger, hunger!"[101]

Usually nobody emphasizes these words so much during the prayer. This shows their special meaning for Kyivan Jews. A Jewish woman told Lang that her children were starving during Passover. At that time, a rabbi whose children were swollen from hunger came to her home and asked her if she had a little bit of bran to cook something like matzah for both her and his children.[102]

According to Lang's evidence, one of the Kyivan cemeteries had a special section for those who died from hunger in 1932–33, where Lang saw hundreds of fresh graves. Perhaps there were also similar sections at the other Kyivan cemeteries.

Lang wrote:

> I went to one of the Kiev cemeteries which had a special famine section. As far as the eye could see, hundreds of new graves stretched before me. They held the victims of starvation of part of 1932 and part of 1933. They were like the graves which follow a war or an epidemic. There were no headstones, only wooden sticks with numbers.
>
> During the critical famine months, there were scores of daily burials. Sometimes the corpses would lie in the open on the grass for days until their turn came to be interred.[103]

Lang said that he saw at the cemetery many people who "begged the dead for bread."[104] Some even asked the dead to take them away with them, to end their sufferings. Lang wrote: "The entire cemetery was peopled with such scenes."[105] Many were so exhausted from their sufferings that they preferred death to such a horrible life.

AID FROM ABROAD: TORGSIN STORES

Kyivans tried to pass the word about the Holodomor to their relatives abroad and to the world. Lang reported that during his trip to the Soviet Union, people asked him many times to tell the truth in America about their lives.[106] When Lang visited a Kyiv cemetery, a gravedigger came to him and "started a conversation. 'You are looking at our fresh graves?' he said. 'You see, Kiev has also made its contribution to the second five-year plan. Tell my brothers in America about it.'"[107]

What was behind this black humor? Perhaps the gravedigger hoped for some aid from abroad. Sometimes such aid from relatives could save lives. Naum Korzhavin describes how he and his parents did not starve during the Holodomor due to the help of their relatives from abroad.[108] People who had hard currency could buy food in the Torgsin stores. The All-Union Association for Trade with Foreigners (Torgsin) functioned in the Soviet Union in 1931–36. Torgsin stores sold food to foreigners and Soviet citizens for hard currency, or exchanged food for gold, silver, and precious stones. The Soviet authorities used Torgsin stores to raise more foreign currency for industrialization. Some emigrants sent hard currency to their relatives in the Soviet Union. Elena Osokina wrote:

> Money transfers to Belorussia and Ukraine were mostly Jewish, it was the aid from those who left from these regions to the US and Canada before the revolution.... In 1932–1933 more than half the money (60 percent) from the US came from New

York City. Significant help, also mostly Jewish money, came from Poland and the Near East.[109]

Korzhavin wrote that Torgsin stores "had everything, including meat and sausages."[110] But his family could afford to purchase "only a little bit of butter and a little bit of porridge"[111] However, not all Jewish families had relatives abroad, which caused jealousy among their Jewish and gentile neighbors. Soon this help from relatives abroad was turned against the people who received it. Lang reported that during his visit to Kyiv he spoke with a Jew who worked at OGPU. He told Lang that the "dollar inquisition" mostly affected Jews, because the OGPU believed that Jews had connections with their relatives abroad. So, the OGPU arrested many Jews and demanded a ransom in dollars (they did not take rubles) from their families for their release. Lang wrote that fear ruled over Kyiv in 1933. Those who had been arrested at least once by the OGPU "don't go to sleep without putting near their bed a packet with underwear and a piece of bread," because they awaited a new arrest, and nobody knew when they would be arrested again.[112]

On the first night of Rosh Hashanah (the Jewish New Year) police arrested an elderly rabbi and his wife in Kyiv. Lang was an eyewitness of some Kyivan Jews walking from door to door and begging Jews to give some money for the liberation of the rabbi and his wife. By the next morning, the Jews had gathered seventy dollars; the OGPU wanted more, but were satisfied with this ransom, and the rabbi and his wife were released.[113] Lang wrote that the OGPU members kept for themselves part of the seized dollars and the rest was shared with the local authorities.[114]

Trying to get the attention of Americans, Lang published his article "Soviets Seized Cash Sent by U.S. Kin to Starving Russians" in the *New York Evening Journal* on April 23, 1935. He wrote:

> The G.P.U.[115] then launched an organized campaign to extort the American dollars as a source of government revenue.
>
> This "Dollar Inquisition" caused the American Jewish Congress, led by Rabbi Stephen S. Wise, to call meetings of protest.
>
> The Hebrew poet laureate in Palestine, Chaim Nachman Bialik, had gathered a mass of authentic evidence proving conclusively that the G.P.U. was terrorizing all the Jewish communities in Russia, imprisoning people just because they had relatives in America, and holding them as hostages until ransom arrived.[116]

Later, during the repression of the second half of the 1930s to 1953, many of those who received aid from abroad and were in correspondence with their relatives abroad were arrested as spies of foreign intelligence services.

RELATIONS BETWEEN JEWS AND NON-JEWS IN KYIV

Jewish-gentile relations were quite complicated in Kyiv in the interwar period. Judeophobia and anti-Semitism in Kyiv have deep historical roots. Religious intolerance of Jews in this holy Orthodox Christian city, envy of their professional success, and later political and racial anti-Semitism contributed to the hatred of Jews by much of Kyiv's gentile population. Thus, anti-Jewish pogroms occurred in Kyiv in 1881, 1905, and several times during the civil war (1918–20). The blood libel Beilis Affair (1911–13) was initiated by the Kyiv Black Hundreds organization Two-Headed Eagle. Kyiv was an outpost of Russian nationalism and chauvinism before the February 1917 Revolution. From prerevolutionary times, there were also Judeophile Russian and Ukrainian intelligentsia, but many gentiles in Kyiv were prejudiced against Jews.[117]

During the interwar period, the Soviet authorities suppressed popular anti-Semitism, but it continued to persist in everyday life. For example, my late high school history teacher Alexander Kravets (1929–2006) told me how he learned that he was Jewish. Once when he was six years old his parents went to the theater and left him at home in the communal apartment under the care of their roommates (usually three to five different families lived in a communal apartment). One of the roommates told another her recollections from the civil war. She vividly described how *petliurovtsy* (as members of the Ukrainian National Army were called) put a "Yid" on a pike and gleefully mimicked how the "Yid" pitifully screamed and tried to escape. Kravets told me that everybody in the apartment was laughing at the story, except him, because he did not understand the meaning of the word "Yid." So, he asked the woman, "What does the word 'Yid' mean?" The roommates all began to laugh at him, because he was Jewish and did not understand the meaning of "Yid."

The Holodomor badly affected relations between Jews and gentiles in Kyiv before and during World War II. It made the prejudice against Jews even stronger. The participation of a member of the Soviet Politburo, Lazar Kaganovich (who was Jewish), in the organization of the Holodomor, along with Josef Stalin, Vyacheslav Molotov, Pavel Postyshev, Stanislav Kosior, Vlas Chubar, and Mendel Khataievich, allowed anti-Semites to claim that the Jews organized the genocide in Ukraine in 1932–33. Of course, anti-Semites did not admit that many Jews starved and died during the Holodomor in Ukraine along with the rest of the population.

Famine increased tension in the city between Kyivans and newcomers. Korzhavin wrote that native Kyivans did not like the uneducated and rude newcomers, and many newcomers—Ukrainian peasants—did not like Kyivans, who lived better than they did, especially the Jews.[118] Kyivans lived in communal apartments, while the newcomers settled in the basements of the apartment buildings. According to Korzhavin, a person's place of living became the indicator of their social and cultural status. Peasants felt disrespected in Kyiv.[119] Korzhavin pointed out:

> But these people, who had self-esteem, who were before the owners of farms, had gotten used to being respected. In their eyes, a city was a place from which all their calamities came, from which all these collectivizators and dekulakizers came....
>
> And now this city, which had destroyed their world, made senseless their labor, expelled them from their houses and villages, in addition to all, yet arrogantly towered above them....
>
> For these recent peasants, Jews were the ultimate embodiment of the city, which had abused them.[120]

Jews felt the hostile attitude of some gentiles and had "bad premonitions of how these people would behave during a war."[121] Thus, the hostility between Jews and gentiles existed before the war; however, Soviet authorities suppressed popular anti-Semitism in the 1920s and 1930s. The Bolsheviks declared anti-Semitism to be a shameful remnant of the Tsarist regime. So, anti-Semites were afraid to attack Jews openly, as the attackers could be accused of counterrevolutionary activities and could be prosecuted as "enemies of the people." Popular anti-Semitism was usually limited in the prewar years to personal insults of Jews and did not typically acquire a violent character.

Anatoly Kuznetsov wrote in *Babi Yar: A Document in the Form of a Novel* that people who lived in the Soviet Union during the Holodomor and Stalin's repression of the 1930s got used to being silent. They knew that any protest could cost them their lives. When the repressive Soviet system was replaced by the Nazis, and the Nazis killed Jews in Babyn Yar, the rest of the Kyivan population remained silent and indifferent.[122] Kyivans got used to seeing dying people on the streets during the Holodomor, and they got used to the disappearance of their neighbors and friends during Stalin's repression. If they had remained silent previously, it would be naïve to anticipate that they would have more compassion for Jews during the Holocaust.

CONCLUSION

The Jewish population of Kyiv grew rapidly after the abolition of the Pale of Settlement on account of the newcomers. Jews were attracted to the city by better prospects for education and a professional career than in provincial cities and shtetls, and by the vibrant urban cultural life. Kyiv became the center of Soviet Jewish scholarly life and culture in the 1920s and 1930s as a result of a combination of factors. Of course, the large number of Jews in the city and the high percentage of Jewish intelligentsia among them played a significant role. The existence in the city of the "old" Jewish cultural and scholarly institutions was also important. The personal factor also played its role: the director of the Kyiv Institute of Jewish Proletarian Culture, Joseph Liberberg, was an ambitious administrator with strong connections with the Soviet authorities that allowed him to centralize all Jewish scholarship in Kyiv within a short time.

Jewish scholarship and culture in the Soviet Union never developed under conditions of political freedom. The Soviets always defined what areas of Jewish culture should be developed and which ones should be banned. However, the 1920s were still a comparatively liberal time for Soviet scholarship and culture, and the "old" cultural and scholarly organizations continued to function under the supervision of Soviet censorship.

Jewish proletarian organizations founded by Evsektsiia and the Soviet authorities focused on the destruction of the "old bourgeoisie" scholarly and cultural institutions. When they, together with their creators, had fulfilled their functions and had destroyed the "old" Jewish scholarship and culture in the Soviet Union, the authorities liquidated them too.

In the second half of the 1930s, the Soviet policy toward all national minorities, including Jews, abruptly changed. Instead of encouraging the development of various national cultures of the multinational population of the Soviet Union, the authorities decided to emphasize the dominant Russian culture and suppress all others. The typical expression of the official policy toward the national minorities of the Soviet Union in the second half of the 1930s was the speech by a Soviet apparatchik, Alexander Shlikhter, at the Thirteenth Congress of the Communist Party of Ukraine (May–June 1937) about "the wrecking activity of the various nations."[123] Thus the Soviets spread their repression from individuals to entire nations that were accused of the harmful activity.

The Holodomor had a severe impact on the entire population of Ukraine. In rural areas the death rate was higher, but in Ukrainian cities and towns many thousands also died from starvation. Among the victims of the Holodomor were people of all nationalities.

Jews starved and died during the Holodomor in Kyiv, in provincial cities and towns, and in agricultural settlements. Unfortunately, the theme of the Holodomor and Jews has not yet received its deserved attention by historians. Most histories describe the first half of the 1930s as a period of development of Soviet Jewish cultural and educational institutions, and a flourishing of Yiddish culture in the Soviet Union. But these institutions were just official "cultural toys," while many Jews were starving and dying from hunger. Hungry people could not utilize these cultural and educational institutions. My paternal grandmother, Dvoira Feldman, studied in the early 1930s in a Yiddish college in the town of Bila Tserkva. She told me that she never starved so severely as in those years. She had to quit her education because she fainted from hunger during her classes. She managed somehow to escape to Kyiv, where her oldest brother lived, during or soon after the famine. He helped my grandmother establish her life in the new place.

The Holodomor embittered many people, made them indifferent to the suffering of others, and created more tension between Jews and gentiles in Kyiv and Ukraine. In this way, the Holodomor prepared the ground for the Holocaust of Jews in Kyiv.

During the Holodomor and the Holocaust, the same repressive mechanisms operated: dehumanizing enemies and starving them to death (during the Holocaust the Nazis used these methods in the ghettos and concentration camps). However, the ultimate goals of these two genocides were different: the suppression of resistance to collectivization during the Holodomor versus the extermination of the entire Jewish people during the Holocaust. But, by suppressing the peasants' resistance to collectivization, the Soviets also starved much of the population.

2

THE BABYN YAR MASSACRE: THE HOLOCAUST OF JEWS IN KYIV

POINT OF NO RETURN

Many Jews remained in Kyiv at the time of the Nazi occupation on September 19, 1941, because they did not have any opportunity to leave the city. First, they were misled by Soviet propaganda that claimed until the surrender of Kyiv that the Red Army would never give up the city, that "Kyiv was and is Soviet," and that "the enemy will never drink water from the Dnipro."[1] Soviet leaders did not intentionally mislead the Kyivans. Stalin gave the order to hold the city by all possible means. The Red Army defended the city until over 600,000 Soviet troops were encircled and forced to surrender. Thus, when Kyivans realized that the Nazis were on the outskirts of the city, it was already too late to leave.[2]

Evacuation from Kyiv to the eastern part of the Soviet Union was organized only for military plants and their workers, Soviet leaders, prominent scholars, cultural figures, and their families. Nobody evacuated women, children, and the elderly. Most Jews who remained in Kyiv at the time of the Nazi occupation belonged to these categories. Almost all men eighteen to forty-five years old had already been drafted into the Red Army in the first days of the war.[3]

In the first weeks of the Soviet-Nazi war, when there was still some possibility of escaping from the city, many elderly Jews preferred to stay. They remembered the Germans as "civilized people" from their occupation of Kyiv during World War I. During the occupation of Kyiv in 1918, the Germans established order, stopped Jewish pogroms, and encouraged private business. So, many elderly Jews and gentiles thought that the Nazis would be better rulers than the Soviets.[4] My great-grandmother Ester

Vons implored her husband, Iosif Polinovsky, to evacuate with her from Kyiv, but he refused to go. Polinovsky told her, "I remember the Germans well from the First World War. They are civilized people. I will open a store with my son [from his first marriage] and will trade with him." Ester went to evacuation with her daughter, who was the wife of a Soviet officer, and granddaughter. Polinovsky and his son remained in Kyiv, and they perished at Babyn Yar.

The Nazi occupation of Kyiv continued for 778 days from September 19, 1941, to November 6, 1943. The murder of Jews in Kyiv began one week after the occupation. On September 26, 1941, the Nazis arrested 1,600 Jews and executed them the next day at Babyn Yar.[5] On September 26 and 27, 1941, the Nazis killed Jews not only at Babyn Yar, but also in other parts of Kyiv. *The Black Book* describes some of the murders:

> On September 26–27 (Friday–Saturday), Jews who had gone to the synagogue disappeared. Yevgenia Litoshchenko, a resident of Kiev, testified that her neighbors—an elderly man named Schneider and a couple by the name of Rosenblat—did not return from the synagogue. Later she saw their corpses in the Dnieper. Her testimony was supported by T. Mikhasev.[6]

On September 28, Einsatzgruppe C, located in Kyiv, reported to the chief of the Security Police and Security Service in Berlin, "There are probably 150,000 Jews in Kyiv. To check this information has been impossible thus far."[7] The report stated: "Execution of at least 50,000 [Kyivan] Jews planned."[8] Nazis chose the Babyn Yar ravine as the mass execution site for Kyivan Jews because of its remote location and large size: 2.5 kilometers (1.5 miles) long and 50 meters deep. Babyn Yar is located about six miles from downtown on the outskirts of Kyiv. Before the war, the Babyn Yar ravine was the site of a sandpit and a garbage dump[9] (figure 2.1).

To trick the Jews and make them come to the place of their massacre, the Nazis spread the rumor that "all the Jews of Kiev would be moved to another place."[10] The Ukrainian police helped bring Jews to Babyn Yar. Karel Berkhoff wrote:

> On Sunday, September 28, 1941, the newly installed Ukrainian police posted 2,000 copies of a Russian-, Ukrainian-, and German-language order to the Jews of Kiev and the surrounding area. It instructed them to appear the next day before 8:00 a.m. at a specified intersection and to bring along "documents, money, valuables, warm clothing, and underwear." ... The announcement added that those Jews who disobeyed would be shot; the Russian text employed the word "Yids."[11]

Jewish women, children, and elderly people who remained in Kyiv during the Nazi occupation could not resist the armed Nazis and Ukrainian police. Most of them did

Figure 2.1. Babyn Yar before World War II. (Unidentified photographer.)

not have any place to hide and could not escape from the city. Many Kyivan Jews believed the rumors that they would be resettled. The Lukianivka freight train station was near the Nazi-assigned gathering place. So, most Jews who remained in Kyiv submitted to the Nazi order to come to the assigned place at the corner of Melnikov and Dekhtirivska Streets, which merge at Lukianivka Square. *The Black Book* describes the last road of Kyivan Jews:

> At dawn of September 29 Kiev's Jews were moving slowly along the streets in the direction of the Jewish Cemetery on Lukyanovka [Lukianivka] from various parts of the city. Many of them thought they were to be sent to provincial towns, but others realized that Babi Yar meant death. There were many suicides on that day.[12]

On Monday morning, September 29, Fedir Pihido was on Lviv Street, and he saw how many thousands of people, mainly old ones—but middle-aged people were also not lacking—were moving toward Babi Yar. And the children—my God, there were so many children! All this was moving, burdened with luggage and children. Here and there old and sick people who lacked the strength to move by themselves were being carried, probably by sons or daughters, on carts without any assistance. Some cry, others console. Most were moving in a self-absorbed way, in silence and with a doomed look. It was a terrible sight.[13]

On the next day Jews continued to walk toward the assigned place of gathering from which they were ushered to Babyn Yar. Early in the morning of September 30, Fedir Bohatyrchuk saw many Jews walk to the assigned gathering place. The Jews had

> stony faces, paralyzed with fright. They already instinctively foresaw what was going to happen to them. Only the children did not suspect a thing and walked business-like, with bags in their hands or knapsacks on their shoulders. I remember a group of Jews who carried a gray-haired old man, apparently a rabbi, on a stretcher and were singing a sad song.[14]

A guard of the Lukianivka Jewish cemetery, Sergey Lutsenko, was an eyewitness of the tragedy. He testified that arriving Jewish people filled Lukianivska, Dekhtirivska, Lagerna, and Melnikov Streets and the three cemeteries that are located near Babyn Yar.[15]

Crowds of Kyivans observed the procession of Jews to Babyn Yar.[16] Oleg Minsky, an eyewitness of the Babyn Yar tragedy, recalled:

> Jews who walked to Babyn Yar in the afternoon already knew that they are walking to their execution. They looked around, looking for help. But there was no help, people [gentiles] looked down, left for home, not because they did not want to help the miserable, but because it was impossible.[17]

However, not all Kyivan gentiles felt compassion toward the Jews. Some expressed their satisfaction that they were getting rid of the Jews in the city and insulted Jews on their final road; some even stole their belongings along the way. Bohatyrchuk recalled, "Unfortunately and to my shame, I have to say that I saw quite few of my co-religionists watching this exodus with a happy face. These short-sighted people, blinded by hatred, simply did not realized what was going on."[18]

Kuznetsov recalled that as a twelve-year-old, he observed the last walk of the Jews to Babyn Yar. He wrote:

> The closer I got to Podol the more people I found out on the streets. They were standing in the gateways and porches, some of them watching and sighing, others

jeering and hurling insults at the Jews. At one point the wicked-looking old woman in a dirty head-scarf ran out on to the roadway, snatched a case from the elderly Jewess and rushed back inside the courtyard. The Jewess screaming after her, but some tough characters stood in the gateway and stopped her getting in. She sobbed and cursed and complained, but nobody would take her part, and the crowd went on their way, their eyes averted. I peeped through a crack and saw a whole pile of stolen things lying in the yard.[19]

When Jews came to the assigned point at Lukianivka Square, they were ordered to continue walking on Melnikov Street toward the Lukianivka Jewish Cemetery. According to Holocaust survivor Dina Pronicheva, this was the point of no return, because this part of Melnikov Street had a fence of barbed wire and anti-tank hedgehogs. Germans and Ukrainians stood at the entrance to this part of the street. They allowed everybody to come in, but did not allow anybody to exit, except the drivers. There was "a dense police cordon along the Jews' entire route and around Babyn Yar."[20]

From the direction of Babi Yar could be heard the barking of many dogs, the crackle of automatic-rifle fire, and the cries of the dying. The crowd moved toward them, and the road was packed. Loudspeakers bellowed dance melodies which drowned out the screams of the victims.[21]

Babyn Yar survivor Geniia Batasheva testified:

Both sides of Dorogozhytska Street [where Jews were forced to turn from Melnikov Street] were densely planted with young trees and between them stood Hitlerites armed with automatic weapons and sticks. Many had dogs.... Those who tried to move aside... were beaten severely with sticks and attacked by dogs. People were also beaten without any reason.[22]

Pronicheva confirmed this testimony: "If someone fell, a dog was let loose which ripped things and the body, the person just had to get up and run downward and fall into the hands of [non-German] policemen."[23]

The Military Police divided arriving Jews into groups of 100 to 150 people and pushed them further along for "registration."[24] The "registration" tables were near the Bratske (Brotherhood) Cemetery. There the Nazis took the Jews' documents away from them and immediately burned them.[25] Then Jews were pushed to the other tables where the Nazis confiscated the Jews' belongings and forced them to undress. "The survivor, Ruvim Shtein recalled in 1996 that men and women undressed separately, and the Nazis put them in separate lines and then conveyed them to Babi Yar."[26] The Ukrainian auxiliary police sorted the Jewish belongings.[27]

The Jews were then chased to the edge of Babyn Yar ravine through a "double row of SS men with the dogs" who beat people with rubber clubs. "Bleeding and very scared, the victims came to the edge of the ravine and there the German and Ukrainian policemen even more brutally beat the people."[28] Jews came to the top of the hill and by trails they came down to the ravine.

The execution of Jews at Babyn Yar was done by "Sonderkommando (special unit) 4a, a subunit of Einsatzgruppe (taskforce) C, a mobile killing squad of the Security Police (Sipo) and Security Service (SD), and by Order Police battalions 45 and 303 of the regular German police. Also present were Ukrainian auxiliary police."[29] The Nazis shot Jews in three different locations at Babyn Yar.[30] Sergey Lutsenko, the guard of Lukianivka Jewish Cemetery, witnessed from his guardhouse the Germans shooting people at Babyn Yar using automatic rifles and machine guns. Young children were thrown into the pit alive.[31]

The Nazis shot the Jews on the edge of the ditch and their corpses fell into the pit. A few Jews who survived the massacre fell or jumped into the pit alive and some crawled out later that night. That is how Dina Pronicheva, Nesya Elgort and her son Ilia, Elena Borodiansky-Knysh and her daughter Ludmila survived.[32]

Executions took place from 10 a.m. to about 5 or 6 p.m.[33] Einsatzgruppe C reported that on September 29, 1941, 22,000 Jews were killed at Babyn Yar.[34] The Germans locked the rest of the Jews in the empty garages of a tank repair plant at night. Lutsenko testified that the mass murder continued for five days. The Nazis brought more and more people to Babyn Yar, and from there returned only trucks with people's clothes. "Every five minutes a new truck left. The corpses were thrown into the ravine. The Nazis at night exploded the steep slope to cover by earth the dead and wounded."[35] On September 30 approximately 12,000 Jews were executed at Babyn Yar.

The Operations Situation Report, Einsatzgruppe C, from October 7, 1941, stated:

> In collaboration with the Einsatzgruppe staff and 2 commandos of the Police Regiment South, the Sonderkommando 4a executed 33,771 Jews on September 29 and 30. Money, valuables, underwear, and clothing were confiscated and placed in part at the disposal of the NSV for the use of Volksdeutsche and in part given to the city's administrative authorities for the use of the needy population.[36]

The execution of Jews at Babyn Yar continued until mid-November 1941. Nachmanovich wrote: "German police battalions of Regiment South carried out executions until 15 October. By early October they were joined by Einsatzkommando 5, which had remained in Kyiv and formed the nucleus of the local security police and the SD."[37] The Nazis and Ukrainian police searched for Jews in Kyiv and the countryside. "The Germans not only searched apartments, but also inspected cellars and caves, and even used explosives to blast open floors, suspicious walls, attics, and chimneys."[38] They found and killed hundreds of hidden Jews.

After the mass murder of Jews, the Nazis forced Soviet prisoners of war to cover the corpses at Babyn Yar by half a meter of sand and earth. Before their retreat from Kyiv, the Nazis decided to destroy the evidence of the mass murder at Babyn Yar. Berkhoff wrote: "For six weeks from the middle of August 1943, the Security Police attempted to erase the crime scene: it forced hundreds of mostly Jewish prisoners to dig up corpses and incinerate them."[39]

HOW MANY JEWS PERISHED AT BABYN YAR?

Debate among historians persists regarding the widely varying estimates of the number of Jews murdered at Babyn Yar.[40] Estimates range from 33,771 to over 100,000. Many scholarly publications use the number of 33,771 Jewish victims of Babyn Yar, which Einsatzgruppe C provided in the report on October 7, 1941. But this number included only Jews who were killed at Babyn Yar on September 29–30, 1941. Alexander Kruglov wrote that for the entire period of the Nazi occupation of Kyiv, 39,000–40,000 Jews were killed at Babyn Yar.[41] Nachmanovich estimated that by mid-November 1941 "up to 65,000 Jews from Kyiv and surrounding towns and villages were shot [at Babyn Yar]."[42] Felix Levitas writes that over 100,000 Jews might have perished at Babyn Yar.[43]

Statistical data that would allow calculation of the number of Jewish victims of Babyn Yar does not exist. It is impossible to know with any precision how many Jews were in Kyiv when the Nazis occupied the city on September 19–20, 1941. We do not know how many Jews were able to evacuate, how many Kyivan Jews were mobilized into the Red Army, or how many Jewish refugees from other places were in the city. At the time of the chaotic retreat of the Red Army, nobody thought about collecting such statistics.

Soviet press and official documents provide varied data about the number of Babyn Yar victims. V. Stepanenko wrote in the article "Chto proiskhodit v Kieve" (What is going on in Kyiv) in *Pravda* on November 29, 1941, "History has never known such pogroms and slaughter as the Hitlerites organized in Kyiv. 52,000 people were shot within a few days. Fascists[44] organized the Jewish pogrom, during which they also killed Russians and Ukrainians."[45]

Soviet foreign minister Vyacheslav Molotov used the number 52,000 victims of Babyn Yar in a memorandum "sent on January 6, 1942, to all countries with which the USSR maintained diplomatic relations":

> A frightful slaughter and terror action were committed by the German invaders in the Ukrainian capital of Kiev. During three days the German robbers shot and killed

52,000 men, women, old people and children, mercilessly killed Ukrainians, Russians and Jews who showed their loyalty to the Soviet government.[46]

Certainly, "loyalty to the Soviet government" was not important in the case of Jews, who were killed based on their ethnicity. Jews, who were listed as the main victims of the Nazi massacre in the newspaper *Pravda*, were mentioned as Babyn Yar victims after Ukrainians and Russians in Molotov's memorandum.

Berkhoff wrote that after the liberation of Kyiv,

> the Soviet Secret police (NKVD) organized five of its own excavations of mass graves at Babi Yar, including the former Syrets camp, and concluded that in 1943 that the Nazis had attempted to burn 100,000 corpses at Babi Yar. The NKVD's analysis also correctly noted that "displaying a special hatred toward the Jewish nationality, the German-fascist bandits in the city of Kiev annihilated almost all the Jews." The death count included, in September 1941 alone, "about 70,000 Jews at Babi Yar."[47]

The number of 100,000 victims of Babyn Yar was used in the report of the Extraordinary State Commission for Investigation of German-Fascist Crimes Committed on Soviet Territory at the Nuremberg trial. The commission reported that during the occupation of Kyiv over 195,000 Soviet citizens were killed, including

1. at Babyn Yar—over 100,000 men, women, children, and elderly people;
2. in Darnytsa (district of Kyiv on the left bank of the River Dnipro)—over 68,000 Soviet prisoners of war and civilians;
3. in an anti-tank trench and near the Syrets concentration camp and on the territory of the camp—over 25,000 Soviet citizens and prisoners of war;
4. on the territory of Kyrylivsky Hospital—800 mentally ill people;
5. on the territory of Kyiv-Pechersk Lavra—about 500 civilians;
6. at Lukianivka Cemetery—400 civilians.[48]

The Extraordinary State Commission data regarding the Kyiv loss of population during the Nazi occupation was based on data revealed by the NKVD excavations of the killing sites and on the testimony of Holocaust survivors and eyewitnesses of the events.

The large loss of Kyivan population during the war indirectly confirms the statistics of the Extraordinary State Commission. The total population of Kyiv decreased from 930,000 inhabitants in 1940 to 704,609 in 1947.[49] So, Kyiv lost over 225,000 inhabitants during the war. There are no statistics on how many Kyivans perished at the front, how many died during the Nazi occupation, and how many did not return from evacuation. The Kyivan Jewish population decreased during the war by 91,769 people compared to the census of 1939 (on January 1, 1947, 132,467 Jews lived in Kyiv, or 18.8 percent of the city's inhabitants).[50] Perhaps about 10,000 to 20,000 Kyivan Jews were killed at the front, several thousand did not return from evacuation, and the rest perished at Babyn Yar. So, we can estimate that about 50,000 to 70,000 Jews were killed at Babyn Yar during the Nazi occupation of Kyiv.

There were many victims of the Nazi occupation regime in Kyiv; however, most victims at Babyn Yar were Jewish. Roma, mentally ill people, Soviet prisoners of war, members of the Soviet underground movement, and members of the Organization of Ukrainian Nationalists (OUN-M) were also executed at Babyn Yar.[51]

WHY DID BABYN YAR BECOME THE LARGEST HOLOCAUST SITE IN THE SOVIET UNION?

There were several reasons why the largest massacres of Jews in Nazi-occupied Soviet territory occurred in Kyiv. The Nazis blamed Jews for massive explosions and fires in downtown Kyiv in the first days of their occupation of the city. Before retreating from Kyiv, an NKVD diversionary group hid remote-controlled explosives and incendiaries in the buildings and squares of downtown Kyiv. On September 24, 1941, explosions and fires began in downtown Kyiv, which continued for several days. The explosions and fires destroyed 940 buildings in Kyiv, including those where the offices of the staff of the German Army and the Nazi city commandant were located and five hotels where many German officers were billeted.[52]

Einsatzgruppe C reported on September 28, 1941:

> Up to now 670 mines detected in buildings, according to a mine-laying plan which was discovered: all public buildings and squares are mined, among them, it is alleged, also the building assigned to this office for future use. Building being searched most assiduously. In the course of this search, 60 Molotov cocktails of explosives were detected and removed. In the Lenin Museum, 70 hundredweights [8,000 lbs.] of dynamite discovered which were to be touched off by wireless. It was repeatedly observed that fires broke out the moment buildings were taken over. As has been proved, Jews played a pre-eminent part.[53]

The explosions killed many Nazi officers and soldiers, which made the Nazis furious and seeking revenge. The Nazis needed scapegoats, and while they could not retaliate against the real culprits, the Jewish population of Kyiv was an easy target.

Writer Yuri Shcheglov (pen name of Yuri Varshaver) recalled that he asked his friend, the writer Victor Nekrasov, whether the explosions and fires in Kyiv were the real reason for the execution of Jews at Babyn Yar. Nekrasov told him that this was the Nazi justification of the Babyn Yar massacre. Nekrasov said that the occupation authorities needed to explain to the Wehrmacht High Administration and Hitler why they could not prevent the explosions and destruction in Kyiv and show that the culprits had been punished. So, the Nazis blamed the Jews for everything and executed them at Babyn Yar, claiming to their superiors that they had punished the culprits of the destruction of downtown Kyiv.[54]

Certainly, the racist Nazi ideology and the extermination of Jews, which had already begun on occupied Soviet territory, shows that Kyivan Jews were already doomed regardless of the explosions and fires downtown. The "Holocaust by bullets" began from the first days of the Nazi occupation of Soviet territory. By the end of June 1941, about 1,500 Jews in the L'viv, Drogobych, and Volhynia regions had been murdered. Alexander Kruglov estimated that the death toll of Jews in the Nazi-occupied territory of Ukraine was 38,000–39,000 in July 1941 and 61,000–62,000 in August.[55] However, Kyiv became the first large European city where almost all Jews were exterminated. That the Holocaust of Kyivan Jews was preplanned is proven by the arrival in the city of special extermination task forces together with the rest of the Nazi troops. Sonderkommando 4a arrived in Kyiv on September 19, 1941. Einsatzgruppe Headquarters was established in Kyiv on September 24.[56] On September 26 representatives of the Nazi occupation forces and the SS had a meeting in the staff quarters of the city commandant, where they decided not to establish a ghetto in Kyiv, but instead to exterminate all Jews at Babyn Yar.[57] So perhaps the explosions and fires in Kyiv just accelerated the Nazi decision to exterminate Kyivan Jews.

In their planning for the mass murder of Jews at Babyn Yar, the Nazis considered Kyiv's sizable Jewish population, one of the largest in occupied Soviet territory. The Nazis also counted on the anti-Jewish sentiments of a significant number of Kyiv gentiles. Anti-Semitism in Kyiv was always stronger than in other places of the Russian Empire. Kyiv had a long history of pogroms, Jewish expulsions, religious intolerance, and the chauvinistic Black Hundreds organizations, which instigated the Beilis Affair in 1911–13.[58] According to the Einsatzgruppe C report dated October 7, 1941, Kyiv's gentile population "was extremely infuriated against the Jews because of their preferential economic status under Soviet rule."[59]

As mentioned in the previous chapter, "privileged status" in Kyiv meant merely having a room in a communal apartment instead of living in the basement, a distinction that nevertheless fueled jealousy among neighbors. So, the Nazis anticipated correctly that much of the local gentile population did not like Jews and would not resist their extermination. Before the execution of Jews at Babyn Yar, the Nazis spread rumors that Jews would be resettled elsewhere. Einsatzgruppe C reported on October 7, 1941, "The population agreed with the plan to move the Jews to another place. That they were actually liquidated has hardly been made known. However, according to the experience gained so far, this would not meet with any opposition."[60]

While the Nazis may have overstated the extent of anti-Jewish sentiment among Kyiv's gentiles, it is true that the execution of Jews at Babyn Yar failed to provoke any public protest either during or after the horrifying events. Certainly, the entire gentile population was not hostile toward Jews, and many felt compassion for them, as did Anatoly Kuznetsov's family and the Kyivan artist Irina Khoroshunova. Khoroshunova expressed in her diary how terrified she was by the murder of Jews at Babyn Yar. She mentioned that the Kyivan gentile population believed the Nazi rumors about the resettlement of Jews, and that when the execution of Jews at Babyn Yar began, they could not change anything. Khoroshunova wrote in her diary on October 2, 1941:

> I write because it is necessary that people around the World know about this horrible crime and retaliate against it.
>
> While I write the mass murder of defenseless, innocent children, women and elderly people is continuing at Babyn Yar. Many of them were buried semi-alive, because the Germans are thrifty, and they do not like to spend extra bullets....
>
> We are absolutely, absolutely powerless!...
>
> This is it. And we are still alive. And we do not understand, why we suddenly have more right for life, because we are not Jews. Damn century, damned monstrous time![61]

Kuznetsov blamed Kyivan gentiles and Jews for their passivity and submission to Nazi orders. In *Babi Yar: A Document in the Form of a Novel*, he wrote that people who lived in the Soviet Union during the Holodomor and Stalin's repression had become accustomed to keeping quiet. They knew that any protest could cost them their lives. When the repressive Soviet system was replaced by the Nazis, and the Nazis killed Jews at Babyn Yar, most Kyivan gentiles remained silent and appeared indifferent.[62] Kyivans had gotten used to seeing people dying on the streets during the Holodomor, and they got used to the disappearance of their neighbors and friends during Stalin's repression. If they had remained silent previously, it would be naïve to expect that they would protest the murder of Jews at Babyn Yar.

It is hard to judge whether Kyiv gentiles, who were taken by surprise by the mass murder of Jews at Babyn Yar on September 29–30, 1941, could have resisted more and if their protests would have made any difference. But it is obvious that several thousand Kyivan Jews who disobeyed the Nazi order to come to Babyn Yar and instead hid or tried to escape from the city would have had a much better chance of survival during the Nazi occupation if local collaborators had not frequently betrayed them (figures 2.2 and 2.3).

Figure 2.2 Portrait of three-year-old Anna Glinberg, a Jewish child who was killed at Babyn Yar. (Unidentified photographer.)

Figure 2.3 Portrait of four-year-old Malvina Babat and three-year-old Polina Babat, who were killed at Babyn Yar. (Unidentified photographer.)

BETRAYAL AND RESCUE OF JEWS IN NAZI-OCCUPIED KYIV: INDIVIDUAL COLLABORATORS

By all accounts, it appears that significantly more gentiles betrayed Jews during the occupation of Kyiv than rescued them. Motivations for betrayal varied: Traditional anti-Semitism was reinforced by Nazi propaganda; some gentiles desired to enrich themselves with Jewish property, to occupy Jewish apartments, or to demonstrate their loyalty to the Nazis. Betrayal of Jews was encouraged and rewarded by the Nazis and the Ukrainian police, while the rescue of Jews put gentiles and their families under mortal risk.

Unfortunately, the bad premonitions of many Jews were realized during the Nazi occupation of Kyiv. Anti-Semitism exploded in the city from the first days of the Nazi occupation. Korzhavin wrote that the janitor of his apartment building, Mitrofan Kudritsky, so sadistically tortured his elderly Jewish family members during the first nine or ten days of the Nazi occupation that their subsequent execution at Babyn Yar was seen as a liberation.[63] Korzhavin described how Kudritsky organized "a personal Auschwitz in their home" for Korzhavin's relatives:

> Every day, every morning he came to our apartment ... with one purpose, to commit outrages against them. He tortured these elderly people creatively, in many ways, beat them, forced them to clean the restroom in the yard with their bare hands and to do many other jobs that were humiliating and beyond their strength. He punished them if they did not fulfill his orders well enough. He was their master, and he enjoyed this situation.[64]

Kudritsky had appeared in Kyiv with his family in 1934. He had been "dekulakized" and hated everybody who, in his opinion, lived better than he did. He was happy when people were arrested during Stalin's repression. Kudritsky also hated the Soviet regime, which had spoiled his life. He rejoiced when Nazi Germany attacked the Soviet Union and when Nazi aircraft bombed Kyiv. But why did Kudritsky choose elderly Jews who did not have any connection with the Soviet authorities as his victims? Notably, one of Korzhavin's uncles had owned a building in which he shared an apartment with his brother's family that was confiscated after the revolution.[65] For Kudritsky, the Soviet authorities were distant and unreachable, and so he directed all his anger toward his Jewish neighbors, turning their lives into a nightmare. In addition to Korzhavin's relatives, Kudritsky also sadistically tortured two other Jewish families that lived in the building: an elderly couple and a mother with her child. He outlived his Jewish victims but did not survive the war. The Nazis, whom Kudritsky had praised at the beginning of the occupation, executed him for stealing from them.[66]

The Nazis encouraged local gentiles to denounce Jews hidden in the city. Holocaust survivor Veniamin Liberman testified that on the fifth day of the occupation of Kyiv (September 24, 1941) he saw on Khreshchatyk Street "a car with a huge megaphone making frequent stops; a loud voice was coming over the megaphone, shouting, 'Report the where-abouts of communists, partisans, and Jews to the Gestapo and to the police! Report them!'"[67]

The similar call to gentiles to inform the German authorities about Jews, partisans, and communists was posted around Kyiv and promised a reward for their denunciation. Kuznetsov wrote:

> Notices were posted on the hoardings saying that anyone who informed the German authorities about Jews or partisans in hiding, about important Bolshevik officials who had not reported for registration as Communists, **or about other enemies of the people** [bold in the original], would receive ten thousand roubles in cash or in the form of foodstuffs or a cow.[68]

Kuznetsov recalled that many Kyivan Jews did not obey the Nazi order and did not go to Babyn Yar but hid in basements and storerooms. He wrote:

> In most cases the hidden people were discovered, because there were plenty of people glad enough to have the money or the cow. Near our market in Kurenyovka, for instance, there lived a certain Praskovya Derkach. She would nose around until she found out where some Jews were hiding and then go to them and say:
>
> "Aha! So there you are! So you don't want to go to Babyn Yar? Out with your gold! Let's have your cash!"
>
> They would hand her over all their valuables. Then, in spite of this, she would make a statement to the police and demand another reward. Her husband Vasili had a horse and cart, and they usually took the Jews off to the Yar on it. On the way Praskovya and her husband would be snatching clothes and watches off the people, saying:
>
> "You won't need them anymore!"
>
> They carted off sick people, children and pregnant women.[69]

Most Kyivan Jews, quite acculturated in the interwar period, dressed and looked like gentiles. So, without the help of local gentiles the Nazis would not have been able to identify and kill so many Jews hidden in Kyiv. According to Timothy Snyder, "In Kyiv, Ukrainians and Russians helped the German Order Police find and register Jews before the mass shooting at Babyi Iar."[70]

Kruglov and Umansky pointed out that some Kyivan gentiles detained Jews before the Babyn Yar massacre, gathered them in one place, and then passed them to the German police. During the mass shooting these gentiles themselves delivered Jews to Babyn Yar. Historians assume that their main motivation was greed and a desire to enrich themselves with Jewish property.[71]

The reaction of Kyiv's gentile population to the massacre of Jews at Babyn Yar varied from compassion for Jews to satisfaction with their death. Minskiy recalled that the Nazi shooting of Jews at Babyn Yar became known in the city by 11 a.m. on September 29, 1941.[72] There were people who looked upon the execution of Jews as an opportunity to obtain for free some Jewish property. He said that they were not numerous, "but their greed did not know any bounds. Without shame they put on themselves the still warm clothes of murdered Jews."[73] Minskiy wrote in his memoirs that on October 1 and 2, 1941,

> these people stood in front of the row of German policemen and soldiers on Makarovska and Melnikov streets and asked to be given a coat, jacket or skirt from the huge pile of clothes [which belonged to executed Jews] laid on the street.... Germans threw the clothes into the crowd. People in the crowd caught them in the air, pulled them from each other and asked for more.[74]

This scene poignantly underscores the desperate poverty among Kyiv's gentiles, competing for used clothing, juxtaposed with a disturbing lack of compassion for the fate of the Jews who had just been executed at Babyn Yar.

The local population helped the Nazis "cleanse" Kyiv of Jews who defied the Nazi order and did not report to Babyn Yar on September 29, 1941. On September 30 and October 1, 1941, a mob of several dozen individuals carried out a violent pogrom against Jews in Podil.[75] Oleksandr Melnyk wrote: "While protocols of the [Soviet] interrogation of defendants and witnesses leave little doubt that participating in the pogrom in one way or another were dozens of Kyivans, only the three most active perpetrators were brought to trial."[76] In his article, Melnyk employed pseudonyms for defendants, witnesses, victims, and NKGB investigators. He justified his decision "by a combination of ethical considerations ... and the possibility of false statements during NKGB interrogations."[77] However, Kruglov and Umansky, who describe the same pogrom in their book *Babi Yar: zhertvy, spasiteli, palachi* (Babyn Yar: Victims, rescuers, perpetrators) used the real names of the perpetrators. To avoid further confusion, I use the real names of the perpetrators or, when I quote Melnyk's article, I provide the real names in parentheses.

After the liberation of Kyiv by the Red Army, three pogrom perpetrators, Egor Ustinov (born in 1905), Nikifor Yushkov (born in 1905), and Venedikt Baranov (born in

1900), were charged with the murder of Jews during the pogrom on September 30–October 1, 1941, in Podil and betrayal to the Nazis of Jews and gentiles hidden in the city.[78] They received death sentences and were publicly hanged in Kyiv on January 23, 1944, but other gentiles who participated in Jewish pogroms in Podil did not receive any punishment whatsoever.[79]

During his interrogation, Yushkov testified that several dozen gentiles, including children, participated in the Jewish pogrom in Podil:

> On 30 September 1941 at around 4–5 p.m. I was walking along Mezhyhirs'ka Street towards 33 Nyzhnii Val Street when I noticed a crowd of people heading toward Nyzhnii Val.... In front of 37 Nyzhnii Val Street there sat a citizen of Jewish nationality. Children that surrounded her (10 in total, I do not know their names) hit her with stones, dispersed her belongings and otherwise abused her. On seeing this Grigorii (I do not know his surname), Ushakov [Ustinov], and myself approached the woman and started to beat her. I kept punching the old woman in the face until she fell to the ground. Grigorii, Ushakov [Ustinov], and I lifted her and hit her head several times against the lamp post. Together with Ushakov [Ustinov] and Grigorii we kicked the woman in the face and in the chest. As we beat her, we yelled "Iids sucked our blood for 23 years. Now it is our turn." The crowd that gathered there cheered us on with jokes and shouts.[80]

Eyewitness Evgeniia Beliaeva provided a harrowing account of how these three perpetrators stopped tormenting an old woman, named Schwartz, only when they saw new victims: "an old Jewish man, old woman and a young girl whom somebody had brought 'from the lower numbers of Nyzhnii Val.'"[81] Beliaeva also confirmed that many perpetrators participated in the Jewish pogrom in Podil. During her interrogation she provided "an extremely graphic and detailed account of the torture" of Jews. Beliaeva described "how Chusov [Yushkov] ordered his [ten-year-old] son and other children to bring sand, which he stuffed into victims' mouths or about how adult perpetrators instructed children to throw heavy rocks at Jews inside the grave in order to kill them before the burial."[82]

Ustinov boasted to his neighbors that "he personally buried alive three Jewish women, 'he organically hated all Jews' and that he would 'happily exterminate their entire nation.'"[83] Ustinov testified during his Soviet interrogation on December 21, 1943, that he with several other gentiles buried Jews alive in a garden in Kyiv. Ustinov stated:

> We buried six or seven people total, some of them were still alive, they screamed and asked us not to bury them, but we hit them with shovels on their heads and buried

them. A young girl about 20 years old and an old woman, who was dragged to the pit with a broken head, were especially screaming and begging us not to bury them.[84]

Yushkov, who also participated in the murder of Jews in the garden, testified that the murders continued the second day with the participation of German soldiers. Yushkov said, "On the next day in the morning the janitor of the apartment building on 37 Nizhniy Val Street, whose name is Aleksei, dragged beaten semi-alive Jews from the apartment building 37 to another pit in the same garden and Nazis shot the Jews in the pit."[85]

The torture and murder of Jews occurred openly on the city streets and in the garden during the day in front of their gentile neighbors. Among the many testimonies of eyewitnesses of the pogrom in Podil only three claimed that they were "opposed to the Nazi policies toward the Jews and openly castigated the 'bandit' Bulanov [Baranov] for his actions. In his turn, Bulanov [Baranov] responded with the threats also to bury them, the 'defenders of the iids.'"[86]

During the pogrom in Podil on September 30 and October 1, 1941, as in the October 1905 pogrom in Kyiv, a small group of active pogrom-makers beat and killed Jews. Meanwhile, a larger group of gentiles robbed Jewish apartments and stole Jewish property, and an even larger crowd of gentiles watched the pogrom, cheering the perpetrators on "with jokes and shouts."[87] In this way the behavior of the pogrom-makers and bystanders had changed little since the 1905 pogrom. However, the presence of the Nazis in the city in combination with the local anti-Semites almost did not leave Kyivan Jews any chance of survival. During the pogrom in Podil on September 30–October 1, 1941, at least seven Jews perished who had not obeyed the Nazi order and had not come to Babyn Yar on September 29, 1941.[88] They were tortured and killed by their gentile neighbors.

Jews in hiding faced grim prospects of survival during the Nazi occupation of Kyiv, largely due to widespread denunciations by their gentile neighbors. Dr. Schumacher, as a member of the Einsatzkommando 5, had been in Kyiv in January–February 1942. As a defendant, Schumacher testified in court in Karlsruhe in 1961:

> Due to the small number of members of the Einsatzkommando 5, and the urgency of other tasks, it was impossible to search for Jews on territory of Kyiv or organize round ups of them. And it was really unnecessary; the hostility toward Jews in wide circles of the Ukrainian population was so strong, that the people [i.e., gentiles] continuously revealed Jews and passed them to the German military, civil and police agencies, who delivered Jews to the former NKVD prison on Korolenko Street, 33 [during the Nazi occupation the Gestapo office and prison were located there].[89]

Historian Mordechai Altshuler wrote that "informers assumed a monstrous form" as they denounced not only adult Jews, but also Jewish children as shown in the case of a Kyiv orphanage: "The Germans took all the Jewish children and killed them. Four Jewish children, ten and eleven years old, were hung... in the orphanage yard. A woman doctor who worked in the orphanage had informed on them."[90]

THE UKRAINIAN POLICE AND THE BUKOVINIAN BATTALION

The Ukrainian police played a crucial role in identifying Jews in Kyiv and facilitating their subsequent murder at Babyn Yar. The Nazis created the Regional Administration of Ukrainian police as soon as they occupied Kyiv. They needed the assistance of the local population to detect Jews, NKVD workers, and communists. Only volunteers from the local population served in the Ukrainian police. The Nazis announced the call to serve in the Ukrainian police in the newspaper *Ukrains'ke Slovo* (Ukrainian word), published in the Ukrainian language. The announcement invited Ukrainian men younger than 35 years old, not shorter than 165 centimeters, with an education of at least four grades, who did not have previous criminal charges, had not served in the NKVD, and were not members of the VKP(b) (All-Union Communist Party, or Bolsheviks) to serve in the Ukrainian police. People with higher education and former members of the Ukrainian National Army of Simon Petliura (*petliurovtsy*)[91] were appointed to command positions in the police. Deserters from the Red Army, prisoners of war, criminals, and people who hated the Soviet regime volunteered to serve in the Ukrainian police. The policemen were often dressed in a Soviet uniform with yellow and blue stripes attached to their hats and a white arm band (*poviazka*) with yellow and blue stripes. They were armed with Soviet rifles.[92]

> The Commandant of the Ukrainian Police of City Kyiv, Orlik, required in his order that all managers of apartment buildings provide before midnight lists of **all Yids, NKVD workers and members of the VKP(b)** [bold in the original], who live in their apartment buildings to the closest Commissariats and to the administration of the Ukrainian police of city Kyiv on 15 Korolenko Street, second floor.
> **Hiding of these people will be punished by the death sentence** [bold in the original].
> The managers of apartment buildings and janitors had the right themselves to deliver Yids to the Yid's [concentration] camp, which was located at the POW camp on Kerosynna Street.[93]

This document is without a date, but by its content and location among other Nazi orders written in fall 1941, it seems likely that the order was issued in September or October 1941, just before or immediately after the Babyn Yar massacre.

Ukrainian police guarded Jews walking on their last road to Babyn Yar and prevented any escape attempts.[94] Nachmanovich wrote that members of Ukrainian police, Sirosh, Muzyria, Grigor'ev, Shcherbina, and Grishka (whose last name he does not mention), gathered fifteen Jews in a basement on September 29, 1941, brought them to Babyn Yar, and passed them to the Nazis. Then these Ukrainian policemen helped the Nazis undress the Jews before their murder.[95]

Dina Pronicheva was one of very few Jews who escaped from Babyn Yar. She testified that "the auxiliary policemen readied the Jews for their murder by stripping them." The Ukrainian policemen, according to Pronicheva, "chased the fully undressed people one by one up a hill [to the place of shooting]."[96] German and Ukrainian policemen beat Jews on the way to execution. After the end of the shooting "Germans assisted by non-Germans walked across the bodies of the victims; with flashlights they sought out survivors and finished them off."[97]

Historians Karel Berkhoff and Per Anders Rudling assumed that the Bukovins'kyi Kuren' (Bukovinian Battalion) participated in the execution of Jews at Babyn Yar. Berkhoff wrote:

> Newly found Ukrainian sources also named paramilitary and auxiliary police formations that were in Kiev at the time of the massacre: a squad of what was then simply called the "Ukrainian police" and the Bukovinian Battalion. Both were created or commended by activists of the Mel'nyk faction of the Organization of Ukrainian Nationalists (OUN-M), a militant group dominated by western Ukrainians who saw themselves engaged in a struggle to free Ukraine from "Muscovite-Jewish gangs."[98]

Several sources mentioned that the Ukrainian police and the Bukovinian Battalion, which had 700 to 800 members, arrived in Kyiv in the first days of the Nazi occupation. "Several newcomers took jobs in the city administration or went to create police units in the towns Vasylkiv, Bila Tserkva, and other places near Kyiv, but others joined Kyiv's 'Ukrainian police.'"[99] Per Anders Rudling wrote:

> The participation of the Bukovyns'kyi Kuren' in massacres in Babyn Yar cannot be ruled out, as executions in Babyn Yar continued every Tuesday and Friday for the next 103 weeks, during which between 50 and 60 thousand people were murdered. After reinforcement by volunteers from Galicia and other parts of Ukraine, the Bukovyns'kyi Kurin' had a total number of 1,500–1,700 soldiers by early November [1941].[100]

According to the order of Reichsführer-SS and Chief of the German Police Heinrich Himmler from November 6, 1941, the Ukrainian police were renamed as "Schutzmannschaft" (Auxiliary Police) and were subordinated to the German police ("Ordundspolizei"). In January 1942, Schutzmannschaft received their police identification cards and began to receive a salary of 30 Reichsmarks per month plus provisions. *Schutzmanns* (policemen) also received special benefits: the right to use city transportation for free, to rent an apartment for half price (the rest was paid by the city council from the city budget), and to move freely in Kyiv at any time, while other Kyivans lived under martial law. Most of the policemen were non-Kyivans.[101] Ivan Dereiko wrote that in 1942 the total number of policemen in Kyiv General District was over six thousand. "About one thousand policemen were German, 200 Baltic German (Volksdeutsche) and the rest, about five thousand, Ukrainians."[102] So the Auxiliary Police, formed mainly from Ukrainian collaborators, played a crucial role in the establishment of the new Nazi order and in revealing and exterminating Jews, Roma, and other undesirables.

After the massacre on September 29–30, 1941, *schutzmanns* delivered hidden Kyivan Jews and Jewish prisoners of war to Babyn Yar for execution. Dereiko wrote that one of the *schutzmanns* testified that the *schutzmanns* convoyed to Babyn Yar columns of Jews from the concentration camp on Kerosynna Street.[103]

OUN-M AND THE PRO-NAZI UKRAINIAN PRESS

The brutal Soviet policy in interwar Ukraine, the Holodomor, repression, and the suppression of the Ukrainian national movement created strong hatred among much of the Ukrainian population toward the Soviet regime. Perhaps this explains why some Ukrainians welcomed the Nazi invasion and collaborated with the Nazis. Oleksandr Melnyk pointed out that 320,000 individuals were charged with collaboration by Soviet military tribunals and other special courts between 1943 and 1953. "About 90,000 of these cases originated on the territory of the Ukrainian Soviet Socialist Republic."[104]

According to historian Paul Robert Magocsi, "Initially, some Ukrainians welcomed the German invasion, because they hoped that with the end of Soviet Rule their country would enjoy a better life and perhaps some form of national sovereignty."[105] Thus, two factions of the OUN, the Banderites and the Melnykites, initially cooperated with the Nazis. However, cooperation of the Banderites with the Nazis was cut short because the Banderites unwisely declared an independent Ukrainian state on June 30, 1941. Ukrainian independence did not at all fit the Nazis' plans. So, the Germans quickly arrested the faction leader, Stepan Bandera, and other leading Banderites. They spent the remainder of the war in German prisons and concentration camps.[106]

The Nazis tolerated the OUN-M faction (the Melnykites) longer because they offered their cooperation in the struggle against the Soviet Union. Magocsi wrote: "The faction leader, Andrii Mel'nyk, was joined by former officers from the army of the Ukrainian National Republic, who on July 6, 1941, appealed to Hitler to allow them to take part in the 'crusade against Bolshevik barbarism.'"[107] The German military considered cooperation with OUN-M useful in the occupied territories. At first the Nazis supported the activities of OUN-M, especially their efforts at "cleansing" Kyiv and Ukraine of Jews. The German military also counted on the assistance of Ukrainian nationalists in their struggle against the Red Army and Soviet partisans. But the Nazi leadership "rejected on racially motivated ideological grounds... any serious cooperation with the local ethnic Ukrainian population, which it believed should be conquered and remain totally subordinated within Nazi Germany's new world order."[108]

However, OUN-M formed the Ukrainian National Council and continued to promote the Ukrainian national idea and culture, which contradicted Nazi plans. So, the members of the Ukrainian National Council and one of the OUN-M leaders and editor of the newspaper *Ukrains'ke slovo*, Ivan Rogach, were arrested by the Gestapo and executed in December 1941–February 1942.[109] Mel'nyk was kept under house arrest in Berlin until January 1944 and then taken with the other leading members of the OUN-M to the Sachsenhausen concentration camp.[110]

Members of both OUN factions viewed Jews and other national minorities as enemies of Ukraine. OUN members participated in the murder of Jews and the spread of anti-Semitic propaganda. The OUN-M newspaper *Ukrains'ke slovo* and other pro-Nazi Ukrainian press further fueled anti-Semitism in the city by blaming Jews for all the crimes of the Communist regime and called upon readers to denounce them and cleanse the city of "Yids." A few days after the mass murder of Jews at Babyn Yar, on October 2, 1941, the newspaper *Ukrains'ke slovo* published an article, "The Foremost Enemy of Ukraine—the YID!,"[111] which claimed that Jews had brutally ruled Ukraine for twenty-three years and deserved to be killed. On October 9, 1941, *Ukrains'ke slovo* published an article, "Malen'kyi budynochok" (The little house), which stated that many Jews still were hiding in the city, "who disguised themselves as Greeks, Armenians, Ukrainians, Russians and paying thousand rubles for such documents and make diversions."[112] The article called on all Ukrainian patriots to report Jews to the "little house" at 48 Taras Shevchenko Boulevard.

Nazi propaganda depicted all Jews as Bolsheviks and exploiters of the gentile population. Nazis and their local collaborators also blamed Jews for organizing the Holodomor in Ukraine in 1932–33 and claimed that Jews had not suffered from the famine themselves. The newspaper *Vidrodzhennia* (Revival), which was published under Nazi rule in occupied Ukraine, wrote on December 6, 1942:

> Only one part of the population did not feel the famine. Those were the Jews. They calmly used the services of "Torgsin,"[113] in whose stores there was everything one could want, including produce. But it could only be bought with gold and foreign currency. And the Jews lacked neither gold, nor dollars.[114]

Similar publications, which blamed Jews for the famine, appeared in *Dnipropetrovs'ka hazeta* (Dnipropetrovsk gazette) during the Nazi occupation of Ukraine.[115]

Kyivan Valentin Terno "recalled seeing in Kyiv... in the summer of 1942 a feature film in Ukrainian called *Ostannii udar* (The last blow), about collectivization and the famine."[116] Terno described the film "as fiercely anti-Semitic, it showed corpses of famine victims and ended with the killing of a Jewish NKVD officer."[117]

After the liberation of Kyiv by the Red Army only a small percentage of collaborators faced criminal charges. Eighty-two policemen were accused of collaboration crimes in Kyiv. Among them were 73 Ukrainians, 6 Russians, 2 Germans, and 1 Pole.[118] Many civilians who denounced Jews and stole Jewish property avoided any punishment whatsoever.

In 1966 Kuznetsov wrote:

> It is a curious fact that Praskovya [Derkach, who denounced hidden Jews in Kyiv to the Nazis] continues to flourish to this day. She lives on Menzhinsky Street and has never been punished in any way, maybe because she did not betray any NKVD agents or Communists, but only a few Jews. She is, of course, older now, but only in her body, not in her mind. The neighbors often hear her giving her views: "You think that's the end of the war? Oh, no, not yet. The Germans will come back from over there, and the Chinese will come from over there—then we'll give the Yids something worse than Babyn Yar!"[119]

The communist leaders of Ukraine were quite lenient regarding collaboration crimes, especially if they were directed only against Jews. Volodymyr Shcherbytsky, the First Secretary of the Communist Party of Ukraine from 1972 to 1989, appealed to the Party Central Committee with a request to keep secret information on the involvement of his countrymen in the brutal slaughter of civilians.[120] The request was taken "with understanding" and information about local collaborators was classified as secret in Ukrainian archives until the collapse of communism.

In contemporary Ukraine, some collaborators have been glorified as fighters for Ukrainian independence. Ukrainian nationalists commemorated the seventy-fifth anniversary of the Babyn Yar massacre by erecting at Babyn Yar a memorial display to the editor of the anti-Semitic, pro-Nazi newspaper *Ukrains'ke slovo*, Ivan Rogach.[121] They claimed that he was also a Babyn Yar victim, although in fact the place of his execution is unknown. This memorial display provoked a strong protest by Jews in Kyiv and abroad.[122]

RESCUE

Gentiles who rescued Jews faced mortal danger, especially if they were denounced. This perhaps explains why only a small percentage of gentiles participated in the rescue of Jews and only a few hundred Jews survived in Kyiv during the Nazi occupation. Some Jews lived under false identities, being listed as Russian, Ukrainian, or Armenian. Others were hidden by colleagues, friends, neighbors, and gentile relatives. In several cases Jewish children were adopted by gentile families.

One hundred and fifty gentiles from Kyiv received the title "The Righteous Among the Nations" from Yad Vashem, the World Holocaust Remembrance Center, Israel.[123] The Ukrainian foundation Memory of Babyn Yar gave the title of "The Righteous of Babyn Yar" to 662 gentiles and claimed that they participated in the rescue of Jews during the occupation of Kyiv.[124] However, in many cases, the Ukrainian foundation awarded the title "The Righteous of Babyn Yar" based solely on the personal recollections of self-identified rescuers or their children, without the testimonies of the survivors and, in some instances, without even knowing the names of the rescued Jews.[125] Certainly, information about gentiles who rescued Jews in Kyiv was collected many years after the war, when the Soviet ban on research of Holocaust topics was lifted. So, information about the righteous gentiles and the Jews whom they rescued is incomplete. But, in any case, there were only a few hundred gentiles who rescued Jews in Kyiv during the Nazi occupation.

In Kyiv gentiles most frequently hid children of Jewish and partially Jewish descent. In several cases Jewish mothers, instead of taking their children to the place of gathering assigned by the Nazis, left them with their gentile friends and relatives. Most Jews did not know their fate until they arrived at Babyn Yar. Many thought that they would be deported from Kyiv to some other place. However, they could observe the rabid Nazi anti-Semitism from the first days of the German occupation of Kyiv and did not expect anything good even in the case of their deportation.

To save Jewish and partially Jewish children (who had one Jewish parent), their gentile rescuers sometimes baptized them. For example, Igor' Ageev was baptized. He had a Jewish mother, Ida Ageeva (née Belozovskaia), and a gentile father, Aleksander Ageev. Aleksander and his relatives hid his wife, Ida, and five-year-old son, Igor'. But soon a danger appeared: When Igor' played in the yard the children of the janitor called him a Yid. So, the relatives baptized Igor' and hung a cross over his bed.[126]

Some gentiles in Kyiv, fearing their Christian neighbors, sent Jewish children to their relatives in smaller towns and villages, where there were fewer police. Thus, Valentina and Ludmila Sviridenko (born in 1937 and 1939) were rescued by gentile relatives and friends who lived in a rural area. Their mother, Rebekka Yakovlevna Sapir, was Jewish and their father, Ivan Petrovich Sviridenko, was Ukrainian.[127] The gentile family Belostotsky hid their friend's grandchild, Ella Gershman (born in 1936), whose father was Jewish.[128] Victor Radetsky, whose mother, Klara Iorish, was Jewish and perished at Babyn Yar, was rescued by his gentile grandmother in the city of Uman'. Victor was first hidden by his gentile relatives in Kyiv, but they were afraid of denunciation by their neighbors and sent the boy to his grandmother.[129]

Family ties and romantic relationships often served as powerful motivations for the rescue of Jews. Some gentiles hid their wives and husbands, girlfriends and boyfriends. Thus, Valentina Berezleva saved her Jewish friend Veniamin Liberman for whom she was able to get bogus documents that he was a Karaite. Later they escaped together from Kyiv where somebody might denounce them. After the war Berezleva and Liberman married.[130]

Gentile Tamara Bozhkova married the Jew Abram Yakovlevich Rubinshtein before the war. He was drafted into the Red Army and captured by the Nazis in the first months of the war. Tamara received a note that her husband was in the concentration camp in the village of Gogolevo. Tamara went to the camp and bribed a policeman, who released her husband and one other Jewish prisoner of war. She was able to obtain through the manager of an apartment building a bogus passport for her husband in the name of Arseny Mikoian (an Armenian last name). But to stay in Kyiv even with this passport was too dangerous; somebody could denounce them. So, Tamara and Abram escaped from Kyiv to the village of Bol'shaia Saltanovka and stayed with distant relatives of Tamara, who hid them and another Jewish couple.[131]

In several cases Kyiv gentiles hid their Jewish colleagues. Thus, during the Nazi occupation of Kyiv several colleagues hid a Jewish medical doctor, Kuperman, who worked with them before the war at the clinic on Boulevard Shevchenko. Kuperman moved several times from one gentile family to another. She survived until the liberation of Kyiv and worked at the clinic for many years after the war.[132] Jewess E. Iskol'skaia worked as chief physician at the tuberculosis hospital in Darnitsa (then a suburb of Kyiv). During the Nazi occupation, her gentile colleague Shumilo helped her obtain documents for entrance to Kyiv.[133]

Philosemitic traditions often passed in gentile families from generation to generation. Thus, the Orthodox priest Alexander Glagolev saved Jews during the 1905 pogrom in Kyiv; his son Aleksey rescued Jews during the Nazi occupation. Alexander Glagolev was a professor at Kyiv Theological Seminary who testified as a religious expert at the

Menachem Mendel Beilis blood libel trial in 1913, when Beilis was accused of the ritual murder of the Christian boy Andriusha Yushchinsky. Glagolev gave expert evidence at the trial that Judaism does not include any rituals that require Jews to use blood in their food. On October 20, 1937, Alexander Glagolev was arrested by the NKVD. He was tortured and died in prison on November 25, 1937.[134]

His son Aleksey Glagolev was an Orthodox priest at the Pokrov Church in Podil. Aleksey lived in Kyiv with his wife, Tatyana, and three children during the Nazi occupation.

In early October 1941, the Glagolevs were visited by Mariya Yegorycheva, Aleksey's sister-in-law, who pleaded that they help Izabella Mirkina, her brother's Jewish wife. Mirkina was hidden in Yegorycheva's house, but it was too dangerous to remain there. Tatyana Glagoleva proposed that they switch the photograph in her identity card with one of Mirkina, which was successfully accomplished. Provided with the ID as well as with Tatyana's baptism certificate, Mirkina then left Kiev, but one month later she returned to the Yegorychevs' home. Her sister-in-law then approached the Glagolevs again, and they welcomed the Jewish woman into their home, introducing her to people as Aleksey's niece. In 1942, Mirkina's daughter Irina, who had been hiding in the Yegorychevs' home until then, joined her at the Glagolevs'.[135]

Kruglov and Umansky described two cases in which Nazis supposedly helped Jews escape from Babyn Yar. In the first case Nazis Paul Worzberger and Johann Koller released from Babyn Yar two Jewish girls: seventeen-year-old Genia Batasheva and fourteen-year-old Mania Palti, who claimed that they were Ukrainians and came to Babyn Yar out of curiosity. Both girls were blond and had blue eyes, so they did not "look Jewish," and the Nazis believed them. Some gentiles saw off their Jewish relatives and friends to Babyn Yar and the Nazis released them also. So, it was not a special merit of Worzberger and Koller that they released Batasheva and Palti, and helped them leave Babyn Yar, because they most likely believed that the girls were Ukrainians and therefore should not be executed.[136]

The second case that Kruglov and Umansky described is even less reliable. They cited the testimony of a member of the Sonderkommando 4a, Richard Kerl, who claimed that he was a guard on the road on which Jews came to Babyn Yar and let a Jewish family, a mother with two adult girls, escape. However, there is no evidence to support this story.[137]

In many cases rescuers were motivated by altruism and compassion for Jews. However, in some cases Jews paid their rescuers. Arkadiy Wiesbreim (born in 1869) worked as a dentist before the war. He paid the gentile family who hid him and his family in golden crowns.[138] His daughter Raisa and granddaughter Lidia (born in 1935) were hidden by the gentile Akulina Sukalo. But Akulina's husband, Roman Sukalo, was against hiding Jews at home and threatened to denounce them to the police. Raisa and Lidia moved to Akulina's gentile neighbor Polina. But Roman Sukalo continued to threaten to denounce them. So, Raisa and Lidia had to move three more times. Finally, in the spring of 1942, Raisa, Lidia, and Raisa's sister Berta settled in the village of Matveikha in the Kyiv region, where German soldiers seldom came. Raisa, Lidia, and Berta survived the war.[139]

If the Nazis detected hidden Jews, they severely punished their rescuers, as in the case of Vladimir and Pelageia Savitskiy and Pelageia's sister Natalia Tkachenko. Savitsky's family and Tkachenko hid their Jewish acquaintance Isaak Brodsky. He was drafted into the Red Army at the beginning of the war and was taken into captivity, but two weeks later he escaped from the POW camp. Natalia Tkachenko obtained for Brodsky documents in the name of a Ukrainian, Konstantin Balatsenko. Brodsky lived with these fake documents in occupied Kyiv for over a year. But Brodsky's acquaintance Shimans'ka recognized him on Glubochitse Street on January 17, 1943, and denounced him to the police. Brodsky was arrested and severely beaten by the police. He was then taken to the Gestapo and interrogated by Shimans'ka's husband, who worked there. After the interrogation Brodsky was sent to the Syrets concentration camp.[140] His rescuers, Vladimir and Pelageia Savitskiy and Natalia Tkachenko, were also arrested. Vladimir and Pelageia Savitskiy were interrogated, tortured, and sent to Germany for forced labor, but they escaped from the train on the way and secretly returned to Kyiv. Natalia Tkachenko was placed in the Syrets concentration camp.[141] "There she encountered Isaak [Brodsky] again, who was enslaved in Unit 1005, which has the task of burning the bodies of those murdered at Babi Yar."[142] Isaak Brodsky was one of the few prisoners of the Syrets concentration camp who participated in the Babyn Yar uprising on September 29, 1943, and survived. After the liberation of Kyiv, Brodsky joined the Red Army; he was killed in 1944 fighting on the front in Poland.[143] Vladimir and Pelageia Savitskiy and Natalia Tkachenko survived the war and received the titles of the Righteous Among the Nations and the Righteous of Babyn Yar.[144]

Among the rescuers were people from all social strata: peasants, workers, intelligentsia, and nobles. There were Russians, Ukrainians, Poles, and Germans who rescued Jews in Kyiv. Gentiles who rescued Jews put in mortal danger their own lives and the lives of their family members. During the occupation, the Nazis repeatedly confiscated provisions from the Kyiv civilian population. Kyivans were starving and those who rescued Jews usually needed to feed them also. Hidden Jews in most cases could not leave the homes of their rescuers and find a job or any provisions for themselves for the entire period of the occupation. The brutality of the Nazi regime in Kyiv, where most Kyivans suffered from a shortage of food, fuel, and clothes, and could not freely move about the city due to martial law, also explains why only several hundred gentiles in the city rescued Jews.

JEWISH RESISTANCE TO THE HOLOCAUST AND SELF-RESCUE

Jews who survived in Kyiv relied heavily upon their gentile rescuers. However, some Jews who survived the Nazi occupation put considerable effort into rescuing themselves. Some of them did not obey the Nazi order and did not come to the place of gathering for the shooting at Babyn Yar; rather, they went to their gentile friends and relatives. Often, these Jews lived with false documents in occupied Kyiv, frequently moved from place to place, or settled in some remote village where the Nazis did not come so often. Jewish prisoners in the Syrets concentration camp participated in an uprising against the Nazis, and several of them ran away from the camp and survived.

Escaping from Kyiv helped Jews survive in several cases. Elena Borodiansky-Knysh, with her five-year-old daughter Ludmila, fled from Babyn Yar. During the shooting she jumped with her daughter into the pit, and they were not hurt by the bullets. Elena and her daughter waited among the dead until the Nazis were gone and then they escaped in the darkness. They were hidden for one month by Elena's gentile friend Valentina Litvinenko. But it was too dangerous to stay in Kyiv due to the Nazi roundups and possible denunciation. So, Borodiansky-Knysh moved with her daughter to the village of Minkovtsy, in the Kyiv district, and settled in an abandoned house. Their new neighbors, peasants Mikhail and Luker'ia Grigorenko, shared with them their food and clothes.[145]

Solomon Gorodetsky was hidden for one month by the above-mentioned gentiles Pelagea Savitskiy and Natalia Tkachenko during and after the Babyn Yar massacre. Natalia then obtained for Solomon documents in the name of a Russian, Konstantin Shirkatnyi, and he escaped from Kyiv. Gorodetsky crossed the front line and joined the Red Army. He came to the sisters to express his gratitude after the liberation of Kyiv.[146]

The uprising of the prisoners in the Syrets concentration camp on September 29, 1943, which will be discussed in the next chapter, was a special case of resistance and self-rescue of prisoners of war, among whom were many Jews.

CONCLUSION

Kyiv was under Nazi occupation for over two years. Most Kyivan Jews who remained in the city were killed at Babyn Yar on September 29–30, 1941. Several thousand Jews who hid in the city were arrested and killed later; many of them perished due to denunciation by local gentiles. Only a few hundred Kyivan Jews survived the Nazi occupation. They were rescued by their gentile colleagues, relatives, friends, and neighbors. Some Holocaust survivors exerted lots of effort to rescue themselves: They changed location many times, lived under bogus identities, and escaped from concentration camps and from Nazi-occupied Kyiv.

Betrayal of Jews was easy and well rewarded by the Nazis; rescue was difficult and dangerous. With these stark alternatives, significantly more gentiles denounced Jews in Kyiv than saved them. There were about 6,000 members of the Auxiliary Police (all of them volunteers), the Bukovyns'kyi Kurin' of 1,500 to 1,700 soldiers, and many neighbors who denounced Jews to the Germans or even personally participated in their murder. The number of righteous gentiles in Kyiv varies according to different calculations: Yad Vashem recognizes 150 righteous gentiles, while the Ukrainian foundation Memory of Babyn Yar recognizes 662 righteous gentiles. But in any case, only a few hundred gentiles dared to rescue Jews in Kyiv.

Righteous gentiles were motivated by compassion, family and romantic relations, and the idea of resistance against the Nazi regime. However, despite all their efforts, they were not always successful in saving Jews. Often their anti-Semitic neighbors threatened to denounce them or actually did so. In such cases, not only the hidden Jews, but also their saviors and all members of the savior's family were under mortal threat. Due to the Nazi confiscation of provisions, gentiles starved in occupied Kyiv. Therefore, it was difficult for them to find food for hidden Jews. Some gentiles believed that they had already done enough if they knew about hidden Jews and did not denounce them. The Nazi regime was much more brutal in Eastern Europe than in the West. So, many gentiles were terrified in Kyiv and primarily just thought about their own survival and that of their family. This explains why most gentiles remained passive bystanders during the execution of Jews in Kyiv.

Widespread anti-Semitism played a significant role in the betrayal of Jews. Some gentiles began to kill Jews in Kyiv on their own initiative before or during the massacre at Babyn Yar. They brutally tortured Jews before their murder. The participation of gentiles in the Holocaust of Jews in Kyiv was crucial. Without their denunciations and help, the Nazis would not have been able to recognize and exterminate almost all Kyivan Jews who were in the city during its occupation. Many Kyivan Jews submitted to the Nazi order to come to the assigned place on September 29, 1941, because they understood that their gentile neighbors would hand them over to the Nazis in any case. The Ukrainian police shared responsibility for the Holocaust of Jews in Kyiv. Ukrainian policemen searched for Jews, conveyed them to Babyn Yar, beat them, and participated in the massacre. The brutality of the Nazi occupation, pervasive anti-Semitism, and widespread hostility from gentiles left Kyivan Jews little chance for survival.

3

OTHER VICTIMS OF THE NAZI REGIME IN KYIV

OVER 100,000 GENTILES PERISHED DURING THE NAZI OCCUPATION OF Kyiv, the majority of whom were prisoners of war. Many died from starvation and disease in Nazi concentration camps. Kyivans were also starving in the city due to continued Nazi confiscation of civilian provisions. Some gentiles were executed for resisting the Nazis, as were some prisoners of war, members of the underground, partisans, Ukrainian nationalists, and Orthodox priests. Roma and mentally ill people were killed due to Nazi racial policies. Some of these victims were executed at Babyn Yar, others in different locations in Kyiv.

During Soviet times, official propaganda glorified heroic struggle and death on the front, in the underground movement, and in partisan resistance on occupied territories but kept silent about all other victims of the Nazis. For a long time, Soviet authorities considered prisoners of war to be traitors and had a suspicious attitude toward the entire population that remained on Nazi-occupied territories. Research about the victims of World War II who were not represented in Soviet historiography began in Ukraine only after the collapse of communism; by that time many eyewitnesses of these events were gone. Thus, we have today limited sources and testimonies of some groups of victims of the Nazi regime in Kyiv.

ROMA VICTIMS OF BABYN YAR

The Nazis annihilated Roma, like Jews, based on their ethnicity and justified by the Nazi racist ideology. In Ukraine, the Porajmos (the Romani genocide) "happened at the same time as the Shoah."[1]

In the occupied Soviet Union including the annexations of 1939–40, German military and SS-police units shot over 30,000 Roma, whereby Einsatzgruppen and other mobile killing units murdered Roma at the same, or almost the same time that they killed Jews and other victim groups. The vast majority were killed in Ukraine, which was the destination for many Roma deported from Romania.[2]

Unfortunately, there are almost no documentary sources about the life of Roma in Kyiv before the war or about their murder at Babyn Yar. So, we know little about their life and the Romani genocide in Kyiv. Andrej Kotljarchuk wrote:

> In 1937, a Romani craft cooperative, *Trudnatsmen* [Labor of national minorities], was established in Kurenivka near Babi Yar that united 27 Roma families. In 1941 an administrative building for the Romani cooperative was situated in Babi Yar in the former NKVD shooting range. There is no evidence about the existence of the Romani craft cooperative in Kyiv after WWII. However, neither scholars nor Roma of Kyiv can compile a list of the victims.[3]

Kuznetsov wrote about the murder of Roma at Babyn Yar:

> The Germans hunted down gypsies [Roma] like wild animals. They were due for the same immediate liquidation as the Jews....
>
> The gypsies were taken off to Babi Yar, whole camps at a time; and it appears, moreover, that they too did not realize until the last moment what was happening to them.[4]

A few testimonies of eyewitnesses of the Romani genocide at Babyn Yar were recorded several years after the war. However, there are no exact dates for when the massacre of the Roma happened. Nachmanovich wrote:

> Liudmila Zavorotna, recalled that the Roma were shot in Babyn Yar, and she herself saw gypsy wagons driving past her house, although this was a long time after the mass shooting of the Jews. Volodymyr Nabaranchuk, whose family escaped death, also recalls that the Germans began shooting the Roma in late October 1941. It was not just the Roma living in their encampments who were shot but also those who lived conventional lives in the city. Nabaranchuk stated that, in addition to Babyn Yar, Roma encampments were destroyed in what then were the Kyivan suburbs of Sviatoshyn and Berezniaky. In any case, we can confirm that at least 150 Roma were killed in Babyn Yar because nearly 50 people usually lived in the Roma encampment.[5]

The number of Roma victims of Babyn Yar could be at least twice higher than Nachmanovich estimated, because any number from fifty to over a hundred people could live in a Romani encampment.[6] In recent years the Ukrainian press has stated that the Nazis exterminated Roma from five encampments at Babyn Yar.[7] However, the publications do not provide sources for this information.

EXECUTION OF MENTALLY ILL PEOPLE IN KYIV

"Between 1939 and 1945, in a campaign sanctioned by the signature of Hitler himself, the Nazis murdered an estimated 300,000 people with disabilities, of whom 216,000 were in Germany and annexed Austria, and around 70,000 elsewhere in Europe."[8] They believed that these people were an excessive burden on society and were therefore "unworthy of life." Kyiv was not an exception to this brutal Nazi policy. The Nazis first killed mentally ill Jews at the Pavlov Psychiatric Hospital. Several months later, they liquidated the rest of the mentally ill patients of the hospital.[9]

Before the war, the Pavlov Psychiatric Hospital in Kyiv had 1,500 beds, and, according to Professor E. A. Kopystinsky, who worked there, the hospital applied the latest methods of medical treatment.[10] The hospital treated patients not only from Kyiv, but also from other cities and towns of Ukraine. The director of the hospital before the war was a Jew, Lev Zak; he left Kyiv on September 17, 1941, two days before the Nazis occupied the city, and disappeared.[11] Perhaps he perished, because at this time the city was encircled by German troops and most likely he would not be able to go far. Before his departure, Zak passed his responsibilities to the vice director of the hospital, Pavel Chernai. At the end of September 1941, the Nazi authorities approved Chernai's appointment as director of the hospital.[12]

The Nazis robbed the hospital soon after the beginning of their occupation of Kyiv. They took a significant part of the hospital provisions, starving the patients.[13] At the end of September, the German garrison doctor, Rakovsky (according to other sources Rikovsky[14]), came to the hospital with four German correspondents, who took pictures of undressed women patients, selecting those who looked the worst. Such pictures were supposed to illustrate, in accordance with Nazi ideology, the utterly worthless lives of mentally ill people.[15]

On October 14, 1941, the Nazis again came to the hospital with Doctor Rakovsky and ordered that all Jewish patients be gathered in one building (the hospital had several buildings) "for their deportation to a labor colony in Vinnytsia."[16]

The medical personnel of the hospital doubted that the Nazis really planned deportation of the Jewish patients, because the order was issued just two weeks after the

Babyn Yar massacre. However, the director of the hospital, Chernai, reassured them that the Nazis really planned to deport the Jewish patients. The chief medical doctor of the hospital, Musii Tantsiura, asked Chernai whether the Nazis were going to deport the Jewish patients or murder them. Chernai told him that "ill people are not divided by nationalities and never in the history of humankind was there a case when ill people were executed."[17]

Historian Andrii Rukkas wrote that Chernai knew in advance the real Nazi plans for the Jewish patients. In the first week of October, the Nazis came to the hospital and Chernai helped them find a convenient place for the execution of Jewish patients in the Kyrylivsky (also known as Gorikhovyi) grove. It was just 400 meters (a quarter mile) away from the hospital. The Nazis sent some Soviet prisoners of war to the grove, who dug a big pit for the execution. The hospital provided food for the prisoners of war while they dug the pit.[18]

On October 15, 311 Jewish patients were transferred to Building No. 8, according to the Nazi order, where they were held for three days. The building was overpacked with patients because its capacity was for 170 people. Many patients had to share one bed for two people. The medical personnel could not provide necessary treatment for the sick people. By the order of the head medical doctor, Tantsiura, two mentally ill Jewish patients, who were in the best condition, were secretly released from the hospital at night with orders that they must immediately leave Kyiv. The medical personnel reported to the Nazis that they had died. Only one Jewish patient really died before the execution; the remaining 308 Jewish patients were killed by the Nazis on October 18, 1941, in the Kyrylivsky grove.[19]

At 8 a.m. on October 18, 1941, a group of Gestapo officers with 200–300 SS troops arrived at the psychiatric hospital. They encircled Building No. 8 and stood in two lines along the road from the building to the shooting pit. The Nazis ordered that the medical personnel of the hospital accompany the patients to the grove and undress them before their murder. The shootings began at 10 a.m. and continued for six hours.[20]

Rukkas wrote that the medical personnel obediently followed the order. Later, during the Soviet investigation of Nazi crimes, the medical doctors, nurses, and aides justified their behavior by their fear of the Nazis.[21] It seem likely that if they had refused the Nazi orders they would have been summarily shot.

After the murder of the Jewish patients, the hospital's medical personnel felt that the rest of the patients were also doomed.

> The hospital's medical doctors, by their own initiative and with risk to their own lives, began to release the patients. About 400 patients were released from the hospital. But then the Gestapo issued an order to stop the release of the patients. Without provisions, the remaining ill people died in large numbers.[22]

The Nazis came to the hospital several times for extermination of the mentally ill gentile patients. On January 7, 1941, Gestapo members arrived at the hospital. They put guards at all entrances to the hospital and forbade anybody from entering or leaving. Professor Kopystinsky recalled:

> A Gestapo member demanded that chronically ill people be selected for deportation to Zhitomir. The Nazis made an exact record of all patients and told the hospital administration that any disappearance of mentally ill people would be severely punished, and absent patients would be substituted by medical personnel.[23]

Then special vans arrived at the hospital. The Nazis pushed 60 to 70 patients inside each van and killed them by carbon dioxide gas.[24] The corpses were thrown out under the windows of the hospital. The murder of mentally ill people continued for two days, during which 365 patients were killed. Other patients and the medical personnel could observe the murders that took place under the windows of the hospital. According to Professor Kopystinsky, "The Nazis warned all medical personnel that any criticism or expression of dissatisfaction are inappropriate and would be considered as sabotage."[25]

The Nazis murdered mentally ill people at the hospital two more times. On March 29, 1942, they killed 90 people, and on October 17, 1942, they killed 30 people. All attempts of the hospital personnel to rescue at least some patients were unsuccessful. The Nazis themselves made the ultimate decision about who should be exterminated. Thus, Professor Kopystinsky personally petitioned the Nazi authorities to leave alive the mentally ill wife of Professor Mozhar and a daughter of medical assistant Kolendo. Kopystinsky wrote to the Nazi authorities that their conditions were improving and their medical cases had scientific-pedagogical interest. He was told that there would be no exceptions for these patients and threatened Kopystinsky that his petitioning for patients could finished badly for Kopystinsky.[26] When the medical doctors asked why the Nazis killed the mentally ill patients, they received "some incomprehensible answers about cleansing of the race."[27]

According to the Extraordinary State Commission report on February 29, 1944, the Nazis killed a total of 800 mentally ill patients of the Pavlov Psychiatric Hospital.[28]

PRISONERS OF WAR AND NAZI CONCENTRATION CAMPS IN KYIV

The Nazis encircled a massive group of Soviet troops near Kyiv and took into captivity 665,212 Soviet soldiers.[29] In late September to early October 1941, "prisoner marches through Kiev took place almost every day."[30] The treatment of the Soviet POWs was brutal. The Nazis did not feed them for many days and did not allow the local population to provide any help. Kyivan artist Irina Khoroshunova wrote in her diary about the POWs, whom she saw on September 24, 1941: "They look so terrible that our blood turns cold. It is very clear that they don't get food." The local women threw the POWs food. "The prisoners throw themselves at the offered food like animals, they grab it and rip it apart. But the Germans beat them on the head with rifle-butts. They beat them and the women too."[31] On September 28, 1941, the newspaper *Ukrains'ke slovo* published a Nazi order promising the death penalty for hiding or supporting soldiers of the Red Army.[32]

Berkhoff wrote that "Jewish prisoners of war suffered the worst treatment."[33] Khoroshunova noted in her diary on October 2, 1941, "The Nazis are chasing endlessly through the city the prisoners of war. Jews are chased undressed. The Nazis kill them if they ask for water or bread."[34] While gentile POWs were placed in concentration camps, most Jewish POWs and military commissars were shot right away or soon after their captivity. According to Berkhoff, "An estimated three thousand Jewish POWs were marched toward Babyn Yar in late September and early October 1941."[35] The Nazis used Babyn Yar as the killing ground for Red Army commanders, military commissars, members of the underground movement, and other political opponents. In January 1942, the Germans executed at Babyn Yar 65 captive Soviet sailors. Perhaps the Nazis decided to execute the sailors due to their resistance to the German occupiers. An eyewitness, Nadiia Horbacheva, recalled:

> Their [the sailors'] arms and legs were so heavily chained that they could barely move. The completely undressed and barefoot prisoners were driven through the snow during the severe frost. Local residents threw shirts and boots at the column of the prisoners, but the prisoners refused to take them.... You can tell they were sailors by their sailors' caps. After they were brought to Babyn Yar, the sailors were shot by the Germans.[36]

The Nazis also executed Soviet POWs at other sites in Kyiv. Soviet POWs Vladimir Davydov and Yakov Steiuk testified after the liberation of Kyiv that they saw in an anti-tank trench thousands of shot people in the uniforms of Red Army commanders. However, they provided quite different numbers of how many corpses they saw in the trench. Davydov testified that he saw 20,000 corpses of the shot commanders, while Steiuk stated that he saw 2,000 corpses.[37] Perhaps it was hard to correctly estimate the number of the corpses in the piles.

The Nazis originally sent the POWs

> on foot to camps in or near other cities, such as Zhitomir. On these death marches ... a significant percentage [of POWs] perished.... By October 1941, the POW camps in or near Zhitomir were unable to accept any more prisoners, and therefore many captive Red Army soldiers were left in camps in Kiev and its environs (such as Darnitsa).[38]

The Nazis created several concentration camps in occupied Kyiv: in the Darnytsia and Syrets districts, on Kerosynna Street (now Sholudenko Street), and on Instytutska Street.[39] The majority of the inmates were Soviet POWs, but there were also members of the underground movement, Jews, and some gentile civilians. Civilians were placed in a concentration camp for violation of Nazi orders or as political opponents. There were also criminals in the camps.

The Nazis had a genocidal policy toward concentration camp inmates. The occupiers considered Slavic and Jewish people inferior and often kept them under the open sky or in dugouts, without sufficient food or any medical aid. As a result, the prisoners died in thousands from typhus and other contagious diseases.

Kyivans knew about the terrible situation of inmates in the Nazi concentration camps. Some Kyivans had members of their families, relatives, and friends imprisoned in the camps and tried to help them. On October 5, 1941, the head of Kyiv city administration, Oleksadr Ohloblyn, signed a resolution establishing the Ukrainian Red Cross. The main goal of the organization was "to provide a variety of aids to POWs and medical aid to Kyiv and the population of the city suburbs."[40] The newspaper *Ukrains'ke slovo* appealed on October 30, 1941, to the Kyivan population:

> The Ukrainian Red Cross began to collect donations for POWs and our wounded brothers-Ukrainians among the population of the Ukrainian capital.... Every conscientious Ukrainian and citizen must donate everything possible. Nobody can ignore the "Brothers to Brothers" appeal.[41]

The Ukrainian Red Cross gathered food, warm clothes, and medication for Ukrainian POWs. The Red Cross also petitioned the Nazis to release at least Ukrainian-Kyivans from the concentration camps.[42] The liberation of Ukrainians and other non-Russian POWs from the concentration camps briefly coincided with Nazi policies. Thus, many ethnic German, Baltic, Belarussian, and Ukrainian POWs were released in the first months of the war.[43] Berkhoff wrote:

> On September 29, [1941] Hitler personally spoke out in favor of letting go a large number of Ukrainians. Russians were deliberately omitted from these orders. But several weeks later (on November 7), Reich Minister Goering told a conference of officials that Hitler had ordered an end to the release of Ukrainians, though without giving Hitler's reasons, which remain unknown.[44]

The end of the liberation of Ukrainians from the concentration camps happened at the same time as a change of Nazi policy toward all Ukrainians. In the first months of the war, the Nazis flirted with the Ukrainian national movement and tried to use it to support the Nazi regime in Ukraine. But then the Germans became irritated by the promotion of the Ukrainian national idea and by the struggle of Ukrainian nationalists for independence. Nazis began to close all Ukrainian national organizations and to arrest the Ukrainian nationalists. The Ukrainian Red Cross functioned for just over two months. The Nazis abolished it on December 10, 1941.[45]

Nobody cared at all about the non-Ukrainian inmates of the concentration camps. There were many thousands of Russians and a few thousand Jews and POWs of other nationalities. The Soviet government considered Soviet POWs to be traitors and did not provide them with any aid. So, they died in large numbers from starvation and diseases in the Nazi camps.

The concentration camp on Kerosynna Street was organized soon after the beginning of the Nazi occupation of Kyiv on the territory of the military barracks next to the Zenit stadium. The Nazis kept in the camp POWs, communists, and Jews who had escaped the original execution at Babyn Yar. The camp had a Jewish Department due to the large number of Jewish prisoners. After the liberation of Kyiv, David Budnik, who was a prisoner in the concentration camp on Kerosynna Street, testified that the Nazis held in the camp "over three thousand Jews—elderly people, women and children."[46] But the concentration camp on Kerosynna Street was only a holding point for captured Jews before they were sent to their execution at Babyn Yar.[47] Almost every day the Nazis executed 200–300 prisoners from the camp.[48]

While most Kyivan Jews were killed at Babyn Yar in the end of September to mid-November 1941, several thousand Jews were killed there later.[49] The concentration camp on Kerosynna Street functioned from September 1941 to spring 1942. The camp prisoners were then transferred to the newly established Syrets concentration camp, which was located next to Babyn Yar (figure 3.1).[50] The concentration camp on Kerosynna Street was not far from downtown Kyiv. So, perhaps the Nazis decided to move the camp further away from downtown and use the Zenit stadium for sport competitions.

The Syrets concentration camp functioned from spring 1942 until the liberation of Kyiv in November 1943. The Nazi kept 2,000 to 3,000 prisoners in the camp at a time. The male inmates lived in dugouts, while the females were kept in wooden barracks. There were thirty-two dugouts, with seventy to eighty men living in each of them. "According to the testimony of former inmates, the dugouts in the men's section had names: the Jewish, Soviet, partisan, and Communist dugouts, the team leaders' dugout, and the medical dugout."[51]

It was difficult to escape from the concentration camps. The Syrets concentration camp was encircled by three rows of high fences made from barbed wire and wires with high-voltage electricity. The camp was guarded by 120 to 150 *polizai* (policemen) per shift and several dogs.[52] All camp inmates were divided into brigades of 15 to 20 people led by brigadiers and hundreds led by *sotniks*. The brigadiers and *sotniks* were selected mostly from criminals and they helped the Germans watch and torture other

Figure 3.1 Soviet prisoners of war covering the bodies of Jews killed at Babyn Yar. (Photo by Johannes Hähle. Courtesy of the Hamburger Institut für Sozialforschung.)

prisoners.[53] The brigadiers and *sotniks* were supposed to watch that no prisoners escaped during their shift and that the prisoners fulfilled their work assignments. They had the right to physically punish prisoners. They often beat the prisoners with stakes.[54]

The commandant of the Syrets concentration camp was Sturmbannfuhrer Paul Radomski,

> a cruel Nazi whose own brothers-in-arms nicknamed him "mad dog." One former prisoner described him as a man who "had the look of a cocaine addict in a pince-nez, with a red face and a shaven head, almost always drunk." He frequently appeared with his favorite dog, a German Shepherd named Rex, whom Radomski occasionally commanded to attack inmates. He himself took part in beating and killing prisoners.[55]

The Nazis established collective responsibility for the concentration camp inmates. When three prisoners of the Syrets concentration camp dug under the fence and escaped, Radomski announced that for each escaped prisoner ten others would be executed. Then he selected thirty prisoners, twenty-eight of whom were executed. When another three prisoners escaped during their work outside the camp, the Nazis executed thirty-five concentration camp inmates.[56]

Berkhoff wrote: "Behind the guidelines for the POW camps was the idea that feeding those inside amounted to stealing from the German people."[57] Many prisoners died from starvation and exhaustion in the Syrets concentration camp. *Sotnik* I. Morozov[58] testified about the strict regime in the Syrets concentration camp:

> The prisoners woke up at 4 am, at 4:30 was breakfast, at 5 am in a column they went to work. 12 noon was lunch, they went to work again at 1 pm and worked until 9 pm. They received in the morning a cup of so-called coffee, but this was really boiled water with a taste of some grass. They received for dinner a liter (quart) of *balanda* [gruel]—it was just water with a few grains of millet. The prisoners received 200 grams of bread per day made from millet flour. There was no dinner. The prisoners ate rats, dogs, cats and various grasses. Some prisoners were swollen from starvation. Such prisoners were taken to the so-called hospital-dugout, where they did not receive any medical treatment, and they died themselves or were shot by the commander of the camp German Radomsky. In 1942 Radomsky shot sick people almost every day. He came to the hospital-dugout, gave the order to carry out the sick people and there outside of the dugout he shot them.[59]

Ten to fifteen inmates of the Syrets concentration camp died from starvation every day. They were buried either in pits on the territory of the camp or their corpses were carried by other prisoners to Babyn Yar.[60]

In the most difficult situation in the Syrets concentration camp were the Jewish inmates. They were tortured and killed not only by the Nazis but also by the brigadiers and *sotniks*. *Sotnik* Morozov testified, "In July to August 1942 [the prisoners] cut trees on the territory of the camp. Konrad and Kuripko forced Jews to climb up the trees. Then tree was then pulled down by a rope and fell to the ground with the prisoner."[61]

Leonid Ostrovsky, a Jewish prisoner of the Syrets concentration camp, provided similar testimony in 1944:

> They [*sotniks*] beat us with sticks for any small violation: 25 sticks were the system. The main tortures: they forced the prisoner to climb a tree and then cut down the tree. If the prisoner was not killed falling with the tree, he was buried alive or was beat by a stick 200–300 times to death. He was beat by the other prisoners.[62]

Historian Stanislav Aristov wrote: "Over the course of two days the Sotniki Kuripko and Kolbas'ev killed twenty-three of the forty-two members of a Jewish work team uprooting trees at Babyn Yar. The remaining prisoners were subjected to perverse humiliations."[63]

Jewish prisoners of the Syrets concentration camp received even less food than other prisoners. They were constantly tortured and beaten by *sotniks* and brigadiers.[64] Thus *sotnik* Victor Konrad created for Jews a special "exercise," which he forced them to do after their long and exhausting workday. The "exercise" was the following: "The prisoners should stand in a circle and hold each other by their hands. On the shoulder of each prisoner sat one more man and they were forced to dance with a song. They should sing songs only in the Jewish language [i.e., Yiddish]."[65] *Sotnik* Morozov forced Jews "to run around and head-butt one another."[66] Those who refused were brutally beaten with sticks.[67]

The prisoners of the Syrets concentration camp were forced to do various jobs in the camp and in the city. The prisoners "felled trees in the surrounding woods, built dugouts, and worked at carpentry, excavation, or saddlery for their German masters."[68] They were also forced to toil in the city removing the ruins of exploded buildings, and they did construction work and paved the streets. The women prisoners did cooking, sewing, and "they were set to whatever needed to be done."[69] Often the camp inmates were forced to do pointless jobs. Five camp prisoners who survived, D. Budnik, V. Davydov, Z. Trubakov, I. Doliner, and V. Kukhlia, testified in 1945:

> Often the work was absolutely exhausting, tortures pointless, people were forced to move soil from one place to another, putting on stretchers eight-ten *puds*[70] of soil and forced to run. The guards beat us by shovels and shot us. They killed people and buried people alive. One such, Efim Vilkis, was buried alive and survived. He fled later with us from Babyn Yar.[71]

When the Nazis thought in August 1943 that they might not be able to hold Kyiv for long due to the offensive of the Red Army, they "rushed to hide every sign of mass execution at Babi Yar."[72] The Nazis formed "two Sonderkommandos for carrying out Action 1005.... The Security office and policemen were responsible for directing the exhumation and burning of the corpses, guarding the laborers put to the task, and keeping the operation as secret as possible."[73]

On August 18, 1943, the Germans took 327 prisoners from the Syrets concentration camp and "shackled them in leg irons."[74] The prisoners were moved to Babyn Yar and received the order to dig up and burn the corpses of the executed people. Among the prisoners who were brought to Babyn Yar were people of different nationalities: Jews, Russians, Ukrainians, and Armenians.[75] Most of the prisoners were men, but there were also thirteen Jewish women.[76]

Leonid Ostrovsky, a prisoner who worked at Babyn Yar, testified that the Nazis forced the prisoners to dig up the corpses, burn them on stone platforms, and "scatter the ashes through the ravine so that no traces of the corpses would remain."[77] The prisoners realized that when they finished their job the Nazis would exterminate them also to not leave any witnesses of their crimes. So, the prisoners began preparations for a mass escape. They brought to the dugout where they lived tools for opening their leg irons, metal and heavy objects for attacking the guards, and keys for opening the lock on the dugout gate. Most of these items the prisoners found among dug up corpses.[78]

Jewish prisoner Yakov Kaper found a key to the lock of the dugout and checked that it worked during lunchtime on September 27, 1943.[79] One of the prisoners, a Jew, Vladimir Davydov,[80]

> found a pair of scissors in a dead woman's pocket. With those rusty scissors he unlocked his leg irons. Then the other prisoners did the same. At dawn on 29 September 1943, exactly two years after the mass murder of Jews in Kiev, Davydov and his comrades ran from the bunkers and raced toward the walls of their cemetery. Stunned by the sudden escape, the SS were unable to open fire with their machine guns right away. They killed 280 men. But Vladimir Davydov and eleven other men managed to climb the walls and run away. Residents in the area near Kiev sheltered them.[81]

Different sources provide varied numbers of the uprising survivors, from twelve to eighteen men.[82] Among those who escaped from Babyn Yar and survived were Jews Vladimir Davydov, Isaak Brodsky, Semen Berliant, Leonid Ostrovsky, Yakov Steiuk (Shtein), David Budnik, and Yakov Kaper.[83]

During the uprising, prisoners ran in different directions so that it would be more difficult for the Nazis to find and catch them. Certainly, none of the escaped prisoners would have survived without the support of the local gentile population. Natalia Petrenko hid Davydov and Kharash. Feofan Vlasiuk hid Budnik, Vilkis, Kotler, Ostrovsky, Kaper, and Berliand in the pipe of the nearby brick factory. N. Kozlovskaia hid Doliner. Several other escaped prisoners hid elsewhere in Kyiv.[84] From the escape of the prisoners from Babyn Yar until the liberation of Kyiv, there remained a bit more than a month. Kyivans knew about the approaching Red Army, so perhaps this encouraged some gentiles to help the escaped prisoners.

Immediately after the liberation of Kyiv the escaped prisoners reported about the Nazi crimes at Babyn Yar and the Syrets concentration camp to the Extraordinary State Commission for Investigation of German-Fascist Crimes Committed on Soviet Territory (ChGK). Furthermore, on November 11, 1943, Davydov "personally reported about the German crimes to Nikita Sergeevich Khrushchev and showed him all the sites where Germans committed the crimes."[85]

In September 1943, when the Red Army was approaching Kyiv, the Nazis began liquidation of the Syrets concentration camp. On September 22, 1943, they sent many prisoners in freight trains to forced labor in Germany. The Syrets concentration camp officially functioned until late October 1943. According to ChGK records, 25,000 concentration camp inmates, POWs and civilians, perished at the Syrets concentration camp.[86]

The Darnytsia concentration camp was organized for POWs in fall 1941 in Darnytsia, then a suburb of Kyiv, now a district of the city. About 300,000 POWs went through the concentration camp and 68,000 prisoners perished there. Starvation in the Darnytsia concentration camp was so severe that the inmates ate all the grass in the camp.[87] Malnutrition and contagious diseases were the main causes of death of the prisoners, most of whom were between 20 to 40 years old. The Kyiv District ChGK found many corpses of prisoners who had been shot. Conditions in the camp were so horrible and the treatment of the prisoners so brutal that some of the concentration camp inmates committed suicide by throwing themselves against the camp fence's high-voltage wires.[88] In June 1943, the camp inmates were transferred to Berdychiv.

Unfortunately, we know significantly less about the Darnytsia concentration camp than about Syrets, although more prisoners perished there. In general, former POWs were kept under suspicion in the Soviet Union even after Stalin's death. Soviet historians avoided writing about the POWs. The surviving Soviet POWs usually did not talk about their war experiences publicly during Soviet times. By the time communism collapsed, many of them had already passed away. So, some aspects of the history of the Darnytsia and other Nazi concentration camps is likely lost forever.

It is also unknown if the ChGK intentionally elevated the number of victims of the Nazi regime in the occupied territories, or if there was a problem with the calculation of the number of victims. The corpses of the prisoners of war were buried in mass graves, so to calculate how many people died there was difficult. Different sources provide widely varying estimates of the number of POWs who perished in the concentration camps in Kyiv. For example, according to ChGK, 93,000 people perished in the Syrets and Darnytsia concentration camps, the vast majority of whom were POWs. Martin Blackwell wrote: "Privately, the Ukrainian government noted in October 1944 that 127,273 civilians and 69,021 Red Army POWs were killed in German occupied Kyiv."[89] Although the exact number of victims of the concentration camps in Kyiv is unknown, certainly tens of thousands of POWs perished there.

THE MATCH OF DEATH: MYTH OR TRUTH?

Among the concentration camp inmates, there were many civilians who were arrested for disobeying Nazi orders or because of denunciation. Some local celebrities, as well as several soccer players from the Dynamo-Kyiv team, were imprisoned. This soccer team was one of the best in the Soviet Union and Europe before the war.[90] During the war, several team members were mobilized into the Red Army and taken into Nazi captivity. However, by request of the head of the Kyiv city administration, Oleksader Ohloblyn, they were released and soon reappeared on a newly created soccer team, Start, which belonged to Kyiv Bakery No. 1. One of the administrators of the bakery, Czech Iosef Kordik, who claimed during the Nazi occupation that he was a Volksdeutsche, was a big soccer fan. Kordik invited nine soccer players formerly on the Dynamo-Kyiv team to work at the bakery. Working at the bakery helped them survive in starving Kyiv,[91] although several of the players who worked at the bakery recalled that they were often hungry. As porters they worked outside the bakery and were not supposed to have access to bakery products. The Germans threatened bakery workers with summary execution for stealing absolutely anything from the bakery. However, the workers received at least some salary and were protected by their work from deportation to Germany for forced labor, where the unemployed were sent.

So, the soccer players worked at the bakery and trained in their free time. On May 27, 1942, the bakery soccer team, Start, was officially registered, and the soccer season was opened in Kyiv on June 7, 1942. All games took place in Zenit Stadium (Kerosynna St., 24) after the concentration camp was moved from the stadium. From June 7 to August 16, 1942, Start played ten matches against Ukrainian, German, and Hungarian teams and won all of them, with a total score of 56 to 11. The Start victories were expected: the team had professional players from one of the best soccer teams in Europe, while the other Ukrainian teams were newly formed, and the German and Hungarian teams were composed of troops billeted in the city.

Start had two matches against the best German team on the Eastern Front, Flakelf,[92] on August 6 and 9, 1942. The rematch of Start versus Flakelf on August 9, 1942, was later called the Match of Death. According to legend, an SS officer came to the Dynamo-Kyiv players before the match and demanded that they lose to the Germans, or they would be put in a concentration camp. This myth was created in Soviet times to show the heroic behavior of the Start players, who won the match despite the Nazi threat. However, Start player Makar Goncharenko denied that German officials threatened the team: "Nobody from the official administration blackmailed us to give up the match."[93] Goncharenko said that some private people, either provocateurs from the competing soccer team, Rukh (Movement), or somebody who was really concerned about the Start soccer team, suggested that they should lose the game to avoid irritating the Nazis. Goncharenko recalled that before the game an SS officer came to the Start team changing room and "in pure Russian language politely introduced himself as the referee of the game."[94] He asked the players to greet the German team with the Nazi salute. But the Start soccer players did not follow his suggestion and greeted Flakelf with the standard Russian sports greeting *"Fizkult-privet!"* ("Fizkult-Hurrah!" or "Long live sport!").[95]

The German soccer players were brought to the stadium by bus, while the Start soccer players walked a long distance to the stadium. Goncharenko recalled, "With our malnutrition to play serious matches with a two-day break was pure torture."[96] Start player Mikhail Sviridovsky recalled, "A German general came to the match and brought a bouquet of flowers, oranges, lemons and chocolate. This really hurt us a lot."[97] The Start soccer players did not have enough bread in everyday life, and they had not seen such exotic food since prewar times.

There were about 2,000 spectators in the stadium, including many German soldiers and officers, and Kyivans. The match finished with a 5 to 3 victory by the Start team. Goncharenko, who scored two goals, said that it was a difficult match, because the Flakelf team played well.[98] Nobody arrested the Start soccer players after the Match of Death, unlike the Soviet legend.

One week later, on August 16, 1942, the Start soccer team played its last match against the Ukrainian team Rukh and won 8 to 0.[99] On August 18, 1942, nine Start players were arrested by the Gestapo. According to Sviridovsky, the players were arrested because of a denunciation by the Nazi collaborator Georgy Viachkis. Before the war, the Lithuanian Viachkis lived in Kyiv and was champion of Ukraine in swimming. During the Nazi occupation, Viachkis worked for the Gestapo. Sviridovsky testified that on December 16, 1943, Viachkis participated in his interrogation.[100] Goncharenko stated that the Rukh soccer team's coach, Georgy Shvetsov, wrote in a denunciation of the Start soccer players that they "made propaganda of Soviet sport."[101] It is possible that the Nazis received more than one denunciation of the Start players. Many were jealous of the team's repeated victories and may have tried to eliminate their competition. After the arrest of the nine players, the Start team folded.[102]

Goncharenko said that the Nazis checked who played for the Dynamo-Kyiv team by looking at prewar team posters and arrested those players.[103] Two days later, the Gestapo released Vladimir Balakin, who played for the Lokomotiv soccer team before the war. On September 6, Nikolai Korotkikh, who had played for Dynamo-Kyiv, was arrested.

During their interrogation, the Nazis accused the arrested soccer players of playing before the war on the Dynamo-Kyiv team, which belonged to the People's Commissariat of Internal Affairs (NKVD). So, the Nazis claimed that the Dynamo-Kyiv team members also worked for the NKVD. According to Oleg Yasinsky, the Dynamo-Kyiv team belonging to the NKVD was rather a formality. The soccer players did not work for the NKVD, and only one of them, Korotkikh, was a member of the Communist Party.[104] Korotkikh died from torture during his interrogation.[105]

One of the arrested soccer players, Aleksandr Tkachenko, collaborated with the Nazis before his arrest and worked in the Kyiv branch of the German military intelligence service, Orion. According to Viacheslav Sabaldyr', Tkachenko was a double agent who also worked for the Soviet intelligence service and sent important information to Moscow.[106] Tkachenko was a player for Dynamo-Kyiv before the war and then he played for the Start soccer team. But he did not participate in the Match of Death. Tkachenko was arrested simultaneously with other Start players on August 18, 1942. He was killed during his attempt to escape from the Gestapo prison on September 8, 1942, in front of his mother's eyes, when she brought him a package.[107]

After Gestapo interrogation, the seven other players were sent to the Syrets concentration camp. Ultimately, four players survived and three were killed in the concentration camp. Three players, Nikolai Trusevich, Ivan Kuzmenko, and Aleksei Klimenko, were executed on February 24, 1943. There are various versions of why the soccer players were executed. Syrets concentration camp survivor Isaak Brodsky testified on November 29, 1943, that some prisoner tried to kill a German, in retaliation for which twenty-five prisoners were executed.[108] Another version is that some prisoner tried to escape during work outside of the camp and twenty-five prisoners were executed as punishment. Yet another version stated that a prisoner hit the dog of the commandant of the concentration camp, Radomski, with a shovel, because the dog stole his food. In revenge Radomski ordered the execution of twenty-five prisoners.[109]

Dynamo-Kyiv soccer team founder Lazar' Kogen also perished in the Syrets concentration camp, and the first administrator of Dynamo-Kyiv, Lev Chernobyl'sky, was killed at Babyn Yar. Both were Jews.

After the war (in 1974–76 and in 2005), German prosecutors attempted to find out why the Dynamo-Kyiv soccer players were arrested and who executed them. The investigations did not finish with any particular result. But it seems likely that the soccer players were arrested due to the denunciations of local collaborators, who were responsible, along with the Nazis, for the soccer players' deaths.

After the war, the Dynamo-Kyiv players who perished were glorified as Soviet heroes, and the myth of the Match of Death with the German soccer team Flakelf was created. Several monuments to the Dynamo-Kyiv players were erected in Kyiv. However, the true story of the arrest and death of the Dynamo-Kyiv team members was revealed only after the collapse of communism.

MEMBERS OF THE UNDERGROUND MOVEMENT

Unlike the neglected history of the prisoners of the concentration camps, the history of the underground movement was written and glorified in Soviet times. Soviet historians usually depicted the underground movement in Kyiv as heroic resistance that caused significant harm to the Nazi occupiers. The real story of the Kyiv underground movement was quite different: Most of the members of the movement perished due to betrayal by local informers. The Gestapo killed 617 members of the underground movement during the Nazi occupation of Kyiv.[110] It took the Nazis over two years to detect, arrest, and execute most of the underground movement members.

The underground movement organized diversions and sabotage of industrial equipment, exploded freight trains and destroyed railroads, spread pro-Soviet leaflets and killed Nazis.[111] The activities of the underground members are well described in historical literature. However, Soviet historians always omit one courageous member of the movement, Tatiana Markus, because she was Jewish. In the best case, Soviet historical publications just mention her name, without any description of her contributions to the resistance against the Nazi occupation.

Tatiana was born in 1921 to a large Jewish family in the provincial Ukrainian town of Romny. Also called Tania, she was the fifth of six children in the family. In the 1920s, her family moved to Kyiv. Tania grew up in Kyiv, where she studied at school. Her parents were quite poor and after the ninth grade Tania began to work as a secretary in the Human Resources Department at South-Western Railroad. She married Grigory Levitsky in 1940.[112]

When Kyiv was occupied by the Nazis, Tatiana refused to go with her mother and siblings to evacuation. Tatiana, her husband, Grigory, and her father, Iosif, joined the underground resistance movement. The members of the underground created a "legend" for Tatiana that she was a Georgian, Princess Tatiana Markusidze, whose father had been executed by the Bolsheviks. Tatiana moved to another district of the city so that her neighbors would not recognize her and stayed in the house of Nataliia Dobrovol'skaia. Tatiana, her father, Nataliia Dobrovol'skaia, and Nataliia's sister helped hide Jews and wounded Red Army soldiers. They rewrote the medical documents of mentally ill patients in the Psychoneurological Institute to hide which of them was Jewish.[113]

Tatiana and other members of the underground movement killed Nazi officers and soldiers in Kyiv. During a Nazi parade in occupied Kyiv, Tatiana threw a grenade hidden in a bouquet of flowers from a balcony and killed four German soldiers. She escaped and soon began to work in a dining hall for Nazi officers, where she put poison into the food. Several Nazi officers died from the poison, but nobody suspected the young "noble" girl.

Tatiana was a beautiful young girl, and her appearance helped her get the attention of Nazi officers. By order of the underground movement, Tatiana began to "date" Nazis. She arranged rendezvous with German officers in places where other members of the underground movement waited and killed the Nazis. Tatiana Markus and her comrades killed thirty-three Nazis, six of whom Tatiana personally killed.[114]

Tatiana was able to elude the Nazis for a while, because they were searching for male partisans and did not suspect the attractive young girl of committing the murders. However, her husband, father, and many other members of the underground were caught and killed by the Nazis. On July 17, 1942, the pro-Nazi newspaper *Nove Ukrains'ke Slovo* wrote about the execution of "communist bandits," among whom was Tatiana's husband Grigory Levitsky.

Tatiana sought revenge for the death of her husband, father, and many thousands of Jews in Kyiv. She told her friend that her life would be justified by the number of Nazis she killed. Without her husband, who helped and protected Tatiana during her underground operations, she became more careless. Perhaps her young age (she was twenty-one years old) can explain her courageous but reckless behavior. When Tatiana killed Obersturmbannführer Carl Stuckert in his house, she left a note: "All of you, fascist reptiles are awaiting the same fate. Tatiana Markusidze."[115] Thus she revealed herself to the Nazis. The underground movement leadership decided to send Tatiana out of the city to the partisans. But when Tatiana and her comrades tried to cross the Dnipro River on August 22, 1942, they were captured by the Nazis. She was subjected to brutal torture by the Gestapo for five months, but she did not betray anyone. Tatiana was executed by the Nazis on January 29, 1943, at Babyn Yar.[116]

On September 21, 2006, the president of Ukraine, Victor Yushchenko, awarded Tatiana Markus the title of Hero of Ukraine with a Golden Star. In December 2009, a monument to Tatiana Markus was unveiled at Babyn Yar.[117]

DESTRUCTION OF THE UKRAINIAN NATIONALIST UNDERGROUND IN KYIV

The complicated relations of the Ukrainian nationalist movement with the Nazis were described in the previous chapter. The efforts of the Ukrainian nationalists to create an independent state were suppressed by the Nazis, and many members of the movement were arrested and killed during the German occupation of Ukraine.

Historian Sergii Kot provides the following periodization of the Ukrainian nationalist movement under Nazi rule:

- The first period (September 19–December 13, 1941) was when members of the OUN-M arrived in Kyiv and functioned legally in the city. They created various municipal institutions and public organizations.
- In the second period (December 13, 1941–February 9, 1942) the Nazis arrested many OUN members in Kyiv and the OUN went underground.
- During the third period (February 9, 1942–November 6, 1943) the OUN underground movement was active in occupied Kyiv and in confrontation with the occupiers.[118]

Contemporary works of Ukrainian historians show that the OUN-M members worked in Kyiv in the first period to create Ukrainian national institutions and that a group of OUN-M members joined the City Council, and they "really influenced its work."[119] On October 5, 1941, the OUN-M created the Ukrainian National Council in Kyiv, which was supposed to spread its activity to central, eastern, and southern Ukraine. The members of OUN initiated the creation of the Kyiv police.[120] In the first period of its activity, the OUN-M collaborated with the Nazis and participated in the murder of Jews and of opponents of the Nazi regime.

"The main ideological tool of OUN at this time was the newspaper *Ukrains'ke slovo*."[121] The first issue of the newspaper was published on the day when the massacre of Kyivan Jews began at Babyn Yar, September 29, 1941. As noted above, the newspaper spread violent anti-Semitic propaganda and called upon its readers to denounce Jews hidden in the city. *Ukrains'ke slovo* was quite popular among Kyivans and from 20,000 to 50,000 copies were published per issue.[122] Thus the newspaper had a significant impact on public opinion.

But later, when the Ukrainian nationalists went too far with their striving for independence, the Nazis arrested many members of the OUN-M movement, while others switched to underground activities. Nachmanovich wrote:

> Between 1941 and 1944 the Organization of Ukrainian Nationalists lost 4,756 members, including 197 leading staff members, 6 homeland (*krai*) leaders, and 5 members of the OUN leadership. Of all the Ukrainian lands where OUN structures operated, the organization suffered the greatest losses in occupied Kyiv, where 621 Ukrainian patriots were killed.[123]

There were many Ukrainian intellectuals among the executed members of the OUN. The most prominent among them was the Ukrainian poet Olena Teliga, who published the literary journal *Litavry* (Timpani) in occupied Kyiv and was the head of the Union of Ukrainian Writers. In her publications in *Litavry*, Teliga called for the independence of Ukraine. As a result, the journal was closed and Teliga was arrested by the Gestapo on February 9, 1942. According to one account, she was executed with other members of the OUN at Babyn Yar on February 22, 1942. By another account, Teliga and other members of the OUN were killed in the Gestapo prison and buried at Lukianovsky Cemetery, where a mass grave of 400 people was recently found.[124]

One of the authors of *Litavry* was the Russian Ukrainian poet of Jewish origins Yakov Gal'perin (1921–43), who published his works under the pseudonyms Yakov Galich and Mykola Pervach. Gal'perin was born to a Jewish family and studied in a Ukrainian school in Kyiv. From his school years, he wrote poetry in Russian and Ukrainian. In 1939, the eighteen-year-old Gal'perin won an all-Ukrainian literary competition devoted to the 125th anniversary of Taras Shevchenko's birth. The jury recognized Gal'perin's poems as the best poetry about Taras Shevchenko.[125] In 1940, Gal'perin became a student at the Philological Department of Kyiv University.

When Nazi Germany began the war against the Soviet Union, Gal'perin was not mobilized into the Red Army due to his severe lameness, which was a consequence of childhood polio. He remained in Kyiv during the Nazi occupation. The twenty-year-old Yakov initially had a somewhat romantic attitude toward the war, and like many Kyivan Jews, he did not comprehend the mortal danger of the Nazi regime. He said, "Ehrenburg was the only Soviet writer, who saw the German troops enter Paris, I want to see how they enter Kyiv."[126] When the Nazis occupied Kyiv, Gal'perin pretended that he had lost his passport, which, according to the Soviet standard, showed his nationality as "Jew." M. Berdichevsky wrote that some Ukrainian intellectual helped Gal'perin obtain a new passport in his pen name, Yakov Galich. Oleksandr Kucheruk claimed that the Ukrainian writer Izydora Kosach-Borisova, sister of the renowned Ukrainian poet Lesia Ukrainka, helped Gal'perin. Kosach-Borisova had connections with OUN members, and through the Kyiv City Council they obtained a new, non-Jewish passport for Gal'perin.[127]

Under a new literary pen name, Mykola Pervach, Gal'perin wrote articles for the newspaper *Ukrain'ske slovo* and poetry for the literary journal *Litavry*. Olena Teliga mentioned in her letter to OUN member O. Lashchenko that Yakov provided her with lots of his "very good poems devoted to her or not, but all of them are completely 'our' [i.e., Ukrainian nationalist] poems."[128] It is difficult to say if Gal'perin was really inspired by the ideals of the Ukrainian national movement or if it was just gratitude to the OUN members who saved his life.

Gal'perin was betrayed by his girlfriend Nadiia Golovatenko and his acquaintance Levitin. Levitin was half Jewish (he had a Ukrainian mother and a Jewish father) and served, according to one version, as a translator for the Gestapo, according to another for the police. Nadiia knew Levitin from prewar times. They revealed to the Nazis that Gal'perin was a Jew. Gal'perin had quarreled with Nadiia not too long before his arrest, because he had seen her in the company of Hungarian officers. Gal'perin left Nadiia and moved to live with a friend. Nadiia sent Gal'perin a note asking him to meet with her. When Gal'perin came out from the house where he was staying, Gestapo officers and Levitin were waiting for him. Gal'perin was arrested and killed by the Gestapo in April 1943.[129]

The Gal'perin case shows that OUN-M members, who were in general quite hostile toward Jews because they believed in the Judeo-Bolshevik myth, could make some exceptions for Jews who served Ukrainian national interests. This shows that OUN-M anti-Semitism was political, not racial. The members of the OUN-M collaborated with the Nazis in the beginning of the war, as they thought, for the sake of the creation of an independent Ukraine. However, the OUN-M members did not foresee the future of Ukraine under Nazi occupation, nor their own future. Common Kyivans understood the brutality of the Nazis much more quickly than the OUN-M members. After the murder of the Jews and Roma at Babyn Yar, Kyivans anticipated that the Nazis would not feel mercy for Slavic people either, and certainly, the German occupiers would not allow Ukrainian independence. Kuznetsov recalled that after the Babyn Yar massacre, "People started repeating a jingle: 'The Jews are done for and so are the Gypsies. Next on the list are the Ukrainians.'"[130]

ORTHODOX CLERGY

Three members of the Russian Orthodox clergy were executed at Babyn Yar on November 6, 1941. Archimandrite Aleksandr (Vishniakov), archpriest Pavel (Ostrensky) and schema nun Esfir' were motivated by Christian principles and hid Jews in Nazi-occupied Kyiv. Archimandrite Aleksandr and archpriest Pavel also distributed Metropolitan Sergiy Stragorodsky's epistle to believers, which called for resistance against the Nazi regime.[131] While almost no information is available about archpriest Pavel and schema nun Esfir', there are several publications about Archimandrite Aleksandr.

Archimandrite Aleksandr (1890–1941) was born to a clerical family. He participated in World War I as an army chaplain. In one battle, he substituted for a perished squadron commander and led soldiers on an attack. Vishniakov was awarded the Cross of Saint George for his courage.[132]

During the civil war, Father Aleksandr saved Jews during pogroms in Kyiv. In 1934, his church was closed by the Soviet authorities. Father Aleksandr was arrested several times in the 1920s and 1930s. In 1937, he was sentenced to three years' forced labor in a Soviet concentration camp. During Aleksandr's sentence, his wife divorced him.[133] In the 1930s, it was a common practice for husbands and wives to denounce and divorce their arrested spouses. If they did not do so, they were under risk of arrest as family members of an "enemy of the people."

After Vishniakov's release, he became a monk and received the title of archimandrite from Metropolitan Sergiy Stragorodsky. Archimandrite Aleksandr preached before the war in various parishes in Kyiv. When the war began, rumors about the execution of Jews in Zhytomyr and Vinnytsia reached Kyiv. Some local Jews began to ask Archimandrite Aleksandr to convert them to Russian Orthodox Christianity, naively believing that conversion would help save their lives. Unfortunately, the previous experience of Jews, when conversion helped save Jewish lives during pogroms, did not work for Nazi racial anti-Semitism. However, in some cases, converted Jews pretended that they were Russians or Ukrainians and as proof showed the Nazis documents about their baptism with Christian names. If nobody denounced their Jewishness to the Nazis, they might survive in occupied Kyiv. Vadim Maksimov and Konstantin Kapkov wrote that several Jewish families survived the Nazi occupation in this manner.[134]

On September 29, 1941, when the Babyn Yar massacre began, a neighbor, converted Jew Ian (his last name is not recorded) ran for help to Archimandrite Aleksandr and asked him to save his wife and three children whom the Nazis had taken to Babyn Yar. In the first months of the war, Archimandrite Aleksandr had baptized all of Ian's family. Aleksandr wore his priest's cassock and the Cross of Saint George and went to Babyn Yar. When Archimandrite Aleksander came to Babyn Yar, the execution of Jews had already begun. He wandered until nightfall among the frightened and despairing people who awaited their execution. Aleksandr talked to people and tried to comfort them. He found Ian's wife, Sima, and two of her children, and persuaded the Germans to release them. Aleksandr spoke fluent German, so he communicated with the Nazis without a translator. But he could not find the third child.

Archimandrite Aleksandr was shocked by the scenes of execution and the doomed people at Babyn Yar. He prayed for a long time that night. The next day he preached in the church against the enemies of the Fatherland. Somebody denounced his preaching to the Gestapo, and Archimandrite Aleksandr was arrested soon thereafter.

According to Kirill Frolov, Archimandrite Aleksandr was executed by Ukrainian *polizai* (policemen) at Babyn Yar on November 6, 1941. Frolov wrote that the *polizai* made a cross from cut trees and crucified Archimandrite Aleksandr, attaching him to the cross with barbed wire. They poured gasoline on him and threw him with the burning cross into the Babyn Yar pit.[135] The crucifixion of Archimandrite Aleksandr may be a legend, but several sources state that he was executed at Babyn Yar for resistance to the Nazi regime and hiding Jews.[136]

PROSTITUTES AND WOMEN WITH VENEREAL DISEASES

During the Kyiv occupation, some young gentile women had affairs with Nazis. Perhaps behind these affairs were not romantic relations, but rather pragmatic motivations to get money and food from the Germans. In the starving city, morals were quite low, and people attempted to survive by all possible means. As a result, venereal diseases spread in Kyiv among the local population and German troops. Medical doctor and professor N. A. Shepelevsky testified that German men infected women without any punishment:

> However. they severely punished women if they were infected themselves. They created a special organization, which investigated who infected this or that German.... They created a Venereal Department for sick women, where they were held behind bars as arrested criminals.[137]

The Germans executed women who were sick with syphilis. But the Nazis did not seem interested in punishment or even treatment of their sick men. When a doctor of the October Hospital in Kyiv asked the German garrison doctor what they should do with the sick men, the garrison doctor replied: "We are not interested what should be done with the men. It is important to us to find a solution only regarding the women."[138] And soon the Nazis found a solution:

> From early 1942, prostitution was severely persecuted if it took place outside the official brothels. All prostitutes found to have venereal disease were very likely to be killed.... It is not clear if that was the alleged reason for the gassing in Kyiv in the fall of 1943 of about a hundred naked young women, which was witnessed by Jewish survivors at Babi Yar. These women are said to have been from a brothel.[139]

Thus, prostitutes and women sick with venereal diseases also became victims of the Nazi regime in Kyiv and their corpses were thrown into Babyn Yar.

HOSTAGES

During the Nazi occupation, at least 800 hostages were executed in Kyiv. According to the Extraordinary State Commission report, on February 29, 1944, the Nazis caught random people on the streets and

> shot them in large groups or individually. For intimidation of the population, the Nazis put up announcements about the execution of hostages: "As punishment for the sabotage, 100 Kyiv inhabitants were shot today. This should serve as a warning. Each Kyiv inhabitant is responsible for sabotage. Kyiv, October 22, 1941. Commandant of the city." Or "Due to the increased number of cases of arson and sabotage, I must use the strictest measures. Therefore, 300 Kyiv inhabitants were shot today. For each new case of arson or sabotage, significantly more Kyiv inhabitants will be executed. Kyiv, November 2, 1941. Eberhard, Major General and City Commandant."[140]

This was not merely a threat, as the number of executed hostages increased with time. On December 2, 1941, the newspaper *Ukrains'ke slovo* published an announcement by City Commandant Kurt Eberhard[141] dated November 29, 1941:

> Somebody intentionally destroyed the communication equipment (phone, telegraph, cable). Because saboteurs cannot be tolerated anymore, 400 MEN WERE

SHOT IN THE CITY [text capitalized in the announcement], this should be a warning for the population.

I order that everyone immediately inform the German troops or German police about any suspicious cases so that the perpetrators can be immediately punished.[142]

VICTIMS OF FAMINE

Karel Berkhoff gave a comprehensive picture of the famine in Kyiv during the Nazi occupation in his book *Harvest of Despair: Life and Death in Ukraine Under Nazi Rule*.[143] The famine is also well described by Kuznetsov in his book *Babi Yar: A Document in the Form of a Novel*.[144] Here I will summarize this topic to show how the famine was deliberately created by the Nazis and how many Kyivans perished during the famine.

Kyiv stores were looted by the city inhabitants in the short period when the Red Army troops had retreated from the city, but the Germans had not yet arrived. Kuznetsov wrote that in his first order, German commandant Eberhard required that Kyivans return all stolen goods to "the place they were taken from" and hand over to the Germans their entire food supply: "The whole population must hand over all surplus of food. It is permitted to retain only supplies sufficient for twenty-four hours. Anyone failing to carry out this order will be SHOT."[145]

The day after the announcement, German soldiers came to Kuznetsov's house, but they did not find any food. Anatoly's grandfather had hidden their food "in the shed under the straw." But, in any case, Kuznetsov's family had food for only ten days and soon began to starve. Kuznetsov recalled that Kyiv shops "were deserted" from the time of their looting, "their windows broken, and nothing was being sold anywhere except at the market."[146] However, prices were so high at the market that common Kyivans could not afford to purchase enough food for themselves. For example, the price of bread increased more than a hundred times the prewar price. Kuznetsov wrote that bread before the war cost "ninety kopeks a kilogram." At the market during Nazi occupation, homemade bread cost 90–120 rubles per kilogram.[147] This was almost as much as the monthly salary of Kuznetsov's mother. So, Kuznetsov, his mother, and his grandparents severely suffered from famine, as did most Kyivans during the Nazi occupation. Only the Volksdeutsche were in a better situation, because special food shops were opened for them in Kyiv.

Kuznetsov recalled that for many days he was "eating hardly anything but [horse] chestnuts."[148] But the bitter-tasting horse-chestnuts were a seasonal food. Kuznetsov wrote that at some point he began to swell from starvation. He survived because his mother and grandmother gave up their food for him. Kuznetsov's grandmother died during the Nazi occupation. In Kyiv cannibalism appeared.[149] There was a similar situation in other Nazi-occupied cities of Ukraine: "City streets and roads into the city sometimes were littered with the corpses of starved people. Informed estimates are that at least 30,000 residents of Kharkiv and 10,000 residents of Kyiv starved to death."[150]

Berkhoff shows that the famine in Kyiv was artificially created, because there was a good harvest in 1941, but the German Economy Inspectorate South "callously banned the supply of food to Kyiv. Ukrainian émigré memoirs reveal that beginning in October, policemen barred people from entering the city and confiscated food that people attempted to take there."[151] The Nazis established bread rationing in Kyiv, and the daily amount of bread for common people "ranged from 125 grams in late 1941 to 400 grams in the middle of 1942.... Kievans with jobs received small amounts of flour, barley, and vegetables and were authorized to buy or receive an extra loaf once or twice a month."[152] However, in many families, only one person worked, and they were starving as severely as Kuznetsov's family. Many died from famine. Kyiv, according to Kuznetsov, was turned into "a city of beggars."[153]

Top Nazi authorities knew about the famine in Kyiv, but this fit well in their plans to get rid of "extra" Slavic people. "On October 3, [1941] SS chief Heinrich Himmler visited Kyiv as part of a city tour in central and southern Ukraine." On October 5, he shared his impression from the tour with Hitler during dinner. Himmler reported that he saw many poorly dressed Kyivans and "they looked awfully 'proletarian.' One can easily do without eighty to ninety percent of them."[154] The Nazi authorities characterized the Kyivan population as "racially very bad" and supported the policy of their death from famine.[155]

THE OCCUPATION REGIME AND SLAVE LABORERS

Over the two years of Nazi occupation, most Kyivans lived in constant fear. The commandant of the city, Eberhard, imposed upon Kyivans more and more restrictive measures and threatened immediate execution for disobedience. On October 16, 1941, Eberhard ordered a curfew in Kyiv from 6 p.m. to 5 a.m. (German time). The order said that everybody who did not follow the rule would be shot.[156] On October 26, 1941, Eberhard ordered, "All pigeons in the city and suburbs must be destroyed immediately. Anyone found still keeping pigeons after October 26th will be SHOT as a saboteur."[157]

Another order of the city commandant stated:

> All felt boots now in the possession of the civilian population, including children's sizes, are to be requisitioned immediately. The use of felt boots is forbidden and will be punished in the same way as the use of weapons without permission.[158]

All adult Kyivans were required to work. The newspaper *Ukrains'ke slovo* published on October 8, 1941, an announcement that all adults who can work must come "every day 7 AM to the Employment Exchange." On October 23, 1941, *Ukrains'ke slovo* reported that about 55,000 unemployed people, among whom 60 to 65 percent were women, registered at the Employment Exchange.[159] On January 10, 1942, the newspaper *Nove ukrains'ke slovo* (New Ukrainian Word) published an announcement signed by the general-commissar of the Kyiv region of the Reichskommissariat Ukraine SA-Brigadenführer, Helmut Quitzrau:

> According to the laws of wartime, everybody is required to work at the place where the authorities send you (the Employment Exchange). People who do not come to the assigned workplace or leave the assigned workplace without the agreement of the employers or the Employment Exchange will be punished. They will be sent to forced labor camps, if they do not receive more serious punishment.[160]

However, the Employment Exchange could not provide work for so many unemployed people in the war-torn city, from which the most significant plants and factories had been evacuated to the eastern regions of the Soviet Union. Unemployment reached 20 to 25 percent in Kyiv during the Nazi occupation. So, the Nazi authorities decided to send unemployed people to work in Germany.

First, the Nazi authorities invited volunteers to go to work in Germany. The newspaper *Nove Ukrains'ke slovo* published on January 11, 1942, an announcement signed by the general-commissar of the Kyiv region, Quitzrau, which proposed that all Ukrainians from seventeen to fifty years old should go to work in Germany, promising them good living conditions and a salary. However, after several months of occupation, Kyivans had little trust in Nazi promises and were not eager to move to Germany.

The occupation authorities then established a norm for each Kyiv district of how many workers it must provide for Germany. To fulfill the norms, the Nazis and their auxiliaries conducted roundups on Kyiv streets and markets and caught all adults; they selected the unemployed and sent them to Germany.[161] Malakov wrote that only an *arbeitskarte* (work card), with a stamp showing current employment, could protect adults from being sent for forced labor in Germany.[162] From January 1942 until the end of the Nazi occupation, 50,000 Kyivans were sent to the Ostarbeiter program in Germany.[163] The Nazis forced Ukrainian Ostarbeiters to work in plants, farms, and households throughout Germany. They lived in varied conditions and the attitudes of Germans toward them were also quite varied. After the war, some of them came back to Kyiv, some remained in the West, and some may have perished. The forced laborers were ultimately recognized as victims of the Nazi regime, and in the early 2000s the German government paid them compensation.[164]

THE RETREAT OF GERMAN TROOPS AND THE DESTRUCTION OF KYIV

From late September 1943, the Nazis began their preparations for retreat from Kyiv. The well-known Kyivan artist Nikolai Andrianovich Prakhov testified:

> On September 25, 1943, they [the Nazis] announced on radio that all inhabitants of Pechersk, Lipki, Podil and the Old City districts must leave the fighting zone no later than September 26, 1943. All this territory was encircled by barbed and thick steel wire, on which were hung posters "Fighting zone. Those who enter without special permission will be shot." De facto this "fighting zone" turned into a "thieves' zone"—the Germans broke the doors of apartments and took away everything that they liked.[165]

Prakhov reported that despite the ban, he visited the forbidden zone six times and saw how the Nazis took from apartments the furniture and all valuable things. "What the Germans did not take, local marauders robbed."[166] Prakhov also testified that the Nazis took all valuable property from Jewish apartments after the execution of Jews at Babyn Yar.[167]

A professor at the Kyiv Forestry Institute, I. N. Zhitov, testified on November 30, 1943, "It is hard to find even one Kyiv inhabitant from whom the Germans did not steal something. Particularly, they stole from my apartment much of the furniture and even the tub from the bathroom."[168]

Kuznetsov wrote that the Nazis did not limit their looting of the city to robbing apartments; they also took everything they could from city plants, factories, and offices: "Everything that could be removed from the factories was carried away; in the offices they even unscrewed the door handles and window catches and removed the lavatory basins."[169]

The Nazis took all the art works from the Russian Art Museum and Museum Khanenko (Western and Oriental Art Museum) in Kyiv.[170] During their retreat, the Nazis destroyed the buildings of Kyiv University, the City Public Library, two power plants, two departments of the plant Bolshevik, industrial bakeries, all city bridges, and many apartment buildings.[171]

The Nazis forced Kyivans to go to so-called evacuation. Germans tried to chase away the entire population from Kyiv. They called it a "voluntary evacuation," but Kuznetsov described how it worked in practice:

> Using the butts of their rifles and their fists, and firing into air, they drove out on to the streets everybody who could walk and even those who couldn't. They gave them

one minute to gather their things and then announced: The city of Kiev is being evacuated to Germany; the city itself will exist no more.

It was horribly like the procession of Jews in 1941. Masses of people were on the move, with howling children, old people and invalids. Bundles hastily tied up with string, broken ply-wood suitcases, shopping bags and boxes of tools.[172]

Gentile Kyivans were horrified because they remembered well the execution of Jews at Babyn Yar, which occurred two years prior to the city "evacuation." The Nazis promised that they would resettle Jews in some other place, but instead massacred them. So, gentile Kyivans did not believe any promises and were afraid that the Nazis had prepared the same fate for them as for the Jews. Some Kyivans, such as Professor Lozinsky and his wife, committed suicide instead of going to "evacuation."[173] Many Kyivans hid in wells, basements, and attics. The Nazis searched for them with dogs specially trained for catching people.[174]

If the Nazis caught Kyivans and they refused to go to "evacuation," they executed them on the spot. When the Red Army liberated the city, troops found many corpses of people who had been executed by the Nazis on the city streets. The Soviets reported that the Nazis succeeded in chasing away from Kyiv most of the population. After liberation, "Kyiv made the impression of a dead city."[175]

Fortunately for most Kyivans, the Nazis retreated in such a rush that they were not able to chase the Kyivans far away from the city and so they returned soon after its liberation. Yet, Kyivans who survived the Nazi occupation looked upon their survival as a miracle, because they could have been executed many times for the slightest disobedience of Nazi orders. Kuznetsov, who was fourteen years old by the time of the liberation of the city, wrote that he could have been shot twenty times during the Nazi occupation. Among his "offences" he listed "1. Not informing on a Jew (my friend Shurka), 2. Concealing an escaped prisoner (Vasili), 3. Wearing felt winter boots, 4. Being out after the curfew."[176]

CONCLUSION

Babyn Yar became the symbol of terror and suffering for the entire population of Kyiv. Although a significantly larger percentage of Kyivan gentiles survived the Nazi occupation than Jews, most Kyivan gentiles lived in continuous fear during the occupation and suffered from hunger and humiliation. The massacre of Jews at Babyn Yar opened the eyes of most of the gentile population to Nazi brutality and terrified Kyivans. Many Kyiv gentiles lived during the Nazi occupation with the notion that they could be the next victims and could be killed at any instant for any minor infraction.

Babyn Yar became a mass grave not only for Jews, but also for Roma, mentally ill people, prisoners of war, Ukrainian nationalists, members of the underground movement, athletes, priests, and prostitutes. The Nazis killed people for their ethnicity (Jews and Roma), those who resisted the Nazi regime, and even those who attempted to collaborate with the Nazis but showed too much independence in their actions, or broke some rules and regulations, or just became unnecessary for the Nazis.

Many Kyivans and prisoners of war were killed during the Nazi occupation in the concentration camps, in the Gestapo prison, or on the city streets. About 10,000 Kyivans died from famine during the Nazi occupation. Babyn Yar became the symbol of the massacre for them too because the places of burial of many of these people are unknown. So, there appeared two distinctly different narratives of the Babyn Yar massacre: Babyn Yar became the symbol of the Holocaust for Jews as well as the symbol of universal suffering for the gentile population. This dichotomy of comprehension of the Babyn Yar massacre created heated debates regarding its commemoration and memorialization that continue until the present.

It is hard to reach a consensus between these two opposing narratives and points of view. Certainly, it is possible to provide statistics and show that only Jews and Roma were totally exterminated by the Nazis. Based on the statistics that I provided in the previous chapter, from 1940 to 1947, Kyiv's gentile population decreased from 706,000 to 572,000, by about 134,000 people, or 19 percent of the gentile population. Certainly, a significant percentage of Kyiv's gentile population perished during the war. Some Kyiv gentiles died at the front, some during the Nazi occupation, and some people might not have returned to the city after the war for many different reasons. The Kyivan Jewish population in the same years decreased by 41 percent. Almost all Jews who remained in Kyiv during the Nazi occupation were killed at Babyn Yar. The 59 percent of Kyivan Jews who survived the war were either in evacuation or at the front.

However, for those who lost their relatives, friends, or national heroes, statistics mean little. In 1996, at the request of the Shoah Foundation, I prepared to record a video interview with Ivan and Anastasiya Bondarenko, who saved the life of Raisa Dashkevich (her real name was Revekka Kogut) after she escaped from Babyn Yar. The entire Bondarenko family (a total of six people) received the title Righteous Among the Nations from Yad Vashem.[177] When I came to the Bondarenko family, Anastasiya told me: "Why should we talk about Raisa Dashkevich? She survived the war. Let's talk instead about my father and brother, they were partisans, and the Nazis burned them alive. Why does nobody want to hear about them?" The tragic fate of her father and brother was much more important for Anastasiya Bondarenko than the story of the rescue of Raisa Dashkevich and the Babyn Yar massacre. When I saw the reluctance of the Bondarenko family to talk about the rescue of Raisa Dashkevich, I decided not to insist upon my planned interview.

The commemoration process, if it is not politically biased, is based on people's personal memories and emotions, so it is clearly more subjective than objective, and personal tragedy and trauma always outweigh statistics or historical arguments. The only way to satisfy people's expectations is to incorporate their personal stories into one narrative about life and death in Kyiv during the Nazi occupation. I hope that the future Babyn Yar Holocaust Memorial Museum will fulfill this difficult task.

4

JEWISH LIFE AND ANTI-SEMITISM IN POSTWAR KYIV

TEVYE RETURNS HOME: THE RETURN OF JEWS TO KYIV

Kyiv was liberated on November 6, 1943. After the liberation of the city, Kyivans who had hid from the Nazi "evacuation" of the city returned to their homes. Nikita Khrushchev, who arrived with the liberation troops, wrote: "Kyivans returned to the city in big groups from the nearby woods, swamps, ravines and cemetery tombs [where they hid from the forced evacuation]. They made a difficult impression from their ordeals, tortures and depravations."[1] Before the war, 930,000 people lived in Kyiv; by December 1, 1943, only 220,000 remained.[2] The city, especially its downtown, was in ruins; there was no bread, water, heat, or electricity; and public transportation was not operating (figure 4.1).[3] It seems that returning Kyivans and the authorities were initially overwhelmed by the problems of restoring everyday life.

However, on the second day after the liberation of the city, on November 7, 1943, the Kharkiv Ukrainian Theater of T. G. Shevchenko performed the play *Tevye the Dairyman*[4] in Kyiv. The play is based on Sholom Aleichem's stories, written at the turn of the twentieth century. The main character, Tevye, was a dairy supplier to the inhabitants of Boyberik (Boiarka), a suburb of Yehupets (i.e., Egypt, as Sholom Aleichem called Kyiv in his works). Sholom Aleichem's works were written with great humor and his characters often show an ability "to laugh through tears" even in difficult life circumstances. Sholom Aleichem's humor was supposed to improve people's mood and lift their spirits, to help them overcome difficulties and return to normal life. It was a perfect choice of play for Kyivans devastated by the war. Sholom Aleichem's works were

Figure 4.1 Liberation of Kyiv, Khreshchatyk Street, November 1943. (Unidentified photographer.)

enjoyed not only by Jews, but also by liberal gentile intelligentsia, who often attended theater performances.

The well-known Ukrainian actor Marian Krushel'nitsky played Tevye.[5] Ukrainian actors performed Sholom Aleichem's story to a gentile Kyivan audience, because no Jews were left in the city by the time of its liberation: Those who remained in the city during the Nazi occupation were killed; the others had not yet returned from evacuation and the front. There could have been some Jewish soldiers present who had liberated the city the day before, but most people in the audience were gentiles.

This was quite a symbolic gesture by Ukrainian liberal intelligentsia: They brought the play *Tevye the Dairyman* back to the city where its author lived for over a decade, to the city where the Nazis exterminated almost all Jews, and where for two years Nazi anti-Semitic propaganda prevailed. Certainly, the theater's repertoire was confirmed with the authorities and no doubt the performance was an attempt to combat Nazi propaganda and to prepare an appropriate public mood for the return of Jews to Kyiv.

The Ukrainian State Jewish Theater brought the play *Tevye the Dairyman* to Kyiv during its long jubilee tour from August 30 to mid-October 1945, devoted to the twentieth anniversary of the theater.[6] Moisei Loev wrote that the play had "unprecedented success. The famous Ukrainian actor Marian Krushel'nitsky, who had himself played Tevye in the Kharkiv Ukrainian Theater ... was delighted by the brilliant performance of [Moyshe] Goldblatt and applauded the entire troupe."[7]

In the summer of 1947, the Kharkiv Ukrainian Theater again came on tour to Kyiv with the play *Tevye the Dairyman* along with other plays. There is an excellent photo by American war photographer and photojournalist Robert Capa that shows three men reading announcements on the semi-ruined wall of a building in Kyiv.[8] Capa did not know Russian or Ukrainian, but perhaps he was struck that people in the ruined city, which faced so many problems, were still interested in the arts. The picture shows a poster with the repertoire of the Kharkiv Ukrainian Theater and among the Russian and Ukrainian plays is listed *Tevye the Dairyman*. So, *Tevye the Dairyman* returned to Kyiv several times with great success (figure 4.2).

However, the return of Jews to Kyiv was not so easy and triumphant as the return of Sholom Aleichem's fictional character. Jews faced many difficulties, including a severe

Figure 4.2 Kharkiv Ukrainian Theater poster for *Tevye the Dairyman*, Kyiv, 1947. (Photo by Robert Capa.)

shortage of apartments in the ruined city, poverty, and popular and state anti-Semitism. Many Jews and gentiles in Kyiv suffered from postwar traumatic syndrome; they had lost their relatives, friends, and neighbors at the front and during the Nazi occupation.

Commemoration of the Babyn Yar massacre depended upon Soviet government policy, interethnic relations in Kyiv, and the collective memory of Jews and gentiles. To understand how the collective memory formed, we should discuss how Jews and gentiles lived in postwar Kyiv, what their interethnic relations were, as well as the changing government policy toward Jews.

THE STRUGGLE FOR APARTMENTS

Some Jewish and non-Jewish evacuees returned to Kyiv soon after the liberation of the city, but before the end of the war. Although Kyiv was in ruins, the conditions of life in evacuation were harsh, so many evacuees hoped for a better life and to recover their property when they came back to their native city. Leonid Bodankin and Emilia Osterman (née Ostrovskaia), who were children during the war, recalled that they returned to Kyiv with their mothers in March 1944, when Nazi aircraft were still bombing the city.[9]

However, when to return from evacuation to Kyiv was often not a personal decision. Usually, workers returned to the city together with the plants and factories where they worked. The authorities decided when and who should be allowed to return. A daughter of the well-known Ukrainian poet Andriy Malyshko, Valentina, recalled that she and her family returned from evacuation from the city of Ufa (Bashkiria) on March 8, 1944: "We went in a freight train for two weeks. It was the first train from Bashkiria, it brought the partisans' families to Kyiv."[10]

Historian Solomon M. Schwarz wrote:

> Generally, return without special permission was not authorized until August 1945; from then on, organized re-evacuation was carried through by special trains. Its start was reported late in August from Kazakhstan and Uzbekistan. A correspondent from Tashkent wrote:
>> These last days the mass re-evacuation of Uzbekistan's Jewish population has begun. In addition to those hundreds and thousands who moved westward with the regular railroad traffic, special trains for re-evacuated are now being dispatched from time to time.
>
> This Tashkent correspondent witnessed the departure of a special train that took 2,500 Jews from Tashkent to the Ukraine and White Russia; several more special trains were scheduled for the following weeks. Similar reports abounded.[11]

However, when surviving Jews came back to Kyiv and other Ukrainian cities, they encountered an utterly new level of vicious, violent anti-Semitism that did not exist in Ukraine before the war. This eruption of popular anti-Semitism can be explained partly by the influence of Nazi propaganda on the local gentile population, and partly by the awful living conditions in the ruined cities and towns. According to the report of the Extraordinary State Commission for the Investigation of German-Fascist Crimes Committed on Ukrainian Territory (ChGK), over 6,000 apartment buildings and houses (over 40 percent of all living accommodations) were destroyed in Kyiv during the war, and over 200,000 Kyivans were homeless in 1944.[12]

In this situation, many gentiles in Kyiv broke into the empty apartments of the evacuees and then refused to return them to their legal residents when the evacuees returned home. When Jews came back and attempted to return to their apartments, this provoked a sharp anti-Semitic reaction. Thus, most "re-evacuated" Jews in Kyiv failed to regain their apartments and other property. Appeal to the authorities or even official court orders to return their property to Jews usually did not work. For example, when my maternal grandparents returned to Kyiv with their two children in 1946, they found their apartment occupied by gentiles. My grandfather, Il'ia Brovarnik, appealed to the court. The judge decided that, due to the shortage of apartments in Kyiv, one of two rooms in the apartment would be returned to my grandparents and the other room left to the gentile family, which settled there during the war. However, when my grandparents tried to move into their officially allocated room, the head of the gentile family threatened that he would slaughter my grandparents' children (my mother and her sister) at night if my grandfather dared to move into the room. My grandparents decided that it would be impossible to live with such rabid anti-Semites in one apartment and looked for an alternative place to live.

Through the personal connection of my grandfather with the mayor of Kyiv, Fedor Chebotarev (my grandfather was an excellent dentist and had treated Chebotarev), they received a basement on Andriivskyi Descent that they only had to share with big rats. Even such a place as that was difficult to obtain in Kyiv after the war. My mother, Ludmila Brovarnik, recalled that the rats made holes in the ceiling and came into their basement apartment from the first and second floors and ran on the walls and ceiling. After the war, Andriivskyi Descent had a bad reputation, and there were many hooligans (*shpana*). When my mother returned home from her elementary school, the local boys often scared her with their German shepherd by commanding the dog, "Go get the Jew!"

My paternal grandparents were luckier: they were able to regain their one-room apartment. My grandfather, Boris Khiterer, was a senior lieutenant in the Red Army and fought at the front for the entire war. When his wife and son returned to Kyiv in 1944, their apartment was occupied by gentiles, who refused to leave, so they stayed for five months in the apartment of their friends. My grandfather then received a ten-day leave, came to Kyiv to visit his family, and was able to retrieve his apartment. My father, Mikhail Khiterer, told me that his father was able to recover their apartment because he was an officer who came from the front, and because the head of the gentile family that occupied the apartment was a Nazi collaborator who had previously been arrested. So, when my grandfather came to the apartment with a policeman, the Nazi collaborator's wife and other family members quickly disappeared without further resistance.

My paternal grandfather was the luckiest person in his extended family. None of his and his wife's relatives were able to return to their apartments after the war. So, they all came to live with my grandfather's family, and ultimately thirteen people were living in his one-room apartment. They stayed there until Khrushchev began his mass apartment construction program at the beginning of the 1960s. My aunt Elena Sokolovsky recalled that the one large room (before the revolution there was a bakery in the house) was divided into cubicles by plywood boards, but not to the ceiling, because the room had only one fireplace. The two restrooms for the six apartments in the building were outside: one for men and one for women.

Most surviving Kyivan Jews were unable to get their apartments back. Their appeals to the authorities, where they mentioned their family members killed at the front or who perished during the Holocaust, did not help much, if at all. Six members of Tsil'ia Sokolovsky's family were killed at the front during the war: her husband, stepson, and all four of her brothers. She returned to Kyiv with her two children from Siberia after the war and applied to the authorities asking to return to her apartment or at least be provided another apartment or room. However, all her requests were denied. So, she rented a room, and her teenage son had to go to work so that they could afford it.[13]

Sofia Kuperman wrote from Kyiv to a lawyer applying for legal assistance on February 22, 1946, saying that she went

> from office to office for action on the court decision that allowed her to move back into the apartment that once belonged to her. Using not only legal arguments but emotional ones, Kuperman wrote that eleven members of her family were killed by the Nazis during the occupation. The first secretary of the Party in their region, whom she finally got to see (she does not give his name), replied, "Who supplies you with hostile disinformation on the alleged martyrdom of Jews? Why don't you look for your tortured relatives in Tashkent somewhere? They just changed their names and are living happily ever after. And where did you hide? Not in partisan trenches, I'll bet. You fed your face in the rear of the front and now you want an apartment too. I'll pass your complaint on to the NKVD, they'll take care of it for sure."[14]

JEWISH POGROM IN KYIV

After the liberation of Kyiv from Nazi occupation, popular anti-Semitism erupted in the city without the permission, encouragement, or approval of the local or higher authorities. Ukrainian authorities were concerned about how to deal with this phenomenon, not so much due to their compassion for Jews, but more likely because they were afraid of their responsibility to Moscow for street disorders. The Security Service of Ukraine (NKGB) admitted there was a rise of popular anti-Semitism in Ukraine after its liberation from the Nazis. According to a top-secret report of the people's commissar of the Security Service of Ukraine to Khrushchev, the chair of the Council of Ministers of Ukraine and the First Secretary of the Communist Party of Ukraine in 1944–47, "About Anti-Semitism in Ukraine," dated September 13, 1944, the Kyiv population had called for a pogrom on June 22, 1944 (the third anniversary of the beginning of the Nazi-Soviet war), and the local gentile population attacked and beat Kyivan Jews on the streets.[15]

Jews who returned to Kyiv from evacuation were deeply traumatized by the loss of their relatives and friends in Babyn Yar. They felt that they needed to do something to commemorate the victims of the massacre. However, when the Yiddish poet David Hofshtein attempted to organize "a mass demonstration [according to another source, a meeting[16]] of the Jewish population on the anniversary of the German massacre at Babyn Yar" in 1944, the authorities forbade the demonstration, claiming that it might "provoke anti-Semitism."[17] And probably they were right. Considering the militant anti-Semitic mood of much of the gentile population, such a demonstration could have provoked a pogrom in the city. But a Jewish pogrom broke out in Kyiv anyway in the following year.

On September 5, 1945, the vice commissar of interior affairs of the Ukrainian SSR, I. L. Loburenko, reported to the secretary of the Central Committee of the Communist Party of Ukraine, D. Korotchenko, about the pre-pogrom situation in Kyiv after NKGB Lieutenant Iosif Rozenshtein killed two local anti-Semites the prior day.[18] The events developed as follows.

During the war Ivan Grabar and his mother occupied the apartment of the Jewish Rybchinsky family, who evacuated to Uzbekistan. Grabar was drafted into the Red Army at the beginning of the war, but soon deserted out of the Nazi encirclement and returned to Kyiv. He stayed with his mother in Kyiv during the Nazi occupation. After the liberation of Kyiv, Grabar was again drafted into the Red Army in November 1943. The Rybchinsky family returned to Kyiv from evacuation in February 1945 and, through the court, got their apartment back. Grabar's mother and his relatives wrote letters to Ivan, demanding that he come to Kyiv and help them recover the apartment from the "Yids." So, Ivan Grabar and his friend Nikolai Melnikov received leave from the army from August 16 to September 8, 1945, and came to Kyiv. However, Grabar's hopes of getting the Rybchinskys' apartment back were dashed.

A few days before his murder, Grabar came to the Office of the Public Prosecutor and told the prosecutor, "We fight on the front and Yids occupy our apartments."[19] Grabar stated his anti-Semitic views openly and said he dreamed about revenge against all Jews. On September 4, 1945, Grabar and Melnikov were drunk when a Jew, Iosif Rozenshtein, walked past.

At 5:30 p.m., Rozenshtein, who worked for the NKGB as a radio technician, was returning home from the grocery store dressed in civilian clothes. Grabar and Melnikov insulted and beat Rozenshtein. Some passers-by came to Rozenshtein's aid, and he was able to get home. However, he saw where the anti-Semites went. At home, Rozenshtein put on his uniform, took his service pistol, and went to the courtyard of Grabar's mother's house, where Melnikov was also present. Rozenshtein's wife followed him.[20] Rozenshtein demanded that Grabar and Melnikov come with him to the police station. But they refused and continue to insult Rozenshtein. Rozenshtein lost control and shot and killed his abusers in the courtyard of Grabar's house. Hearing the screaming of Grabar's mother, a large crowd gathered, shouting anti-Semitic slogans and severely beating Rozenshtein's wife and a passing Jew named Boris Spektor.[21]

Kyiv police quickly arrived and attempted to pacify the crowd that had gathered there, but the crowd resisted the authorities. Mounted police then came and restored order.[22] Rozenshtein was immediately arrested and was soon executed according to the decision of a military tribunal.[23]

The funeral of the anti-Semites shot by Rozenshtein, which took place on September 7, 1945, turned into open violence against Kyiv's Jews, with some three hundred rioters participating. Kyiv Jews Kotliar, Zabrodin, Pesin, and Miloslavsky wrote a letter on October 16, 1945, addressed to the "Central Committee of the Communist Party, Comrade I. V. Stalin, the NKVD USSR, Comrade Beria, and the editor of the newspaper *Pravda*, Comrade Pospelov," noting that the funeral had transformed into a pogrom:

> The funerals were organized in a special way. The coffins were carried on the most populous streets [downtown Kyiv] and then the procession went to the Jewish market. This procession was set up by pogrom-makers. They began to assault Jews. One hundred Jews were beaten up on this day, thirty-six of them were taken to Kyiv hospitals with serious injuries, and five of them died on the same day.[24]

Solomon Schwarz reported that sixteen Jews were killed during the pogrom in Kyiv.[25] Kotliar, Zabrodin, Pesin, and Miloslavsky lamented in their letter that they could not recognize their city "not only by its outlook, but also due to the existing political situation there."[26] They said they felt the strong influence of Nazi propaganda:

The words "Yid" or "Let's beat the Yids" you can hear everywhere in the capital of Ukraine: in trams, trolleybuses, stores, markets, and even in some Soviet offices.

In some more latent form, it [anti-Semitism] is present in Communist organizations, up to the Central Committee of the Communist Party of Ukraine.[27]

The authors of the letter wrote that the pogrom was a result of the rabid anti-Semitism that raged in Kyiv. They stated that every day many Jews were insulted and beaten in Kyiv and the authorities did not defend them.[28]

Ukrainian authorities also reported the pogrom mood in the city and took measures to reinforce security.[29] As shown on September 8, 1945, in a secret report of the people's commissar of internal affairs of the Ukrainian SSR, V. Riasnoi, to the secretary of the Central Committee of the Communist Party of Ukraine, Korotchenko, the local authorities took seriously the threat of an even larger pogrom in Kyiv. Riasnoi wrote:

> Considering the inflamed condition of some part of the population of the city due to the spreading of bogus rumours and agitation directed against Jews, we reinforced patrols in the city, moreover, giving special attention to the markets, gathering places, and the places of residence of relatives of the murdered Grabar and Mel'nikov.[30]

It is obvious that without the measures taken by the Soviet authorities, the anti-Jewish violence in the city would likely have taken on even larger dimensions.

The demobilized veteran M. Vaslits wrote in his letter to the newspaper *Pravda* that the housing question was the main reason for the rise of anti-Semitism in Kyiv. He pointed out that "those who had been here with the Germans had already in most cases succeeded in settling. The effort to evict these settlers has led to spread of anti-Semitism everywhere and in everything."[31]

Unfortunately, the Kyiv pogrom was not unique. Anti-Jewish violence occurred in other Ukrainian cities and towns, although on a smaller scale. Anti-Semitic violence was often sparked by the attempts of Jews to return to the apartments where they lived before the war. Even if Jews came to their apartments with court orders, the occupants often refused to move out. On August 25, 1944, the Jewish dentist Yuzef Markovich Petelevich attempted to return to his apartment in Dnipropetrovsk, where Pelageya Orlova had settled. Petelevich had a court order giving him the right to the apartment, and Orlova, according to the court's decision, was to be resettled in a less comfortable apartment. During her forced move, which was demanded by "administrative order," Orlova resisted, and at the sound of her screaming, a crowd of about two hundred people gathered, shouting, "Beat the Yids, save Russia!," "Death to the Yids," "Thirty-seven thousand Yids were slaughtered [by the Nazis in Dnipropetrovsk]; we'll kill the rest," and so on.[32]

Then several members of the crowd attacked Petelevich with stones and tried to break into a neighboring apartment in which a Jew named Ulanovsky lived: "Because the apartment was locked, the above-mentioned group of people brought an axe, broke the door, and burst into the apartment, where they danced and shouted antisemitic slogans while setting about smashing the furniture."[33] The Dnipropetrovsk police dispersed the crowd and arrested the three most active pogrom-makers.[34]

In March 1945, the *Bulletin of the Rescue Committee of the Jewish Agency for Palestine* published the testimony of a Ukrainian Jew who had escaped from Kharkiv and the Soviet Union in 1944. He stated:

> Ukrainians meet returning Jews with animosity. In the first weeks after the liberation of Kharkiv [the city was liberated on August 23, 1943], no Jews dared go onto the street at night. The situation improved only after the intervention of the authorities, who reinforced police patrols in the city. There were many cases where Jews were beaten up on the market squares, and, in one incident, a Jew was killed in the market by a Ukrainian. The police were summoned to the spot of the crime; however, the peasants who were present during the murder began to quarrel with the police; all of them were arrested together with the killer....
>
> Returning to their apartments, Jews received only a small portion of their belongings. When they appealed to the court against the Ukrainians who had possession of their items, other Ukrainians supported the thieves and provided false testimony in the court.
>
> The Ukrainian authorities are infected to a significant extent with antisemitism. Appeals made by Jews are not considered in an appropriate way. When the [Kyiv] Commercial Institute returned from Kharkiv to Kyiv, Jewish professors asked for permission to return also. Their request was rejected.... The Jewish Theatre did not receive permission to return to Kharkiv. The radio programme in the Jewish language [Yiddish] was not revived. The official reply to all complaints by Jews stated that antisemitism, through which the Germans had poisoned the mentality of the population, could be eradicated only gradually.[35]

POPULAR ANTI-SEMITISM AND THE SOVIET AUTHORITIES

The authorities explained that the increased popular anti-Semitism in Kyiv was due to the influence of Nazi propaganda and the "provocative behaviour" of the Jews themselves. This latter explanation had often been used by the czarist government to justify anti-Jewish pogroms. The people's commissar of state security (NKGB) of Ukraine,

Savchenko, wrote in his secret report "About Anti-Semitism in Ukraine" on September 13, 1944, to Khrushchev, the First Secretary of the Central Committee of the Communist Party of Ukraine, that some Jews provoked anti-Semitism themselves. According to the report, Jews spread "provocative rumors" that anti-Semites, including Khrushchev, would be dismissed from the Ukrainian government.[36] Savchenko reported that Genia Izrailevna Brand, who had returned to Kyiv from evacuation and failed to regain her apartment, allegedly told her neighbors, "All of the population who lived in occupied territory will be expelled and Ukraine will be settled by Jews."[37] Brand was arrested by the Ukrainian NKGB.[38]

Savchenko also reported the provocative behavior of Senior Lieutenant Petr Mikhailovich Kovtun, vice commander of the 191st aircraft regiment, a Jew who had come to Kyiv from the front on an official visit. Kovtun arrived in an intoxicated condition at the NKGB office in the Zaliznychnyi district of Kyiv, bringing with him a woman named Chemikhova. In the presence of NKGB personnel, he attacked Chemikhova and tried to shoot her. When the NKGB members disarmed him, he called them "fascists and anti-Semites." Kovtun stated: "I came from the front to defend Jewish people. I will dispose of the Union of Russian People, which exterminated Jews."[39] Kovtun was detained and sent to the Kyiv garrison's military tribunal.[40]

Soviet authorities were especially concerned about Jewish intellectuals who called for a Jewish national revival, claiming that the expression of Jewish nationalism would provoke further tension between Jews and gentiles. Thus, the vice heads of the organizational and propaganda, and the human resources departments of the Central Committee of the Communist Party (Bolsheviks) of Ukraine KP[b]U wrote in a secret report to the secretary of the Central Committee, Korotchenko, on October 28, 1944, that the Yiddish poet David Hofshtein said that the suffering of Jews "will restore their national consciousness, which was previously lost."[41] The Yiddish poet Itsik Fefer, who came to Kyiv for the Congress of the Union of Writers, reportedly told the journalist Chaim Tokar', "We, Jews, should have our own state, otherwise there won't be a future for us."[42] The people's commissar of state security of Ukraine, Savchenko, and the vice heads of departments of the Central Committee (KP[b]U) concluded that Zionist and nationalist ideas were spreading among some Jewish circles.

The Holocaust and the rise of popular anti-Semitism were turning points for many Jews, who previously had been quite assimilated and considered themselves Soviet citizens, but now returned to their national roots. These phenomena provoked a Jewish national awakening and a desire to restore and preserve their national culture and the memory of Jews who had perished. Many Jews attempted to combat the rampant popular anti-Semitism in Kyiv using a variety of methods: by appealing to the local and higher authorities of Ukraine and the Soviet Union; by fighting with anti-Semites on the streets; and by supporting the creation of a Jewish state.

Jewish intellectuals took a prominent role in the revival of Jewish culture. They called for the commemoration of Holocaust victims and the restoration of Jewish scholarly, cultural, and educational institutions. At the same time, anti-Semitism metastasized in all strata of Ukrainian society. On a popular level it was often more open and violent, while in the government it was more covert. The above cited letters from Kyivan Jews showed that they tried to struggle against anti-Semitism, appealing to higher authorities in Moscow and for help from lawyers. They were certain that anti-Semitism contradicted socialist internationalist principles and that the higher authorities would restore order.

However, the authorities received complaints not only from Jews, but also from anti-Semites. For example, Ivan Soloviev, a Russian born in 1902, wrote to the chair of the Party Control Commission of the Central Committee, A. A. Andreev, that the Russian people always "was and is the leading nation" in the country:

> We saw who sold and betrayed the Motherland—it is the damn Yids, seated in the rear, in the second echelons, and receiving orders for alien blood....
>
> What is going on here in Ukraine? How did the Jews come to own all of Ukraine? It is they, with their Yids' snouts, who torture Russian people in Ukraine. For money, they purchased many people, even Ukrainian district and city leaders. Who sells passports on the markets? Jews. Who is selling awards? Jews. Who is killing the Russian people? Jews. Who is throwing people out of their apartments in the winter in Kyiv? Jews.[43]

Soloviev wrote that Jews threw him, a disabled veteran of World War II, out of "his" apartment in the winter. But he also mentioned that before World War II he lived in Siberia and settled in Kyiv after the liberation of the city. Soloviev presumably occupied an apartment that belonged to some Jewish family before the war. He wrote that "it is necessary to exterminate all of these parasites (i.e., Jews)." Soloviev also said that he gathered a meeting of twenty people, and they decided to begin a "ruthless struggle with these parasites." He claimed that this opinion was shared by many people in Kyiv. He said that there were signs appearing in the city: "Beat Yids, save Russia!" and he asked why the government in Moscow ignored this will of the people.[44]

Soloviev proposed his solution for the Jewish question:

1. Exile to the last men all Jews to Siberia, and then resettle part of Siberians to Ukraine so that Siberian Russian people can taste life.
2. Perform the cleansing of Jews from all state offices of Ukraine ... and the Army.[45]

Martin Blackwell wrote that the rise of anti-Semitism in Kyiv "left the Stalin regime ... with little choice but to ratify the marginalization of Jewish interests in that city."[46] The Ukrainian authorities tried to limit the return of Jews to Ukraine, following the policy of fewer Jews, fewer problems. Lieutenant General Pavel Sudoplatov of the NKVD wrote in his memoirs that he was present in the office of the First Secretary of the Communist Party of Uzbekistan, Usman Yusupov, during a telephone conversation that Yusupov had with Khrushchev:

> Khrushchev complained to him [Yusupov] that Jews evacuated during the war to Tashkent and Samarkand "are flying to Ukraine like ravens." In this conversation, which took place in 1947, he [Khrushchev] claimed that he did not have room to accept all of them, because the city [Kyiv] was in ruins, and it was necessary to stop this flood; otherwise, pogroms would begin in Kyiv.[47]

Ukrainian authorities tried to prevent the further influx of Jews into the city. They required for return documents proving that the Jews had lived in Kyiv before the war and that they were needed at their workplaces. So, it was quite difficult for many Jews to return from evacuation to Kyiv.

Despite all the obstacles, most Kyivan Jews who survived the Holocaust returned to the city. The Jewish population of Kyiv increased rapidly after the war. By January 1, 1947, Jews already constituted 18.8 percent of the Kyiv population: 132,467 of 704,609 city inhabitants.[48] In 1959, 153,466 Jews (13.8 percent of the total population) lived in Kyiv.[49] Many of these Jews moved to Kyiv (often without authorization) from provincial towns and shtetls after the war.

Thus, the Soviet authorities failed to prevent the influx of Jews into the city; nor did they prevent violent anti-Semitic incidents. Obviously, Khrushchev was having problems handling the situation regarding anti-Semitism in Ukraine. Popular anti-Semitism in Kyiv and Ukraine appeared to be stronger than the powerful Soviet repression machine. Solomon Schwarz wrote:

> The Communist Party did not fight openly against Ukrainian anti-Semitism, but considering the danger of anti-Semitism, as the most popular form of the Ukrainian anti-Soviet mood, began a campaign against anti-Semitism in a covert manner, slowly adjusting the population to the fact of the promotion of Jews to important positions in different lines of work, including particularly [Communist] party work. ... It is possible that the realization of this policy was one of the goals for which Kaganovich was sent to Ukraine.[50]

In March 1947, Khrushchev was dismissed from his position as the First Secretary of the Communist Party (Bolsheviks) of Ukraine (KP(b)U) and Lazar Kaganovich was appointed. The official explanation for this change was "the need to separate the posts of premier and First Secretary of the republic, but criticism of [Khrushchev's] agricultural performance appeared in the press as well."[51] Certainly, when Stalin sent Kaganovich to Ukraine, the Jewish question was not his main consideration. The crop failure and famine in Ukraine in 1946–47 were the main reasons for Stalin's dissatisfaction with Khrushchev's performance. The struggle against all kinds of nationalism and chauvinism was a secondary consideration.[52]

After Kaganovich arrived in Kyiv at the end of February 1947, Khrushchev disappeared from public view until September. Khrushchev retained the post of Ukrainian premier but did not participate in politics while Kaganovich was in Ukraine.[53] Khrushchev later wrote in his memoirs that he had been ill with pneumonia. However, Khrushchev's biographers suggest that his "illness" had more to do with politics. Perhaps Khrushchev feared that his dismissal from his position as First Secretary was the beginning of the end of his political career.[54]

In May 1947, Kaganovich proposed a resolution, which was approved by the Central Committee of the KP(b)U, "on the improvement of ideological-political work with personnel and on the struggle against manifestations of bourgeois-nationalist ideology," stating that nationalist forces in Ukraine use "the most disgusting weapon of fascist obscurantism—anti-Semitism."[55] On May 29, 1947, this document was sent to Stalin.

It is hard to say how successful Kaganovich would have been in suppressing anti-Semitism in Ukraine had he stayed longer in his post. His term as First Secretary of the KP(b)U continued for less than a year: "On December 15, 1947, he received the order to transfer his position as the First Secretary of the KP(b)U back to Khrushchev and return to Moscow and again take up the position as Deputy Chairman of the Council of Ministers of the USSR."[56]

Why did Stalin recall Kaganovich to Moscow so soon? Perhaps one of the reasons was the explosion of popular anti-Semitism in Ukraine. With the arrival of Kaganovich in Ukraine, popular anti-Semitism became even stronger. From December 1946 to the beginning of summer 1947, there was a new famine in Ukraine. This was the result of the poor harvest of 1946 when, due to drought, the plan for the collection of grain in Ukraine was only 52 percent fulfilled.[57] When Kaganovich arrived in Ukraine, the famine had already begun. The central Soviet government did not provide any help with grain, so Ukrainian leaders could not do much to improve the situation before the new harvest. Bread was distributed by vouchers, allowing only 100–200 grams (approximately from a quarter to a half pound) per person per day. However, the bread vouchers were received only by working people, while children, pensioners, and disabled people did not receive vouchers. The authorities organized free dining halls, which provided one poor meal per day for starving people, which did not help much. By summer 1947, over one million people in Ukraine were suffering from starvation. In 1946 to 1947, approximately 800,000 died from famine in Ukraine. The situation improved only after the next harvest in 1947.[58]

Paradoxically, the gentile population blamed their horrible living conditions and famine not on the higher Soviet authorities, but on Jews and speculators. This was "a popular motif in ballot inscriptions and anonymous notes" during the municipal elections in December 1947.

"Jews live well," "Down with the Yids," and "Beat the Yids" appeared regularly on ballots. There were also longer letters that combined, as does this one from December 1947, Bolshevik language with the language of prejudice: "I give my vote to the block of the communist and non-party people, and thank the Government, the party, and Comrade Stalin for abolition of rationing and the currency reform. However, there is one more request, namely, to remove Jewish speculators from Soviet trade." The same year other voters expressed this sentiment in cruder terms: "We are voting for you, but how long will you torment us; you have allowed the Yids to live [well], while the workers are starving." "It would be good if the Jews worked more and drank the workers' blood less." Since some of the hundreds of candidates in the municipal election of 1947 had Jewish names, seeing them on ballots prompted anti-Semitic voters to write things like "Yid, to Palestine!" "Against. Not sure about her nationality," or "We don't need them."[59]

Anti-Semites in Kyiv were not afraid to openly demonstrate their hatred toward Jews who occupied high government positions, particularly the member of the Presidium of the Central Committee of the Communist Party of Bolsheviks of the Soviet Union, Lazar Kaganovich. The following anti-Semitic incident occurred just before the appointment of Kaganovich as the First Secretary of the KP(b)U in March 1947. The head of the Administrative Department of the Central Committee of the Communist Party of Ukraine, I. Golynnyi, wrote in a secret report to the secretary of the Central Committee of the Communist Party (Bolsheviks) of Ukraine (KP(b)U),[60] L. G. Mel'nikov, on February 23, 1947:

> The Head of Police Administration of Ministry of State Security (MGB), Ukrainian SSR comrade Rudenko, informed me by phone about an incident that occurred yesterday at the 175th elective district of the city Kyiv.
> Ermakov, a blind worker of the Association of Blind People, born in 1903, came to vote in an intoxicated condition, with his wife.
> They received ballots for the election with the name of L.M. Kaganovich on one of them. Ermakov tore up the ballots and made anti-Semitic pronouncements in the presence of voters and members of the [election] commission.
> The Regional Administration of the MGB is checking the situation.[61]

Perhaps the Soviet government considered the widespread anti-Semitic mood when they switched from the suppression of popular anti-Semitism to the policy of state anti-Semitism. After the war, the Soviet authorities lost total control over the population. To reestablish control, they needed to flow with, not against, the popular mood. This was clearly understood by the First Secretary of the KP(b)U, Khrushchev, who allegedly said: "This is Ukraine! And it is not in our interest that Ukrainians should associate the return of Soviet power with the return of the Jews."[62] The suppression of popular anti-Semitism and the protection of Jews would further undermine the prestige of the Soviet authorities. On the contrary, by supporting the popular anti-Semitic mood, the Soviet authorities satisfied the desire of much of the gentile population and thus became closer to their people. The use of popular anti-Semitism was also convenient, because it diverted people's anger about the famine and their miserable poor life from the Soviet authorities toward "Jewish bloodsuckers and speculators."[63]

THE STATE ANTI-SEMITIC CAMPAIGNS IN KYIV

Despite strong popular anti-Semitism after the war, Jews hoped for the restoration of normal life and of Jewish cultural and educational institutions in Kyiv. Itsik Kipnis wrote in his essay "Babi Yar," "And a native city, like a mother, should hug us, encourage us and return us to life."[64] This was undoubtedly an idealistic and naïve view, but such idealists attempted to revive Jewish life and culture in the ruined city. However, the Jewish national revival was overwhelmed by rising popular and state anti-Semitism.

State anti-Semitism did not develop in the Soviet Union overnight. It slowly grew from the late 1930s, and then erupted during the campaigns against "bourgeois nationalism" and cosmopolitanism in the second half of the 1940s. These two campaigns were part of the nascent Cold War. Jewish and gentile liberal intellectuals became targets for attack because they allegedly shared Western ideas. Many Jews had relatives abroad with whom they were in correspondence and had shown patriotic feelings toward the newly created State of Israel. Rising Jewish national consciousness after the Holocaust clashed with the rise of Russian nationalism. These factors turned the entire Jewish population into a potential fifth column in the eyes of Soviet authorities. They directed their state campaigns against "bourgeois nationalism" and cosmopolitanism, primarily against Jewish intellectuals.

According to Benjamin Pinkus:

> Although campaigns against Jewish nationalism and Jewish cosmopolitanism were frequently carried out simultaneously, we believe that three main periods can be distinguished: (a) 1946–8, when a campaign was waged against all forms of bourgeois nationalism; (b) 1948–9, when the campaign was mainly against cosmopolitanism; and (c) 1950–3, which saw a campaign against both "deviations."[65]

The campaign against bourgeois nationalism began in August–September 1946 with the resolution of the Central Committee of the Communist Party concerning the journals *Zvezda* and *Leningrad,* and the accompanying speech of Central Committee secretary Andrei Zhdanov. The new Soviet doctrine (*Zhdanovshchina*) condemned liberalism, modernism, sympathy with the West, and "servility before contemporary bourgeois culture."[66] The anticosmopolitan campaign, which began two years later with an anti-Western focus, was very soon redirected against Jews. Many Jewish intellectuals were labeled as rootless cosmopolitans and "bourgeois nationalists." According to Pinkus, "The fiercest campaign was conducted in the Ukrainian Republic."[67] Blackwell wrote that these state campaigns in Ukraine were inspired by strong popular anti-Semitism and were enthusiastically supported by the gentile population. He wrote that the government's "new line, however, paradoxically meant that Jews would need to swallow the fact that to the regime Ukrainians' interests were more important than their own."[68] So, Jewish interests were marginalized, and anti-Semitism was disguised under campaigns against "bourgeois nationalism" and cosmopolitanism.

Ukrainian and Jewish writers, scientists, and artists participated in the campaign against "Jewish bourgeois nationalists and cosmopolitans" in Kyiv. Gentile intellectuals mostly did this voluntarily, and some even with personal anti-Semitic motives. However, many Jewish intellectuals "were forced to participate occasionally in various meetings to condemn cosmopolitanism, but this was mainly by way of 'self-criticism.'"[69] Thus, at the Second Plenum of the Board of the Union of Soviet Writers of Ukraine on March 2, 1949, the Jewish-Ukrainian poet and writer Leonid Pervomaisky (Ilya Shlyomovich Gurevich, 1908–73), "fully admitted the mistakes, which he had made in his works. He said, 'I reread my essay about Lesia Ukrainka,[70] and I should frankly admit that I have not read such harmful writings for a long time.'"[71] However, even such "self-criticism" did not protect Pervomaisky from further persecution.

In 1948 to 1949, Jewish scholarly and cultural organizations were liquidated throughout the Soviet Union. On November 20, 1948, the Jewish Anti-Fascist Committee was dissolved as a "center of anti-Soviet propaganda that regularly provided anti-Soviet information to foreign espionage agencies."[72] By Stalin's order, on February 2, 1949, the associations of Jewish writers were dissolved in Moscow, Kyiv, and Minsk, and the Yiddish literary periodicals *Heimland* in Moscow and *Der Shtern* in Kyiv were closed.[73] On June 10, 1949, the Lithuanian Jewish Museum in Vilnius, which had operated in the city since 1944, was also shut down.[74]

The struggle against "Jewish bourgeois nationalism" continued in Ukraine under Kaganovich's leadership, now orchestrated by the Ukrainian Ministry of the State Security (MGB). According to Gennady Kostyrchenko, Kaganovich suppressed Jewish nationalism in Ukraine, because this was required by his position and insisted upon by the Ministry of State Security.[75] However, the arrests of "Jewish nationalists" and "cosmopolitans" began later, in 1948 and 1949, after Kaganovich had already returned to Moscow.

The MGB of the Ukrainian SSR characterized the prominent Jewish poets and writers David Hofshtein, Itsik Kipnis, academic of the Academy of Sciences of the Ukrainian SSR, M. M. Gubergrits, and the linguist Elie Spivak, chair of the Department of Jewish Culture of the Academy of Sciences, as "informal leaders of Jewish nationalists in Kyiv."[76] The MGB of the Ukrainian SSR reported that in his works the "Zionist" Hofshtein had called for the creation of a Jewish state in Palestine and had given nationalist speeches during a trip to Chernovtsy in April 1947.[77] In 1948, the MGB of the USSR fabricated "the affair of the Jewish anti-Fascist Committee," and the minister of state security, Viktor Abakumov, reported to Stalin about the "Jewish nationalist group in Kyiv which is led by a member of the Presidium of the Jewish Anti-Fascist Committee, Hofshtein D. N."[78] Hofshtein was arrested in Kyiv on September 16, 1948, and in November the Jewish Anti-Fascist Committee (JAC) was closed and hundreds of Jewish intellectuals were arrested, "including many people associated with the JAC." The members of the JAC were accused of espionage, treason, and "bourgeois nationalism." After a secret trial in Moscow, Hofshtein was executed along with twelve members of the committee on August 12, 1952.[79]

In the late 1940s to the early 1950s, several dozen Yiddish writers, poets, and scholars who had promoted Jewish culture in their works were arrested in Kyiv. Many of them openly supported the creation of the State of Israel, attempted to struggle against anti-Semitism in Kyiv, and had participated in unsanctioned Holocaust commemoration meetings at Babyn Yar. They were Jewish patriots and nationalists who had done everything possible for the revival of Jewish national life and culture after the Holocaust. This attempted revival was now violently suppressed.

In January 1949, the last Jewish scholarly institution in the Soviet Union, the Department of Jewish Culture of the Academy of Sciences of Ukraine, was closed.[80] Study of the Holocaust had dominated the work of the department since its return from evacuation to Kyiv in 1944. The department had organized several ethnographic expeditions in the postwar years to various regions of Ukraine. Their purpose was to collect songs from Jewish survivors that were sung in the ghettos and concentration camps. E. M. Beregovsky wrote that her father, Jewish folklorist and ethnomusicologist Moisei Beregovsky, recorded seventy songs from Jewish survivors during these expeditions that became the basis of his work about Jewish war folklore.[81] According to the introduction to the liner notes for the CD *Yiddish Glory: Life and Fate of Soviet Jewish Folk Music During World War II*, the ethnographical expeditions "recorded hundreds of new Yiddish songs: tunes that detailed Soviet Jewish wartime service in the Red Army, survival and death in Nazi-occupied Europe, and stories from those working in the Soviet home front in Central Asia, the Ural Mountains and Siberia."[82]

Despite the important scholarly work of the Department of Jewish Culture, the interim president of the Academy of Sciences of the Ukrainian SSR, Evgenii Oskarovich Paton, and academy secretary N. P. Semenenko wrote to the secretary of the Central Committee (TsK) KP(b)U, L. G. Mel'nikov, on January 13, 1949, that the department "has not done any useful work for several years." They claimed that the work of the department "divided the Soviet people [into national groups] and because of this, it is harmful." They proposed "liquidation of the Department of Jewish Culture as an unnecessary and useless office."[83] On the same day, the Council of Ministers of the Ukrainian SSR and the Central Committee (TsK) KP[b]U decided to close the Department of Jewish Culture and proposed that the Academy of Sciences of the Ukrainian SSR complete the elimination of the department by January 20, 1949.[84]

Almost all members of the Department of Jewish Culture were arrested soon thereafter. The chair of the Department of Jewish Culture, linguist Elie Spivak, died in prison in 1950. The NKVD collected compromising materials on Spivak in advance, including his statements about anti-Semitism in Kyiv. The following statement by Spivak was recorded:

> I received dozens of letters with requests for protection [from anti-Semites], complaints about the de facto reestablishment of the old "percentage norm" [i.e., quota] that came by order of the Central Committee [Communist Party] not to appoint Jews to leading positions, which people in Kyiv and district centers met with joy. Anti-Semites are celebrating. Many administrative offices in Kyiv became quite anti-Semitic.[85]

The peak of the campaign against "cosmopolitanism" in Kyiv was in March 1949. A general meeting of the unions of writers, composers, and artists denounced "rootless cosmopolitans" and, as a result, many Jewish writers, composers, and artists were expelled from the unions, fired from their positions, and some were arrested.[86] During the campaign against bourgeois nationalism, Jewish intellectuals who specialized in Jewish studies and Yiddish culture suffered the most. During the anticosmopolitan campaign, many Jews who contributed to Russian, Ukrainian, or Jewish culture were denounced and fired, often accused of trying to destroy Russian and Ukrainian culture from within. An employee of the Institute of Folklore and Ethnography of the Ukrainian Academy of Sciences, N. Gordeichuk, described the situation in the Kyiv Conservatory as follows:

> A band of rootless cosmopolitans and formalists operated in the Kyiv Conservatory for a long time. I. Belza, A. Gozenpud, M. Geilig, L. Khinchina, M. Beregovsky and others were the members of this group and they caused great harm to Ukrainian national Soviet culture.[87]

Mikhail Mitsel writes that the population perceived the anticosmopolitan campaign as a purification of Soviet culture, arts, and science from the "antipatriotic" influence of Jews because "cosmopolitans" were identified as Jews. Thus, the campaign against "cosmopolitans was the first publicly organized action in which the ideology of the state and public mood coincided."[88]

THE FUSION OF STATE AND POPULAR ANTI-SEMITISM IN KYIV

The state campaigns against bourgeois nationalists and cosmopolitans reinforced popular anti-Semitism in Ukraine and gave anti-Semites a convenient rationale for attacking Jews. Solomon Schwarz warned in 1952 that "in the tense situation in Ukraine, where an anti-Semitic mood there still persists..., the ruling authorities should know that such a struggle against Jews as 'anti-patriots' is social-psychological dynamite."[89] But the Ukrainian authorities seemed to instigate popular anti-Semitism by organizing show trials against Jews and by inflammatory publications in the local press.

In fall 1951, the so-called Textile Affair began. This was a case of embezzlement in the textile industry in Kyiv. Over 100 people were involved in the affair, thirty of whom were arrested.[90] The main defendant was Khanan Khain, the "director of a bulk textile distributor (Glavlegsbyt), which provided cloth to the Kyiv region, receiving an income of more than two billion rubles and employing 160 people. He was accused of stealing, with his accomplices, seven million rubles."[91] Glavlegsbyt received cloth from Moscow, Leningrad, Kharkiv, Odesa, Summy, Boguslav, and Georgia. The cloth was distributed among Khain's cohorts, who sold it in stores and on the black markets at significantly higher than state prices. Khain and his colleagues divided the profits and used it for bribes for local authorities, police, and textile factory administrators to get the illicit goods. Khain provided stolen goods to the wife of one of the secretaries of the Central Committee of the Communist Party of Ukraine.[92] Due to Khain's good connections, local authorities turned a blind eye to his illegal operations for several years. Khain and his companions made illegal trades from 1946 until Khain's dismissal from his position in fall 1951. While the majority of Kyivans lived in poverty in communal apartments in the first postwar years, Khain had a luxurious apartment and a Mercedes with a personal driver.[93]

Originally the Zaliznychnyi District Prosecutor's Office began an investigation of Khain's activities in 1950 after an inspection by the Control-Revision Commission of the Ministry of Finance of Khain's textile warehouse. However, the investigation suddenly stopped, because Khain bribed the investigator by paying her 3,000 rubles and providing some fabric. Soon the investigator became Khain's lover. The City Kyiv Prosecutor's Office began a new investigation of Khain's activities in 1951. Khain again bribed the investigator, used his high connections in the Central Committee of the Communist Party of Ukraine, and the investigation was stopped. However, Khain was transferred to another place of work. Finally, in 1952, the Ministry of State Security (MGB) of the Ukrainian SSR began an investigation of the Textile Affair.[94]

This time, his connections with the authorities did not help Khain and he was arrested in January 1952. Later, Khain's collaborators were also arrested. In August 1952, MGB agents reported that during the investigation they confiscated 14 kilograms of gold, 5 kilograms of silver, 600,000 rubles, and property worth several hundred thousand rubles.[95] Khain denied his guilt until the end. After all, it was well known that MGB agents fabricated many affairs. However, Khain's luxurious way of life and the confiscated precious metals, money, and property indicated that this affair was most likely real.

Presumably, Khain and the other defendants committed economic crimes such as bribery and "theft of socialist property," but in the "spirit of the time," they were also accused of anti-Soviet crimes such as "sabotage of Soviet trade." So, the economic criminal case was turned into a political "anti-Soviet" Jewish nationalist affair. Juliette Cadiot wrote:

> During the investigation, some defendants had to answer for their "nationalist views," particularly Gerzon, who faced condemnation for his alleged desire to leave the country. Discussions around their Jewish names, reports of their criticisms of shifts in official Jewish policy, such as the closing of Jewish theaters, turned around the question of their loyalty toward the Soviet State. The general atmosphere of paranoia was also visible when Khain was accused of using a Jewish community arbitration court (*treteiskiy sud*) to force one of his creditors to give him the bribe they had agreed upon.[96]

The defendants were judged by the Kyiv Regional Military Court because the defendants were accused not only of economic crimes, but also of anti-Soviet activity. The trial took place in Kyiv on November 20–26, 1952. According to Kyivan Ion Degen, the public Khain trial was a convenient occasion for demonstrations of anti-Semitism in downtown Kyiv. All the defendants were Jewish. The tickets for the Khain trial were distributed via trading institutions and receiving them was "harder than getting tickets" for the Bolshoi Theater tour.[97] During the trial, "ordinary female Ukrainian peasants" blamed the Jewish defendants, saying that they could not find clothes and other goods in stores, but everything was available on the black market, where the goods were sold for higher prices.[98]

The court verdict characterized the defendants as a "band of parasites" and as an "anti-Soviet group." Three defendants, Khanan Khain, Iakov Iaroshetskiy, and David Gerzon, were sentenced to capital punishment and were executed on February 4, 1953. Moisei Grushko and Lev Teplitskiy received twenty-five years in corrective labor camps.[99]

The Khain trial was one of many trials in which Jews were accused of economic crimes. In the second half of 1952 and early 1953, the Soviet press often published articles that claimed Jews were involved in economic crimes. Benjamin Pinkus wrote that in economic "trials reported in the press, the number of Jews exceeded that of non-Jews. The 'map' of economic crime encompassed all the Soviet republics, but it was the Ukrainian Republic that had a particularly high percentage of trials involving Jews."[100] Pinkus pointed out that the economic trials were used for political purposes, "with the emphasis placed on defendants' Jewishness."[101] The purpose of these trials was to further instigate popular anti-Semitism. This was a prelude to and preparation of the appropriate anti-Semitic atmosphere for the "Doctors' Plot," which was announced on January 13, 1953.

Immunologist Oskar Rokhlin (1937–2018), who grew up in Kyiv, recalled that during the Textile Affair, the newspaper *Vecherniy Kiev* (Evening Kyiv) published detailed reports "from the courthouse," where the Jewish names of the defendants were listed, and explained that due to their criminal activities, Ukrainian people still lived in poverty and could not buy goods in stores.[102] Such publications fomented violent anti-Semitism in Kyiv. Rokhlin wrote:

> The fusion of the state and popular anti-Semitism brought the anticipated remarkable results. . . . The scream "Beat the Yids" hangs in the air and anti-Semites beat the Jews: children, women, elderly people on the streets, in the stores' queues, in parks and on the Dnieper beaches. Police pretended that they don't see anything, and nobody appealed to the police, because to be detained by police was even worse than to be beaten on the street.[103]

Not the police, but the criminal world, provided protection for Jews in some areas of Kyiv. Rokhlin recollected that Tarasivska Street, where he lived, was controlled by criminals who lived in empty carriages at the nearby freight station. Most of the criminals were quite young, fourteen to thirty years old, and many were Jews. Almost all the criminals were armed with knives, and many had pistols. So, the anti-Semites did not dare to attack Jews in the area controlled by the criminals. The criminals chose their victims not by nationality, but for pragmatic reasons. They beat and robbed well-to-do people, among whom there were almost no Jews, since the Jews had returned impoverished from evacuation.[104]

REACTION IN KYIV TO THE "DOCTORS' PLOT" AND STALIN'S DEATH

The culmination of state anti-Semitism in the Soviet Union was the "Doctors' Plot." On January 13, 1953, the central Soviet newspapers *Pravda* and *Izvestiia* published articles about the "plot of the doctor-wreckers." Many prominent Jewish doctors were arrested and accused of conspiracy with American and British intelligence services, and of intentional mistreatment of Soviet leaders, which caused their deaths.[105] The news about the arrest of the "doctor-wreckers" created real panic in Kyiv. Patients refused to come for treatment to Jewish doctors or to purchase medicine in drugstores where Jewish pharmacists worked. My maternal grandfather, Il'ia Brovarnik, was a dentist, and during the "Doctors' Plot" his patients suddenly disappeared. Many mothers refused to hospitalize their children with serious illnesses due to fear of the "Jewish doctors-murderers."[106]

Soviet state anti-Semitism unleashed even more rabid and violent public anti-Semitism in Kyiv. Anti-Semites openly called not only for the execution of the "doctor-wreckers," but also for the exile or extermination of all Jews. Sometimes the bloodthirsty desires of Kyivan anti-Semites were even a bit much for the Soviet authorities. For example:

> On January 14, 1953, Ivan Loshak, the guard at the 4th [Kyiv] Shoe Factory said, "I have a pistol with seven bullets, and with pleasure I would kill seven Jews." Because of this, Loshak was summoned to the Podil District Department of the MGB and strictly cautioned.[107]

Over the next few days, after publications about the arrest of the "doctor-wreckers" in *Pravda* and *Izvestiia,* hand-written leaflets appeared on the streets of Kyiv that called for the expulsion of all Jews from the city. The wording of these leaflets was reminiscent of those that the Nazis posted in the city a few days before the execution of Jews at Babyn Yar. There were two versions of the announcement. Both appeared in the Zaliznychnyi district of Kyiv on January 14–15, 1953. The first leaflet said:

> Announcement!!! Expulsion of Yids! Comrades, despise all Jews, submit the addresses of all Abrams to the Second police station. Chase them away so that their stench will not remain on our land. This is the order of the City Main Administration.[108]

The second leaflet said:

> Announcement!!! Expulsion of Yids! Chase away Yids! Jews are our enemies and traitors of our beloved Motherland.[109]

On January 17–18, 1953, police spotted three copies of another anti-Semitic leaflet ("Jews! Get out of Ukraine!") on different Kyiv streets. Two weeks later, on February 1, 1953, police found fourteen handwritten leaflets in the Jewish district of the city, Podil. The leaflets were hung on houses, fences, and booths and called: "Beat Yids, save Russia!" "Beat Yids, spies," and "Beat Jewish spies."[110] On the same night, the police also found three copies of an anti-Semitic leaflet at the Besarabskyi market (ironically, this market was built by a behest in the will of the Jewish millionaire Lazar Brodsky in 1910–12) and the Sinnyi and Zhytniy markets in Kyiv, writing about the "brutality of the doctors-murderers" and calling for vigilance. The leaflet ended with the words "Long live Great Stalin! And glory for him."[111] Kyivan anti-Semites were creative in their propaganda: On January 15–16, 1953, they wrote their slogans "Beat Yids!" in large letters on four trams on four different city routes.[112]

The pogrom atmosphere again appeared in the city. Kyivan Jews lived in constant fear of a pogrom and possible expulsion during the "Doctors' Plot." Rumors appeared in the city that soon all Jews would be expelled to Siberia. During Stalin's funeral radio broadcast in Kyiv on March 9, 1953, Jews avoided coming out to the crowded streets, because they were afraid of being beaten by anti-Semites. Jews either stayed home or sought protection by gathering at the only open synagogue in Kyiv in Podil.

The commissioner for the Council for the Affairs of Religious Cults (CARC), A. Oleinikov, accused Kyivan Jews of a lack of Soviet patriotism, because they did not come to listen with others to the broadcast of Stalin's funeral. He reported on April 7, 1953, about what he considered the inappropriate behavior of Kyivan Jews on the day of Stalin's funeral:

> On March 9 of this year, on Monday, a day unusual for religious service, an unusually large number of Jews visited the Jewish synagogue in Kyiv. Over five thousand Jews came to the synagogue, among whom the majority were unbelievers or those who seldom come to the synagogue (only on Yom Kippur).
>
> Exactly on this Monday, on March 9 this year, the funeral of I.V. Stalin took place. Due to this, a huge number of Soviet people gathered to listen to the radio broadcast [of Stalin's funeral] on Khreshchatyk [Street] and other large squares of Kyiv.
>
> Why did a significant part of Jews not come to Khreshchatyk to be with all the people there, but instead concentrated at the synagogue?
>
> I assume that this happened (the concentration of Jews at the synagogue on that day), because the synagogue is the center for all Jews, not only the prayer house for observant Jews. Synagogues are really the place of concentration and gathering of almost all the local Jewish population.
>
> The above listed facts show that "behind the shoulders and backs" of the registered Jewish communities and their synagogues, hide some dark forces and possible

nationalists, who use Judaism as a curtain for some specific purposes. I hope that our state security will pay attention to this.[113]

A Jewish pogrom did not occur in Kyiv at that time, because the authorities suppressed such initiatives by local anti-Semites. Soon after the war, Soviet power was still rather weak, and a pogrom was ignited spontaneously in Kyiv in September 1945. But by 1953, the situation was totally under control in Kyiv, and the authorities prevented a Jewish pogrom that was unnecessary for them, especially on the day of Stalin's funeral.

Soviet propaganda disguised state anti-Semitism under the slogans of state campaigns against bourgeois nationalists, cosmopolitans, and "doctors-wreckers." So, anti-Semites, who extended their efforts to struggle against Jews too far and called for the killing of all Jews, were arrested. Thus, a group of Kyivan youth who created "The Ukrainian Social-Communist People's Party" were arrested for counterrevolutionary propaganda. The members of this "party" had distributed leaflets that called upon gentiles to take up weapons and "exterminate the lousy Yid nation—the world's worst scoundrels." All three variations of the leaflet were handwritten in Ukrainian and ended with the words, "Long live the Soviet Union! Forward to the victory of Communism!"[114] In May 1953, a court sentenced thirteen members of the Ukrainian Social-Communist People's Party to terms of six to ten years in corrective labor camps.[115]

Why did the authorities accuse the members of this group with "counterrevolutionary propaganda" instead of anti-Semitism? Because the Soviet authorities did not want to admit the existence of anti-Semitism in the Soviet Union. Foreign politicians and journalists often asked Soviet leaders and diplomats about anti-Semitism in the Soviet Union and always received the answer that there was no anti-Semitism in the country.

To the disappointment of anti-Semites, all state campaigns against Jewish bourgeois nationalists, cosmopolitans, and the "Doctors' Plot" were stopped almost immediately after Stalin's death on March 5, 1953. The "Doctors' Plot" was repudiated by Soviet authorities. On March 31, 1953, thirty-seven arrested doctors were released and rehabilitated.[116] On April 6, 1953, the newspaper *Pravda* published the article "Soviet Socialist Law Is Indestructible," which said that the "Doctors' Plot" was falsified by the Ministry of State Security, doctors were arrested "incorrectly, without any lawful basis," but that justice had been restored.[117]

CONCLUSION

The trauma of the Holocaust caused many Jews who had been indifferent to their culture before the war to turn toward their roots. During and after World War II, the Holocaust and its commemoration became a central preoccupation for Jewish scholars, writers, musicians, and artists. However, the Jewish national and cultural revival lasted only a few years (1944–48) before it was crushed by the Soviet authorities. During this short period, Jewish intellectuals showed a strong desire to rebuild their scholarly and cultural institutions in Kyiv and to remake the city as a center of Jewish culture, as it had been during the interwar period. The Jewish national and cultural revival was brutally suppressed by the Soviet authorities, who promoted Russian nationalism and implemented the policy of state anti-Semitism from the late 1940s.

The Russian Jewish poet Naum Korzhavin (pseudonym of Naum Mandel), who lived in Moscow and visited his native Kyiv in the summer of 1946, recalled in his memoirs that he encountered there "hard, overwhelming anti-Semitism, which in such concentration and absolute power I never saw anywhere again."[118] Several factors overlapped in Kyiv and made anti-Semitism so virulent: the long-lasting local anti-Semitic tradition, Nazi propaganda during the war, the postwar struggle for apartments in the ruined city, and Soviet state anti-Semitism. Horrible living conditions and the famine of 1946–47 embittered and brutalized the local gentile population. Anti-Semitism in Kyiv took more violent forms than in other places in the Soviet Union.

The Soviet authorities tried, but failed, to suppress popular anti-Semitism in Ukraine after the war. They then adopted a policy of state anti-Semitism in 1948–53. They decided to flow with the mood of a significant part of the gentile population who wanted to see Jews suppressed and humiliated. State anti-Semitism was mainly directed against the Jewish national awakening in the Soviet Union after the war, against Jewish culture and Jewish intellectuals. The state-initiated campaigns against "bourgeois nationalists," "cosmopolitans," and "doctors-murderers" inspired anti-Semites to make new attacks on Jews. In Kyiv, however, the local anti-Semites exceeded the acceptable limits for attacks allowed by the authorities and called in their leaflets for the expulsion or extermination of all Jews. The authorities, who understood the real threat of a new Jewish pogrom in the city, arrested and imprisoned the most rabid anti-Semites. So, to compare state versus popular anti-Semitism in Kyiv, the latter was more violent and directed against all Jews, while the state authorities selected their victims mostly among the Jewish intelligentsia.

After Stalin's death, the level of state and popular anti-Semitism decreased in the Soviet Union, as well as in Kyiv. Anti-Semites lost official justification for their attacks on Jews. Furthermore, they saw that the most rabid anti-Semites, those who called for the murder of Jews, were arrested and received long sentences in corrective labor camps. Certainly, both state and popular anti-Semitism continued to exist in Kyiv and the Soviet Union, but in more latent forms, often disguised under the struggle against Zionism and Judaism.

5
AFTERMATH OF THE BABYN YAR MASSACRE

PROPAGANDA AND OBLIVION

Initially, the Soviets widely publicized the Babyn Yar massacre, and Soviet propaganda turned it into a symbol of Nazi brutality against a peaceful population, like the Khatyn[1] massacre in Belarus and the siege of Leningrad. The Soviet press published numerous articles about the Babyn Yar massacre during the war. The Soviets publicized the Babyn Yar massacre so much, not because of their compassion for Jews or its other victims, but rather to rouse the wrath of the country and abroad against Nazi brutality and to increase support for the Red Army.

The Soviet press published several articles about the Jewish victims of Babyn Yar in 1941–42. The first official short notes about the execution of Jews at Babyn Yar appeared in the two main Soviet newspapers, *Pravda* and *Izvestia*, on November 19, 1941. The newspapers based their stories "on a report filed with the Overseas News Service in New York" and announced that "information has been received that in Kiev Germans executed 52 thousand Jews—men, women and children."[1]

Ten days later, on November 29, 1941, *Pravda* published an article by V. Stepanenko, "Chto proiskhodit v Kieve" (What is going on in Kyiv) about the Babyn Yar massacre. Stepanenko wrote: "History has never known such pogroms and slaughter as the Hitlerites organized in Kyiv. 52,000 people were shot within a few days. The Fascists[2] organized a Jewish pogrom, during which they also killed Russians and Ukrainians."[3] Stepanenko called the Babyn Yar massacre a Jewish pogrom, because in 1941 neither of the terms genocide nor Holocaust had yet been created, and the only historical parallel that the correspondent could provide was the Jewish pogroms in the past.

The Soviet description of the Babyn Yar massacre was already modified when People's Commissar for Foreign Affairs Vyacheslav Molotov described Nazi atrocities on occupied Soviet territory in his diplomatic note to the British and American representatives in Moscow. The note was sent on January 6, 1942, and published in *Pravda* on the next day. The note said:

> A frightful slaughter and terror actions were committed by German invaders in the Ukrainian capital of Kiev. During three days the German robbers shot and killed 52,000 men, women, old people and children, mercilessly killed Ukrainians, Russians and Jews who showed their loyalty to the Soviet government.[4]

The note listed Jews as the third national group among the victims of the Babyn Yar massacre. This appears to have been an intentional distortion of the truth, because from September 29 to the beginning of October 1941 the Nazis, with the assistance of their Ukrainian collaborators, almost exclusively killed Jews. Soviet prisoners of war and members of the Soviet underground and of the Ukrainian nationalist movement were later executed by the Nazis at Babyn Yar.

The Yiddish newspaper *Eynikait* (Unity) of the Jewish Anti-Fascist Committee (JAC) published several articles about the execution of Jews at Babyn Yar. Two of these articles were written by the Soviet writer Ilia Ehrenburg in Russian and published in translation in Yiddish in *Eynikait*: "Gebentshte erd" (Obetovannaia zemlia, Promised land) on October 15, 1942, and "Di daytshishe fashistn tor nit lebn blaybn" (Nemetskie fashisty ne dolzhny zhit', German fascists should not live) on November 4, 1943.[5] *Eynikait* also published articles by Yiddish writer Ikhil Falikman in February 1944 and Yiddish literary critic Moishe Mizhiritsky in March 1945 about the uprising at Babyn Yar of the prisoners of the Syrets concentration camp.[6] Falikman's article contains the memoirs of Yakov Kaper, a prisoner of the Syrets concentration camp, while Mizhiritsky's "Uprising at Babyn Yar" was based on materials gathered about the Holocaust in Kyiv by the Department of Jewish Culture of the Ukrainian Academy of Sciences.

Itsik Fefer, Yiddish poet and vice chair of JAC, titled his speech at the Third Plenum of the Jewish Anti-Fascist Committee in Moscow on April 2, 1944, *Pepel Babiego Yara zhet nashi serdtsa* (The ashes of Babyn Yar burn our hearts).[7] His relatives perished at Babyn Yar.[8] Fefer said:

> Before their retreat from Kyiv, the Nazis dug up and burned the remains of our fathers and mothers, brothers and sisters and scattered their ashes to the wind, hoping that the wind would hide the secret of their crimes. But the ashes of Babyn Yar burned our hearts, the flame burns in our eyes, the ashes lay on our burning wounds;

and do not give us any rest. And we will be unworthy to walk upon the earth if we do not destroy these cannibals with the bayonets of our hatred, if we do not burn them on the fires of our revenge, if we do not turn our tears into crushing projectiles.[9]

The speeches of the members of the JAC at the Third Plenum of the Jewish Anti-Fascist Committee were published as a book by Der Emes Publishing House in Moscow in 1945.[10]

By the end of the war, the Soviet Russian and Ukrainian press stopped reporting the nationality of the victims of Babyn Yar, calling them Kyivans or Soviet citizens. Perhaps this switch in the Soviet approach to the Holocaust happened due to the rise of popular and state anti-Semitism in the Soviet Union. So, the Soviets usually avoided talking about the Holocaust, especially in Ukraine, because the level of anti-Semitism there was higher than in other Soviet republics.

The draft report of the Extraordinary State Commission for Investigation of German-Fascist Crimes Committed on Soviet Territory (ChGK), which was disseminated among its members, mentioned the extermination of the Jewish population at Babyn Yar. The draft report stated:

> The Hitlerite bandits committed a mass brutal destruction of the Jewish population. They hung announcements ordering all Jew to go to the corner of Melnikova and Dokterivska [actually Dekhtirivska] streets on September 29, 1941, taking with them documents, money and valuable items. The executioners herded the Jews who had assembled to Babyn Yar, they confiscated all their valuables and then shot them.[11]

However, the official report of the ChGK, "About Destruction and War Crimes Committed by German-Fascist Occupants in City Kyiv," described the Babyn Yar massacre without mentioning the nationality of the victims. The report, which was first published in the newspaper *Krasnaia Zvezda* (Red star) on February 29, 1944, said:

> Hitlerite bandits gathered thousands of peaceful Soviet citizens on September 29, 1941, on the corner of Mel'nik and Dokterivska Streets. The executioners brought the people to Babyn Yar, took all their valuables and then murdered them. Citizens N.F. Petrenko and N.T. Gorbacheva, who lived near Babyn Yar, testified that they saw how Germans threw into the ravine live babies and buried them together with their killed and injured parents.[12]

Ilia Altman wrote that the Soviet tendency to keep silent about the Holocaust began in 1943. Thus, the publication of the text of official information about the victims of Babyn Yar in the collection of the acts of the Extraordinary State Commission "was discussed at high party and state levels."[13] The head of the Department of Agitation and Propaganda of the Central Committee of the Communist Party of the Soviet Union, Georgy Aleksandrov, edited the text of the official information, and he replaced the word "Jews" that appeared in the original text many times with "peaceful Soviet citizens."[14] "This happened in February 1944, with the consent of V. Molotov, A. Shcherbakov, and the leader of Ukraine, N. Khrushchev."[15]

In accord with "political expediency," the Soviets avoided mentioning Jewish victims of the Nazi regime in some regions but allowed mention of them in others. Thus the ChGK official report describes many times the Jewish victims of the Nazi regime in other places but did not mention them in Kyiv.[16] The ChGK report was based on reports of local commissions, some of which reported about the Jewish victims of the Nazis and some that did not, or such mentions were removed by Soviet censors. The Special Commission led by the First Secretary of the Communist Party of Ukraine (CPU), Nikita Khrushchev, also avoided mentioning Jewish victims in its report.[17] Perhaps the authorities were afraid that writing about the mass murder of Jews at Babyn Yar could provoke an explosion of popular anti-Semitism in Kyiv and incur the wrath of the gentile population against Soviet officials who emphasized the suffering of Jews.

BABYN YAR AFTER THE LIBERATION OF KYIV

Many Kyivans recalled that in the first years after the liberation of the city, Babyn Yar looked appalling: human bones, skulls, and belongings protruded through the sandy ground showing the huge dimension of the tragedy that had occurred there. Russian Soviet writer and war correspondent Boris Polevoy, who visited Babyn Yar soon after the liberation of Kyiv, observed:

> We entered Kyiv with the first Soviet units. The city was still burning. But all of us correspondents were eager to visit Babyn Yar. We had heard enough about it in those years, but we had to see everything for ourselves.... We came to Babyn Yar and were horror-struck. Huge deep ditches. The day before, the city was bombed, and one of the bombs hit the edge. The explosion knocked down a piece of the slope at the bottom. And we saw the incomprehensible: a geological deposit of death—between layers of the earth was found a level of human remains. Even in our worst dreams, we had not envisaged anything like this.... I couldn't believe that something like this could exist. Scary.... It's very scary to even remember it.... I have seen the worst of the whole war. There were Auschwitz, Dachau, Buchenwald, dozens of other places

of the mass destruction of people. But the most terrible, the incomprehensible to the mind was there, in Babyn Yar.[18]

Mykola Bazhan, Ukrainian poet and deputy chair of the Council of Ministers of the Ukrainian SSR (1943–48), who visited Babyn Yar soon after the liberation of Kyiv, provided a similar picture of horror:

> There, on the outskirts, in the most nightmarish ravine of our planet rows of charred human bodies mixed with yellow sand met the eye—that was Babyn Yar.... At the time we knew neither of Auschwitz, nor Treblinka, nor Dachau, nor Buchenwald. And one of the foreign reporters whom I brought to Babyn Yar in the first days after the liberation of Kyiv, was overcome, trembling and suffocating [figure 5.1].[19]

Ukrainian Soviet leader Nikita Khrushchev visited Babyn Yar in November 1943, soon after the liberation of Kyiv. Leon Leneman, *Forward*'s Paris correspondent, described Khruschev's visit to the site:

> "While Khrushchev was at the death-pit of Babyn Yar, one could still recognize traces of the cruel, bestial slaughter."... "Beneath fresh hastily scattered loose earth even

Figure 5.1 A press party being taken through the Babyn Yar site after the liberation of Kyiv. (Unidentified photographer.)

now, one could see victims' limbs protruding." According to Leneman, Khrushchev was saddened by the site, and committed that the Soviet regime would ensure a monument to the memory of the slaughter.[20]

Another *Forward* correspondent, Sholem Rosenfeld, described a visit by Khrushchev to Babyn Yar in 1943. "Rosenfeld, like Leneman before him, reported that Khrushchev had then given a stormy speech acknowledging the Jewish victims and swearing a monument would be erected in their memory."[21] Unfortunately, this promise was not fulfilled for many years.

Soviet Ukrainian officials paid great attention to the Babyn Yar massacre after the liberation of Kyiv because they used the Babyn Yar tragedy for the purposes of Soviet propaganda. In November 1943, the Soviets brought American and British correspondents to Babyn Yar to show them the dimensions of the Nazi crimes, to horrify the world, and to garner support for the Soviet Union from the Western allies. Their guide in Kyiv was Pavel F. Alyoshin, the former chief architect of Kyiv. Alyoshin took the correspondents to Babyn Yar on the first day of their visit to Kyiv and told them about the Babyn Yar massacre.[22] However, despite all the evidence provided by the Soviets at Babyn Yar, including human remains and belongings, the foreign correspondents were reluctant to believe the magnitude of the massacre that had occurred there. Alyoshin was not an eyewitness of the Babyn Yar massacre, and the foreign correspondents remained skeptical. They asked "the Soviet authorities if there were any witnesses still in Kiev who might provide testimony about some of the crimes alleged against the Germans."[23] The next day the correspondents from the *New York Times*, *Newsweek*, and the *Daily Worker* were again brought to Babyn Yar by Alyoshin and Bazhan. There "the atrocity commission was meeting," and the foreign correspondents heard the testimony of eyewitnesses, former prisoners of the Syrets concentration camp, who had escaped from Babyn Yar:

> Efim Vilkis, 33; Leonid Ostrovsky, 31; and Vladimir Davidoff [Davydov], 28, who said they were Soviet soldiers who had been captured by the Germans and forced to take part in the disinterment and burning, and who were among the handful of prisoners who escaped [figure 5.2].[24]

Vilkis, Ostrovsky, and Davydov showed the foreign correspondents the wounds on their legs caused by the shackles placed on them by the Nazis.[25] However, despite the efforts of the Soviets, some foreign correspondents still doubted the scale of the massacre. Thus, W. H. Lawrence wrote in his article "50,000 Kiev Jews Reported Killed" in *The New York Times*, on November 29, 1943:

Figure 5.2 In liberated Kyiv, Jewish prisoners of war who escaped from Babyn Yar: Efim Vilkis, Leonid Ostrovsky, and Vladimir Davydov, 1943. (Unidentified photographer.)

Kiev authorities asserted today that the Germans had machine-gunned from 50,000 to 80,000 of Kiev's Jewish men, women and children in late September 1941....

On the basis of what we saw, it is impossible for this correspondent to judge the truth or falsity of the story told to us....

If this was the Germans' intent, they succeeded well, for there is little evidence in the ravine to prove or disprove the story.[26]

The *Buffalo Courier-Express* newspaper republished Lawrence's article under the title "Little Evidence Supports Story of Nazi Atrocity" on November 29, 1943 (figure 5.3).[27] Such mistrust of the Soviets was typical in the West. David Shneer wrote that during World War II, the Soviet press published "photographs of Nazi mass murder of Jews and others."[28] But Soviet photojournalism and the Soviet media in general were "considered unreliable from a Western standpoint."[29] Soviet propaganda had often lied before the war, so Western correspondents cautiously processed information they received from the Soviets. When the correspondents heard about the Babyn Yar massacre in November 1943, not much was known about the Holocaust, because the major Nazi concentration camps had not yet been liberated.

Foreign correspondents perceived information provided by the Soviets according to their political views. Thus, pro-socialist journalists usually trusted the Soviets more than others. For example, Bill Downs, who was criticized for his sympathy toward

Figure 5.3 W. H. Lawrence's article "Little Evidence Supports Story of Nazi Atrocity" published in the *Buffalo Courier-Express* on November 29, 1943.

the Soviets, wrote in his article "Blood at Babii Yar—Kiev's Atrocity Story" that he was "convinced that one of the most horrible tragedies in this Nazi era occurred" at Babyn Yar.[30]

In 1946, the Soviets brought Fiorello La Guardia, the ex-mayor of New York City (1934–46) and the director general of the United Nations Relief and Rehabilitation Administration (UNRRA), to Babyn Yar during his visit to Kyiv and filmed his arrival at the ravine.[31] It seems that Babyn Yar was turned by Soviet propagandists into one of the must-see places for important guests of the city. Such an approach was used by the Soviets until the Cold War gained momentum and visits of Western politicians and journalists to the Soviet Union were curtailed until after the death of Stalin.

In any case, Soviet efforts to publicize abroad information about the Babyn Yar massacre and other Nazi crimes were not without results. Gradually, the foreign audience learned more about the Holocaust and other war crimes committed by the Nazis in the occupied territories.

Due to strong popular anti-Semitism in Kyiv and other liberated territories, Soviet ideologists often provided different accounts for foreign and local audiences. While foreign correspondents were told that most victims of the Babyn Yar massacre were Jews, Soviet propaganda directed toward the internal audience described the victims as either Kyivans or "peaceful Soviet citizens," neglecting to mention their ethnicity. Obviously, the Soviets omitted writing about Jewish victims so as not to irritate the part of the local gentile population that was hostile toward Jews.

INVESTIGATION OF THE BABYN YAR MASSACRE AND TRIALS

After the liberation of Kyiv from the Nazi occupation on November 6, 1943, the Extraordinary State Commission for Investigation of German-Fascist Crimes Committed on Soviet Territory (ChGK) began to work in the city. Hrynevych wrote that the ChGK "undertook practically no large-scale excavations and exhumations of human remains in Babyn Yar."[32] Probably the large-scale excavations would not provide any significant evidence of the Babyn Yar massacre, because most of the corpses were exhumed and burned by the order of the Nazis before their withdrawal from Kyiv. The ChGK used as evidence of the Nazi crimes at Babyn Yar the testimony of witnesses of the Babyn Yar massacre and testimony of surviving prisoners of the Syrets concentration camp who participated in the exhumation and burning of the corpses and succeeding in escaping from Babyn Yar.[33] The NKVD closely cooperated with the ChGK and provided the commission evidence of Nazi crimes.[34] Thus, on December 12, 1943, the head of the Kyiv district NKVD directorate (UNKVD), Mykhailo Bondarenko, sent to the people's commissar of state security of the Ukrainian SSR, Serhii Savchenko, a memorandum "About the Atrocities of the German-Fascist Occupiers in the City of Kyiv," in which he indicated that Jews were the main victims of the Babyn Yar massacre.[35] Bondarenko wrote:

> A mass murder of Jews was carried out in Babyn Yar....
> Thus, in Babyn Yar in late September 1941, nearly 70,000 Jews were shot over the space of several days.
> During the entire period of the German occupation of Kyiv, Babyn Yar was a permanent site where the shootings of Soviet people were carried out.
> According to preliminary estimates, it has been determined that, in addition to 70,000 Jews, nearly 20,000 captured fighters and commanders of the Red Army and nearly 10,000 communists, Komsomol members, [and] non-party Soviet patriots were shot in Babyn Yar during the occupation.[36]

The mass murder of Jews at Babyn Yar and other Ukrainian cities and towns was discussed at the Kyiv Military District Tribunal (the Kyiv trial), which took place in the Red Army Hall (now the Officers' House) on January 17–28, 1946. This was a public trial of fifteen Nazi perpetrators who committed crimes on the territory of occupied Ukraine.[37] Martin Dean wrote:

> The trial in Kyiv, like many others, was filmed and used for propaganda purposes, to demonstrate that some Germans were being held responsible for the crimes committed against the Soviet people. At the Kyiv trial Dina Pronicheva gave moving testimony about her escape from the mass grave and survival of Babyn Yar. However none of the German defendants in Kyiv could be linked directly to the Babyn Yar killings [figure 5.4].[38]

According to Dean, the reason that the main culprits of the Babyn Yar massacre did not appear at the Kyiv trial was that "very few of the German lead perpetrators of the Holocaust fell into Soviet hands."[39] Only one of the lead perpetrators of Babyn Yar, Fridrich Jeckeln, "was tried and executed in Riga, mainly for his organization of the mass shooting of some 30,000 Jews in Riga in late November and December 1941."[40]

Nevertheless, the Kyiv trial addressed questions of the Babyn Yar massacre. Several eyewitnesses of the Nazi crimes provided their testimony about the mass murder of Kyivan Jews at Babyn Yar. The deputy prosecutor-general of the Red Army, General

Figure 5.4 Dina Pronicheva, a Jewish survivor of the Babyn Yar massacre, testifies about her experiences during a war crimes trial in Kyiv. (Unidentified photographer.)

Major Aleksandr Cheptsov, talked about the crimes of the Nazis against Jews and the Babyn Yar massacre in his verdict. Cheptsov said:

> The capital of Soviet Ukraine long-suffering Kyiv will not forget the tragedy of the Babyn Yar—the tragedy of the mass extermination of the Jewish population of Kyiv: women, elderly people, children walked there; the Germans undressed them, drove them into a prepared pit and shot them in cold blood, tore children from their mothers and threw them alive into their graves.[41]

Prosecutor Cheptsov frankly characterized the Babyn Yar massacre as "the mass extermination of the Jewish population of Kyiv." He also mentioned in his speech how the Nazis tried to destroy the evidence of their crimes at Babyn Yar:

> The witness Berliant depicted a terrible picture of the burning of the corpses of Babyn Yar in order to destroy the traces of mass executions, the Germans shackled innocent Soviet people, who for a long time removed corpses from the graves of Babyn Yar and burned them.[42]

Twelve Nazis were sentenced to capital punishment and three to long terms of forced labor from fifteen to twenty years.[43] The twelve convicted Nazis were publicly executed the next day, January 29, 1946, at 5 p.m. at Kalinin Square (now Maidan of Independence) in the presence of 200,000 Kyivans.[44] The central and Ukraine republic press extensively covered the Kyiv trial, which raised public awareness of the Babyn Yar massacre and other Nazi crimes in the territory of Ukraine. The Kyiv trial and the execution of the Nazi criminals were filmed by Soviet documentary filmmakers. Based on this Soviet documentary footage, Ukrainian film director Sergei Loznitsa prepared his documentary *The Kiev Trial* in 2021.[45]

Why was the execution of Jews openly discussed at the Kyiv trial in January 1946, while the ChGK report published in February 1944 talked about the execution at Babyn Yar of "thousands of innocent Soviet citizens"? Perhaps the authorities could not totally control the testimony of the witnesses of the Babyn Yar massacre, who openly talked about the execution of Jews. Or the Soviet authorities, who felt that their power in the city was still quite weak in February 1944, just a few months after the liberation of the city, were much more confident that they were in control of the situation in Kyiv by January 1946. So, they allowed the witnesses to tell the full truth about the Babyn Yar massacre.

Three weeks after the completion of the Kyiv trial, materials about the Babyn Yar massacre were discussed at the Nuremberg trials in mid-February 1946.[46] The deputy prosecutor of the Soviet Union, Lev Smirnov, "presented a document numbered

SSSR-9, an announcement published earlier by the NKVD about the events that took place on September 29, 1941 at Babyn Yar, where 'thousands of innocent Soviet civilians' were killed."[47] Pavel Polian wrote that the preliminary list of witnesses who were supposed to testify at the Nuremberg trials was discussed and approved by the People's Commissariat of State Security of the USSR at the end of November 1945. It was planned that three people from the Kyiv district would testify at the Nuremberg trials: David Budnik and Vladimir Davydov, who escaped from Babyn Yar, and poet Pavlo Tychina, the minister of education of the Ukrainian SSR. But only Budnik came with the Soviet delegation to Nuremberg. "The delegation arrived in Nuremberg on February 21, [1946] after Babyn Yar was discussed on February 19. Thus Budnik did not personally testify at the trial, but his testimonies were read and taken into account."[48] An episode of a documentary film about the Babyn Yar massacre was shown at the Nuremberg trials on February 19, 1946.[49] But the Babyn Yar massacre was not a focal point of the Nuremberg trials.

Polian wrote that along with the public trials of Nazi perpetrators, many closed trials took place in different locations. On July 31, 1947, a trial took place at NKVD special camp #7, located at Sachsenhausen, the former Nazi concentration camp in Oranienburg, Germany. The fifteen defendants were Police Battalion #9 members, and they were accused of war crimes committed in the occupied territory of the Soviet Union, including Kyiv. They were sentenced to twenty-five years in a concentration camp. Among them was SS Obersturmfuhrer Walter Ebeling, former head of section IV (Gestapo) at the security police SD (KdS) in Kyiv, who participated in the Babyn Yar massacre.[50]

The main Babyn Yar perpetrators were tried at the Einsatzgruppen trial. It was the ninth of the twelve trials that the US authorities conducted in their occupation zone in Nuremberg. The trial was held from September 29, 1947, to April 10, 1948. The defendants were twenty-four former commanders of the Einsatzgruppen, which committed war crimes and crimes against humanity in the occupied Soviet territory. Fourteen of them received capital punishment, but ten were pardoned. Among those who were not pardoned was SS Standartenfuhrer Paul Blobel—the head of Sonderkommando 4a of Einsatzgruppe C, which executed Jews at Babyn Yar. Blobel was also the head of Sonderkommando 1005, which organized the exhumation and burning of the corpses. Blobel said about Babyn Yar at the trial, "Here lie my Jews...," because he was in charge of the massacre of Kyivan Jews. Later, on June 25, 1960, Viktor Trill, who participated in the execution of Jews at Babyn Yar, testified that Blobel was present at the Babyn Yar massacre and personally led it. Trill stated: "During the shooting Blobel stood watching with his commanders from the edge of the ravine. He constantly found something to criticize and shouted unceasingly into the ditch. Most likely the shooting was not going fast enough."[51]

Figure 5.5 Defendant Paul Blobel is sentenced to death by hanging at the Einsatzgruppen trial. (Unidentified photographer.)

However, Blobel did not consider himself guilty; he claimed at the trial that he was just following orders (figure 5.5).[52] Blobel was executed at Landsberg Prison on June 7, 1951. His last words were: "I die in the faith of my people. May the German people be aware of its enemies!"[53]

The defendants at the Einsatzgruppen trial included other Babyn Yar massacre perpetrators: SS-Sturmbannführer Waldemar von Radetzky, deputy chief of Sonderkommando 4a of Einsatzgruppe C, and the commanding officer of Einsatzgruppe C, SS-Brigadeführer Otto Rasch.[54] Radetzky was sentenced to twenty years' imprisonment on April 10, 1948. He was released on February 3, 1951, after his remaining prison time was forgiven.[55] Otto Rasch was removed from the trial on February 5, 1948, for medical reasons. He died in the prison hospital in Nuremberg on November 1, 1948.[56]

Two trials of Babyn Yar massacre perpetrators took place in Darmstadt in 1967–68 and in Stuttgart in 1968–69. At the Darmstadt trial ten SS officers of Sonderkommando 4a were accused of participating in the Babyn Yar massacre. The main defendant was SS-Sturmbannführer Kuno Callsen, deputy chief of Sonderkommando 4a of Einsatzgruppe C.[57] He was one of the organizers of the Babyn Yar massacre. Callsen was sentenced to fifteen years' imprisonment but was released from prison early in 1981. Six other defendants received from four to eleven years of imprisonment; three were acquitted.

> Adolf Janssen and August Häfner, Blobel's adjutant, received 11 and 9 years, respectively, Victor Woithon 7 years, and Christian Schulte got a term of 4 years and 6 months [for participation in the Babyn Yar massacre]. Two other former members of Sonderkommando 4A received prison sentences for crimes committed elsewhere.[58]

Among those who were acquitted at the trial was Viktor Trill. He participated in the mass shooting at Babyn Yar on September 30, 1941.[59] Trill testified at the trial, "It is possible that on this day I shot between around 150 and 250 Jews. The whole shooting went off without incident. The Jews were resigned to their fate like lambs."[60] Trill "was not punished by the West German court, as in his case according to German law no 'base motive' could be proven for his admitted participation in the killings."[61]

A trial of Sonderkommando 1005 members was held in Stuttgart.[62] The four SS officer defendants oversaw destruction of the evidence of the mass extermination at Babyn Yar and other places in Ukraine. Two defendants were sentenced to imprisonment of four and two and a half years "for accessory to murders"; the other two defendants were acquitted.[63]

There was a shocking contrast between the Soviets' harsh punishment of Nazi perpetrators and the lenient attitude toward the Nazi criminals by the West German legal system. The Soviets sent victims and witnesses of the Nazi crimes at Babyn Yar to testify at the Darmstadt and Stuttgart trials. Dina Pronicheva testified at the Darmstadt trial and Vladimir Davydov, David Budnik, and Yakov Kaper testified at the Stuttgart trial.[64] However, their testimonies did not change the leniency of the West German courts.

On the eightieth anniversary of the Babyn Yar massacre, the Babyn Yar Holocaust Memorial Center (BYHMC) released 161 names of Nazis who murdered Jews at Babyn Yar.[65] The 161 Nazis who participated in the massacre were

> from over the whole of Germany and other countries under Nazi control, and they were between 20 and 60 years old [the oldest perpetrator in the released list was 67]. They were educated and uneducated, they included engineers and teachers, drivers and sales people. Some were married and some were not.... They testified at trial and were found not guilty, except for very few commanders, not the soldiers who carried out the horrific massacre.[66]

The search for the Babyn Yar massacre perpetrators is ongoing research, and the list of the perpetrators is perhaps not complete. BYHMC "estimated that hundreds of German soldiers, policemen, and SS personnel were complicit in the massacre."[67]

Father Patrick Desbois, head of the BYHMC Academic Council, pointed out that among the 161 names of the Babyn Yar perpetrators that were revealed,

> some were shooters, others extracted the Jews from their homes, others took their belongings and their luggage. Others armed the weapons while others were serving sandwiches, tea and Vodkas to the shooters. All of them are guilty. In a mass crime anyone who was involved in any way, directly or indirectly, must be considered guilty.[68]

Historian Andrej Umansky wrote:

> Few of these men were bothered by justice after WWII.... From the SS, only Paul Blobel,[69] Kuno Callsen, August Häfner, Adolf Janssen and Christian Schulte were sentenced [to] jail time for Babyn Yar. Engelbert Kreuzner was the only policeman sentenced for his participation. No other SS member, policeman or Wehrmacht soldier was ever sentenced for his role in Babi Yar, although many admitted in post war depositions their involvement. All these men lived a calm and normal life after the war.[70]

Thus for many perpetrators and collaborators the Babyn Yar massacre became a crime without a punishment. Some of the perpetrators lived a long and comfortable life like Waldemar von Radetzky, who after his release from prison had a good professional career and became an art collector. The von Radetzkys' collection of Baltic silversmiths' art has been exhibited in the Haus der Deutsch-Balten in Darmstadt since 2008.[71] It seems that a guilty conscience did not bother the Babyn Yar perpetrators. None of them considered himself guilty and they never apologized for their participation in the Babyn Yar massacre.

CRYSTAL VASE FULL OF TEARS: FIRST ATTEMPTS TO COMMEMORATE THE BABYN YAR TRAGEDY

Commemoration of the Babyn Yar tragedy began soon after the liberation of Kyiv from Nazi occupation, and it was initiated and organized by Kyivan Jews. Commemoration of those who perished in the Holocaust was of foremost importance for Kyivan Jews, because every Jewish family lost their relatives, friends, and neighbors at Babyn Yar. It was an emotionally difficult and traumatic experience for Kyivan Jews to visit Babyn Yar, especially due to the awful condition of this valley of death after the liberation of Kyiv. But many survivors thought that it was their moral duty to visit Babyn Yar soon after their return to Kyiv. Doctor Gutin (his first name is missing) came to Kyiv with a military hospital on April 15, 1944. He came to Babyn Yar directly from the train station. Gutin recalled what he saw there:

> Near Babyn Yar, some Ukrainian was standing at a booth, which he had built, like a real guide, telling the Jews surrounding him about what he had seen, and for greater effect, he lit a fire on the bottom of the ravine so that the people could see the ashes, he was talking and stretching out his straw hat, demanding payment. The people surrounding him were catching his every word in hope of at least finding out something about their loved ones.
>
> I came down to the ravine. A young woman was screaming, crying, and tearing out her hair. "Thirteen," she was screaming, "thirteen relatives and friends are here, I remained alone." Another woman told everyone again and again that she left [to evacuation] with a military plant. "Those who had money or connections could evacuate, these was necessary to push into the train carriage, and you did not have them, my dears," (she seems to have lost her mind, she spoke to those around her, then to herself, then to those, whose bones were under her feet). [She said] "It would have been better if I had died with you."
>
> A Jew stood on the side and read the prayer for the dead "El Malei Rachamim" [God, full of Mercy], read it many times, each time he pronounced a different name, apparently many of his relatives remained here.[72]

Yiddish poet David Hofshtein recalled:

> I prepared myself for months [for my visit of Babyn Yar]. I prepared myself for shock, for suffering. For months I suppressed the first cry that was supposed to break out of me at the very moment that I would see everything that I already knew: our calamity, our catastrophe in its fullest extent.[73]

Kyivan Jews attempted to organize the first commemoration meeting at Babyn Yar on the third anniversary of the massacre, September 29, 1944. However, when David Hofshtein attempted to organize "a mass demonstration [according to another source, a meeting], the authorities forbade the gathering, claiming that it might "provoke anti-Semitism."[74]

Despite the warnings of the authorities, many Jews who had returned to Kyiv from evacuation came to Babyn Yar on that day. Among them was the Yiddish writer Itsik Kipnis. On the same day, he wrote his essay *Babyn Yar (On the third anniversary of the massacre)*.[75] The essay was written in Yiddish; in it Kipnis appeals to Kyivan Jews. According to him, many Jewish women came to Babyn Yar, because the men were still fighting at the front. He proposed that Jews walk on foot to Babyn Yar (rather than take the tram) "on the same streets, which were completely filled up by our then still alive brothers and sisters."[76]

Eleven months after the liberation of Kyiv, the Babyn Yar ravine remained a terrifying place. Perhaps the Soviet authorities were too busy with war needs, or maybe they intentionally did not rush to cover the human remains at Babyn Yar, to expose them to Soviet and foreign correspondents as evidence of Nazi crimes. Kipnis wrote that, on the third anniversary of the massacre, Babyn Yar "looked worse than death."[77] On the bottom of the ravine, the sandy ground had washed away, revealing bones, scalps and the hair of murdered people, and the abandoned belongings of the victims. The weeping of Jews who came to Babyn Yar was heard from a distance.[78] The trauma of the Babyn Yar tragedy was still very fresh, and many Jews could not control their emotions: they cried for their beloved ones whom they had lost there.

In this atmosphere of grief and despair, Kipnis called on Kyivan Jews to undertake a national revival. In his words: "Let's rise from the earth, draw ourselves up to our full height and raise high our banner! … A people half and three-quarters of which have been annihilated, is like a globule of mercury. Wrench half of it away, and the other half will become round and whole again."[79]

Kyivan Jews also considered it their duty to bury the bones of the Babyn Yar victims, which were scattered around the ravine. Sara Tartakovskaia wrote that she returned from evacuation to Kyiv in 1944. On the third anniversary of the Babyn Yar massacre, she went to the ravine where her parents, sister, and other relatives perished. There she saw the burned human bones. Sara recalled that, together with other Jews, she gathered "a mount of bones, we buried them near the house of the rabbi, which was near Babyn Yar [perhaps she meant that they buried the bones in the nearby Jewish cemetery]. The entire year 1944, I went to Babyn Yar every day, we buried and buried the bones."[80]

Soviet Jews perceived the Babyn Yar massacre as a tragedy of the entire Jewish people. Many Jewish intellectuals believed that it was their moral obligation to commemorate the victims of Babyn Yar. In 1945, Solomon Mikhoels, artistic director of the Moscow State Jewish Theater (Moscow GOSET) and chair of the Jewish Anti-Fascist Committee, came to Kyiv to celebrate the twentieth anniversary of the Ukrainian State Jewish Theater (Ukrainian GOSET). The celebration took place in the building of the Kyiv Operetta Theater on Sunday, October 7, 1945.[81] Mikhoels spoke first. He congratulated the Ukrainian GOSET troupe on its anniversary and presented a crystal vase with flower seeds to its artistic director, Moisei Goldblatt (who was his student).[82] In his address, Mikhoels said:

> The vase, as you can see, is full of seeds. I brought these seeds so that you can plant them at Babyn Yar, where innocent Jewish blood flowed abundantly. Let the flowers

that grow from these seeds remind people about the victims of the most awful crime of the Nazi miscreants, people should remember this forever. And let the vase fill up to the brim with the tears of your audience, but only when you perform a play about Babyn Yar.[83]

Mikhoels had a prophetic vision: Performances about Babyn Yar created a "curtain of tears" in Kyiv. However, Kyivans had to wait many years for these performances, because all Jewish culture was suppressed in the Soviet Union during the anticosmopolitan campaign in the late 1940s to early 1950s. Mikhoels was killed by Soviet secret police (which received the order from Stalin) late on the night of January 12, 1948, and his murder was disguised as a traffic accident.[84] Many Yiddish cultural figures became victims of Stalin's repression during the anticosmopolitan campaign. Only during Khrushchev's Thaw were some Jewish performances allowed again.

In 1959, the hundredth anniversary of the birth of the Yiddish writer Sholom Aleichem was celebrated in the Soviet Union. The authorities permitted "a relatively large number of Yiddish concerts."[85] Soviet Yiddish singer Nehama Lifshitz came to Kyiv with her concerts in December 1959.[86] Yaacov Ro'i wrote that Nehama Lifshitz's concerts "were not only cultural events, but 'happenings' of great national significance."[87] Yiddish writer Itsik Kipnis, the poet Riva Balasnaia, and Feige, the widow of David Hofshtein, came to Lifshitz's concert in Kyiv in December 1959. Nehama brought her Jewish concerts to Kyiv, Odesa, Kharkiv, and other Ukrainian cities several times in the 1960s before her immigration to Israel in 1969. But the strongest impression was made by her first performance of the "Lullaby to Babyn Yar" in Kyiv in December 1959. The lyrics to the song were written by the Yiddish poet Shyke Driz, with music by composer Riva (Reveka) Boyarskaia. Driz's poem depicts a mother who lost her children at Babyn Yar, and she sang her lullaby to the ravine, where her children perished:

> *Had I fastened*
> *The cradle on a rafter,*
> *And rocked it and rocked it,*
> *My little son, my Yankl.*
>
> *But the house has vanished*
> *Into a fiery dome,*
> *How then can I rock*
> *My little son, my own?*
>
> *Had I fastened*
> *The cradle on a little tree,*

And rocked it and rocked it,
My little son, my Shleyml.

But nothing was left,
Not a thread from a sheet;
Nothing remained
Not a shoestring for my feet.

Had I shorn my long braids,
My hair untended,
Upon them the cradle,
The cradle suspended.

But where can I search for
The little bones to find them,
The little bones the dear ones,
Of both my precious children.

Help me mothers, help me
My mournful song to weep;
Help me, mothers, help me,
So Babi-Yar may sleep.[88]

Performing this song in 1959 in Kyiv created a shocked reaction among the audience. There were many people who lost their beloved ones at Babyn Yar. Ro'i wrote:

> Jewish cultural events were very rare in the Ukrainian capital. The large hall was so packed that there was no standing room at all. Nehama concluded her concert with the "Lullaby to Babii Iar" by a Jewish poet from Kiev, Shayke Driz, set to music by Riva Boiarskaia (also of Kiev). Nehama usually sang this particular song last, as she found it difficult to continue singing after it. But to sing about Babii Iar in Kiev was not like singing about it elsewhere. Here no one applauded. The hall seemed to be electrified. The entire audience rose to its feet like one man and stood in absolute silence, in the atmosphere of fear that characterized the Jews of Kiev. In Nehama's words, this was a "curtain of tears." As she left the hall people stood outside, still silently weeping, in order to touch her hand or sleeve as though she were some holy person.[89]

According to Vladyslav Hrynevych, "The next day the singer was invited to the Central Committee of the Communist Party of Ukraine (CPU), after which the rest of her concerts in the Ukrainian capital were cancelled, and she was forbidden to perform for a period of one year."[90] Nehama Lifshitz recalled that it was her first and last performance in Kyiv.[91]

THE FIRST LITERARY WORKS ABOUT THE BABYN YAR MASSACRE

During the war and in the postwar years, several Jewish, Russian, and Ukrainian writers and poets depicted the Babyn Yar massacre in their works. Their publications raised awareness about the Babyn Yar tragedy. Perhaps the largest contribution to preserving memory about the Babyn Yar tragedy and gathering the evidence of its eyewitnesses was by Ilya Ehrenburg and Vasily Grossman, who initiated and edited *The Black Book*, about which I wrote in the introduction.[92] Ilya Ehrenburg also depicted the Babyn Yar massacre in his poetry and fiction. The Babyn Yar tragedy was especially meaningful for Ehrenburg because he was born in Kyiv in 1891. Although Ehrenburg moved with his parents to Moscow in 1894, he returned to Kyiv many times to stay with his grandparents during the summer, and he lived in the city during the civil war in 1918–20.[93] Yevgeny Yevtushenko devoted his poem "Kreshchatitskii Parizhanin" (Khreshchatyk's Parisian) to Ehrenburg.

Ehrenburg most likely knew some Kyivan Jews who perished at Babyn Yar. He visited Kyiv in spring 1941 and read to the public at the Lenin Museum (now the Teachers' House) chapters from his new novel *Padenie Parizha* (The fall of Paris) about the Nazi occupation of Paris. As a Soviet correspondent in France, he was an eyewitness to this event. Mikhail Kalnitsky wrote: "In the Spring of 1941 Soviet propaganda praised the Soviet-German agreement [of 1939]."[94] However, listening to the chapters from Ehrenburg's new novel, "even the most cheerful optimists" felt the approach of the war.[95] As a Jew and liberal, Ehrenburg hated the Nazi regime from its beginning to the end and tried to show in his works all the dangers of Nazism.

Ehrenburg was a war correspondent, and he impatiently waited for the liberation of his native city. He came to Kyiv soon after its liberation, but it was a different city: All downtown was in ruins, including the house on Instytutska Street where he lived with his parents in his childhood, and tens of thousands of Kyivan Jews had perished at Babyn Yar.[96] Hirsh Smolar, a partisan commander from Minsk, recalled visiting Ehrenburg in Moscow in 1944: "Ehrenburg had just returned from Kiev, and he was in a rotten mood.... 'This was my hometown,' he told me, 'and I will never go back there.'"[97] Ehrenburg broke his promise never to return to Kyiv only once, in 1952, when he visited soon after receiving the International Stalin Prize "For strengthening peace among nations."[98]

Maxim D. Shrayer wrote that the destruction of Ehrenburg's native city, Kyiv, and the Babyn Yar massacre were a "personal wound" for the author.[99] Deeply traumatized by these events, Ehrenburg described them several times in his writings. He published in August 1941 and November 1942 two articles about the extermination of Jews by the Nazis in occupied Soviet territory.[100]

Ehrenburg wrote his poem "Babi Yar" in 1944 and described the Babyn Yar massacre in his novels *Buria* (*The Storm*, 1945–47) and *Deviatyi Val* (*The Ninth Wave*, 1951). Ehrenburg was not alone in devoting works to the Babyn Yar massacre during the war and in the first postwar years. The Ukrainian poet Mykola Bazhan and the Russian poet of Jewish origins Lev Ozerov wrote their poems about Babyn Yar in 1943 and 1946. However, Ehrenburg, Bazhan, and Ozerov depicted the Babyn Yar massacre in their poems as a universal, even cosmic tragedy, and none of them mentioned that primarily Jews were killed there. Such a blatant omission is unlikely to have been accidental. We don't know for sure whether the poets did this due to censorship demands or if they intentionally tried to present the Babyn Yar tragedy as universal, appealing to a general audience and trying to get its attention to the Babyn Yar massacre. There are arguments in support of both these points of view. A new Soviet doctrine emerged during the war, which required that war victims not be divided by nationalities. Since 1943, Soviet official reports and propaganda talked about the Babyn Yar tragedy without mentioning its primarily Jewish victims.[101] This approach was used by most Soviet poets and writers.

However, Sava Holovanivsky, a Ukrainian poet of Jewish origins, wrote in 1943 in his poem "Abraham" about the murder of Jews in Babyn Yar. The poem depicts "an old Jew, Abraham, whom the Germans marched through the streets of Kiev to be shot."[102] Soviet censorship allowed publication of the poem. But Holovanivsky was punished later: During the anticosmopolitan campaign, he was "violently berated for having spread 'nationalist slander.'"[103] Holovanivsky showed in his poem the indifference of the local gentile population to the fate of Kyivan Jews. He wrote that "Russians and Ukrainians—turned their backs on the old Jew, Abraham," when the Nazis pushed him toward Babyn Yar. *Literaturnaia Gazeta* wrote about Holovanivsky's poem on March 9, 1949, "This is a terrible defamation of the Soviet nation, which has succeeded, after a hard and bloody struggle and by dint of great sacrifice and effort, in upholding the freedom and independence of Soviet people of all nationalities."[104]

Ehrenburg, who did not mention the Jewish victims of Babyn Yar in his poem, did this later in his novels *The Storm* and *The Ninth Wave*. He knew a great deal about the Babyn Yar tragedy from eyewitness testimonies and other documentary materials that he collected for *The Black Book*. Ehrenburg published his novel *The Storm* in 1947. He depicted in his novel the lives of two brothers, Osip Alper in Kyiv and Leo Alper in Paris, "who represent two widely separated branches of the same family."[105] During the war Osip's family perished at Babyn Yar, while his brother Leo was sent to Auschwitz. Thus,

Ehrenburg's description of the common fate of Jews during the Holocaust "joins Kiev with Paris, Babi Yar with Auschwitz."[106] This connection had a personal meaning for Ehrenburg, who showed that the Holocaust brought the same fate to all European Jews.

Joshua Rubenstein wrote: "*The Storm* was severely criticized in the official press before he received the Stalin Prize."[107] However, the novel had not only critics who denounced it, but also admirers among literary circles, because it was nominated for and received a Stalin Prize. The last word in the discussion of whether the novel deserved the prize belonged to Stalin himself. Ewa Berard wrote that Stalin read attentively all literary works nominated for the prize in his name.[108]

Konstantin Simonov, who was a secretary of the Union of Writers of the USSR in 1946–50, recalled that during the discussion of the novel *The Storm*, Stalin told the novel's critics, "No, in my opinion, it is not correct that French people are depicted in Ehrenburg's novel better than Russians.... Perhaps Ehrenburg knows France better, this is possible. He certainly has faults, he does not always write well, sometimes he is rushing, but *Buria* is a great novel."[109]

Berard wrote that Stalin defended Ehrenburg and his novel because he needed Ehrenburg to keep good connections with France, particularly with the French Communist Party.[110] Ehrenburg, who lived nine years in France and visited the country several times thereafter, had many friends and connections there. But it was also possible that Stalin really liked the novel. The main topic of the novel was World War II and the struggle with the Nazi regime. Perhaps Stalin believed that the novel, which glorified the Soviet victory in the war, also glorified him.

Ehrenburg's novel *The Ninth Wave* is a sequel to *The Storm*, in which the writer depicted several of the same characters. The Jewish character Major Osip Alpert returned to Kyiv after the war. His mother and daughter had been killed at Babyn Yar. Looking for his friend in Kyiv, Osip was insulted by his friend's anti-Semitic neighbor, who shouted at Osip, "Why don't you go to Palestine now you've got a State of your own?"[111] Rubenstein pointed out that this was "the only literary depiction of popular anti-Semitism to appear in a Soviet novel" during the rise of state anti-Semitism in the Soviet Union.[112]

Considering his important political and cultural connections, Soviet authorities allowed Ehrenburg "to preserve his individuality and not flow with the stream."[113] Taking advantage of his situation, Ehrenburg discussed themes in his works that were really important for him: the Holocaust, anti-Semitism, and the fate of the Jewish people. The paradox of Ehrenburg is that despite being an adherent of Jewish assimilation, he wrote a great deal in his works about the lives and persecution of Jews. And Jewish people saw in Ehrenburg their defender. Many Soviet Jews wrote to Ehrenburg about their participation in the war, the Holocaust, anti-Semitism, and the revival of Jewish national life. They asked Ehrenburg for help and advice. Some of these letters are published in the book *Sovetskie evrei pishut Il'e Erenburgu, 1943–1966* (Soviet Jews write to Ilya Ehrenburg, 1943–1966).[114] As a member of the Jewish Anti-Fascist Committee during the war, deputy of the Verkhovnyi Sovet (the Supreme Council) of the Soviet Union, and a person with good connections in Soviet high circles, Ehrenburg often attempted to help his Jewish correspondents.

PIONEERS OF THE BABYN YAR THEME IN FILM, VISUAL ART, AND MUSIC

The Babyn Yar massacre was first depicted in the Soviet feature film *The Unvanquished*, which was released in October 1945. The film was based on the eponymous novel by Boris Gorbatov. The renowned film director Mark Donskoi, who was Jewish himself, turned the Jewish doctor, Aron Davidovich, into the main character in the film. The film was shot at the Kyiv Movie Studio and the main characters were performed by distinguished Jewish and Ukrainian actors: Yiddish actor Veniamin Zuskin played the medical doctor Aron Davidovich, and the Ukrainian actor Amvrosii Buchma played the Ukrainian main character Taras. While Aron Davidovich perished at Babyn Yar, Taras hid Davidovich's Jewish granddaughter from the Nazis.[115] Olga Gershenson wrote:

> A key scene in the film was the mass execution of Jews by a German firing squad (this scene was filmed on location in Babi Yar, a place that came to symbolize the Holocaust in the Soviet Union). Remarkably, this film, representing a Nazi massacre of Jews in the Soviet Union, was ... even sent to represent the USSR at the 1946 Film Festival in Venice. According to the critic Miron Chernenko, *The Unvanquished* was the first film to depict the Holocaust on Soviet screens, and one of the first such films worldwide.[116]

Jeremy Hicks and Gershenson mentioned that Donskoi used Nazi photographs made in the ravine and "his interview with witnesses and survivors in the newly liberated Kiev" to depict the execution of the Jews at Babyn Yar.[117] The scene of the Jewish massacre that was shot at the Babyn Yar ravine is quite recognizable. Nevertheless, the depiction of the execution of the Jews in the film, which lasted less than two minutes, is quite tragic, but far from reality. We see the suffering Jewish faces and the shooting Nazis in the film; the shooting is accompanied by dramatic music and thunderclouds in the sky. Nobody undressed Jews before the shooting and divided them into groups in the scene as the Nazis did before the Babyn Yar massacre. In the film, all the Jews stand together facing their executioners and some even could walk toward them. In reality the Nazi shot Jews in the back. The shooting is depicted as somewhat chaotic. If the shooting was done in this way, more Jews would have had a chance to escape. Unfortunately, the Nazis organized the massacre much better than what is depicted in the movie. Perhaps Donskoi attempted to show a symbolic scene of Jewish suffering during the Holocaust, rather than exactly reconstructing the historical events at Babyn Yar.

But even such a short and symbolic scene of Jewish execution at Babyn Yar irritated the anti-Semites. Hicks and Gershenson describe the heated debates of the Artistic Council of the Film Committee about the entire film and particularly about the scene of the execution of Jews at Babyn Yar. The opinion of the committee members was divided. Writer Konstantin Simonov and renowned movie directors Mikhail Romm and Sergei Eisenstein spoke in favor of the film. Simonov emphasized the importance of the film "for the collective memory of war crimes."[118] Romm predicted that the film would be a great success in the Soviet Union and abroad. But the movie directors Ivan Pyr'ev and Boris Babochkin demanded removal of the scene of the execution of Jews at Babyn Yar. Babochkin argued that this scene "does not have any elements of art … which cannot leave one indifferent, but it is not art. I believe we don't have the right to show our audience scenes like that." Babochkin stated that "the audience will not accept this picture."[119]

Pyr'ev was more openly anti-Semitic in his criticism of the film. He denounced the scene of the execution of Jews in the film "because it sidelined the sufferings of others, Slavic characters. In other words, Donskoi's depiction of the Jewish victims' death steals from the wider Soviet and Russian suffering."[120] Many of these arguments were used later by the officials when they refused to build a monument at Babyn Yar and commemorate the victims of the Holocaust.

The Babyn Yar tragedy was a dangerous theme not only in literature and film, but in all kinds of arts. The pioneers of the Babyn Yar theme in visual art and music, artist Vasily Ovchinnikov and composer Dmitry Klebanov, were accused of Jewish nationalism and cosmopolitanism.

Vasily Ovchinnikov was director of the Museum of Western and Oriental Art in Kyiv from 1936 until his death in 1978. During World War II, Ovchinnikov fought at the front. He was a Ukrainian, but he had many Jewish neighbors before World War II. When Ovchinnikov returned from the front to Kyiv, he found that all his Jewish neighbors had perished at Babyn Yar. His daughter, Elena Ovchinnikova, wrote in her memoirs about her father:

> The Babyn Yar tragedy was not an abstraction for him. It had specific faces of people who lived nearby. The next day [after his arrival in Kyiv], he wandered at Babyn Yar, walked around and drew clay ravines, the trunks of fallen trees, and old monuments in his little album. How can an artist communicate his shock?—with a pencil.[121]

Ovchinnikov's series *Babyn Yar* includes four works. His daughter wrote:

The first picture is called "September 29." It shows a corner of a Kyiv apartment somewhere in Lukyanovka. Outside the window floats a mournful procession of people driven into the unknown. There is a crying woman on a stool by the window, clinging to a girl who is dumbfounded and anxious. Who are they? A Jewish woman and her child who are going to join the death row? A Ukrainian woman mourning her fellow countrymen?

The central painting "Road of the Doomed" has a long horizontal format. People did not know where they were being driven, it was a monstrous Nazi deception. People flocked in streams from the hilly streets of Kyiv, rose from Podil, flowing into the common river. And this mournful river flowed to the Lukyanivsky cemetery. In Ovchinnikov's painting, against the backdrop of an alarming sunset sky, the blocks of the Lukyanivsky hills float like darkening ships, crowned with the silhouettes of the monuments of the old Jewish cemetery. And the mourning stream of people slowly floats into the unknown, into inevitability. A baby stroller is rolling like a wounded bird, a disabled person is limping on crutches, dragged by the crowd, a pregnant woman is looking around with an anxious, melancholy look [figures 5.6 and 5.7].[122]

The third and fourth paintings perhaps were not completed, but their sketches were described by D. Fedorovs'ky in the complementary article "Bab'iachyi Yar: V maisterni khudozhnyka Ovchynnikova" (Babyn Yar: In the studio of Artist Ovchinnikov) published in the newspaper *Radians'ke Mystetstvo* (Soviet art) on July 30, 1947. The third painting showed the execution of Jews at Babyn Yar and "the fourth painting called 'Retribution' depicted a German sitting in a trench with a machine gun in his hands but without a head. His head is lying at his feet."[123]

Ovchinnikov's painting *Road of the Doomed* was shown at the Ninth Ukrainian Art Exhibition in November 1947 in Kyiv. Elena Ovchinnikova recalled:

The scandal over the display of this painting began even before its exhibition. After preparing the exhibition, all the employees left, and, when they arrived in the morning, Ovchinnikov's painting "Road of the Doomed" was cut with a knife. It was hastily taped at the back; there was no investigation. By order of the Central Committee [of the Communist Party of Ukraine, the paintings] "Christ on Majdanek" by Zinoviy Tolkachev and "Babyn Yar" [by Ovchinnikov] were removed from the exhibition.[124]

After the exhibition, Ovchinnikov was accused of "cosmopolitanism," "bourgeois nationalism," and "anti-patriotism." Elena Ovchinnikova wrote:

Figure 5.6 Vasily Ovchinnikov, *September 29*.

Figure 5.7 Vasily Ovchinnikov, *Road of the Doomed*.

In the huge hall of the Academy of Sciences (artists did not have a spacious room after the war), open party meetings and processes began one after another. They [Ovchinnikov and Tolkachev] were accused of "distortion of reality," "decadent mood," and "harmful and dangerous tendencies in art." "Why are only Jews shown?"—"Yes, because there was an order from the commandant 'to all Jews of the city of Kyiv.'" On September 29, only Jews went [to Babyn Yar], and then Ukrainians, Poles, Romas, and prisoners were shot at Babyn Yar. "The Soviet people could not go to their death without resisting!" "Who was supposed to resist the hellish war machine—helpless old people, children, disabled people?" When Tolkachev tried to interject: "This is a universal human grief..."—"Oh, a universal human one? Cosmopolitan!"

Ovchinnikov portrayed Jews—a "Jewish nationalist!" "Nationalist," "cosmopolitan," "dissident"—this was already smoothly turning into "an enemy of the people." ... Ovchinnikov "silently left the meeting, slamming the door."[125]

But harassment of the artist was not limited to meetings of the local committee of the Communist Party. His daughter wrote: "At night at the office of the director of the Museum of Western and Oriental Art, searches took place, in the morning he found everything turned upside down. What were they looking for?"[126] Perhaps the NKVD officers were searching for some compromising documents so they could arrest Ovchinnikov, or it was psychological pressure so that the artist would not dare to create any painting about Babyn Yar in the future. In May 1949, the Sixth Plenum of the Union of Artists of Soviet Ukraine made a statement regarding Ovchinnikov's painting *Road of the Doomed*: "This formalistic work is based on the false idea that supposedly only the Jewish population, and not all Soviet people, were victims of German fascism."[127]

Jewish composer Dmitry Klebanov (1907–87) wrote his *The First Symphony: In Memory of the Martyrs of Babyn Yar* in 1945, after his return from evacuation to Kharkiv.[128] The composer used Jewish folk melodies, ancient religious chants, and hymns in the symphony. Its culmination was a mournful vocalization reminiscent of Jewish prayers. The symphony was criticized by Soviet censors during its final rehearsal for its "nationalistic sound."[129] However, in 1947, the Soviet censors did not ban the symphony. The first performances took place in 1947 in Kharkiv.[130] In 1948, it was performed in Kyiv "under the direction of the acclaimed conductor Natan Rakhlin."[131] In 1949, during the peak of the campaign against cosmopolitanism, Klebanov's symphony became a target for ideological attack. Natalia Symonenko explains that the symphony "was condemned as a work 'imbued with the spirit of bourgeois nationalism and cosmopolitanism' and that was 'replete with biblical motifs and steeped in tragic doom.'"[132]

Pavel Polian describes how the critic and composer Valerian Dovzhenko viciously attacked Klebanov's symphony as being antipatriotic at the Congress of the Union of Composers of Ukraine in March 1949. Dovzhenko said:

Klebanov wrote a symphony imbued with the spirit of bourgeois nationalism and cosmopolitanism, which he based on old Jewish religious songs. Ritual rites of ancient Palestine, "The Lament of Israel," synagogue intonations—these are the sources that inspired Klebanov to create this anti-patriotic symphony.... The composer slanders the Russian and Ukrainian people. In this symphony, filled with biblical motifs and imbued with tragic doom, Klebanov forgets about the friendship and brotherhood of the Soviet peoples and pursues the idea of the complete loneliness of the people murdered by the Germans at Babyn Yar.[133]

As a result of this critique, Klebanov was dismissed from his position as chair of the Department of Composition at the Kharkiv Conservatory and head of the Kharkiv branch of the Union of Composers of Ukraine.[134] Klebanov's symphony *In Memory of the Martyrs of Babyn Yar* was forbidden to be performed. The symphony was next performed after the death of the composer, during the perestroika years, when the ban on the Jewish and Holocaust themes was finally lifted in the Soviet Union. On September 29, 1990, the National Symphony Orchestra of Ukraine, under the direction of conductor Ihor Blazhkov, performed the symphony in Kyiv. Symonenko wrote that Blazhkov was a friend of Klebanov, and he considered "the revival of the Babyn Yar symphony as his own moral obligation in tribute to the memory of its creator.... Eventually, Ukrainian radio made a recording of the symphony."[135]

CONCLUSION

During and immediately after World War II, the Soviet press wrote many times about the Babyn Yar massacre and Soviet propaganda made Babyn Yar a symbol of Nazi brutality against civilians in the occupied territories. Soviet journalists described the massacre of Jews at Babyn Yar in their early publications, but they later avoided mentioning the nationality of the Babyn Yar victims under the pressure of Soviet ideology, or perhaps censors removed the word "Jews" from their articles. Ukrainian Soviet authorities visited Babyn Yar immediately after the liberation of Kyiv from the Nazis. They brought foreign correspondents to Babyn Yar, trying to focus the world's attention on Nazi war crimes and gain more support for the Red Army. Thus, the Babyn Yar tragedy was already politicized during the war and was used by Soviet propaganda.

The Soviets used public trials of the Nazi perpetrators for propaganda purposes, where they emphasized Nazi crimes against the civilian population. The Babyn Yar massacre was discussed at the Kyiv trial, Nuremberg trials, and others. However, only a few Nazis who participated in the massacre were sentenced. Most of the Babyn Yar massacre perpetrators did not receive any punishment.

When World War II ended and the Cold War began, publicizing the Babyn Yar tragedy become undesirable for the Soviets. Remembering the Babyn Yar tragedy could not bring any benefit to the Soviet authorities or support from abroad. However, commemoration of the Babyn Yar massacre could provoke irritation and dissatisfaction with the authorities from a significant part of the gentile population who thought that Jewish suffering should not be emphasized, because they too had suffered. The official Soviet representation of the Babyn Yar tragedy as universal suffering did not deceive anyone; Jews and gentiles clearly understood that most of the victims of Babyn Yar were Jewish. Later, the Soviets tried to silence any discussions about Babyn Yar as a place of either universal or Jewish suffering.

Kyivan Jews who survived the war went through a series of shocks: first when they learned about the deaths of their loved ones at Babyn Yar, then when they returned to the city and saw the awful Holocaust site, and finally when the authorities refused to commemorate the Babyn Yar tragedy and persecuted those who did this on their own initiative. However, in the short period when discussion of the theme was allowed during the war and in the first postwar years, there appeared poems, novels, films, paintings, and a symphony about the execution of Jews at Babyn Yar. Many writers and artists who depicted the Babyn Yar massacre in their works were persecuted in the late 1940s through the early 1950s during the peak of state anti-Semitism in the Soviet Union, which was disguised as a struggle against bourgeois nationalism and cosmopolitanism. Babyn Yar became a dangerous topic, which might damage careers and even cause imprisonment for those who dared discuss it. Thus, the Soviets achieved total public silence about the Babyn Yar tragedy until the death of Stalin and Khruschev's Thaw.

6

BROKEN SILENCE OVER BABYN YAR

COMMEMORATION OF THE HOLOCAUST IN THE SOVIET UNION

Despite the general policy of the Soviet government toward Jews, the level of state and popular anti-Semitism varied in the Soviet republics, which affected the commemoration and memorialization of the Holocaust. Zvi Gitelman pointed out in his article "Soviet Reactions to the Holocaust" that historiography in the different Soviet republics treated the theme of the Holocaust quite differently.[1] For example, the *History of Ukraine*, published in Kyiv in 1982, did not mention Jews or the Holocaust even once, despite the large Jewish population of Ukraine. In other Soviet republics (Russia, Belorussia, Estonia, and Lithuania), publications on the Holocaust appeared periodically in the 1960s to the mid-1980s.[2]

Arkadi Zeltser wrote in his book *Unwelcome Memory: Holocaust Monuments in the Soviet Union* that "there were at least 733 cities, towns, or villages in the territory of the Soviet Union where, prior to 1991, Jews themselves established one or more monuments to those killed."[3] Holocaust monuments were usually built on the initiative of Jews and funded by the Jews themselves. Soviet authorities put some restrictions on the design and inscriptions of Holocaust monuments. However, these policies were not consistent. In some places, the authorities allowed inscriptions in Yiddish, while in others, inscriptions could only be in Russian, or the official languages of the Soviet republics. Some monument inscriptions mentioned Jews, others only recognized "peaceful Soviet citizens."

Zeltser wrote that the policies of local authorities toward memorialization of the Holocaust were inconsistent:

> Already in the first years after the war, Jews were refused permission to hold commemorative events or to establish monuments in several major cities, such as Odessa, Riga and Lvov. Concurrently, in other places like Vilnus, Minsk, Ternopol, and Stanislav, the Jews were granted permission to do so, if not at the site of the shooting or in the city itself, then at least at Jewish cemeteries.[4]

The level of popular anti-Semitism seems to have had a major impact on the decisions of local authorities regarding Holocaust memorialization. The main omission in scholarly discussions of the Holocaust commemoration and memorialization policy in the Soviet Union is that historians typically only discuss interactions between the Soviet authorities and Jews. Most scholars ignore the third side in the interaction—the local gentile population, who clearly expressed their attitude toward Jews and Holocaust commemoration and memorialization. In my opinion, the behavior of the local authorities was very consistent: They were afraid of irritating and antagonizing a significant part of the population by their decisions. If they implemented unpopular decisions, they might lose their positions, which was always the main fear of any Soviet official. To build a Holocaust monument would be a very unpopular decision in many places with a high level of anti-Semitism.

Thus, Holocaust monuments were built with Jewish funding and initiative in the shtetls, where Jews made up a significant part of the population, and in some cities where popular anti-Semitism was not so strong. Meanwhile, no Holocaust monument was built in Kyiv, Odesa, Lviv, and other cities where there was a high level of popular anti-Semitism. Furthermore, if a Holocaust monument had been built in these places, it would likely have become a target for anti-Semites to deface and destroy. Officially, anti-Semitism did not exist in the Soviet Union. So, any official who would dare allow a Holocaust monument to be built in such a location would face not only the wrath of much of the gentile population, but would also be blamed by higher authorities for instigating anti-Semitic disturbances.

So, the behavior of the Soviet officials was not determined by emotional factors—whether they liked or disliked Jews—but by pragmatism: how to hold onto power and protect their own positions. The only exception to this rule was during the years of acute state anti-Semitism: 1948 to 1953, when any expression of Jewish national identity was forbidden and construction of a monument to Holocaust victims would not be allowed by any official. In other years, Soviet authorities could, on occasion, authorize the construction of monuments on Holocaust sites.

Holocaust memorialization was a problematic question for Soviet officials because they were under dual pressures from, on the one side, Jews, liberal intelligentsia, and Western countries and, on the other, a significant part of the Soviet gentile population. Jews and liberals wished to commemorate Holocaust victims and build monuments on Holocaust sites. However, in many cities and towns, the local gentile population had their own narrative of the Nazi occupation and usually pointed out that Jews were not the only victims at the massacre sites, since gentiles (prisoners of war, partisans, and members of the underground movement) were also killed there. They insisted that monuments built on such sites should primarily commemorate their fallen heroes. Due to anti-Semitism, many gentiles did not want to see any Jewish monuments in public places. So, the authorities often felt that it was better not to build anything, since any monument was likely to offend one or another segment of the population.

However, the Soviets could not completely ignore the opinion of Jews and the liberal intelligentsia, because it influenced their relations with Western countries. Babyn Yar became not only a symbol of the Holocaust, but also a symbol of the struggle for Holocaust commemoration and memorialization in the Soviet Union. Nevertheless, the authorities needed to consider the mood of much of the population. So, despite all the efforts of Jewish and non-Jewish liberal intelligentsia and Jewish activists, for thirty-five years Soviet authorities did not allow any monument to be built in Babyn Yar. In 1976 a monument was finally erected, which commemorated the suffering of all the Soviet people.

I will explain further why it took so long to build this monument and what roles popular and state anti-Semitism, and the Cold War, played in this process. The reluctance of the Soviet authorities to admit that most victims of the Babyn Yar massacre were Jews and commemorate their memory provoked resistance to Holocaust denial in the Soviet Union that had a strong impact on the memorialization of the site.

THE 1945 BABYN YAR MONUMENT PROJECT

Ukrainian Soviet authorities initially supported building a memorial at Babyn Yar. On March 13, 1945, the Ukrainian government and the Central Committee of the Communist Party of Ukraine decided to build a memorial at the site to be dedicated to "140,000 Kyivans killed by the Nazis."[5] The Jewish victims were not mentioned in the government resolution. In 1946, when Kyiv was still in ruins, the government resolved to provide 2.3 million rubles for this purpose.[6] A model of the monument was created in 1945 by the chief architect of Kyiv, Aleksandr Vlasov, and sculptor Iosif Kruglov, which was envisaged as a black pyramid with white bas-reliefs and two sculptures at the entrance.[7]

On April 4, 1945, *Pravda* published an article, "Pamiatnik pogibshim v Bab'em Yaru" (A monument to the victims of Babyn Yar), by its Kyiv correspondent, whose name was not mentioned:

> Babyn Yar is known throughout the World. Here, at the hands of Hitler's henchman, many tens of thousands of Kyiv residents died a martyr's death. By the decision of the government of the Ukrainian SSR, a monument to the victims of the German barbarians will be erected at Babyn Yar. The design of the monument, developed by architect A. Vlasov, was adopted. The monument will be a prism eleven meters high, lined with polished labradorite.[8] An act of the Extraordinary State Commission on the atrocities of the German occupiers will be engraved on the surface of the monument. A bas-relief made of white marble depicts a mother holding a dead child in her arms. There will be a museum in the basement of the monument. At the entrance, there will be two granite figures holding an eternal flame [figures 6.1 and 6.2].[9]

Figure 6.1 *Babyn Yar Monument* model by Kyiv city architect A. Vlasov and sculptor E. Kruglov, 1945. (Photo from the Central State Archives of the Supreme Bodies of Power and Government of Ukraine [TsDAVO U].)

Figure 6.2 *Babyn Yar Monument* model detail, 1945. (Photo from the Central State Archives of the Supreme Bodies of Power and Government of Ukraine [TsDAVO U].)

Pavel Polian wrote that the image of the mother with a child on the monument indicated the nationality of the majority of the Babyn Yar victims.[10] The article by M. Aizenshtadt, "A denkmol in Babi Yar" (A monument at Babyn Yar), was published on July 7, 1945, in the Yiddish newspaper *Einikait* (Unity) about the planned construction of a memorial to Babyn Yar victims. Aizenshtadt wrote that the monument would be devoted "to 140 thousand residents of Kyiv, mainly Jews—women, old people and children."[11]

However, what Jews considered as an appropriate image for the Babyn Yar monument irritated anti-Semites. The Ukrainian Ministry of Culture denounced the project for its "unimpressive character" and "lack of compositional and ideological direction."[12] Even the personal friendship of the architect, Vlasov, with the First Secretary of the Communist Party of Ukraine, Nikita Khrushchev, could not protect his project from the wrath of officials from the Ukrainian Ministry of Culture.[13] All of Vlasov's other projects were successfully built in Kyiv, among them the reconstruction of the main street of Kyiv, Khreshchatyk, ruined during the war. Stalin recalled Khrushchev to Moscow in December 1949. Soon thereafter, Khrushchev invited Vlasov to Moscow and appointed him chief architect of the Soviet capital in 1950, a post he held until 1955. Vlasov was president of the Academy of Architecture of the Soviet Union in 1955–56 and was awarded Soviet and international prizes for his works.[14]

So, presumably, the problem was not in the "poor" design of Vlasov's monument for Babyn Yar, but rather in the reluctance of the Ukrainian authorities to construct any monument there at all, which they cloaked in their criticism of the design of the monument. This same excuse was used to prevent construction of any monument in Babyn Yar for over thirty years. Thus, in 1959, the Ukrainian authorities claimed that no monument had been built because of the dissatisfaction of the Ministry of Culture of Ukraine with Vlasov's design and the lack of money for its construction.[15] However, these explanations are inadequate.

The absence of funding could have been an issue in the initial postwar years when Kyiv and many other cities and towns of Ukraine were in ruins. But by the 1950s, the economy had recovered from the war and the authorities, if they had wished, could have found funds for construction of a monument in Babyn Yar. In the 1950s, several other monuments to the heroes of World War II were built in Kyiv. Regarding the monument's appearance, if the Ministry of Culture of Ukraine did not like the original monument project, they could have invited other sculptors and architects and organized a design competition for the memorial. But for a long time local authorities resisted the very idea of building any monument in Babyn Yar. The actual reason was the rise of popular and state anti-Semitism in Kyiv and the Soviet Union in the postwar years.

Considering the evident anti-Semitic mood of much of the Kyiv population, it is easy to see why the local authorities felt the need to postpone construction of a monument in Babyn Yar. If a Jewish memorial had been erected in Kyiv in the postwar years, it might have provoked a new explosion of anti-Semitic violence in the city, and the wrath of anti-Semites could have turned against the authorities who allowed construction of the monument. Khrushchev allegedly said: "We are in Ukraine, and it is not in our interest that Ukrainians should associate the return of Soviet power with the return of the Jews."[16]

Ukrainian Jews who survived the war returned home from the front and from evacuation. But it seems that the local authorities did not want to be associated either with the returning Jews, or with the commemoration of the Holocaust victims. More Ukrainian Jews perished during World War II than survived. Alexander Kruglov wrote: "In mid-1941, some 2.7 million Jews lived in the territory of what is today the independent state of Ukraine.... Between 1941 and 1945, more than 1.6 million of them perished at the hands of the Nazis and their accomplices."[17]

However, the surviving Jews received very little compassion from the local non-Jewish population and authorities. To inflict even more pain on the Holocaust survivors, anti-Semites vandalized the mass graves of Jews in many places, turning them into pastures and cesspits.[18] Some even tried to enrich themselves from the accounts of executed Jews. The Russian writer Victor Nekrasov recalled that in the postwar years, "some marginal people crawled on the bottom of Babyn Yar searching for either diamonds or gold tooth crowns."[19]

REVIVAL OF THE BABYN YAR MONUMENT IDEA

During the anticosmopolitan campaign in the Soviet Union (the late 1940s to 1953), all discussion about building a monument in Babyn Yar ceased. These were the years of the most acute state anti-Semitism, when discussion of any Jewish topic could not only ruin the careers of its participants but might even cost them their lives. With the death of Stalin and the subsequent limited liberalization known as Khrushchev's Thaw, Kyivan Jews and liberal gentiles appealed again to the authorities to build a monument in Babyn Yar. Ehrenburg "worked hardest to promote this idea."[20] He sent a letter to Khrushchev asking that a monument be built in Babyn Yar.[21] But Khrushchev replied, "I advise you not to interfere in matters that do not concern you. You had better keep to writing good novels."[22]

Not only Soviet Jews, but also Jews in Israel attempted to memorialize the Babyn Yar tragedy. In 1957, the first chair of Yad Vashem (the World Holocaust Remembrance Center), Professor Ben-Zion Dinur, sent a letter to the Kyiv Jewish Religious Community asking them to send a bag of ashes from Babyn Yar to Yad Vashem.[23] The Yad Vashem Museum and Memorial Complex, which were established in 1953, moved to the Mount of Remembrance (Har ha-Zikaron) in 1957.[24] Professor Dinur, who in his youth lived in Kyiv, wanted to bury ashes from Babyn Yar at the memorial.

The Kyiv Jewish Religious Community forwarded the letter from Professor Dinur to the Soviet authorities. The Ministry of Foreign Affairs of the USSR decided:

> It is advisable to leave the request of Professor Dinur from Israel unanswered.
>
> If representatives of the Jewish Religious Community ask for clarification, it can be answered that the buried Jews, victims of fascist terror, were Soviet citizens and that Soviet organizations object to sending their ashes abroad.[25]

By the 1950s, the Soviet authorities had a new plan for Babyn Yar. They did not plan to build a Holocaust monument there, but instead a monument to the "victims of Fascism" and turn the rest of the ravine into a park and residential district. They also planned to lay a road through the ravine to downtown Kyiv. For this purpose, the Kyiv

Figure 6.3 Babyn Yar in 1959. (Photo by Victor Nekrasov. Source: https://nekrassov-viktor.com/books/nekrasov-articles-ob-antisemitizme/.)

City Council ordered in the 1950s that the Babyn Yar ravine be filled by pumping in liquid mud waste from nearby brick factories, and then building a road through it between the Lukianivsky and Kurenivsky districts (figure 6.3).[26]

Jewish activists and liberal intelligentsia strongly objected to the decision of the authorities to build a road and park at Babyn Yar. The Jewish poet Lev Ozerov, who prepared the chapter "Babyn Yar" for *The Black Book*, proposed to *Literaturnaia gazeta* (Literary gazette) in the late 1950s that he would "write about the need for proper care of the former killing site, including a memorial. Sergei Smirnov, the newspaper editor, approved, but then reneged: Ozerov was unsuitable, he told him, 'for a certain reason that we can guess.'"[27] Presumably, his Jewishness was the unmentionable reason why Ozerov was unsuitable to write about memorialization of the Babyn Yar massacre. If Ozerov wrote an article about Babyn Yar, he would certainly write about the Jewish victims. This was unacceptable to the officials.

The Soviet authorities, who were considering building a monument "to the victims of Fascism" in Babyn Yar, liked to stage "people's initiatives" to show that everything was done by the people's will. In this case, the initiative should belong to a non-Jewish author who would not mention Jews in his publication and who would follow the official concept of the universal suffering of the Soviet people. Karel Berkhoff wrote that the officials asked "several non-Jewish Ukrainian writers" to prepare an article about the need to memorialize the Babyn Yar massacre, but they all declined the offer.[28]

Victor Nekrasov wrote his essay "Pochemu eto ne sdelano?" (Why isn't this done) on his own initiative. His essay was published on October 10, 1959, in *Literaturnaia gazeta* under the rubric "A Writer Proposes." Nekrasov was a veteran of the Second World War and a well-known author. His autobiographical book *V okopakh Stalingrada* (In the trenches of Stalingrad, 1946) was one of the first honest war novels in Soviet literature. His book described the war and the battle of Stalingrad without romanticism, as difficult and dangerous work, where unnecessary risks taken by commanders cost many soldiers' lives. The novel was published in the journal *Znamia* (Banner) and received a Stalin Prize.[29]

Nekrasov was the first who began to talk publicly against the authorities' plan to turn Babyn Yar into a park and who demanded that a monument be built there to the victims of the massacre. Among Victor's numerous friends were many Jews. Vika (as Nekrasov was called by his friends) initiated his friendship with Jews during the years of the most acute state anti-Semitism in the Soviet Union, during the anticosmopolitan campaign in the late 1940s to the early 1950s.

The well-known Kyivan architect Avraam (Ava) Miletsky recalled how his friendship with Nekrasov began. In the beginning of the 1950s, Miletsky, a Jew, was expelled from work on the Hotel Moscow project, and he was not sure if he would ever again be allowed to work as an architect. At this difficult time, Nekrasov came to his apartment to introduce himself. They talked all night about the amorality of current events, the shame of anti-Semitism, about other people's and Miletsky's problems. Miletsky wrote that this was the start of their long and close friendship.[30] Nekrasov inherited his Judeophilia from his mother, Zinaida Nikolaevna. Victor and his mother had many Jewish friends who perished at Babyn Yar. So, they took quite personally everything that was going on with the Babyn Yar massacre commemoration.

Nekrasov wrote in his essay that all Kyivans had lost either relatives, friends, or acquaintances in Babyn Yar. Nekrasov said that he had visited the memorial to the victims of the Nazi concentration camp at Buchenwald. He asked in his article why there was no memorial to the victims of the Nazi regime at Babyn Yar.[31] Nekrasov protested in his essay against the plan of the Ukrainian Soviet authorities to fill in the ravine with mud and build a park and a stadium there. Nekrasov wrote that he heard about this plan at the Architecture Administration and considered it to be a horrible sacrilege of a mass grave:

> Is that possible? Who could think of this—to fill a ravine thirty meters deep and to sport and play soccer on the site of an enormous tragedy. No, this cannot be allowed. When a person dies, he is buried, and a monument is placed on his grave. Is this respect not deserved by the 195 thousand Kyivans, who were brutally killed at Babyn Yar, at Syrets and Darnitsa [concentration camps], at Kirillovsky [Psychiatric] Hospital and Lukianovsky Cemetery?[32]

Nekrasov's essay did not mention Jews but talked about Kyivans and "peaceful citizens" who were killed by the Nazis at Babyn Yar. Such an omission could not have been accidental. Nekrasov always had many Jewish friends and kept a connection with them, and helped them, throughout the worst years of the anticosmopolitan campaign when this was quite dangerous. So, either censorship did not allow Nekrasov to mention Jews, or this was self-censorship, because he understood that otherwise his essay might not be published. Nekrasov's essay also raised another painful problem: For a long time the Soviet authorities did not erect any monuments to commemorate not only murdered Jews, but also the executed prisoners of the Syrets and Darnitsa concentration camps and the patients of the Kyrylivsky [Psychiatric] Hospital. Soviet officials considered only perished heroes of the war worthy of memorialization, but not Jews, Roma, prisoners of the war, or the mentally ill.

Nekrasov's essay was published in a major Soviet newspaper and caught the attention of many Kyivans. So, Kyiv authorities felt obliged to respond to Nekrasov. Their two letters were published in the same periodical. The Kyiv authorities promised in their letters that "a park should be laid out with a monument [to the victims of Fascism] in the center"[33] at Babyn Yar. But the authorities refused to preserve "the ravine as it is," claiming that Babyn Yar was part of a new residential district and that "modern multistoried residential blocks with all conveniences are being built there."[34] So, Nekrasov's article did not prevent the flooding of the Babyn Yar ravine with mud, and consequently, two years later the ravine became the site of a new calamity.

THE KURENIVSKA TRAGEDY

On March 13, 1961, the poorly built dam holding back the mud at Babyn Yar collapsed and a forty-five-foot-high mud wave flowed into the city. Official records show that 150 people in the Kurenivsky district were killed (rumors claimed 1,500 perished); 68 houses and 13 public buildings were destroyed (figure 6.4).[35] Sergei Tiktin, who visited the Kurenivsky district soon after the flood, wrote that some houses were destroyed, others covered by sand up to the second and third floors.

From a phone booth, rescuers pulled out an almost suffocated young man. His first question was "Has Moscow survived?"

> People were evacuated by military helicopters from the top floors of the damaged houses. The soldiers searched for survivors in the rooms. They rescued an old lady from an attic, who screamed [in English] "Don't kill me, don't kill me!" She also took it as an atomic bombing, like the young man, and thought the rescuers in military uniforms were an American airborne assault unit.[36]

When Kyivans were notified by the authorities that it was a mud flood, many saw it as divine retribution for the attempt to erase all traces of the Babyn Yar massacre. Kyivan historian Alexander Anisimov called the Kurenivsky flood a "city-sized Day of Atonement."[37] Berkhoff wrote:

Figure 6.4 Mud flood from Babyn Yar into Kyiv, March 1961. (Unidentified photographer.)

According to KGB reports many Kievan Jews said the ravine should not have been filled; it was an uprising of the dead. A taxi driver said it was revenge of "Jewish blood" for the leveling of Babi Yar. There was anti-Semitic talk along the lines of "At Babi Yar the kike blood began to boil, the kikes are rising." Many talked about an old woman who reportedly screamed in a streetcar that passed the site, "The Jews did this, they are avenging us!"[38]

Thus, whether local gentiles expressed compassion or hatred toward Jews, the Kurenivsky tragedy again directed public attention toward Babyn Yar.

YEVGENY YEVTUSHENKO'S POEM "BABI YAR"

Russian poet Yevgeny Yevtushenko visited Kyiv in August 1961, a few months after the Kurenivsky disaster. Kyivan writer Anatoly Kuznetsov had shared with Yevtushenko his memories about the Babyn Yar massacre and brought the poet to the site. The poet was shocked by what he saw and learned. Yevtushenko recalls, "I anticipated of course that there would be at least some monument—but there was nothing! And suddenly I saw trucks dumping into the [Babyn Yar] ravine garbage—pressed garbage, layer over layer.... It stank terribly, awfully."[39]

That same night, Yevtushenko wrote his renowned poem "Babi Yar." The poem began with the line: "No monument stands over Babi Yar." Yevtushenko told the writer Solomon Volkov that he wrote poetry in two cases: when something really hurt his feelings or from shame. In this case, these emotions overlapped. The next day, Yevtushenko read his poem at a literary evening in Kyiv.[40] When Yevtushenko returned to Moscow, he published "Babi Yar" in *Literaturnaia Gazeta* on September 19, 1961.

Publication of Yevtushenko's poem "Babi Yar" in 1961 had an explosive effect, because it describes the persecution and extermination of Jews, which had been a forbidden topic in the Soviet Union. Publication of Yevtushenko's poem in the popular newspaper *Literaturnaia Gazeta*, which had hundreds of thousands of subscribers, helped widely disseminate knowledge about the Babyn Yar massacre. The poem stirred up a heated debate in the Soviet press. While liberal intellectuals and Jews greeted publication of the poem, conservative and anti-Semitic critics accused Yevtushenko of berating Russians by publishing a poem about Jews, anti-Semitism, and the Babyn Yar massacre. William Korey wrote:

> The storm of criticism that followed the poem's appearance was not unexpected. Five days after "Babi Yar" was published, *Literaturnaia zhizn'* [Literary life], the journal of the Writers' Union of the Russian Soviet Federated Socialist Republic, carried a response in the form of a poem by another Soviet writer, Aleksei Markov, which questioned Yevtushenko's patriotism. "What sort of real Russian are you [when you forgot about your own people]?" asked Markov. By referring to Jewish martyrdom at Babyn Yar and to Russian anti-Semitism, Yevtushenko had attempted to defile (with a "pygmy's spittle") "Russian crew-cut lads" who fell in battle against the Nazis.[41]

Another Soviet critic, Dmitri Starikov, published an article in which he "challenged the view that Babi Yar represented the martyrdom of Jewry."[42] Liberal Soviet writers and poets Ilya Ehrenburg, Konstantin Simonov, Samuil Marshak, and singer Leonid Utesov wrote responses to Yevtushenko's critics, accusing them of anti-Semitism.[43] During the heated public debate about the poem "Babi Yar," Soviet composer Dmitri Shostakovich called Yevtushenko and asked his permission to write a choral symphony using the text of the poem "Babi Yar" and his other poems.[44] Shostakovich's *Thirteenth Symphony*, subtitled *Babi Yar*, with lyrics adapted from Yevtushenko's poems, was first performed in Moscow on December 18, 1962 (figure 6.5).[45]

Trying to calm down the uproar among Soviet intellectuals about Yevtushenko's poem, Communist Party leaders called a meeting "of several hundred intellectuals" in Moscow on December 17, 1962.[46] The chair of the Ideological Department of the Central Committee of the Communist Party, Leonid Ilichev, said that Yevtushenko's

Figure 6.5 Book cover: Yevgeny Yevtushenko, *The Most Famous Symphony of the 20th Century: Dmitri Shostakovich Symphony #13*. (Courtesy of Yevgeny Yevtushenko.)

poem "Babi Yar," which denounces anti-Semitism, "provoked the opposite reaction." Ilichev asked, "Is it appropriate in the situation of our country, which lost twenty million Soviet lives [during World War II],[47] to raise the question [about anti-Semitism]?"[48]

Khrushchev then presented his view of Yevtushenko's poem at the meeting. He said:

> This is a very important question of the struggle against anti-Semitism.... I grew up in Donbas and saw a Jewish pogrom in Yuzovka [now Donetsk] in my childhood, and can tell you that most of the miners, even the miners, were against this pogrom.... There is the poem *Babi Yar*. I worked in Ukraine and visited this Babyn Yar. Many people perished there. But, comrades, comrade Yevtushenko, not only Jews perished there, but others also perished there. Hitler killed Jews. He killed Romas also, next in turn was the extermination of Slavs, he exterminated Slavs also. And if

we make an arithmetic calculation, of which people were exterminated more Jews or Slavs, then those who speak about anti-Semitism will see, that the Nazis exterminated more Slavs than Jews. This is true. Why is it necessary to emphasize [the Jews] and divide [the people]? What goals pursue people, who raise this question? I consider it incorrect.[49]

Khrushchev thus expressed the official Soviet view on the commemoration of World War II and its victims, which did not permit any discussion of the Holocaust. Although the Nazis killed more Slavs than Jews, none of the national groups lost a higher percentage than Jews: two-thirds of European Jews perished in the Holocaust. Only Jews and Romas were totally exterminated by the Nazis for their ethnicity. Soviet authorities knew this but were afraid of allowing "provocative" debates in society about anti-Semitism, Babyn Yar, and Holocaust commemoration. Thus, they tried to reconcile two opposing views of society by compromise.

In the atmosphere of Khrushchev's Thaw, the authorities did not forbid Yevtushenko's poem or Shostakovich's symphony *Babi Yar*. But they forced Yevtushenko to make two additions to his poem. At one point, a line was added: "Here, together with Russians and Ukrainians, lie Jews." A second insertion read: "I am proud of the Russia which stood in the path of the bandits."[50]

The heated public debate about Yevtushenko's poem shows why the Soviet authorities postponed for so long construction of a monument at Babyn Yar. They clearly understood that any monument erected there would provoke sharp criticism from one or another part of society. Nevertheless, Yevtushenko's poem "Babi Yar" broke the silence on the Holocaust theme in the Soviet Union. After the Yevtushenko poem and the Shostakovich symphony, the massacre of Jews at Babyn Yar and the absence of a monument there became well-known to the Soviet public and the authorities could no longer ignore public opinion.[51]

ANATOLY KUZNETSOV'S "BABI YAR" AND THE QUEST FOR A MONUMENT

Five years later, Soviet writer Anatoly Kuznetsov (1929–79) described the Holocaust of Jews in Kyiv in his book *Babi Yar: roman-dokument* (*Babi Yar: A Document in the Form of a Novel*). As a teenager, Kuznetsov was an eyewitness of the Nazi occupation of Kyiv and the Babyn Yar massacre (figure 6.6).[52] His book was originally published in a censored form, in 1966, in the popular Soviet journal *Iunost'* (Youth).[53] Censors cut roughly a quarter of the original text. They deleted discussion about the Holodomor, Stalin's repression, and any comparison between the Soviet and Nazi totalitarian regimes. The censored version of Kuznetsov's novel was praised by liberals and severely criticized by chauvinistic Soviet literary circles.[54] In 1969, Kuznetsov defected to the United Kingdom. He smuggled abroad a microfilm containing the uncensored text of his novel. Kuznetsov's uncensored novel *Babi Yar* was published in the West under the pseudonym A. Anatoli.[55] Korey wrote:

> The open discussion of Kuznetsov's *Babi Yar* [which took place before Kuznetsov's defection abroad] was accompanied by related developments which suggested that strong pressures from the liberal intelligentsia for a memorial to the victims of Babi Yar were having some impact on the political authorities.[56]

Pressure on Soviet officials also came from abroad. Foreign tourists who visited Kyiv in the 1950s to the first half of the 1970s often asked Ukrainian authorities many questions about the absence of a monument at Babyn Yar.[57] Usually, the local officials did not have any clear answer and were in a rather awkward situation. To avoid the unwanted questions, the Soviet Ukrainian authorities issued an order that Intourist[58] guides should not take foreign visitors to Babyn Yar. However, foreign tourists did not know, or care, about this prohibition and attempted to visit Babyn Yar on their own.

Figure 6.6 Anatoly Kuznetsov, author of *Babi Yar: A Document in the Form of a Novel*, 1966. (Unidentified photographer.)

American journalist, writer, political activist, and Holocaust survivor Elie Wiesel, who traveled to the Soviet Union in fall 1965, could not understand why the tourist agency and local Jews ignored his request to take him to Babyn Yar. Finally, Wiesel took a taxi and asked the driver to take him to Babyn Yar. However, the taxi driver cheated him and brought him to the wrong spot. Wiesel said that he was disappointed only for a minute.

> Against his wishes the driver had shown me something that I had unconsciously been aware of for some time. Thanks to him and to his deceit, I was finally able to understand that Babi Yar is not a geographical location. Babi Yar is not in Kiev, no. Babi Yar is Kiev. It is the entire Ukraine. And that is all one needs to see there.[59]

During the official ceremony commemorating the eightieth anniversary of the Babyn Yar massacre (which I attended by invitation of the Babyn Yar Holocaust Memorial Center), U.S. secretary of state Antony Blinken shared a story about his stepfather Samuel Pisar's visit to Kyiv and Babyn Yar in 1971. Samuel Pisar (1929–2015) was a Polish American lawyer, writer, and Holocaust survivor. He came to Kyiv with a U.S. delegation, and members of the delegation asked the local authorities to show them Babyn Yar. But the Soviets, who willingly showed the Americans other World War II sites and monuments, refused to take them to Babyn Yar. The American delegation went there anyway, and so the local Ukrainian Soviet authorities tagged along. Only after this did a productive dialogue between the Soviets and Americans become possible, according to Pisar's memories.

Under pressure from public opinion in the Soviet Union and abroad, the Ministry of Culture of Ukraine called in 1965 for a "closed competition of projects for monuments in the memory of Soviet citizens and soldiers and officers of the Soviet Army—prisoners of the war, who perished during the Nazi occupation of Kyiv."[60] Jewish victims were not mentioned in the call for the competition, because the Holocaust remained a forbidden topic in the Soviet Union. About sixty models of monuments were shown at an exhibition in the Architect's House in Kyiv in December 1965. The exhibition was not widely announced; however, it attracted many Kyivan Jews, members of the gentile intelligentsia, as well as anti-Semites. The exhibition guest book contained not only supportive comments, but also insulting anti-Semitic slurs, so the authorities confiscated it.[61]

The most interesting projects were presented at the exhibition by the architects Iosif Karakis and Avraam Miletsky, together with sculptor Ada Rybachuk and her husband, architect Vladimir Mel'nichenko.[62] Karakis proposed that a memorial park be built over the Babyn Yar ravine. The seven spurs of the ravine would be connected by bridges. According to the concept of the architect, the Babyn Yar ground is a sacred place where nobody should walk. Red poppies would be planted on the bottom of the ravine or red gravel would lie there (figure 6.7).

Miletsky, whose mother and grandmother perished at Babyn Yar, proposed building a memorial complex at Babyn Yar, which would start with a granite block with the sign "Babyn Yar" in several languages and end with a retaining wall with seven artistically decorated spurs between them.[63] Sculptor Rybachuk and architect Mel'nychenko proposed that, inside the spurs of Babyn Yar, a monumental wall be built with bas-relief and steps down to an urn with the "ashes" of the killed (figure 6.8).[64] Both projects used the natural landscape of Babyn Yar, emphasizing and preserving it, showing respect for the sacred meaning of the place. The jury for the competition claimed that the seven spurs in the projects of Miletsky and Karakis represented a Jewish menorah, a symbol of the State of Israel. So, the projects were rejected by the jury as Zionist.[65] In

Figure 6.7 *Babyn Yar Monument* model by Iosif Karakis from the 1965 competition. (Unidentified photographer.)

Figure 6.8 *Babyn Yar Monument* model by Avraam Miletskii, Ada Rybachuk, and Vladimir Mel'nychenko from the 1965 competition. (Unidentified photographer.)

addition, the projects for memorial complexes by Karakis and Miletsky with Rybachuk and Mel'nichenko were both conceived in an abstract style, which was at odds with the officially sanctioned socialist realism artistic style in the Soviet Union.

Many other projects were submitted for the competition of 1965, but none of them satisfied the jury. The jury did not want a Babyn Yar monument that recalled the tragedy of Kyivan Jews. The daughter of the architect Karakis, Irma, also an architect, was present at the public discussion of the competition projects. She recalled that the discussion was marked by both anti-Semitic speeches written in advance and by speeches of the designers of the memorial projects and writers, the majority of whom were Jewish. Irma recalled that Victor Nekrasov gave a brilliant speech about the memorialization of the victims of Babyn Yar. Then the renowned film director Sergei Paradzhanov called for a minute of silence in the memory of the Babyn Yar victims. In the silence that lasted over a minute, the weeping of the Babyn Yar victims' relatives was heard.[66]

A second competition was announced under the title "The Road: Death and Rebirth." The Union of Architects chose as the competition winner a socialist-style project depicting a man carrying a banner, which they thought would gain the support of the authorities. This was sent for approval to the First Secretary of the Central Committee of Communist Party of Ukraine, Petro Shelest, who rejected it saying, "I think this is not for Babyn Yar."[67]

UNAUTHORIZED MEETINGS AT BABYN YAR

Thus, the Holocaust site at Babyn Yar remained without a monument. Khrushchev's Thaw ended the pervasive fear of repression and awoke public initiative. The works of Nekrasov, Yevtushenko, and Kuznetsov raised awareness about the Babyn Yar massacre and the absence of a monument to its victims. Thus, Jewish activists and liberal intelligentsia decided to take the initiative into their own hands. They organized two unauthorized commemoration meetings at Babyn Yar in September 1966, devoted to the twenty-fifth anniversary of the tragedy. Jewish activist Emanuel (Amik) Diamant recalled that a group of Jewish youth organized the first commemoration meeting on September 24, 1966, on the day of the twenty-fifth anniversary of the Babyn Yar massacre, according to the Jewish calendar. The meeting took place at the entrance of the Jewish cemetery next to Babyn Yar at 5 p.m. Diamant recalled: "We announced to everybody to whom we could talk, that at the scheduled time we will gather at the entrance to the old Jewish cemetery [near Babyn Yar] and asked everybody to join us."[68] About fifty to sixty people came to the entrance to the cemetery. Jewish activists hung a large banner on the wall of the cemetery with the inscription "Babyn Yar, September 1941–1966. Remember the 6 million" in Russian and Hebrew.[69] "This banner was hung on a wall facing a major road where passengers on buses and trolleys could easily read the text and see what was going on."⁷⁰

But the Jewish activists did not know what they should do next. They had not discussed this before the meeting and did not want to improvise. Suddenly, some unknown person came to them from the crowd and introduced himself: "I am Nekrasov." Diamant said that they did not need an explanation about who Victor Nekrasov was. Nekrasov was probably the most prominent Kyivan writer and public figure of the time. His literary and publicist works (including his essay "Pochemu eto ne sdelano?" about the absence of a monument at Babyn Yar) were well known to Kyivans, as well as his Judeophile position. However, the Jewish activists did not know what Nekrasov looked like and were afraid of a provocation. Nekrasov asked Diamant if he prepared the banner. Diamant replied, "No." Nekrasov asked him if he was afraid. Diamant replied, "Yes." Nekrasov tried to talk to the other Jewish activists, but the conversation did not go well, because they were afraid to talk to him. Then, Nekrasov gave a note with his phone number to Diamant and asked him to call (figure 6.9). The next day, Diamant called Nekrasov and they agreed to organize another meeting at Babyn Yar on September 29, 1966, at 5 p.m. Nekrasov was concerned about the Jewish activists, who silently stood by the banner during the meeting on September 24. He told Diamant that actions should be developed around a "center of attention" and proposed that a

Figure 6.9 Victor Nekrasov at an unsanctioned meeting at Babyn Yar on September 24, 1966. (Photo from the archive of Emanuel [Amik] Diamant.)

monument be erected at Babyn Yar. Nekrasov said that there should be a monument, "at least temporary, even wooden or from plywood, but some monument."[71]

Since 1959 Nekrasov had argued in his publications and speeches about the need for a monument at Babyn Yar. He watched the ongoing reluctance of the authorities to build it, so he hoped that perhaps it could be done by public initiative. In this manner, Jewish activists had erected a monument to "Victims of Fascism" in Rumbula, Latvia, in 1964, where the Nazis executed the Jews of the Riga ghetto in November and December 1941.[72]

Nekrasov proposed that his friends, the sculptors Ada Rybachuk and Volodymyr Mel'nychenko, could make a plywood monument. Rybachuk and Mel'nychenko had participated in the Babyn Yar monument competition in 1965, and Nekrasov hoped that they could prepare a plywood monument in a few days. Nekrasov asked Diamant to prepare the Yiddish inscription for the monument. Diamant appealed with this request to the Kyiv Yiddish writers Grigoriy (Hirsh) Polianker and Itsik Kipnis. Polianker refused to write the inscription. Kipnis agreed after long persuasion. Both Polianker and Kipnis had been arrested during the anticosmopolitan campaign in the late 1940s and early 1950s and spent several years in the gulag. Polianker "was intimidated to the end of his life."[73] But "Kipnis, who was also Diamant's uncle, agreed and wrote a text."[74] Diamant said that he delivered the Yiddish text and its translation in Russian and Ukrainian to Nekrasov. Meanwhile, Nekrasov, Diamant, and other Jewish activists prepared the meeting. "People passed to each other: 'Come to Babyn Yar on September 29. Nekrasov will be there.'" The name of Nekrasov was the appeal.[75]

Diamant recalled that the banner that they hung on the wall of the Jewish cemetery was there for three days and nobody removed it. "For three days the Shevchenko district residents could see and read it when they went to work and returned home." This gave the rumors about the meeting at Babyn Yar "a legitimate hue."[76]

The Jewish activists made sure that as many people as possible heard about the meeting at Babyn Yar. During Sukkot, on September 28, 1966, three young Jews came to the synagogue during the religious service and demanded that the members of the Religious Board[77] announce to Jews that they should come to the memorial meeting at Babyn Yar at 5 p.m. on September 29, a meeting devoted to the twenty-fifth anniversary of the massacre. The chair of the Kyiv Religious Community, Gendelman, spoke to the congregation in the synagogue on September 29, 1966. He said that the authorities did not allow any meeting at Babyn Yar and rumors about such a meeting were a provocation. Gendelman called upon the congregation not to go to Babyn Yar. Perhaps some Jews in the congregation followed Gendelman's advice and did not go to Babyn Yar. But on the next day, September 30, 1966, a "group of Jews" came to the synagogue and blamed Gendelman for intentionally misinforming them. V. Sukhonin (his position is not mentioned) reported to the secretary of the Kyiv City Committee of the

Communist Party of Ukraine, A. P. Botvin, on September 30, 1966, about the conflict between Gendelman and the Jewish congregation:

> Gendelman told the Jews that the synagogue should not participate in such events, because observant Jews should commemorate the dead according to the religious ritual in the synagogue, but not at a meeting. In response to Gendelman, Panakh called the leaders of the Jewish religious community, the enemies of the Jewish people.[78]

On the twenty-fifth anniversary of the Babyn Yar massacre on September 29, 1966, there was a large unauthorized meeting at Babyn Yar. Yohanan Petrovsky-Shtern wrote about the meeting:

> We do not know how many people gathered for the unauthorized rally that day. The KGB reported five hundred participants. Diamant gave a much higher figure, and Dziuba said that "all hills and mounds were covered by multiple and initially scattered small groups of people—thousands and thousands of them" [figure 6.10].[79]

According to the report of the chief of the KGB, there were many youths among the people who arrived for the meeting. Jewish youth who were born just before, during, or after the war could not know or remember those who perished at Babyn Yar. But the

Figure 6.10 Unsanctioned meeting at Babyn Yar on September 29, 1966.
(Photo from the archive of Emanuel [Amik] Diamant.)

Jewish youth who belonged to the Thaw generation refused to tolerate the absence of commemoration of the Holocaust victims and the lack of a monument at Babyn Yar.

The chair of the Ukrainian KGB wrote in his report, "People who gathered for the meeting waited for the arrival of the city authorities until 5:30 pm, but none of the officials arrived, so the people began their speeches."[80] If the KGB report is correct and people really waited for the city authorities to come to the meeting, it was perhaps naïve to believe that the authorities would participate in a commemoration meeting for the Holocaust victims.

The chair of the Ukrainian KGB reported:

> The speakers and the people who were present at the meeting, along with the commemoration of those who perished there, expressed their dissatisfaction due to the officials not arriving to the meeting, about the absence of a monument and presumably the presence of anti-Semitism in the country, which appeared as the inequality of Jews with other nations and the absence of Jewish schools, theaters, periodicals, etc.
>
> By the end of the meeting, Nekrasov, Dziuba and Antonenko-Davidovich arrived, who got the attention of the audience to the need to struggle with anti-Semitism and unite the efforts of Ukrainian and Jewish people, about saving their own national culture. Their speeches were well received by the audience. Especially, the Jewish youth got excited and expressed a nationalist mood.[81]

The meeting was addressed by Russian and Ukrainian writers Victor Nekrasov, Vladimir Voinovich, and Ivan Dziuba. They talked about the tragedy of the Jewish people and the need to struggle against anti-Semitism, while their friends, the director from the Kyiv documentary studio Ukrkinokhronika, Rafail Nakhmanovich, and the main editor of the studio, Gelii Snegirev, filmed the event. This initiative was swiftly punished by the authorities. According to the memoirs of Ada Rybachuk and Vladimir Mel'nychenko, the police arrived at the meeting, recorded car license plate numbers, made a list of the people who participated in the meeting, stopped the documentary shooting, and dispersed the crowd.[82] The film was confiscated; the director, Nakhmanovich, was fired; and Snegirev was demoted. Later, Snegirev was expelled from the Union of Ukrainian Writers and the Union of Cinematographers, and arrested for his dissident activities.[83] Nekrasov was expelled from the Union of Soviet Writers and later forced to emigrate from the Soviet Union. Several years later, Dziuba was arrested and received five years in concentration camps.[84]

Along with repression of people who spoke at the unsanctioned meeting at Babyn Yar, the meeting had some positive consequences for memorialization of the Holocaust in Kyiv. The Soviet authorities could no longer ignore public opinion, so, two weeks after the meeting, they put a granite stone on the corner of Dorogozhitsky and

Figure 6.11 Official ceremony at the Babyn Yar Massacre stone marker, late 1960s–early 1970s. (Photo from the Central State CinePhotoPhono Archives of Ukraine [TsDKFFA U].)

Mel'nikova Streets with the inscription "On this site a monument will be erected for the victims of fascism during the German occupation of Kyiv, 1941–1943" (figure 6.11).[85]

Another consequence of the unsanctioned meeting at Babyn Yar in 1966 was that the Soviet authorities decided to take commemoration events at Babyn Yar under their control and keep them in the stream of Soviet ideology and propaganda. They declared September 29 (the day of the beginning of the massacre of Jews at Babyn Yar) as "The Day of the Memory of the Victims of German Fascism." On this date, the Soviets held official meetings at Babyn Yar, the scenario and speakers of which were approved in advance by the Central Committee of the Communist Party of Ukraine. At the official meetings, the secretary of the city and district committees of the Communist Party, veterans of World War II, and usually a few Jews loyal to the Soviet regime were invited as speakers. Nekrasov wrote that at such official meetings the speakers denounced "the fascist occupiers" and Zionism. The authorities put wreaths at the stone from the Kyiv Committee of the Communist Party of Ukraine, and from plants and factories of the city of Kyiv.[86] However, the hypocrisy of the Soviet official meetings at Babyn Yar was that they never mentioned the Holocaust nor that the vast majority of victims at Babyn Yar were Jews.

After the end of the official meeting, the common people could put flowers at the stone. Nekrasov mentioned that most people, especially the elderly, were allowed to bring flowers to the stone. The police reluctantly let young people approach the stone, scrutinized the inscriptions on their wreaths, and demanded removal of any text in Yiddish or Hebrew.[87] For such signs, some Jewish activists were jailed for fifteen days. Jewish activists recalled that the police did not allow them to come to the commemoration meetings at Babyn Yar. They were stopped by the police on their way; some of them were detained for ten to fifteen days.

Despite the repression, on every anniversary of the Babyn Yar massacre, people came there for memorial meetings. The most active participants were detained; others were chased away by the police. Thus, Jewish dissident Boris Kochubievsky was accused of "Zionist and bourgeois-nationalist propaganda" for his speech at Babyn Yar in 1968, where he emphasized that most of the victims who perished there were Jews.[88] Kochubievsky received three years in a concentration camp "for slander against the Soviet regime."[89]

> The trial—held ironically, in the same courthouse in which [Menahem Mendel] Beilis had been tried ... [in 1913] was replete, according to samizdat accounts, with numerous instances of anti-Semitism emanating from the bench, the prosecution, the guards, and the persons permitted by the authorities to attend.[90]

Kochubievsky's arrest did not scare the Jewish activists, who continued to organize Holocaust memorial events at Babyn Yar. The KGB reported that in the following years, not only Kyivan Jews, but also Jewish activists from Moscow and Riga participated in the unsanctioned Holocaust commemoration events. All the efforts of the officials to prevent or stop such unauthorized commemoration failed. Furthermore, the authorities compromised their reputation when suppression of the commemoration events at Babyn Yar brought about public confrontations of the officials with Jewish activists. The KGB got used to quietly detaining people one by one, but not publicly fighting with groups of people in front of the eyes of thousands of spectators.

Such a situation occurred during the commemoration events at Babyn Yar on September 29, 1969. Jewish activist Izrail Kleiner, who attended the meeting, recalled that the authorities gathered for their official meeting at Babyn Yar, where they talked about "Soviet citizens, who perished in the struggle with fascism and expressed gratitude to the Soviet Union, who rescued people from the fascist terror."[91] Four young people came to the meeting with two wreaths made from beautiful flowers. The wreaths were made in a very strange shape as equilateral triangles. The crowd split and allowed them to bring the wreaths forward to the memorial stone. Suddenly, they connected the wreaths. Thus, a Mogen David was publicly laid at the memorial stone.

The authorities were at first confused, but then gave the order to the KGB undercover agents, who were present at the meeting, to stop the "Zionist provocation."

The secret agents began to knock people to the ground, trying to get as many people as possible to fall on the wreath. While the agents knocked people down, they screamed heartrendingly, "Police! Help! Save! Hooligans!" Men tried to resist, women screamed from fear, about twenty people fell, including the four men, who brought the Mogen David.[92]

Then policemen ran in to "restore order." They grabbed the smashed wreath from the stone, and it fell apart. The KGB agents pointed out who the police should detain. But people at the meeting did not allow the policemen to arrest anyone. They encircled the people that the police were trying to catch and "several women demanded that the police should instead detain the secret agents, because they knocked people down. Others confirmed this."[93]

Perhaps stunned by the resistance of the crowd, the policemen retreated. Kleiner recalled the inflammatory atmosphere at the meeting:

The crowd exploded in a furious skirmish and shook from frantic Jewish gestures. The secret agents yelled that the Mogen David is a fascist symbol and that under this symbol our brothers were chased to the ovens of crematoriums. The people called the agents turncoats and even by some stronger words. It appeared that people were furious from anger, and they forgot about fear.[94]

The secret agents tried to calm down the crowd for fifteen minutes, but without any success. The people did not let them talk, and some of the agents seemed prepared to retreat. Kleiner reported that a Soviet boss (whose name he did not mention) who was present at the meeting tried to keep his equanimity the entire time, but it seems that he was also nervous. Suddenly, the boss gave the order: "Step aside! Let them lay the wreath!"

The crowd stepped back and the four men who originally brought the wreath put it at the memorial stone. The flowers on the wreath were smashed, the wreath itself partially fell apart, but according to Kleiner, in this way it looked even more symbolic. Kleiner noted that this was "the first time I saw a Mogen David which was laid openly, in front of the eyes of the authorities, and they could not do anything to immediately destroy it."[95]

Thus, the authorities "lost the battle" for Babyn Yar. Similar actions by Jewish activists continued at Babyn Yar throughout the 1970s until most of their participants immigrated to Israel. Hrynevych wrote: "Whereas between fifty and seventy Jewish activists gathered at the marker in 1968, in 1969 this number rose from three to four hundred and in 1970 from seven to eight hundred. The KGB monitored these gatherings closely, invariably calling them 'antisocial actions' and recording all these 'provocative acts' tirelessly."⁹⁶

Thus Jewish activists turned Babyn Yar into a place of public protest and resistance against the official Holocaust amnesia and anti-Semitism in the Soviet Union. Jewish refuseniks also protested at Babyn Yar about the denial of their right to immigrate to Israel. On August 1, 1971, "eleven Kyivan Jews, whose applications to immigrate to Israel were rejected without explanation, tried to organize a protest demonstration and hunger strike at Babyn Yar."⁹⁷ The Jewish refuseniks notified the authorities in advance about their planned action by sending a telegram to the Presidium of the Supreme Council of the Soviet Union. They were called to the Kyiv Office of Visas and Registration (OVIR), where the authorities tried to dissuade them from participation in the action and told them that their requests about leaving to Israel could be satisfied on the condition that "their entire families will leave the USSR, including their parents."⁹⁸ Such a condition was not always acceptable for refuseniks, because some families were split over the decision to go to Israel. Despite the warning of the authorities, the refuseniks came to Babyn Yar on August 1, 1971, and were detained by the police "for causing a public disturbance."⁹⁹

> During the trial that took place the following day militiamen testified that the "arrestees broke flowers and tramped the grass at the monument to the victims of fascism." The ten defendants were sentenced to fifteen days in jail, and one of them was fined ten rubles.¹⁰⁰

Such actions of Jewish refuseniks were monitored by the KGB on the highest level and reported to the Soviet government. Thus, the head of the KGB, Yuriy Andropov, reported on August 10, 1971, to the Central Committee of the Communist Party of the Soviet Union about the gathering of Zionists at Babyn Yar on August 1, 1971, and their detention by the police.¹⁰¹

On the thirtieth anniversary of the Babyn Yar massacre, September 29, 1971, delegations of Jews from Moscow, Leningrad, Sverdlovsk, Odesa, Riga, and several cities in Georgia arrived in Kyiv. The police were only able to prevent a Jewish delegation from Kharkiv from coming to Kyiv. The police forced the delegation to leave a train before its arrival in Kyiv.¹⁰² The *New York Times* wrote:

> About 2,500 Jews from all over the Soviet Union gathered in Kiev today [i.e., on September 29, 1971] to observe the 30th anniversary of the Babi Yar massacre....
> The visiting Jews waited through an official ceremony conducted by the Kiev city government and attended by about 500 non-Jewish citizens, the sources said.¹⁰³

When the official ceremony finished and the non-Jews left, the Jews laid about forty wreaths with signs reading "We never forgive!," "To the children, who were not allowed to grow up!," and other signs.[104]

The presence of Jews from different cities and republics of the Soviet Union at the thirtieth anniversary of the Babyn Yar massacre commemoration shows that Babyn Yar had become a symbol of the Holocaust for many Soviet Jews. Some of them dared to come to the Babyn Yar commemoration ceremony, despite the risk of being detained by the police and coming under KGB observation.

On September 7, 1972, "a group of Kyivan Jews attempted to lay a wreath and bouquets of flowers at Babyn Yar in honor of the eleven Israeli" Olympic team members "who were brutally murdered by terrorists two days earlier at the Munich Olympics." The police and KGB agents

> stopped the mourning ceremony, and the twenty-seven activists were arrested.... Two of [the] arrestees, Yurii Soroko and Zinovii Melamed, recalled afterwards that a KGB officer named Davydenko spoke to them in a threatening tone at the KGB Directorate of Kyiv oblast [region], declaring frankly that the "circumstances had changed." The KGB's hands were now "untied," and if opposition activities continued, the activists would receive lengthy sentences.[105]

The threat from the KGB officer proved to be real, because from 1972, the KGB more brutally suppressed any unsanctioned actions at Babyn Yar. Repression against dissidents became harsher in 1972 because the leadership of the Ukrainian Soviet Republic changed. The First Secretary of the Central Committee of the Communist Party of the Ukrainian Soviet Socialist Republic, Petro Shelest, was transferred to Moscow, and the more conservative Volodymyr Shcherbytsky was appointed in his place. In the same year, "Vitalii Fedorchuk, a stalwart Stalinist, became the chairman of the Ukrainian KGB. Under the auspices of Volodymyr Shcherbyts'kyi ... he initiated what historians referred to as a 'major pogrom.'"[106] Petrovsky-Shtern wrote that "dozens of dissidents and liberal-minded representatives of the Ukrainian intelligentsia" were detained including Ivan Dziuba.[107] Many Jewish dissidents were also arrested.

On September 29, 1972, the official meeting took place at Babyn Yar at the Memorial Stone at 6 p.m. The official meeting

> denounced "Israeli aggression against the Arabs" and mentioned the tragedy of Babyn Yar, where during the war "many Soviet people of various nationalities" were killed. When the official part ended, several hundred Jews tried to pay tribute to their families and friends, but this unofficial part of the ceremony was suddenly

taken in hands by security forces. Numerous militia detachments, stationed earlier on the sidewalk flanking the road leading to the commemorative marker [Memorial Stone], let through only people bearing wreaths decorated with black and red ribbons, barring access to individuals carrying anything decorated with white and blue ribbons and inscriptions written in Hebrew on the ground that "it is not clear what is written on them."[108]

At 7 p.m., the police "began shoving people brutally away from Babyn Yar" and turned off the electric lights at the commemoration site. By 8 p.m., the area was cleared of the people. "Eleven activists who had defied the Soviet government were detained by the militia and jailed for fifteen days on charges of 'violating public order.'"[109]

The brutality of the police and the arrests did not deter the Jewish activists, who continued to organize their Holocaust commemoration ceremonies at Babyn Yar. Considering their 1972 experience, the Jewish refuseniks covertly prepared their 1973 Holocaust commemoration ceremony at Babyn Yar. Genrietta Friedman recalled that they made all their preparations with great secrecy, so that the authorities would not find out about their plans. The refuseniks decided to commemorate the Babyn Yar massacre anniversary in a way that would "remind everybody about the tragic death of the Jews, which never will be forgotten."[110] Several days before the Babyn Yar massacre anniversary, the refuseniks ordered wreaths without signs. On the eve of the anniversary, Friedman wrote signs in blue paint on white ribbons in Hebrew and Russian. The signs said that the people mourn the Jews who perished at Babyn Yar. Friedman recalled:

> We delivered the wreaths to the yard closest to Babyn Yar and took them at the last moment: two men carried each wreath; they were followed by women with flowers.
>
> We passed the ravines where the execution [of Jews in 1941] took place, and many people joined us on the way. On the sides we were encircled by disguised policemen and KGB agents.
>
> When we reached the [memorial] stone, our procession looked like a demonstration.[111]

The police did not stop the procession, because there were already a few hundred people, and they carried the wreaths without any signs, which was not forbidden. But five steps from the stone, the refuseniks pulled the ribbons with signs from their pockets and quickly put them on the wreaths. The policemen were surprised, and it took them a moment to decide what they should do. Meanwhile, the refuseniks put the wreaths and flowers at the Memorial Stone and began to light the candles. Then police attacked the refuseniks, "pulled off the ribbons from the wreaths and trampled the flowers and the candles. But hundreds of people who were there saw it. And they will remember."[112]

While the Soviet authorities did not allow the Holocaust to be commemorated at Babyn Yar, the commemoration of Jewish victims of the massacre took on an international dimension. In 1973, the newspaper *Forward* reported about New York City officials' efforts to memorialize Babyn Yar:

> The city had proclaimed "10 commemorative days." ... City Hall Park was renamed "Babi Yar Park." The opening ceremony, organized by the Greater New York Conference for Soviet Jews, found Deputy Mayor Edward Morrison reading a proclamation on behalf of his boss.[113]

In 1974, the preparation of the Soviet authorities for the Babyn Yar massacre anniversary was reminiscent of the preparation for a major battle. The chair of the Ukrainian KGB, Fedorchuk, reported on September 21, 1974, to the First Secretary of the Central Committee of the CPU, Shcherbytsky, about the

> establishment of an operational headquarters under the supervision of the Vice Chairman of the KGB of the Ukrainian SSR and the Vice Minister of Internal Affairs, for the coordination of the measures of the KGB and MVD [Ministry of Internal Affairs] for prevention of possible hostile and antisocial actions of Jewish nationalists and Zionists on September 29 of this year.[114]

Preventive measures included

> establishment of operational–mobile groups of KGB agents, policemen and vigilantes who are supposed to take all necessary precautions to prevent the infiltration of Zionists to the memorial stone, who are intending to commit provocative actions. In case they attempt to make and deliver to the memorial stone wreaths with Zionists signs on the ribbons, they should be detained on the outskirts of Babyn Yar and delivered to the RO UVD [District Department of the Ministry of Internal Affairs, i.e., the police station] for their identification.[115]

The chair of the Ukrainian KGB, Fedorchuk, and the minister of internal affairs of the Ukrainian SSR, Ivan Golovchenko, informed Shcherbytsky on September 30, 1974, that the KGB took special actions to decrease the presence of foreigners at Babyn Yar on the massacre anniversary date. Fedorchuk wrote:

To prevent the presence of foreigners at Babyn Yar [on the anniversary date] and collection by them of tendentious information, the arrival time to Kyiv of a tourist group from the USA—members [of] the "Association of the District of Columbia Bar"—a total of 76 people, was changed through [the travel agency] Intourist; on the morning [of] September 29, they were sent to Lviv ahead of schedule on a bus with Austrian tourists, and other foreigners were taken under control....

The measures for prevention of planned provocative actions by Zionist extremists at Babyn Yar were carried out under the leadership of the Kyiv City Committee of the Communist Party of Ukraine.[116]

Thus all the might of the state machine was directed against a small group of people who just wanted to commemorate the Jews who perished at Babyn Yar, but the authorities once again failed to prevent the unsanctioned commemoration ceremony. Fedorchuk and Golovchenko reported to Shcherbytsky that despite all the efforts of the authorities, on September 29, 1974, a group of fourteen "Jewish extremists" (nine men and five women) brought to the memorial stone two wreaths, ribbons with Hebrew signs, Mogen Davids, and flowers. Some of these activists arrived from Moscow and Riga, others were local. To get the attention of people gathered at Babyn Yar, the Jewish activists wore black armbands, kipas, and yellow Mogen Davids made from paper attached to their clothes. The Jewish activists attempted to leave at the stone white ribbons with blue Russian and Hebrew signs reading "To the victims of Fascism" and "We won't forget. Jews from Riga and Moscow." They also attempted to leave at the memorial stone two metal Mogen Davids (half a meter each) and "several cardboard Zionist stars and a badge with the flag of the State of Israel."[117]

The police confiscated the Mogen Davids, the ribbons with Russian and Hebrew inscriptions, and other "Zionist symbols." The police also pushed away the "Moscow extremist Begun, who took pictures of the provocative actions of the Zionists."[118] But the police did not detain the Jewish activists at the site, as was planned in the KGB preventive measures.[119] Perhaps the authorities decided that it was inconvenient to arrest people in front of so many observers. Fedorchuk and Golovchenko wrote that when the "Jewish extremists" laid the wreaths at Babyn Yar there were 300 to 350 people from the "unorganized public," mostly elderly, who had arrived at the site on their own initiative. "During the day about 1,500 people came to the memorial stone to honor the memory of the victims of fascism and to lay flowers."[120]

On September 30, 1974, Fedorchuk sent a special message to Shcherbitsky that the Jewish activists who participated in the action at Babyn Yar wrote a letter to the United Nations, and one of them, Tzypin, took it to Moscow for transfer abroad through a foreign correspondent. The KGB did not get a copy of the letter but knew about its contents from one of their informers. According to Fedorchuk, the letter included roughly the following:

> We are a group of Jews, who wanted to commemorate the Jews, who perished at Babyn Yar 33 years ago. However the police, KGB members and vigilantes pulled off the ribbons from our wreaths and the kipas from our heads, by this they desecrated the memory of the perished.
> According to Tsypin, Zionists from the US, Great Britain, Canada and Israel were supposed to call to the "Moscow Jewish extremists" to receive information about Babyn Yar.[121]

It seems that the authorities were so nervous about the "provocative actions of Zionists" that they did not organize any official meeting at Babyn Yar on September 29, 1974, as they did in prior years. Perhaps they were also afraid of questions about the absence of a monument at Babyn Yar. However, the lack of an official meeting at Babyn Yar on September 29, 1974, raised many questions from the public. Fedorchuk and Golovchenko reported to Shcherbytsky that "many people were interested in the reasons for the cancelation of the [official] meeting [at Babyn Yar] and asked when it would take place."[122]

The next official ceremony at Babyn Yar was organized in July 1976, devoted to the opening of the Soviet monument. However, the construction of the monument at Babyn Yar (which will be discussed further) did not change the negative attitude of the authorities to the attempts by Jewish activists to commemorate the victims of the Holocaust at Babyn Yar. The KGB and police took more and more measures to suppress the unauthorized Jewish commemoration ceremonies at Babyn Yar. But, despite all the obstacles and repression, Jewish activists were able to continue their commemoration of the victims of the Holocaust at Babyn Yar. The German newspaper *Allgemeine Zeitung* wrote about this on October 5, 1976:

> Jewish activists from various cities of the Soviet Union were not allowed to participate in the meeting at Babyn Yar.... Anatoly Sharansky was removed from the train on his way to Kyiv, Mikhail Manger from Vinnytsia received the warning that if he went to Kyiv he would be arrested. However, twenty activists from different cities managed to break through and they arrived at the commemoration meeting.
> Refusenik from Kyiv, Itskhak Tsiferblit ... informed by phone the representatives of the New York Student Committee for Aid to Soviet Jews that about 300 Jews were present this year at the memorial meeting at Babyn Yar, and that they laid wreaths at the monument.[123]

Unable to prevent the unauthorized Holocaust commemoration events at Babyn Yar, the KGB attempted to discredit the Jewish activists who organized them. On September 27, 1977, the newspaper *Vecherniy Kiev* published an article, "Kukhnia antisovetchiny" (Anti-Soviet kitchen), "exposing the subversive activities of foreign Zionist centers inspiring anti-Soviet and antisocial actions of 'refuseniks.'"[124]

Soviet officials perhaps tried to persuade the public that there was no state anti-Semitism in the Soviet Union, so they involved some Jews in the official commemoration ceremonies at Babyn Yar. Fedorchuk reported to Shcherbytsky on September 28, 1977:

> A television program was prepared based on interviews taken from one of the eyewitnesses of the mass extermination of Soviet citizens by the Nazis at Babyn Yar, [Zakhar] Trubakov, and a former member of the commission to investigate the atrocities of the fascists, Buryachenko; laying flowers at the monument by the individual citizens of Jewish nationality and foreigners [was also shown].[125]

Fedorchuk wrote that despite the measures taken by the KGB, Kyiv Jewish activists Mizrukhina, Pargamannik, and Gertsberg "did not abandon their provocative intentions" to organize an unauthorized commemoration ceremony at Babyn Yar.

> On September 26 [1977], after visiting the City Council, they prepared a letter to the Central Committee of the CPSU and the Kyiv City Council containing slanderous fabrications about the infringement of their "national rights" and announcing that they would hold a one-day "hunger strike" in protest on September 29 [at Babyn Yar].[126]

Kyiv Jewish activists planned to participate in the commemoration events at Babyn Yar together with Moscow Jewish activists, who were supposed to arrive in Kyiv on September 28, 1977. Fedorchuk wrote to Shcherbytsky that the KGB took all necessary measures to prevent unauthorized commemoration events at Babyn Yar. The KGB established operational surveillance over Kyiv and Moscow Jewish activists and "took measures to prevent arrival to Kyiv of Moscow extremists." Whether the KGB succeeded in preventing an unauthorized Holocaust commemoration ceremony at Babyn Yar in 1977 is unknown. Such a ceremony is not mentioned in either the archived KGB documents or in the memoirs of Jewish activists. There is no information about official or unauthorized commemoration ceremonies at Babyn Yar in the following years. Hrynevych wrote: "Starting in 1977, official rallies were no longer held at Babyn Yar. The Soviet authorities clearly believed that the political potential of such events had been exhausted."[127]

Jewish activists from Kyiv, Moscow, Leningrad, and Odesa again tried to organize a commemoration ceremony on the fortieth anniversary of the Babyn Yar massacre in 1981. The KGB took "preventive measures" and threatened to arrest Jewish activists and deprive them of their emigration visas if they participated in unauthorized commemoration ceremonies at Babyn Yar. On September 24–27, 1981, the KGB arrested Kyiv Jewish activists and activists from Moscow, Leningrad, and Odesa, who arrived in Kyiv for participation in the Holocaust commemoration ceremony at Babyn Yar. Some of these activists received fifteen days' imprisonment for petty hooliganism; some were deported back to their cities. Thus, the Jewish activists from Odesa were detained near Babyn Yar and returned to the airport.

> But the young people returned [at Babyn Yar] and managed to lay flowers in the monument and recited the Kaddish. Later the militia drove them to the train station and waited until the train pulled away. On 27 September at least a hundred militiamen and "people in a plainclothes" were stationed near the monument to the victims of Babyn Yar. In addition four buses were sent to pick up the arrested "hooligans," and the militia and KGB men controlled all the streets leading to Babyn Yar.[128]

On September 29, 1981, the Soviets showed on TV a new propaganda documentary film, *Babyn Yar: Lessons of History*. "The author of the script ... Olexander Shlaien was dismissed from his job [on the film] for refusing to obey the party ideologists' orders that he introduce material aimed at 'unmasking Zionists.'" The director, Volodymyr Heorhienko, included the recommended materials "exposing" Zionists and on the "atrocities committed by the American military clique in Korea and China."[129] "An English version of the film, completed shortly afterwards, contained material on the 'role of Ukrainian policemen.'"[130]

There is no information available about Holocaust commemoration ceremonies at Babyn Yar in 1982–86. Perhaps the Jewish activists could not organize commemoration ceremonies at Babyn Yar after 1981 because of the intensified KGB repression. Also, many Jewish activists emigrated from the Soviet Union in the 1970s. Lucy S. Dawidowicz wrote that in 1971–81 "more than 250,000 Jews have left the Soviet Union."[131] The refuseniks who remained in Kyiv, Moscow, Leningrad, and other cities probably could not break through the KGB and police barriers at Babyn Yar.

THE BABI YAR MEMORIAL PARK IN DENVER

While Soviet Jews were not allowed to commemorate the Holocaust at Babyn Yar, the Babi Yar Memorial Park was opened in Denver, Colorado, on October 2, 1983.[132] The creation of the park with memorial stones took over a decade. "The idea to create a park emerged in the late 1960s and early 1970s."¹³³ "The nucleus of the idea came from the Colorado Committee of Concern for Soviet Jewry (CCCSJ); an organization formed to educate people about the plight of Soviet Jews," particularly refuseniks.¹³⁴ The initiative received support from "the local Jewish community, which included natives of Kyiv whose families were killed at Babyn Yar."¹³⁵ According to Babyn Yar survivor Batya Barg, who visited the Denver park in 1971, it is reminiscent of Babyn Yar in Kyiv.¹³⁶ Jessica Rapson pointed out:

> Both Yevtushenko and Kuznetsov wrote to support the endeavor, in an extension of their existing role in promoting awareness of Babi Yar on the international level. A separate committee, the Babi Yar Park Foundation was formed in 1970 to run the project.¹³⁷

The work on the Denver Babyn Yar memorial was slowed down when a "series of disagreements about the appropriate use of the space led to a rift between the CCCSJ and the newly formed Foundation."¹³⁸

> The idea that the park's landscape in its resemblance to Babi Yar, could bring visitors somehow "closer" to the tragic history of the original ravine, was implicated in the Park Foundation's rhetoric. Plans for landscaped features also included a "Forest that Remembers" and a "People Place," an amphitheater with a cylinder of earth from the original ravine at Babi Yar at its centre.¹³⁹

When Denver state senator John Bermingham visited Babyn Yar in the early 1970s, he scooped up "some soil into his bag to take back to Denver" and presented this soil to the Park Foundation.¹⁴⁰ However, when CCCSJ and the Park Foundation reached their agreement about the Denver Babyn Yar monument model and inscription and they were publicly announced,

> representatives from the local Ukrainian community rose in protest. There was no mention of the massacre of Ukrainians that took place at Babi Yar in 1942, they argued, which included the martyrdom of the nationalist poet Olena Teliha, among others. After several rounds of negotiations between the Babi Yar Foundation and a newly formed committee of Ukrainian Americans, the foundation agreed to change the monument's institutions to reflect the Ukrainian dimension of the killings at Babi Yar between 1941 and 1943. In return the Ukrainian group would contribute $25,000 to finish the memorial. Two massive, polished chunks of charcoal granite at the entrance to the Babi Yar Memorial in Denver now commemorate the "Two Hundred Thousand Victims Who Died [at] Babi Yar, Kiev, Ukraine, USSR. September 29, 1941–November 6, 1943. The Majority Jews with Ukrainians and Others."¹⁴¹

James Young wrote that the process of building the Babi Yar Memorial in Denver

> was occasionally so bruising and contentious that much of the Denver Jewish community grew alienated from the very site that was meant to unify them. In time, wounds may heal and the community may yet return to their Babi Yar Park, but as of this writing, the memorial seems all but forgotten by its community.[142]

Three decades after James Young's book was published in 1993, the Babi Yar Memorial Park continued to function. The Mizel Museum organized Babyn Yar massacre commemoration ceremonies and tribute concerts there. However, the attention of the American Jewish community and world Jewry shifted from the Denver Babi Yar Memorial Park to Babyn Yar in Kyiv when, during perestroika, commemoration ceremonies resumed and the authorities recognized that most of the victims of the Babyn Yar massacre were Jews.

BABYN YAR DURING PERESTROIKA

From 1987, the Soviet authorities did not ban public ceremonies at Babyn Yar anymore. On September 29, 1987, sixteen Jews from Moscow came to Kyiv to hold a memorial ceremony at Babyn Yar. At noon this group came to the monument.

> It was joined by the mostly elderly Jews who were there, the total number of Jews gathered was about 30. In addition, there were several dozen people present who did not look like Jews, but who behaved politely [perhaps there were some KGB agents]. At the beginning of the ceremony, nine women laid two mourning ribbons at the monument, decorated with flowers. The first ribbon was written in Yiddish and stated:
> "Our hearts still ache for your torment, your suffering, we will do everything to ensure that this never happens again.
> Jews of the Entire World."
> On the second tape it was written in Russian:
> "To the generation of calamity from the generation of hope."
> Then they lit candles, a minute of silence was declared after which Laurenson and the Cantor read a funeral prayer.[143]

A. Kholmiansky said, "Every Jew should perceive the tragedy of Babyn Yar as personal."[144] Then he read a paper, prepared by I. Berenshtein, for the group of former Prisoners of Zion. The paper gave an overview of the history of the Babyn Yar massacre and its commemoration. It showed how the Soviet authorities did not allow commemoration of the Holocaust victims at Babyn Yar.[145]

At the conclusion of the meeting at Babyn Yar, the Kyiv and Moscow Jews decided "to appeal to the authorities with a proposal to erect a second monument at Babyn Yar, a monument to the Jewish victims, and build it closer to the place where the executions of Jews actually occurred."[146] They expressed the opinion that many Jewish families would want to donate money for the construction of the monument.[147]

The process of the official recognition of Babyn Yar as a Holocaust site took several years during perestroika. In 1989, a plaque with a Yiddish inscription was added to the monument at Babyn Yar. On September 1990, the Council of Ministers of the Ukrainian SSR issued a resolution about registration of the charter of the Soviet Public Historical-Educational Center "Babyn Yar."[148] The chair of the council of the center was the publicist and scriptwriter Aleksandr Shlaien. The charter of the organization did not mention either the Holocaust or the Jewish victims of Babyn Yar; instead the Soviet term "Fascist genocide" was used. The purpose of the center was "creation of a Memorial Complex, which includes a monument to the victims of Babyn Yar and a scholarly and historical-educational center with an archive and library that would contain materials about the fascist genocide."[149]

An official commemoration ceremony at Babyn Yar took place after a long break in September 1991, when Ukraine had already declared its independence.

THE SOVIET MONUMENT AT BABYN YAR

Under the pressure of public opinion at home and abroad, Ukrainian Soviet authorities ultimately permitted construction of a monument at Babyn Yar. They chose the design of the Ukrainian sculptor Mykhailo Lysenko (1906–72) and his assistants, two young sculptors, Oleksandr Vitryk and Victor Sukhenko. Vitryk wrote that the project was chosen at a competition in 1968.[150] However, no other source verifies that this competition took place. According to Rybachuk, Mel'nychenko, and other sources, the authorities chose the monument project arbitrarily. Most likely, the authorities entrusted the creation of the monument to Lysenko because he was a well-known Ukrainian sculptor who had created several monuments to Soviet heroes in a romantic style marked by great expressiveness.

Lysenko was a student of an Ukrainian sculptor of Jewish origin, Eleonora (Leonora) Abramovna Bloch (1881–1943), who had studied at Auguste Rodin's studio in Paris between 1898 and 1905. Her early works were executed in a style influenced by French impressionism. Bloch wrote a memoir about her teacher, which was published posthumously in 1967 in Kyiv in Ukrainian as *Iak uchiv Roden* (How Rodin taught).

Bloch passed on her admiration of French impressionism to her student Mykhailo Lysenko, who studied with her at the Kharkiv Art Institute in the late 1920s and the early 1930s. Lysenko's admiration for Rodin and the influence of Rodin on his early works caused the sculptor many problems during Stalin's rule. A granddaughter of the sculptor, art historian Lyudmila Lysenko, said that Soviet art critics characterized the works of her grandfather by the words "erotic, *rodenovshchina* (Rodin-like), impressionist."[151] In other countries such a characterization might be a compliment, but not in the Soviet Union during Stalin's years, when only one art style was officially recognized—socialist realism.

However, despite the criticism, Lysenko not only survived, but had a successful career. He taught at the Kyiv Art Institute from 1944 and received the title of professor in 1947 and academic of the Academy of Arts of the Soviet Union in 1970. The secret to his success was his artistic talent combined with sticking to "ideologically correct" subjects, as well as his eclectic mix of realistic and impressionistic styles. Lysenko produced not only erotic statues of couples in love, but also monumental statues of revolutionaries and war heroes with elements of impressionism or in a pure impressionist style, which were usually accepted by the censors.[152]

The original design of the Babyn Yar monument was quite different from its final version. Lyudmila Lysenko wrote that the first version of the monument was created by Mykhailo Lysenko in 1968, and it depicted a group of people carrying a coffin as a symbol of their victimhood.[153] But the sculptor soon rejected this version of the monument himself, because it did not correspond with the Babyn Yar massacre. The second version of the monument by Lysenko was a nude woman with her hands tied behind her back by barbed wire, breastfeeding a baby lying on her knees. This image of a young mother was intended to symbolize the triumph of life over death. However, the officials wanted to see images of resistance in the monument at Babyn Yar. Under their pressure, the sculptor added to the monument a stereotypical group: a worker, a soldier, and a sailor, as depicted in many Soviet monuments. As a result of this addition, the monument appeared eclectic in style, but still quite impressive. In the front of the monument the figures of the worker, soldier, and sailor are sculpted in a realistic style, while other figures on the monument—two nude dying youths who have fallen from a cliff, a young dying woman, and a girl crying over the body of an old man—are depicted in an expressionist style reminiscent of Rodin's work. On the top of the sculpture, Lysenko used his original image prepared for the monument: the young mother with her hands tied behind her back while breastfeeding her baby. The architect Anatoly Ignashchenko proposed partially suspending the monument in the air, which increased the dramatic impact of the sculpture.[154]

Liudmila Lysenko recalled that work on the monument was done under great pressure from the officials. In her words:

Endless directives, orders and fears of party officials roughly broke off the creative process and distorted the original ideas of the artists. Suddenly, in the final stage of work on the project, somebody saw in the six spurs of Babyn Yar, created by nature, the Star of David, disguised by the monument's authors. Immediately 600,000 cubic meters of soil were delivered to the construction site and three spurs of the ravine were engulfed. Because of this, another project was not realized: the bottom of the ravine was supposed to be covered by red powdered glass over which a 350-meter-long thorny branch—a light guide—was supposed to be placed. But perhaps the most ridiculous demand was to dress up the nude figure of the mother in traditional Ukrainian shorts. For Lysenko, this was a brutal blow, because he especially cherished his ideal of a nude woman figure as the symbol of beauty and greatness of the human being [figure 6.12].[155]

The demand of officials that the female figure be dressed in Ukrainian shorts was not just a rejection of nudity; the national shorts symbolized that Ukrainians, rather than Jews, perished there. Certainly, this did not correspond to historical facts, because only Jewish and Roma women and children were executed at Babyn Yar for their ethnicity.

Figure 6.12 1976 Babyn Yar monument detail. (Unidentified photographer.)

However, the Soviets did not need the monument to represent the historical truth; they needed a monument that would fit their concept of the "universal suffering of the Soviet people," which emphasized the suffering of the local gentile population and their resistance to the Nazi regime. Thus, the heroic resistance of Soviet people to the Nazis, their suffering and victimhood became major concepts for the Babyn Yar monument.

The sculptors, who worked on the monument under conditions of strict censorship and great pressure from the officials, suffered tremendously. Several sources suggested that pressure from the authorities and the continuous stress shortened Mykhailo Lysenko's life. He died from a heart attack in 1972 at the age of sixty-five. The monument was erected four years after his death in 1976.

The monument construction was completed by Lysenko's students, sculptors Oleksandr Vitryk and Victor Sukhenko, who were cousins. Vitryk and Sukhenko worked with Mykhailo Lysenko on the monument from the beginning of the project in 1968. Work on the monument dragged on for seven years.[156] Vitryk later wrote that it continued for so long because the officials basically did not allow them to work. He recalled:

> We felt that the high authorities did not want the monument to be built. International Jewish organizations saw it as a monument for the Jewish victims of Nazism. Our officials insisted that Soviet people were shot at Babyn Yar. The members of the artistic council at the Ministry of Culture instructed us as follows: "Executed Jews did not defend the Fatherland and meekly went to their execution. Therefore solders, athletes, communists and partisans should be depicted on the monument. Jews should not be shown on the monument." We, on our own and against the recommendation of the artistic council, depicted in the composition a figure of an old [dead] Jew and bowed over him a crying girl. Certainly, in the foreground, we needed to show the stern faces of communists. But contrary to demands, we considered it our duty to show the Jewish tragedy in the figure of the old man and the girl.[157]

The figures of the old man and girl on the monument are reminiscent of the Pietà motif, only instead of Jesus Christ an old dead Jewish man is depicted, and instead of Mary a crying young girl (figure 6.13). The sculptor Lysenko was born and grew up in a Christian peasant family, and perhaps the Pietà represented for him the universal idea of suffering, including the suffering of Jewish people. However, such a Christian, rather than Jewish, image was still at odds with the official concept of the heroic struggle of the Soviet people. According to Mykhailo Krivolapov, the official from the Ukrainian Ministry of Culture who supervised the work of the sculptors:

> When the project of Lysenko—Sukhenko—Vitryk was presented at the Politburo [of the Communist Party of Ukraine (CPU)] all Politburo members, including the

First Secretary of the Central Committee of the CPU, Petro Shelest, demanded removal of the crying figure on the top of the sculpture and the girl, who bows over the dead old Jew. Obviously, such a "correction" would completely destroy the composition and idea of the monument.... But, in the beginning of the 1970s, the situation suddenly changed — publications appeared in the American press that Soviet leaders were artificially slowing down work on the monument at Babyn Yar, and Jewish organizations in the United States began to collect donations for creation of a gold monument to the executed Jews. On October 4, 1972, the Politburo with the First Secretary of the Central Committee of the CPU, Volodymyr Shcherbytsky, approved the entire monument project.[158]

The "gold monument" was most likely a product of Krivolapov's imagination. But the Jewish initiative to raise funds for construction of a monument at Babyn Yar and publications about it in the Western press accelerated construction of the Soviet monument.

Figure 6.13 1976 Babyn Yar monument detail. (Unidentified photographer.)

Sculptor Vitryk confirmed that work on the monument, which was stopped in the late 1960s, resumed in 1972. He believed that the policy of détente and the improvement of Soviet–American relations played a crucial role in this process. The Soviets tried to show the Western countries that there was no state anti-Semitism in the USSR. Vitryk thus explained the situation with construction of the Babyn Yar monument:

> In the beginning of the 1970s, relations between the USSR and the West were warming up. A delegation from the United States arrived in Kyiv and its members asked the First Secretary of the CPU Shcherbytsky how work was going on construction of the memorial [at Babyn Yar]. He in his turn asked officials from the Ministry of Culture about this. They rushed to resume work on the monument.[159]

Thus, the politicization of the Holocaust is not a recent phenomenon; it was already politicized during the Cold War. Although Soviet officials never admitted that the Holocaust took place, at the same time they allowed memorialization of its victims (usually without mentioning that they were Jewish) when relations with the West improved, to please their Western partners.

Vitryk said that after the visit of the American delegation, work on the monument resumed in a big rush and there was pressure on the sculptors from Soviet officials to complete their work. He recalled:

> In Spring 1972, we were called to the Central Committee [of the CPU] and received the order to immediately continue work on the memorial (by this time Mykhailo Grygorovych Lysenko had already died). For us [i.e., sculptors Vitryk and Sukhenko] began a terrible time. The working model of the monument was ready—we then should create it in bronze. We were lodged in a workshop near Babyn Yar and received campcots so that we would not leave the place at all. We worked day and night.[160]

The sculptors lived and worked under guard. Vitryk recalled that once the sculptors wanted to go to the city for dinner, but an armed policeman appeared at the door of the workshop who would not let them go out. Only when the policeman realized that he and Vitryk were fellow countrymen (both were from Zhytomyr) did he allow the sculptors to leave for a few hours.

Vitryk said that the sculptors worked without rest. They wanted to sleep all the time and so they would not fall asleep during work they drank stronger and stronger coffee. But the young sculptors were inspired and proud that they were creating a large monument in the capital of Ukraine. In the fall the workshop became "terribly cold." Victor Sukhenko became seriously ill and remained disabled for rest of his life.[161]

Why were the authorities suddenly in such a rush to build the monument after over thirty years of not allowing its construction? During the period of détente, the Soviets tried to show the Western countries that they had memorialized the Babyn Yar massacre. The Soviets were also in a hurry to build the monument to preempt the initiative of American and Soviet Jews, and their own dissidents, to build a Jewish monument at Babyn Yar.

In 1974, eighty-six Jews from Kyiv, Moscow, Minsk, and Tbilisi send a letter to the Central Committee of the Communist Party of the Soviet Union regarding the absence of a monument at Babyn Yar. In this letter, they criticized the policy of the authorities regarding commemoration of the Babyn Yar massacre and proposed creating a foundation for construction of the monument at Babyn Yar.[162] The Jews wrote:

> The absence of the monument at Babyn Yar cannot be explained by forgetfulness on the part of the government of Ukraine.... Perhaps it... does not have enough money, but a monument cost much less than one of the thousands of tanks that are supplied [by the Soviet Union] regularly to... Arab countries. If there is still no possibility to economize the deliveries with at least one tank, then... the Jews of the USSR are ready to raise the necessary funds to erect a monument.[163]

The letter was intentionally written in a sarcastic tone, perhaps hoping that the ashamed authorities would either finally build the monument at Babyn Yar by state means or let Jews provide fundraising for this purpose.

The initiatives of American and Soviet Jews to build a monument at Babyn Yar disturbed the Soviet authorities, because it highlighted that officials had failed to build a monument there. Also, if the Jewish activists took the initiative into their own hands and raised the funds for the monument, they would build a Jewish monument at Babyn Yar that did not fit the official concept. So, by finally constructing a monument at Babyn Yar, Soviet officials were able to implement their own concept of what had happened there.

On September 18, 1974, the secretary of the Kyiv City Committee of the CPU, A. Botvin, wrote to the Central Committee of the CPU about the need to inform the public about the monument construction at Babyn Yar:

> Jewish people, so called "refuseniks," have the idea of creating a public committee for fundraising for construction of a monument at Babyn Yar. Because of this, there will be official material published in the newspaper *Vechernii Kiev*[164] on the eve of 29 September about the project of the monument and its construction.[165]

The only Yiddish journal in the Soviet Union, *Sovetish Heymland* (Soviet homeland), published in the June 1975 issue Arn Vergelis's article "Der denkmol in Babi Yar vet shteyn ledoyres" (The Babyn Yar monument will stand forever).[166] The editor of *Sovetish Heymland,* Arn Vergelis, informed readers that a monument would soon be built at Babyn Yar. The article was illustrated by pictures of the model of Lysenko's monument. Vergelis supported in his article the official concept about the universal suffering of Soviet people during the war and justified construction of the monument "for all martyrs." He explained that "the differentiation of victims had been the method of the fascists, a product of 'reactionary nationalism' that has been overcome in the Soviet Union."[167] Certainly censorship, which became stricter during Brezhnev's years than during Khrushchev's Thaw, would not have allowed publication of Vergelis's article if it did not represent the official Soviet concept of the Babyn Yar massacre.

The Soviets began to use the Babyn Yar monument for propaganda purposes even before it was completed. According to Vitryk, when the monument was cast in bronze but not yet assembled, somebody from the KGB called the sculptors and told them: "Representatives from the British Jewish Association[168] are coming to visit you. You should consider what to tell them."[169] The British Jewish delegation came with a rabbi, translator, filmmaker, and representatives of the local Jewish communities. Vitryk recalled:

> It was especially fortunate that we did not follow the recommendations of the members of the Artistic Council and saved the figure of the old Jew and girl [on the monument]. We all together went to Babyn Yar, and the rabbi read a prayer over the figure of the old man. He was very touched. We received another call from the KGB after the departure of the British Jewish delegation and they commended us.[170]

After the visit of the British Jewish delegation, the authorities put strong pressure on the sculptors to complete their work. Vitryk said, "The Chair of the Department of Culture of the Central Committee of CPU, Petro Tron'ko, was begging the sculptors almost on his knees: 'Guys, save us! Here is a piece of paper, write down whatever you need: cars, apartments, money, state awards. You will receive everything!'" However, these promises were never fulfilled. Vitryk returned to his native Zhytomyr after completion of the monument because his request to receive an apartment in Kyiv was denied. Disabled after construction of the monument, Sukhenko committed suicide in 1998 (he was fifty-seven years old) so as not to be a burden on his impoverished family. Sukhenko's image is memorialized in the Babyn Yar monument as a dying young man, because he served as the model for the sculptor Lysenko (figure 6.14).[171] The authorities even forgot, or did not find it necessary, to invite the sculptors to the banquet devoted to unveiling the monument they had created. Furthermore, the names of the sculptors were not engraved on the monument plaque.

The monument was unveiled on July 2, 1976, and was dedicated to "Over one hundred thousand Kyivans and prisoners of war killed in 1941–43 by German fascists." The authorities intentionally chose the date for unveiling the monument in the middle of

Figure 6.14 1976 Babyn Yar monument detail. (Unidentified photographer.)

the summer, during vacation time, to create less public attention for the event. The officials organized a ceremony and military parade to honor "the heroes of Babyn Yar" at the unveiling of the monument (figures 6.15 and 6.16).[172] That most of the victims at Babyn Yar were Jewish was not mentioned either during the unveiling ceremony or on the monument plaque. The monument shows the universal tragedy of the Soviet people, but not specifically the Jewish massacre. Kyivan Jewish activist Emanuel Diamant wrote: "The announced purpose of the erection of the monument was to end 'Zionist propaganda about the Babyn Yar tragedy' and 'Zionist aspersions around Babyn Yar.'"[173]

Jewish activists were not allowed to participate in the official ceremony of the opening of the monument:

Yosif Begun recalled that in Kyiv several dozen Jews from various cities who were getting ready to bring wreaths to Babyn Yar and take part in the official unveiling of the monument were surrounded, thrown into a bus and brought to a police station where they were detained until late in the evening. These young people were released only at 9:00 p.m., when it was already dark on the street and the area around the monument was deserted. (The activists brought the wreath that they had intend to lay at Babyn Yar to Moscow where they showed it to foreign correspondents.)[174]

The two leading Soviet newspapers, *Pravda* and *Izvestia*, wrote about the completion of construction and unveiling of the monument. The article in *Pravda* on June 23, 1976, mentioned Jews among other victims of Babyn Yar:

> In the capital of Ukraine at Babyn Yar a majestic monument was erected.... Tens of thousands of innocent civilians of Kyiv were executed there, among whom there

Figure 6.15 Dedication of Soviet monument at Babyn Yar, July 2, 1976. (Photo from the Central State CinePhotoPhono Archives of Ukraine [TsDKFFA U].)

Figure 6.16 Dedication of Soviet monument at Babyn Yar, July 2, 1976. (Photo from the Central State CinePhotoPhono Archives of Ukraine [TsDKFFA U].)

were many children, women, and old people. The occupiers killed Russians, Ukrainians, Jews, Belorussians and Poles. Over 30 thousand soldiers, commanders, political workers of the Red Army, and sailors of the Dnieper Military Fleet are buried there.[175]

The article in *Izvestia* on July 3, 1976, did not mention Jews, but instead used the Soviet cliché "victims of fascism." The article reported the unveiling of the monument: "On July 2, on the former outskirts of Kyiv at Babyn Yar, a memorial to the victims of fascism was opened. Over 100,000 Soviet people, soldiers, party workers, and civilians of many nationalities were killed there."[176]

The unveiling of the Babyn Yar monument did not go unnoticed abroad: "Foreign radio stations around the world broadcast about it and criticized the monument, which they said did not represent the tragedy that occurred there."[177] Victor Nekrasov, then living in Paris, who never saw the monument in person, only its pictures, wrote: "It took thirty five years to overcome somebody's stubborn resistance for the appearance at the place of the shooting of elderly men and women, of statues of half-naked muscular fighters and underground members, who at gunpoint calmly and confident look to the future."[178] Nekrasov was certainly right about the Soviet stereotypical images of the soldier, partisan, and sailor on the front of the monument, but the monument is not limited to those images. The sculptors also depicted a dead elderly man and crying over him a young girl, and a young mother breastfeeding her baby.

On August 2–3, 1979, a delegation of forty-eight people from the United States visited Kyiv. The group included ten members of the President's Commission on the Holocaust,[179] representatives of Jewish communities, university professors, former prisoners of Nazi concentration camps, as well as journalists, photographers, and others.[180] Edward Sanders, a "leader in the Jewish community who served President Carter as a special advisor on Mideast policy," accompanied the group.[181] Among the members of the delegation was the chair of the President's Commission on the Holocaust, Elie Wiesel. A correspondent of the *New York Times*, Anthony Austin, wrote a detailed article about the visit of the delegation to Babyn Yar on August 3, 1979. The article points out that the members of the US delegation were astonished by the absence of the word "Jews" on the Babyn Yar memorial inscription. Austin wrote:

> The Chairman of the President's Commission, Elie Wiesel, stepped forward, in a yarmulke on his head, and spoke:
> "When I stood here 15 years ago there was no monument at Babi Yar. But we all knew what Babi Yar meant. Now there is a monument at Babi Yar. But what kind of monument is it? We all had hoped to find a memorial for all the Jews who died as Jews, as well as for all the others who died here. But the Jews are not being remembered." ...
> He then laid the wreath, with ribbons brought from the United States and bearing English, Russian, Yiddish and Hebrew inscriptions saying that it was from a Presidential commission formed to establish a memorial "to the catastrophe that overtook European Jewry."
> Cantor Isaac Goodfriend of Congregation Havath Achim of Atlanta conducted a service. In a voice that carried over the landscaped grounds where once a deep ravine was filled high with corpses, he sang: "I believe with perfect faith in the coming of the Messiah. O, though he tarry, yet will I wait for him."
> Mr. Wiesel then asked Bayard Rustin,[182] a commission member and president of the A. Philip Randolph Institute of New York, to sing. Mr. Rustin sang "O Freedom,"

which he said was the favorite spiritual of the late Dr. Martin Luther King Jr.: "We shall remember, we shall remember, we shall remember, O God."

To the rear a handful of Soviet men and women stood listening impassively to the sounds of Jewish prayers and an American Negro spiritual rising from the hillock on which the monument stands.

Intourist guides, questioned persistently by Western reporters, maintained that the Soviet people make no differentiation between the Jews, Ukrainians and Russians who were killed at Babi Yar and say that Jews amounted to perhaps half the total.

Americans with experience in the Soviet Union felt that the authorities of the Ukrainian Republic had made a special effort to accommodate themselves to this unusual mission even though its emphasis on Jewish suffering and Jewish deaths went against the grain of Soviet policy. Mr. Wiesel, saying that he agreed with this assessment, commented: "I am very pleased with the spirit of cooperation we found here in Kiev. The Soviets seem ready to establish a program of exchange of information, archives and other material. This means that for the first time the Soviets recognize the Holocaust as such."

Prior to the visit to Babi Yar, the commission was cordially received by the Mayor of Kiev, Vladimir A. Gusev, who responded warmly to Mr. Wiesel's remarks and requests for exchanges of material and showed a Soviet documentary file of Nazi atrocities perpetrated against the Soviet people in the Ukraine and elsewhere.

At the end of the ceremony, Soviet newsmen asked Mr. Wiesel to explain the nature of the commission and inquired whether Americans realized that the Nazis did not differentiate between Jews, Russians and Ukrainians in their genocidal practices. Mr. Wiesel replied: "That is not what we know from history. I say it not with bitterness but with sadness. In those 10 days that I spoke of, only the Jews were killed, not as citizens of Kiev but as Jews. I would like to see here—please one word about the Jewishness of the Jewish victims."[183]

During détente, Soviet officials allowed members of the US delegation to commemorate the Jews who perished at Babyn Yar, including praying and laying a wreath with inscriptions in Hebrew and Yiddish at the Babyn Yar monument in the presence of the public. The Soviets never allowed their own citizens—Jewish activists—to do this. According to Elie Wiesel, the Soviets were even ready to exchange archival information and other materials with the US delegation. Wiesel believed that this meant that the Soviets recognized the Holocaust. Was this real recognition of the Holocaust by the Soviets? Perhaps not, because during the US delegation's visit, the Soviets continued to insist on their concept of the universal suffering of the Soviet people. Probably, if the policy of détente had lasted longer, the Soviets would have exchanged archival information with the United States for the sake of improving diplomatic relations between the countries. But the policy of détente soon ended with the Soviet invasion of Afghanistan in December 1979.

But, even during détente, discussion of the memorialization of the Babyn Yar massacre between the US delegation and the Soviets was quite difficult, because the Soviets did not want to provide at the monument any inscription mentioning the Jewish victims. The head of the Department for Foreign Tourism under the Council of Ministers of the Ukrainian SSR, V. Dobrotvor, informed the authorities about this:

> Before flying to Moscow, Elie Wiesel expressed sharp indignation that the memorial plaque at the monument does not mention at all that among the civilians shot by the Germans, the majority were Jews. He stated that upon returning to the USA he would raise this issue with his government.[184]

Elie Wiesel wrote in the Report of the President's Commission on the Holocaust about the Babyn Yar monument:

> The monument is most impressive, set in the center of a ravine where the victims were buried. However, in both content and inscription the memorial is devoid of any reference, direct or oblique, to the fact that the Jews were killed at Babi Yar. Shocked by this conspicuous omission, the Commission was alerted to the danger of historical falsification or dilution.[185]

Despite the imperfections of the Soviet Babyn Yar monument and of the official ceremonies organized by the authorities, the monument became a place where Kyivans (Jews and non-Jews) could come to commemorate the Babyn Yar victims and lay a bouquet of flowers or a wreath. Although the monument represents the Soviet concept of universal tragedy, rather than the Holocaust, it was a better solution than to retain an evil-smelling cesspit on the place of the mass murder of Kyivan Jews, Roma, and gentiles. Certainly, it was a step forward in recognition of the tragedy that occurred there. The first Jewish monument was finally built at Babyn Yar only after the collapse of communism in 1991.

CONCLUSION

In an atmosphere of acute popular anti-Semitism, the Soviet authorities did not dare build a monument at Babyn Yar for many years. Perhaps some of them shared these anti-Semitic views, but mostly they worried about retaining their own positions. They feared that construction of a monument at Babyn Yar in the postwar years would have provoked its immediate desecration, anti-Jewish violence, and the wrath of anti-Semites against the authorities. The Soviet authorities could not officially admit the anti-Semitic mood of a significant part of the gentile population, but they expected that the construction of a monument at Babyn Yar would provoke strong popular anti-Semitism. Thus, they postponed construction of a monument for as long as they could, and even unsuccessfully tried to liquidate the Babyn Yar site altogether.

During Khrushchev's Thaw and Brezhnev's years, not only Jews, but also Western politicians and liberal gentile intelligentsia in the Soviet Union and abroad raised their voices in favor of construction of a monument at Babyn Yar. The absence of a monument there was taken in the West as evidence of Soviet state anti-Semitism. During the Cold War, relations of the Soviet Union with the West had a significant impact on Soviet Jewish policy. For example, during détente, to please the West, the Soviets allowed limited Jewish emigration from the USSR and erected monuments on the largest Holocaust sites in Russia, at Zmievskaia Balka in Rostov-on-Don (1975) and in Ukraine at Babyn Yar (1976). The Soviets rushed to bring foreign delegations to the Babyn Yar monument while it was still under construction. The pressure on the sculptors who worked day and night on the Babyn Yar monument also shows how important it was for the Soviets to complete it quickly.

Certainly, the Soviet authorities had to balance, like a tightrope walker, between the different sides who had opposing opinions and attitudes toward memorialization of the Babyn Yar massacre. Thus, the authorities, under pressure from Jews, liberals, and Western countries on the one side and local anti-Semites on the other, accepted a compromise solution: They built a monument at Babyn Yar dedicated to all Kyivans and prisoners of the war who perished there, without obviously Jewish images and without mentioning Jews in the inscription. The same solution was found for construction of the monument at Zmievskaia Balka in Rostov-on-Don, where a monument was erected, dedicated "To the victims of Fascism," although among 30,000 victims executed there, 27,000 were Jews. Commemoration of the Holocaust was forbidden in the Soviet Union until the collapse of communism.

7

BABYN YAR COMMEMORATION IN INDEPENDENT UKRAINE

STATE RECOGNITION OF THE HOLOCAUST AND NEW MONUMENTS AT BABYN YAR

Only after the collapse of communism and the independence of Ukraine, which ended state anti-Semitism, did public discussion of the Holocaust in Ukraine become permissible. On September 29, 1991, the fiftieth anniversary of the Babyn Yar tragedy, the Ukrainian authorities publicly admitted for the first time that most of the victims at Babyn Yar were Jews. Leonid Kravchuk, the head of the Verkhovna Rada (Parliament) of Ukraine and later the first president of independent Ukraine (December 1991 to 1994), participated in the memorial ceremony. He apologized to Jews that the Soviet regime "concealed from the people the historical truth about the Babyn Yar tragedy, about the fact that the majority of the victims of the mass shootings were Jews."[1]

Since then, the anniversaries of the Babyn Yar tragedy have always been commemorated on the state level, usually with the presence of Ukrainian high authorities. All leaders of independent Ukraine have understood that recognition of the Holocaust is a prerequisite for integration with Europe and the West. According to a resolution of the Ukrainian Verkhovna Rada, "On the 70th Anniversary of the Babyn Yar Tragedy," adopted on July 5, 2011, International Holocaust Remembrance Day (January 27) should be commemorated in Ukraine.[2] Many world leaders have visited Babyn Yar and participated in commemoration ceremonies there, including US presidents George W. Bush and Bill Clinton; Israeli presidents Moshe Katsav, Reuven Rivlin, and Isaac Herzog; and Pope John Paul II.

BABYN YAR COMMEMORATION IN INDEPENDENT UKRAINE / 203

Figure 7.1 Memorial *Menorah*, 1991. (Unidentified photographer.)

On the fiftieth anniversary of the Babyn Yar tragedy in 1991, the monument *Menorah* (by architect Yury Paskevich, engineer B. Giller, and sculptors Yakim and Alexander Levich) was dedicated at Babyn Yar (figure 7.1).³ This monument was repeatedly vandalized (six times in 2015 and once in 2016) until a video camera was installed.⁴

Since the collapse of communism, many more monuments have been built at Babyn Yar, dedicated to the memory of members of the resistance movement, Jewish children, the writer Anatoly Kuznetsov, prisoners of war, Roma, and other people murdered there (figures 7.2 and 7.3). Today over thirty monuments and memorial plaques are located at Babyn Yar. Why have so many monuments been built at Babyn Yar since 1991? Perhaps this is a reaction to the long-standing Soviet prohibition against building any monuments there. Postcommunist society was recovering suppressed memories and there was a desire to reevaluate the historical past.

However, this does not mean that there is no longer controversy about Babyn Yar monuments. Some non-Jews have "contested memorializing Babyn Yar as a primarily Jewish place of memory."⁵ Crosses have been erected dedicated to members of the Organization of Ukrainian Nationalists (OUN) and Christian clergy who were killed there.⁶ Monuments have also been erected for victims of the 1961 Kurenivsky flood, for mentally ill people murdered by the Nazis, for imprisoned and murdered members of the soccer team Dinamo, for German prisoners of war who were killed in captivity, and others. Not all these people perished at Babyn Yar, but the ravine was the chosen place

Figure 7.2 Memorial to the children killed at Babyn Yar, 2001. (Unidentified photographer.)

Figure 7.3 *The Roma Wagon* monument, opened September 23, 2016. (Unidentified photographer.)

for all these monuments. However, all these monuments could not tell the entire story of the Babyn Yar massacre. This function can be fulfilled only by the memorial museum.

Originally, in 1945 the Soviet authorities planned to establish a memorial museum at Babyn Yar. But due to the rise of state and popular anti-Semitism, this plan was not realized. The idea of creating a Babyn Yar Memorial Museum reappeared in independent Ukraine in the early 2000s. The American Jewish Joint Distribution Committee (JDC or Joint) declared its intention of providing ten million dollars for the construction of a Jewish Communal-Cultural Center "Heritage" at Babyn Yar.[7] In April 2001, the Kyiv city council resolved to provide land for construction of the center. It was supposed to serve as a major site for revival of the Jewish community in Ukraine. In 2002, the project was presented for public discussion.[8] However, it divided the Ukrainian Jewish community, because "some felt it was inappropriate to have a park and community center on the territory of this mass grave."[9] Ukrainian nationalists protested the memorialization of Babyn Yar "as primarily a Jewish place of memory." According to the Lviv writer Yuriy Vynnychuk, "Jews have no right to privatize Babyn Yar and build a memorial dedicated to a single nation."[10] Because of the public controversy, the proposed center was not built.

In 2003, Ukrainian and Jewish intellectuals created a Public Committee for Commemoration of the Victims of Babyn Yar, which sought to create a national historical-memorial park with a museum and memorial.[11] The discussion continued until September 2005, when Ukrainian president Viktor Yushchenko decreed that a state-controlled historical-cultural sanctuary would be established on the site. In accordance with the desire of Kyivans to make Babyn Yar a memorial place, in 2007 the Ukrainian government declared the ravine a National Historical Memorial Preserve.[12]

In June 2013, the Jewish Agency for Israel, Sochnut, proposed to the president of Ukraine, Victor Yanukovich, a plan for construction of a memorial complex at Babyn Yar. Inside the ravine, at the site of the execution of Jews, there would be an "interactive pavilion with Hollywood special effects, which will immerse the visitors in the atmosphere of the fall of 1941."[13] "Visitors would hear the barking of German shepherd dogs, the commands of Nazi guards, and on the side would walk to the execution of the doomed Jews, Roma and Soviet prisoners of war," Alexander Levin, a representative of the Jewish Agency in Kyiv, briefed Ukrainian journalists.[14] He said that the new memorial complex would include a large pool with fountains and lights in the shape of a candle and "a road of death," as well as a Jewish Community Center. Levin concluded, "At the same spot where the Nazi executed Jews, Jewish children will study the Torah."[15] The 2014 Ukrainian Revolution prevented the fulfillment of this rather vulgar plan.

Many Kyivans criticized this plan because it included construction of the memorial complex on the bones and ashes of Babyn Yar victims, which many saw as a sacrilege. There is, however, enough room around the ravine to build a Babyn Yar memorial museum without disturbing the remains of the victims. The Public Committee for Commemoration of the Victims of Babyn Yar has continuously struggled against various unsuitable construction projects proposed for the site. In addition, the chair of the Committee for the Preservation of Jewish Cemeteries in Europe, Rabbi Elyakim Schlesinger, and the chief rabbi of the State of Israel, Yona Metzger, have stated that construction of any building on a place of massacre contradicts Jewish religious law.[16] So, the major Holocaust site remains without a memorial museum due to the public disagreement about its concept and location.

COMMEMORATION OF THE 75TH ANNIVERSARY OF THE BABYN YAR MASSACRE

In 2016, the Ukrainian government sponsored memorial events devoted to commemoration of the seventy-fifth anniversary of the Babyn Yar massacre, including an official memorial ceremony at Babyn Yar, a competition for the design of a new memorial, a classical music concert, an exhibition, a scholarly conference, and lectures about the Babyn Yar tragedy in schools and universities.[17] Certainly such a commemoration of the Babyn Yar tragedy was a major step forward compared with Soviet denial of the Holocaust and suppression of its commemoration.

However, despite the efforts of the Ukrainian authorities to commemorate the Babyn Yar tragedy on the state level, its commemoration has been accompanied by several public scandals. One scandal occurred after the announcement of a government-backed design competition for a new memorial at Babyn Yar, which was supposed to resolve the "problem" of the "discrepancy between the world's view and Jewry's exclusive view of Babyn Yar as a symbol of the Holocaust."[18] This apparent attempt to diminish the site's Jewish significance infuriated many Jews in Ukraine and Israel. The Ukrainian government was accused of historical revisionism and had to change the language of the competition announcement to emphasize the murder of Jews at Babyn Yar. None of the architectural projects submitted for the competition satisfied the international jury: "The Jury did not feel that any one entry answered the issues raised in the brief in a comprehensive way, and all winning projects left unanswered questions."[19] Fundamentally, the competition could not resolve the issue of whether Babyn Yar should be memorialized as one of the largest Holocaust sites or as a universal symbol of human suffering. These debates about memorialization of the Babyn Yar massacre still continue and represent two diametrically opposed approaches to creation of a memorial museum there.

THE BABYN YAR HOLOCAUST MEMORIAL CENTER (BYHMC) AND ITS OPPONENTS

In 2016, during commemoration of the seventy-fifth anniversary of the Babyn Yar massacre, President Petro Poroshenko of Ukraine "announced that a museum and memorial complex would be built in time for the eightieth anniversary of the massacre."[20] Ukraine was one of the poorest countries in Europe in the early 2000s and could not provide funds for the construction of a multimillion-dollar museum and memorial complex. So, the Babyn Yar Holocaust Memorial Center (BYHMC) project was supposed to be financed by private donations. Among the major donors to the project were wealthy Jewish businessmen: Mikhail Fridman, Pavel Fuks, German Khan, and Victor Pinchuk. All of them are Ukrainian Jews by background, and "all have been involved in other philanthropic projects in the country. Furthermore, Fridman lost eight relatives in the Holocaust in Ukraine and Khan lost thirteen, making the project deeply personal for them."[21] However Fridman, Fuks, and Khan had their businesses and made their profits in Russia, which immediately made the Babyn Yar Memorial project controversial and gave grounds for the accusation that it is a pro-Russian project.

The financial report of BYHMC shows that the center received in 2017–20 about half of the funds from Ukrainian donors and half from abroad.

DISTRIBUTION OF DONOR FINANCING SHARES[22]

	2017	2018	2019	2020
Ukraine	56%	50%	43%	50%
Russia / Israel	44%	50%	57%	49%
USA	0%	0%	0%	1%

In 2021, Fuks left the BYHMC project "after he was accused by the Ukrainian government of having engaged in corrupt business practices, an allegation he denies."[23] With the beginning of the full-scale Russian attack on Ukraine in February 2022, Fridman and Khan also left the project. But the BYHMC continues its work despite the departure of these major donors.

The BYHMC was established in Kyiv in 2016 as "a nonprofit educational institution that documents and commemorates the Holocaust, in particular the Babyn Yar mass shootings of September 1941."[24] The BYHMC had an ambitious plan to create a Babyn Yar Holocaust Memorial Center and Museum in Kyiv near the Holocaust site, which is now indefinitely postponed due to the Russian invasion of Ukraine. The center and museum were intended to

- pay tribute to the victims, to tell the story of their lives and to explain the relationship between Jews and non-Jews in Kyiv and Ukraine;
- become a research center specialized on the Holocaust crimes in the territory of the former Soviet Union and Eastern Europe;
- develop an educational platform, which in addition to teaching about the crimes of the Third Reich, will create a space for discussion and give society the tools to work with topics of Holocaust, in particular, and Human Rights overall.[25]

The Advisory Board of the BYHMC was joined by several well-known politicians and public figures: Belarusian writer and Nobel laureate in literature (2015) Svetlana Alexievich; political prisoner of the Soviet Union (1977–86) and human rights activist Natan Sharansky; Chief Rabbi of Kyiv and Ukraine Yaakov Dov Bleich; former German foreign minister Joschka Fischer; the first president of Ukraine, Leonid Kravchuk; former US senator Joe Lieberman; President of the World Jewish Congress Ronald Lauder; and former Polish president Aleksander Kwaśniewski.[26] The BYHMC project has received support from Ukrainian and Israeli politicians, including the current president of Ukraine, Volodymyr Zelensky; the mayor of Kyiv, Vitaly Klitschko; the president of Israel, Reuven Rivlin; and others. The United States Holocaust Memorial Museum (USHMM) supported the BYHMC project for creation of "a museum and educational center, at one of the most horrendous mass murder sites of the Holocaust."[27]

However, support for the project on the national and international levels does not protect it from attack by some Ukrainian historians, nationalists, anti-Semites, and even competing Jewish organizations. The opponents of the project claim that it is a "foreign, colonial project," although "virtually all of the [BYHMC] full time staff are Ukrainian, as are many supervisory board and scientific [now Academic] council members."[28]

On April 1, 2017, sixteen Ukrainian historians published an open letter in the online periodical *Ukrains'ka Pravda, Istorychna Pravda* (Ukrainian truth, historical truth) under the title "Museum 'Babyn Yar' Open Letter—Warning of Ukrainian Historians." The letter stated:

> We consider harmful the effort to unite Babyn Yar only with the history of the Holocaust, ignoring the other victims and other dramatic moments of its history. This approach just sharpens the war of memories, which has been going on for a long time on the terrain of Babyn Yar.
>
> Although the history of the extermination of Jews perhaps will be the key topic of the Babyn Yar Museum, we consider that a Museum of the Holocaust and Museum of Babyn Yar should be the separate institutions, which reveal different aspects and different contexts of the tragic history of the 20th century.[29]

The Ukrainian historians who signed this letter objected to making the Babyn Yar Museum a Holocaust Museum. Their claim that the BYHMC ignores "other victims and other dramatic moments of its history" is incorrect; the historical narrative prepared for the museum has chapters about all victims of Babyn Yar: Jews, Roma, mentally ill people, prisoners of the war, partisans, civilians, and Ukrainian nationalists. It is symptomatic that the opponents of the project attacked the BYHMC for misrepresenting the history of the Babyn Yar massacre when work on the historical narrative for the future museum had just begun. This clearly shows that their goal was to close the entire project without further discussion.

Two years later, a group of historians at the Institute of the History of Ukraine publicly objected to the creation of the Babyn Yar Museum as a Holocaust Museum. Instead they proposed creating two separate museums: the Museum of Babyn Yar as a place of universal suffering and a separate Ukrainian Museum of the Holocaust. This group of historians published online their *Concept of the Complex Memorialization of Babyn Yar with Extending Borders of the National Historical Memorial Preserve Babyn Yar*.[30] The authors of the *Concept* propose starting with the creation of "a *Memorial Museum of Babyn Yar Victims* in the historic building of the office of the former Jewish cemetery at 44 Melnikova Street."[31] The concept said that this museum "should be viewed only as a pilot project until the complete museum complex is built," "due to the extremely limited exhibition space."[32] The absence of the word "Holocaust" in the proposed title of the future Memorial Museum of Babyn Yar Victims is very much reminiscent of the Soviet approach when the Holocaust victims were referred to as "peaceful Soviet citizens" without mentioning that most of the victims were Jews. It is quite unclear how the Holocaust would be represented in the proposed museum exhibition. The *Concept* only provides an outline of the themes for the intended future exhibition rather than a developed historical narrative. The *Concept* stated that that both museums, the Ukrainian Museum of the Holocaust and the Babyn Yar Memorial Museum, should be funded from the state budget, which was impractical even before the Russian invasion of Ukraine.[33] Also, it is unclear from the *Concept* when the Ukrainian Museum of the Holocaust would be established.

The BYHMC Museum project was in a much more advanced stage of development before the Russian invasion compared to the project of the Institute of the History of Ukraine. The BYHMC has already done extensive work on research and memorialization of the Babyn Yar tragedy. The BYHMC Academic Council (of which I am a founding member) was established in 2017. Within a year, members of the Academic Council and historians from Ukraine, the United States, Israel, Germany, the Netherlands, and Moldova, under the supervision of Chief Historian Karel Berkhoff, prepared the historical narrative for the future museum. The narrative is published online on the BYHMC website. All the work of the center is transparent. The BYHMC developed a high-quality website where everybody who is interested can find all the information about the work of the center, its news, publications, and information about ongoing projects.[34]

In 2019, an international architectural competition for the design of the Babyn Yar Holocaust Memorial Center and Museum took place. On September 6, 2019, the competition jury selected the winning project, which was designed by "the Austrian bureau Querkraft Architekten with the landscape architect Kieran Fraser, Landscape Design (Austria)."[35] The winning project is designed in a modern architectural style with a large public space in the center. The core exhibition would be located 20 meters below ground level. The visitors would come to the museum through "a long ramp resembling a cleft."[36] The future Holocaust Memorial Museum and Center, according to its organizers, should "become a place of memory, a museum and a platform for research, public dialog and reflection on the tragedy, all combined in one."[37]

When the historical narrative was created and the design of the future center and museum chosen, attention shifted to the creation of the future museum exhibits. In November 2019, the financiers of the BYHMC project appointed film director Ilya Khrzhanovsky as artistic director of the BYHMC. Opponents claimed that Khrzhanovsky would build a "Holocaust Disneyland." This accusation resulted in a public scandal and caused three scholars, including Chief Historian Karel Berkhoff, to leave the BYHMC Academic Council.[38] But several other prominent Holocaust historians subsequently joined the project, among them the new chief historian of the BYHMC, Father Patrick Desbois, a French Catholic priest and professor of the practice of forensic study of the Holocaust at Georgetown University; and Norman Naimark, professor of Eastern European studies at Stanford University.

Over the last few years many articles have been published in the Ukrainian and foreign press by both supporters of the BYHMC Museum project and its opponents. According to the BYHMC Digest, in just the two weeks of October 5–19, 2020, "the Memorial Center was mentioned in the information space in a total of 465 materials. These include 359 positive, 113 neutral, and 64 negative materials."[39] The large number of publications shows the great public interest in the work of the BYHMC and heated debates about the future Babyn Yar Holocaust Memorial Museum.

In April 2020, the BYHMC established two institutes: the Institute of Babyn Yar Territory and Memory Studies and the Babyn Yar–East Europe Holocaust Research Institute. "The Institute of Babyn Yar Territory and Memory Studies conducts and supports multidisciplinary research into the history of Babyn Yar and its evolution in the political, economic and cultural aspects as a multidimensional memory space."[40] This institute has also prepared a comprehensive bibliography of works about Babyn Yar in Ukrainian, Russian, English, German, Yiddish, and Hebrew. The bibliography was supposed to be published in 2022, but publication was delayed due to the war. The institute has already begun work on an illustrated encyclopedia, *Babyn Yar: Landscape and Memoryscape*.

The Babyn Yar–East Europe Holocaust Research Institute focuses on the Nazi occupation of Ukraine and Eastern Europe during World War II; regional "features" of the Holocaust in Eastern Europe; the Roma genocide; repressive policies of the occupying Nazi regimes and their allies against civilians and POWs; liberation movements in occupied regions; Jews rescued by local non-Jewish population; survival strategies employed by Jews in the Holocaust; and local population's reactions to the killing of Jews. Aside from its own research, the Institute will build a digital archive, pursue oral history projects, publish scholarly literature, host various scientific, educational events and thematic exhibitions.[41]

Both institutes have published several scholarly articles on the BYHMC website and have conducted scholarly webinars and public lectures. The members of the Academic Council of the BYHMC, Martin Dean and Alexander Kruglov, used a unique spatial 3D modeling technology and defined the exact places of execution at Babyn Yar. They show that "the mass shootings of 33,771 Jews on September 29–30, 1941, took place mainly in the large western spur, and it is possible that some mass shootings also took place at the bottom of the main ravine, near the junction with the western spur."[42] This is an important discovery, because the future Babyn Yar Holocaust Memorial Museum should be built outside of the place of execution.

On September 29, 2020, the BYHMC opened three new memorials at Babyn Yar:

the Menorah Monument Walk Audio Installation, a 300 meter (approximately 1,000 foot) path from the main road to the Menorah monument; the Mirror Field, a disc 40 meters (130 feet) in diameter, with 10 columns, each six meters (20 feet) high and the Monoculars, statues of solid red Ukrainian granite, approximately two meters (six-and-a-half feet) in height, with a form that is reminiscent both of a human body and a gravestone.

The path from the main road to the Menorah monument has 32 pillars, each containing an audio speaker with independent audio channels. As visitors walk along the path, the names of 19,000 victims of the tragedy, compiled by the Babyn Yar Holocaust Memorial Center and recorded by people of different gender and ages, will be played through the speakers, emphasizing both the collective nature of the tragedy and the tragedy of each individual human life that was lost [figure 7.4].[43]

The BYHMC is conducting the project "Names." Within this project, the center's researchers found 867 previously unrecorded names of victims of the Nazi occupation

Figure 7.4 The *Mirror Field* memorial at Babyn Yar, opened September 29, 2020. (Unidentified photographer.)

of Kyiv and created a consolidated list that contains almost 19,000 names of victims.⁴⁴ The archivists of the center are copying documents about the Babyn Yar massacre and on Jewish history in Ukrainian archives and publishing them online. The BYHMC reached an agreement with Yad Vashem about the exchange of databases and testimonies regarding the Babyn Yar massacre.⁴⁵

In 2021, BYHMC established a journal, *Eastern European Holocaust Studies*, with a focus on the Holocaust in Eastern and Central Europe. The center has signed "a cooperation agreement focusing on educational projects with Centropa—one of the core Jewish advocacy organizations committed to preserving Jewish memory in Central and East Europe."⁴⁶ As part of this cooperation, the BYHMC and Centropa plan "to deliver online training workshops for Ukrainian educators, and arrange an exhibition depicting the fate of Ukrainian Jews in the 20th century."⁴⁷ The center has also created a library on Holocaust studies and published books on the Holocaust in Ukrainian.

The BYHMC has collected over one thousand testimonies of Holocaust survivors and righteous gentiles, and it also "delivers necessities and food to the Righteous Among the Nations."⁴⁸ In 2021, as many as thirty elderly righteous gentiles lived in Ukraine.⁴⁹

In July 2020, President Zelensky publicly supported the BYHMC project and Andriy Yermak, Head of the Office of the President of Ukraine, was appointed member of the initiative's supervisory board. In addition, the project received backing from Kyiv's mayor Vitaly Klitschko. The support offered by the authorities was most likely due to the project's grand scale and advanced implementation stage, to the fact that it is not funded from the state budget and to the involvement of world-famous artists, prominent figures and former heads of state in its activities. For Zelensky, who had several family members that perished in the Holocaust, this support likely also has a personal aspect.[50]

In 2021, the Babyn Yar Holocaust Memorial Center announced its plan "for the development of a museum complex, which will stretch over an area of 150 hectares, making it one of the world's largest Holocaust memorial centers. A dozen buildings will eventually be erected as part of the complex, including a symbolic synagogue."[51]

COMMEMORATION OF THE 80TH ANNIVERSARY OF THE BABYN YAR MASSACRE

Preparations for the eightieth anniversary of the Babyn Yar Massacre began well in advance. On June 17, 2021, the head of the Office of the President of Ukraine, Andriy Yermak, noted that the state was preparing a significant action plan regarding the eightieth anniversary of the Babyn Yar tragedy. "Yermak said that President Zelensky has established a task force to complete the entire memorial within a few years and start operating as a museum complex."[52]

The BYHMC built two new memorials at Babyn Yar that opened on the eightieth anniversary of the Babyn Yar massacre: a memorial synagogue by Swiss architect Manuel Herz and the *Crystal Wall of Crying* by Serbian conceptual and performance artist Marina Abramovic.

The synagogue was unveiled in May 2021. Architect Herz designed the synagogue like a book "with a manual mechanism that worshippers will operate."[53]

> The 11 m-high (36 ft) building has a metal frame and is made of Ukrainian oak more than a century old, to reconnect with the old Jewish traditions of the area. The painted constellations on the ceiling also echo the artwork of synagogues destroyed by the Nazis.[54]

The *Crystal Wall of Crying*, an installation by world-renowned performance artist Marina Abramovic, was erected at Babyn Yar. According to the concept of the artist, the *Crystal Wall of Crying* is a "symbolic extension of the Wailing Wall in Jerusalem."[55]

There were several memorial events devoted to the eightieth anniversary of the massacre at Babyn Yar. On September 29, 2021, the BYHMC, together with the Ministry of Education of Ukraine, organized a nationwide online lesson of memory for fifth- to eleventh-grade students in all schools in Ukraine.⁵⁶ On October 3, 2021, the Memorial March to Babyn Yar took place in Kyiv, in which participants walked to Babyn Yar on the same road that Kyivan Jews walked on September 29, 1941.

The international conference on "Mass Shooting During the Holocaust as a Criminal Process" took place in Kyiv on October 5, 2021. Scholars from the United States, Israel, Germany, and France participated in the conference. They discussed the Holocaust by bullets in Ukraine, the personal responsibility of the perpetrators, and postwar investigations and trials. The keynote speech at the conference was presented by Father Patrick Desbois, head of the Academic Council at the Babyn Yar Holocaust Memorial Center and president of Yahad-In Unum.

On October 6, 2021, I participated in the official ceremony of the commemoration of the eightieth anniversary of the Babyn Yar massacre in Kyiv. The ceremony was organized jointly by the BYHMC and the Ukrainian government. The commemoration was delayed for a few days from the traditional commemoration date, September 29 (the day when the massacre began at Babyn Yar), due to Jewish religious holidays. The presidents of Ukraine (Volodymyr Zelensky), Israel (Isaac Herzog), and Germany (Frank-Walter Steinmeier) attended the commemoration ceremony at Babyn Yar and delivered their speeches. US secretary of state Antony Blinken presented his speech on

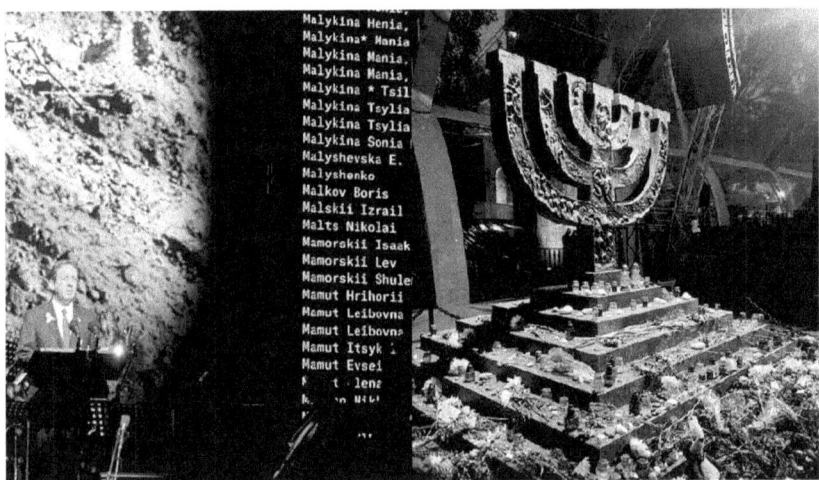

Figure 7.5 The 80th anniversary commemoration of the Babyn Yar massacre. (Photo by Victoria Khiterer.)

Zoom. Throughout the ceremony, the names of the victims of Babyn Yar scrolled continuously on two large display boards (figure 7.5).

The commemoration ceremony was quite involved and over six hours long, from 5 p.m. until after 11 p.m. There was a kaleidoscope of speeches, music and poetry performances, and personal memories of Holocaust survivors, their children and grandchildren. There were many excellent speeches, but three impressed me the most: the speech of the well-known Ukrainian journalist Dmitry Gordon, the speech by President Zelensky, and the speech by US secretary of state Antony Blinken. Dmitry Gordon talked about his grandfather, who perished at Babyn Yar. President Zelensky spoke very emotionally about the Babyn Yar massacre and its personal meaning for him because his great-grandparents were killed during the Holocaust.[57] Antony Blinken shared the story about his stepfather Samuel Pisar's visit to Kyiv and Babyn Yar in 1971, which I described in a previous chapter.

Prominent musicians from different countries participated in the ceremony. The German Symphony Orchestra—Berlin performed Dmitri Shostakovich's Symphony No. 13; a cantor from New York City, who was born on the day the Babyn Yar massacre began, September 29, 1941, sang Kaddish.[58]

For the eightieth anniversary of the Babyn Yar massacre documentary film director Sergei Loznitsa prepared a new documentary, *Babyn Yar: Context*, which was first shown on Ukrainian TV on October 4, 2021. The film is based on documentary footage shot from the Nazi invasion of the Soviet Union to postwar Babyn Yar until 1961.[59] *Babyn Yar: Context* received the Special Jury Prize for Best Documentary at the 2021 Cannes Film Festival.[60]

All the commemoration events that I attended in Kyiv were very meaningful and impressive, as were the future projects. The BYHMC planned to construct the first museum on the Babyn Yar site, Kurgan of Memory, in 2022. The museum model was designed as a kurgan, "a type of tumulus or burial mound raised over a final resting ground, significant to the history of Ukraine."[61] The BYHMC also planned to build the Museum of the Oblivion (of Babyn Yar memory in Soviet times) and several other museums.

The BYHMC wrote about the commemoration of the eightieth anniversary of the Babyn Yar massacre:

> During the days of the anniversary, millions of people around the globe had an opportunity to learn more about the enormity of the tragedy of Babyn Yar. With widespread media coverage, and high-level interest in so many different countries and languages, we were able to begin to give a voice to the victims of those dark days and shine a light on the terrible crimes perpetrated there.[62]

BABYN YAR COMMEMORATION DURING THE RUSSIAN INVASION OF UKRAINE

The Babyn Yar Memorial site suffered from Russian airstrikes twice during the Russian invasion of Ukraine: on March 1, 2022, and on January 2, 2024. During the first airstrike five people walking to Babyn Yar were killed and the Kyiv TV Center, which is located nearby, was damaged, as were the grounds of Babyn Yar.[63] During the second airstrike,

> the missile created a sizeable crater in the midst of the Babi Yar forest, and caused extensive damage to nearby residences and businesses. It was pure luck that the missile struck the woods to the north-west of the Jewish monuments and installations, rather than the monuments themselves [figure 7.6].[64]

President Zelensky wrote on March 1, 2022, "To the world: what is the point of saying 'never again' for 80 years, if the world stays silent when a bomb drops on the same site of Babyn Yar? At least 5 killed. History repeating."[65] The first airstrike caused worldwide outrage and was well covered by mass media. However, the second airstrike "received virtually no coverage in the international press."[66] The attention of the world had shifted to the Israeli-Hamas war and other ongoing conflicts.

On March 20, 2022, President Zelensky presented his speech to the Israeli Parliament, the Knesset, in which he compared the Nazi invasion of Ukraine with the Russian invasion, and the Russian troops' war crimes in the occupied territories with the Holocaust. He also mentioned in his speech that Russian missiles hit Kyiv, including

Figure 7.6 Russian attack on Babyn Yar, March 1, 2022. (Unidentified photographer.)

Babyn Yar.⁶⁷ Israeli mass media "criticized Zelensky for drawing comparisons between the Holocaust and Russia's invasion of Ukraine, and seemingly ignoring some Ukrainians' complicity in the Nazi-led genocide."⁶⁸ It seems to me that such criticism of Zelensky's speech in the first, most difficult month of the war, when the enemy troops were near Kyiv, was not appropriate. We should remember the historical past, but we should also understand that Ukraine is now fighting a war for survival as an independent country against an enemy of overwhelming size and weaponry. Russian troops used genocidal methods and committed thousands of war crimes in occupied Ukrainian territories. Many thousands of Ukrainian troops and civilians have perished in the war.

The BYHMC strongly condemned the Russian aggression against Ukraine in the first days of the war.⁶⁹ Oleh Shovenko, the BYHMC deputy artistic director, reported to the Ukrainian Army. Many projects of the BYHMC were frozen during wartime. Thus the war interrupted the plans for construction of new museums at Babyn Yar. On March 3, 2022, Khrzhanovsky gave an interview to the Russian opposition TV channel *Rain* about a Russian missile strike that hit Babyn Yar. Khrzhanovsky denounced the aggression of Russia against Ukraine and said, "The whole of Ukraine has turned into Babyn Yar."⁷⁰ In September 2023 Krzhanovsky resigned his position as the BYHMC artistic director. He explained his decision to resign:

> The war has changed and will continue to change a lot in the perception and formation of the culture of memory in Ukraine—after the war there will come a stage of rethinking all work with memory. I believe that much of the creative concept developed by our team will be useful in the future, but in the current context I consider my stage of activity completed. Whether or not what we have developed is implemented in reality is a matter for Ukrainian society and future generations.⁷¹

Russian American journalist Masha Gessen published an article, "The Holocaust Memorial Undone by Another War," in *The New Yorker* on April 11, 2022, discussing the destruction of the Babyn Yar Holocaust Memorial project.

But the work of the BYHMC has not stopped during the Russian aggression against Ukraine. It was redirected to other projects that were more appropriate and feasible in the current reality. Since the beginning of the war, the BYHMC has focused on providing aid to the local population and raising funds to help people in Ukraine. In the first month of the war, the BYHMC donated 50 million hryvnias ($1.6 million) to humanitarian aid.

Many of the new scholarly and public projects of the BYHMC focus on resistance to Russian aggression and memorialization of the victims of the war. BYHMC researchers gather information about crimes committed by Russian troops in the occupied territory of Ukraine. Gessen wrote:

Desbois's Ukrainian team of six researchers of mass murder were now interviewing victims and witnesses of new Russian war crimes. By the first week of April, they had completed thirty-seven investigations in Bucha, Mariupol, Irpin, Kherson, and Kharkiv.[72]

Since August 2022, the center has run a new project, "Martyrology: Closed Eyes," about civilians killed during the Russian aggression against Ukraine.[73]

On February 7, 2023, the European Parliament, jointly with the Babyn Yar Holocaust Memorial Center, held a public hearing on "Russia's War Against Ukraine—a War of Ideologies and Cultures." On the first anniversary of the Russian invasion of Ukraine, the BYHMC organized an online conference, "Putin and Hitler: Comparing Propaganda."[74]

The BYHMC continued several scholarly projects that were established before the Russian aggression against Ukraine began. During the war, the BYHMC published several issues of the journal *Eastern European Holocaust Studies*. The center also continues its digital archive project of copying and preserving historical documents in Jewish and Ukrainian history from Ukrainian archives that are now under threat of destruction due to Russian airstrikes.

During the war, the BYHMC organized commemoration ceremonies at Babyn Yar on the anniversaries of the massacre on September 29. Ukrainian politicians, foreign diplomats, clergy of different confessions, and public figures participated in the commemoration ceremonies. On September 29, 2023, the BYHMC together with the March of Remembrance organization conducted a memorial march to Babyn Yar.

On the morning before the Babyn Yar March, the President of Ukraine, Volodymyr Zelenskyy, and the Righteous Among the Nations and rabbis of various cities of Ukraine visited the March [of Remembrance organization]. Later, ambassadors from 47 countries honored the memory of those killed at Babyn Yar. The Ukrainian Institute of National Remembrance, the World Congress of Ukrainians, the State Service of Ukraine for Ethnopolitics and Freedom of Conscience, with the support of the Babyn Yar National Historical and Memorial Reserve, held a joint interreligious event near the Menorah monument.[75]

In 2023, the Babyn Yar Holocaust Memorial Center was awarded the tenth Thomas J. Dodd Prize for International Justice and Human Rights.[76] "The University of Connecticut awards the Thomas J. Dodd Prize in International Justice and Human Rights biennially to an individual or group who has made a significant contribution to the advancement of international justice and global human rights. The Prize commemorates the distinguished public service career of Thomas J. Dodd, who served as Executive

Trial Counsel at the International Military Tribunal in Nuremberg, as U.S. Representative from 1953 to 1957 and as Connecticut's Senator from 1959 to 1971."[77]

The BYHMC received the Dodd Prize for their efforts "to obtain, study, and spread knowledge about the tragedy of Babyn Yar, which is especially relevant more than 80 years after those crimes during the Russian-Ukrainian war."[78]

CONCLUSION

Holocaust research and commemoration that were suppressed in the Soviet Union "occupied an important place in Ukrainian politics of history."[79] The anniversaries of the Babyn Yar massacre were always commemorated on the state level in independent Ukraine. Many monuments were built at Babyn Yar over the past few decades. However, the recognition of Babyn Yar as a Holocaust site on a state level in Ukraine did not stop the bitter war of memory in society. This war of memory did not allow the construction of a memorial complex and museum at Babyn Yar for many years. Vitaliy Nakhmanovych wrote:

> The absence in contemporary Ukraine of a shared memory of World War II and the Holocaust argues against the possibility of eradicating this dispute at least on the internal level within the framework of a joint and universally accepted model.[80]

The other obstacle for creation of a modern memorial complex and museum at Babyn Yar was the absence of funds and lack of specialists on the topic. With the creation of the BYHMC, it seemed that such an opportunity was opened. Wealthy Jewish donors promised to provide the necessary funds and an international group of scholars wrote the historical narrative for the future museum. But the work of the BYHMC was interrupted many times and sometimes paralyzed by public attacks by project opponents. Finally the Russian invasion of Ukraine, in the words of Masha Gessen, has undone the future Holocaust Memorial at Babyn Yar.

It is hard to predict how the project for creation of the Babyn Yar Holocaust Memorial Museum will proceed. It very much depends upon how and when the Russian-Ukrainian war ends and the resulting political situation in Ukraine. However, what has already been done by the BYHMC significantly promotes research of the Babyn Yar massacre and the memorialization of its victims. The BYHMC scholarly publications and public events have had an important impact on Ukrainian society. Thousands of people have visited the new memorials at Babyn Yar. I heard from my Ukrainian friends that they cried when they visited the *Mirror Field* memorial. The BYHMC did more in a few years of its work for research and commemoration of the Babyn Yar massacre than was done in the previous seventy-five years after the tragedy. The BYHMC put a great deal of effort into memorializing the victims of the Russian aggression against Ukraine, preserving Ukrainian and Jewish cultural heritage, and providing aid to people in Ukraine who were suffering during the war. Hopefully, after the war is over, the BYHMC will revive their plans for construction of the Babyn Yar Holocaust Memorial Museum in Kyiv, which will memorialize the victims of the Holocaust and the Russian invasion of Ukraine, and impart a lesson of toleration to society.

CONCLUSION

Before World War II, Kyiv was a center of Jewish cultural and scholarly life in the Soviet Union. The Jewish population of Kyiv was second by size after Moscow. In the interwar period, Jews suffered from pogroms during the civil war and then from the Holodomor and repression under Soviet power. Most Jewish cultural and scholarly institutions in Kyiv and in the Soviet Union were closed by the second half of the 1930s. But Jewish life in the city continued. In the Jewish district of Podil the older generation of Jews spoke Yiddish and celebrated Jewish religious holidays.

When World War II began, Soviet propaganda insisted that the Soviets would never surrender Kyiv to the enemy, misleading many Jews who stayed in the city. Older Jews remembered their experiences of the German occupation of Kyiv during World War I, when the Germans restored order and did not persecute Jews. It was hard for them to comprehend that within twenty years Nazi ideology had totally transformed the German nation. Also, when the Nazis attacked the Soviet Union, it became quite difficult for many people to escape from Kyiv. The Soviet government evacuated military and other important plants with their workers and family members, but not the entire population. So, Kyivan Jews who worked at these plants or had a family member working there were eligible for evacuation, but nobody specifically evacuated Jewish women, children, and elderly. Some Jews fled the city on their own initiative, using all possible means of transportation or bribing authorities to receive space in an evacuation train. The majority of those who fled were either young or middle-aged.

Elderly Jews, many women with small children, and people with disabilities often did not have the opportunity to leave, and so they remained in the city when the

Nazis occupied Kyiv. Almost all of them perished at Babyn Yar. The Nazis, with the support of their local collaborators, executed from 70,000 to 80,000 Jews at Babyn Yar. They also killed thousands of prisoners of war, Roma, members of the Soviet underground movement, Ukrainian nationalists, and other people at the ravine. In total, about 100,000 people were executed at Babyn Yar, which became the largest Holocaust site in the Soviet Union.

The Soviets began to use the Babyn Yar massacre for propaganda purposes during the war to show the world the brutality of the Nazi regime and thus garner more support from the Allies in the war with Nazi Germany. The Soviet press published several articles about the Babyn Yar massacre during the war. The first publications wrote extensively about the Jewish victims. However, by the end of the war, the Babyn Yar massacre was described as a universal tragedy of the Soviet people. Due to the importance of the site for propaganda purposes, Ukrainian Soviet leader Khrushchev visited Babyn Yar in the first days after the liberation of Kyiv from the Nazis. He promised that a monument would be built at the massacre site to commemorate its victims. Local officials brought foreign politicians and journalists to Babyn Yar soon after the liberation of Kyiv.

The Soviets also used the Kyiv, Nuremberg, and other trials for their propaganda purposes. But simultaneously, these trials increased awareness of the Nazi crimes and the Babyn Yar massacre. Soviet prosecutors accused the Nazis of committing crimes against the civilian population at Babyn Yar. However, very few Babyn Yar massacre perpetrators came into Soviet hands and were tried. West German courts showed leniency toward Nazi defendants. Thus, many Babyn Yar massacre perpetrators were never punished.

In March 1945, the Ukrainian Soviet government issued a resolution about the construction of a monument and museum at Babyn Yar dedicated to "140,000 Kyivans killed by the Nazis."[1] However, this project was not realized due to the strong popular anti-Semitism in postwar Kyiv and the state anti-Semitic campaigns in the Soviet Union in the late 1940s and early 1950s.

Kyivan Jews who survived in evacuation and who fought at the front were deeply traumatized by news of the Babyn Yar massacre. Many of them visited the Holocaust site as soon as they returned to the city and participated in unofficial commemoration ceremonies there. Jewish and gentile writers and poets wrote about the Babyn Yar massacre during the war and in the first postwar years; it was also depicted in a film and paintings. Soviet censors did not object to portrayals of the Babyn Yar massacre; however, they made sure that the massacre was depicted as part of the universal suffering of the Soviet people during the war, rather than the specific suffering of Jews during the Holocaust.

But from the beginning of the Cold War, any discussions about Babyn Yar, either as the universal tragedy of the Soviet people or as a Holocaust site, were suppressed in the

Soviet Union. Emphasizing Jewish suffering during the Holocaust could not bring the Soviets any additional benefits and support from Western countries but could provoke the wrath of the Soviet gentile population against the authorities. Many writers, poets, and artists who previously depicted the Babyn Yar massacre were accused of Jewish nationalism and prosecuted. Thus Babyn Yar became a forbidden topic until the death of Stalin and the start of Khrushchev's Thaw.

The Thaw brought new hopes to the Soviet people for social justice and the end of state anti-Semitism. The renowned Russian writer Victor Nekrasov and the poet Yevgeny Yevtushenko questioned in their publications why there was no monument at Babyn Yar. Nekrasov's article "Why Isn't This Done?" and Yevtushenko's poem "Babi Yar" raised awareness about the absence of a monument at Babyn Yar, and Yevtushenko's poem depicted the massacre site as a place of Jewish tragedy. Publication of Yevtushenko's poem provoked a storm of criticism from Russian nationalist circles who claimed that Yevtushenko was a national traitor because he wrote a poem about Jewish but not Russian sufferings during the war. Soviet authorities, including Khrushchev, the First Secretary of the Communist Party of the Soviet Union, tried to reconcile liberal and Russian nationalist circles. The Yevtushenko poem was denounced by Khrushchev and other party ideologues, but not forbidden. The officials asked Yevtushenko to add something positive about Russian people, which he did by adding a verse to the poem. The same stormy reaction of Russian nationalist circles was aroused by publication of the censored version of Kuznetsov's book *Babi Yar: A Document in the Form of a Novel*.

Such a furious reaction by conservative nationalist circles on publications about Babyn Yar alerted the authorities to the danger of building a monument at the Holocaust site. Construction of a monument at Babyn Yar was a much riskier enterprise for the Soviet authorities than any fiction or poetry about the massacre. Yevtushenko's poem and Kuznetsov's novel were published in thousands of copies in periodicals, which were read mostly by the intelligentsia, some of whom shared the anti-Semitic mood, but their anti-Semitism took the shape of debates about patriotism in the Soviet press.

Anti-Semitism often took a violent form in Kyiv in the past: There were Jewish pogroms in the city during imperial Russian times, during the revolution and civil war, and during Khrushchev's rule of Ukraine in 1945. The Soviet authorities put lots of effort into suppressing anti-Jewish violence in Kyiv in the first years after the liberation of the city. So, the authorities were afraid that construction of a monument at Babyn Yar might provoke the wrath of anti-Semites that would be directed against the officials who provided funds for its construction. The Soviet concept of the universal suffering of Soviet people during the war did not mislead either Jews or gentiles. All Kyivans knew that most victims of the Babyn Yar massacre were Jews. Thus, even a neutral monument could be perceived by the local population as a monument to the Jews who perished there. The Ukrainian Soviet authorities understood this very well, thus they repeatedly promised the liberal part of society to build a monument at Babyn Yar but postponed its actual construction for three decades.

By the mid-1960s, Jewish activists and gentile liberals tired of waiting for the monument, and they did not believe that the Soviet authorities were ever going to construct it. Kyivan Jewish activists took the initiative into their own hands and began to organize unauthorized commemoration ceremonies at Babyn Yar. At first the authorities tried to calm down the Jews and liberals by placing a stone marker at Babyn Yar with an inscription promising to build a monument. Jewish activists continued their unauthorized Holocaust commemoration ceremonies at Babyn Yar in the following years. Then the authorities changed their tactics and turned from pacification of the public to repression of the Jewish activists who attempted to commemorate the Jewish victims at Babyn Yar. It took more than a decade until the KGB and the police completely suppressed the unauthorized commemoration ceremonies at the Holocaust site, but the ghost of Babyn Yar pursued them on the international stage.

During détente, the Soviet government could no longer ignore the international protest about the absence of a monument at Babyn Yar, because the rejection of Holocaust commemoration negatively impacted their relations with Western countries. So, a monument was built at Babyn Yar posthaste, and the Soviets began to bring foreign delegations there while it was still under construction. Babyn Yar again became necessary for Soviet propaganda purposes.

The Soviet monument at Babyn Yar did not contain any obviously Jewish images and did not mention Jewish victims in its inscription. It was dedicated to Kyivans and prisoners of the war who perished at Babyn Yar and followed the official concept of the universal suffering of the Soviet people during the war. Jews, liberals, and Western visitors were quite disappointed by the absence of Jewish images and the monument's inscription. But could the Soviets construct a Jewish monument at Babyn Yar, and if so, what would be the reaction of the local gentile population?

After World War II, Kyiv turned into the capital of Soviet anti-Semitism, where traditional imperial Russian anti-Semitism merged with Nazi propaganda and Soviet state anti-Semitism. Jews were often insulted and sometimes attacked on the streets, at schools, in public transportation, at the stores and markets. In this poisonous anti-Semitic atmosphere, erection of any monument at Babyn Yar was risky for the authorities and construction of a Jewish monument was impossible, because it would have been bitterly opposed by a significant part of society. Such a monument with Jewish images and inscription would not last for long. It would soon be turned into a special target for anti-Semites and would be vandalized and destroyed. So the Soviets chose what they considered to be a compromise solution: to build a monument at Babyn Yar to commemorate the victims, but one that did not use any Jewish images or symbols on the monument or its inscription.

With the collapse of communism, state anti-Semitism disappeared in Ukraine and public anti-Semitism significantly decreased. The national mentality of the Ukrainian people changed because most of the population wanted to see their country as a part of the European Union and were ready to accept European values. Thus all the leaders of independent Ukraine understood the importance of recognizing the Holocaust and its commemoration. Most Ukrainians tried to break with the shameful Soviet past and get rid of the stain of anti-Semitism. In 2019, Volodymyr Zelensky, who is ethnically Jewish, received 73 percent of the votes in the presidential election and became the president of Ukraine.

The first president of independent Ukraine, Leonid Kravchuk, publicly apologized that the Soviet authorities concealed the truth about the Jewish victims of the Babyn Yar massacre. Since independence, anniversaries of the Babyn Yar tragedy have always been commemorated on the state level in Ukraine, and the mass media always talks about both the Jewish and non-Jewish victims. Over thirty different monuments to the Jewish and gentile victims have been built at Babyn Yar during the years of Ukrainian independence. However, popular anti-Semitism did not disappear completely in Ukraine, and the Jewish monument *Menorah* at Babyn Yar, built in 1991, has been repeatedly vandalized.

The bitter war of memory over the Babyn Yar site has not yet allowed a memorial museum to be built there. Several projects for construction of the Babyn Yar Memorial Museum collapsed due to the public protests of some circles of society. In Soviet times, only Jews, with the support of a few liberal gentiles, attempted to commemorate the victims of the Babyn Yar massacre. In independent Ukraine, several ethnic groups, national organizations, and religious confessions claimed their rights for the memorial site as a place of their national memory. As historian Nakhmanovich wrote, there is no shared memory of World War II in Ukrainian society, and each ethnic group has own narrative and interpretation of events. Perhaps covert anti-Semitism of some part of the society has also played a role in their rejection of recognition of Babyn Yar as a Holocaust site. Thus, some Ukrainian historians and politicians opposed the idea of the construction of the Babyn Yar Holocaust Memorial Museum because they claimed that it was a place of suffering of different peoples, a concept reminiscent of the Soviet concept of the universal suffering of the Soviet people.

The Babyn Yar Holocaust Memorial Center (BYHMC) made a big step forward in the research and commemoration of the Babyn Yar massacre. A group of Ukrainian and foreign scholars wrote the historical narrative for the future museum, which included information about all the victims of the massacre. However, the comprehensive and inclusive historical narrative for the future museum provoked the same protests as all previous unrealized projects for a memorial museum at Babyn Yar. Heated debates about the concept of the memorial museum at Babyn Yar were interrupted by the Russian invasion of Ukraine. It is quite symbolic that the Babyn Yar site was hit by a Russian rocket in the first days of the Russian aggression against Ukraine. Thus the BYHMC project to build a Holocaust Memorial Museum at Babyn Yar was undone by the war.

As I write this conclusion, Ukraine is fighting a difficult war for its freedom and independence. All the efforts of the Ukrainian people focus on the struggle with Russian aggression. Perhaps one day, when the country recovers from the war, Ukrainian society will return to the idea of constructing the Babyn Yar Holocaust Memorial Museum.

NOTES

INTRODUCTION

1. Alexander Galich, "Zasypaia i prosypaias," https://www.culture.ru/poems/3429/zasypaya-i-prosypayas.
2. Alexander Shlaien, *Babi Yar* (Abris, 1995).
3. Sergiy Karamash, *Babyn yar u tragichnykh podiiakh 1941–1943 rokiv. Istoria i Suchasnist' (istoriko-arkhivne doslidzhennia)* (KMM, 2014).
4. Feliks Levitas, *Babi Yar: Sud'by i pamiat'* (Nash Chas, 2016).
5. Ostap Kin, ed., *Babyn Yar: Ukrainian Poets Respond* (Harvard Ukrainian Research Institute, 2023).
6. Pavel Polian, *Babi Yar: Refleksiia* (Publishing House Zebra E, 2022).
7. Martin C. Dean, *Investigating Babyn Yar: Shadows from the Valley of Death* (Lexington Books, 2024).
8. Dean, *Investigating Babyn Yar*, 5.
9. Il'ia Levitas, *Pravedniki Babiego Yara* (Fund "Pamiat' Babego Yara," 2001); Levitas, *Babi Yar: Spasiteli i spasennye* (Stal', 2005).
10. Vitaliy Nakhmanovich and Mykhailo Tiagly, eds., *Babyn Yar: masove ubyvstvo i pam'iat' pro ni'ogo. Materialy mizhnarodnoi naukovoi konferentsii 24–25 zhovtnia 2011 r., m. Kyiv* (Ukrains'kyi tsentr vyvchennia istorii Golocostu, 2012); Vladyslav Hrynevych and Paul Robert Magocsi, eds., *Babyn Yar: History and Memory* (Dukh i Litera, 2016) (a new extended edition was published by University of Toronto Press in 2023); Yohanan Petrovsky-Shtern, "A Paradigm Changing Day: The Twenty-Fifth Anniversary of Babyn Yar and Ukrainian-Jewish Relations," *Harvard Ukrainian Studies* 38, no. 3–4 (2021): 227–58.
11. Lucy S. Dawidowicz, "Babi Yar's Legacy," *New York Times*, September 27, 1981, A. 48.
12. Jessica Rapson, *Topographies of Suffering: Buchenwald, Babi Yar, Lidice* (Berghahn Books, 2015), 79–132.
13. Richard Sheldon, "The Transformations of Babi Yar," in *Soviet Society and Culture: Essays in Honor of Vera S. Dunham*, ed. Terry L. Thompson and Richard Sheldon (Westview Press, 1988), 125–33; Jeff Mankoff, "Babi Yar and the Struggle for Memory, 1944–2004," *Ab Imperio*, 2 (2004): 393–415; Mikhail Mitsel', "Zapret na uvekovechivanie pamiati kak sposob zamalchivaniia Kholokosta: praktika KPU v otnoshenii Babiego Yara." *Golokost i suchasnist'* 1, no. 2 (2007): 9–30; Jacqueline Cherepinsky, "Babi Yar: The Absence of the Babi Yar Massacre from Popular Memory," in *The Holocaust: Memories and History*, ed. Victoria Khiterer (Cambridge Scholars Publishing, 2014), 143–73.

14. John-Paul Himka, "The Reception of the Holocaust in Postcommunist Ukraine," in *Bringing the Dark Past to Light. The Reception of the Holocaust in Postcommunist Europe*, ed. John-Paul Himka and Joanna Beata Michlic (University of Nebraska Press, 2013), 626–61; Aleksandr Burakovsky, "Holocaust Remembrance in Ukraine: Memorialization of the Jewish Tragedy at Babi Yar," *Nationalities Papers* 39, no. 3 (2011): 371–89; Georgii Kasianov, "Sharing the Divided Past: Symbols, Commemorations and Representations at Babyn Yar," *The Ukrainian-Jewish Encounter: Cultural Dimensions*, ed. Wolf Moskovich and Alti Rodal, *Jews and Slavs* 25 (2016): 281–91.
15. Vladimir Khanin, "Judaism and Organized Jewish Movement in the Public Square of the USSR/CIS After World War II: The Ukrainian Case," *Jewish Political Studies Review* 11, no. 1–2 (Spring 1999): 75–100; Khanin, "Jewish Politics in the Post-Communist World: Personality, Ideology and Conflict in Contemporary Ukrainian Jewish Movement," *Journal of Social, Political and Economic Studies* 25, no. 3 (2000): 319–50; Khanin, "The Postcommunist Order, Public Opinion and the Jewish Community of Independent Ukraine," *Harvard Ukrainian Studies* 23, no. 1/2 (June 1999): 85–108.
16. Ilya Ehrenburg and Vasily Grossman, eds., *The Black Book: The Ruthless Murder of Jews by German-Fascist Invaders Throughout the Temporarily-Occupied Regions of the Soviet Union and in the Death Camps of Poland During the War of 1941–1945* (Holocaust Publications: Distributed by Schocken Books, 1981).
17. Ilya Ehrenburg and Vasily Grossman, eds., *The Complete Black Book of Russian Jewry*, trans. and ed. David Patterson (Transaction Publishers, 2002), xiii.
18. Ehrenburg and Grossman, *Complete Black Book of Russian Jewry*, xv.
19. E. M. Pogrebinskaia, "Istoria evreiskikh nauchnykh uchrezhdenii na Ukraine," in *Ievreis'ki naukovi ustanovi v Ukraieni u 20-30-ti roki XX stolittia*, ed. O. V. Zaremba (Institut natsional'nykh vidnosen' i politologii, 1997), 21–22.
20. Pogrebinskaia, "Istoria evreiskikh nauchnykh uchrezhdenii na Ukraine."
21. Maxim D. Shrayer, ed. *An Anthology of Jewish-Russian Literature: Two Centuries of Dual Identity in Prose and Poetry*, Vol. I: 1801–1953 (M. E. Sharpe, 2007), 573–75.
22. Joshua Rubenstein and Ilya Altman, eds., *The Unknown Black Book: The Holocaust in the German-Occupied Soviet Territories* (Indiana University Press, 2008).
23. A. Anatoli (Kuznetsov), *Babi Yar: A Document in the Form of a Novel; New, Complete Uncensored Version* (Farrar, Straus and Giroux, 1970).
24. Kuznetsov, *Babi Yar*, 14.
25. Kuznetsov, *Babi Yar*, 13.
26. Kuznetsov, *Babi Yar*, 13.
27. David Budnik and Yakov Kaper, *Nothing Is Forgotten: Jewish Fates in Kiev 1941–1943*, ed. Erhard Roy Weihn (Hartung-Gorre Verlag, 1993), 14. According to different sources, between 12 to 18 prisoners survived.
28. Budnik and Kaper, *Nothing Is Forgotten*, 14.

29. Budnik and Kaper, *Nothing Is Forgotten*, 115.
30. Budnik and Kaper, *Nothing Is Forgotten*, 127.
31. Tatiana Evstaf'eva and Vitalii Nachmanovich, eds., *Babi Yar: chelovek, vlast', istoriia. Dokumenty i materialy v 5 knigakh. Kniga 1: Istoricheskaia topographiia. Khronologiia sobytii* (Vneshtorgizdat Ukrainy, 2004).
32. Boris Zabarko, ed., *Holocaust in the Ukraine* (Vallentine Mitchell, 2005); Zabarko, ed., *Life in Shadow of Death: Recent Memories About the Holocaust in Ukraine. Testimonies and Documents*. Vol. II (Melitopol' City Printing House, 2019). Despite the different titles and places of publication of these two books, the introduction to the second volume explains that it is a continuation of the book *Holocaust in the Ukraine*.

CHAPTER 1

1. Gennady Estraikh, "From Yehupets Jargonists to Kiev Modernists: The Rise of a Yiddish Literary Centre, 1880s–1914," *East European Jewish Affairs* 30, no. 1 (2000): 34.
2. I. I. Veitsblit, *Rukh evreis'koi liudnosti na Ukraini periodu 1897–1926 rr.* (Proletar, 1930), 163; Mordechai Altshuler, *Soviet Jewry on the Eve of the Holocaust: A Social and Demographic Profile* (Center for Research of East European Jewry of the Hebrew University of Jerusalem, Yad Vashem, 1998), 277; Antony Polonsky, *The Jews in Poland and Russia, Volume III, 1914 to 2008* (Littman Library of Jewish Civilization, 2012), 275; A. V. Kudryts'kyi, ed., *Kiev: Entsyklopedychnyi Dovidnyk* (Golovna redaktsia Ukrains'koi Radians'koi Entsyklopedii, 1981), 22.
3. Shul'gin's visit had been covertly arranged by the Soviet security police, the GPU, via a bogus monarchist organization called Trust (created so that the GPU could infiltrate émigré circles). The GPU had spread a rumor that Shul'gin's younger son, whom he had not seen since the civil war, was alive and needed his father's help. They expected that Shul'gin would contact other monarchists while in the Soviet Union, which would help the GPU control the émigré movement. Victoria Khiterer, "Vasilii Shul'gin and the Jewish Question: An Assessment of Shul'gin's Anti-Semitism," *On the Jewish Street* 1, no. 2 (2011): 16.
4. Khiterer, "Vasilii Shul'gin and the Jewish Question," 141.
5. Khiterer, "Vasilii Shul'gin and the Jewish Question," 141.
6. Victor Nekrasov, "Iz dal'nikh stranstvii vozvratias', Rim, Parizh, New York, Kamchatka i dalee vezde...," http://nekrassov-viktor.com/Friends/Praxova-Nanina.aspx.
7. A. Anatoli (Kuznetsov), *Babi Yar: A Document in the Form of a Novel; New, Complete Uncensored Version* (Farrar, Straus and Giroux, 1970), 94–95.
8. Fima Zhiganets, "Gop so smykom, istoria velikoi pesni," https://www.proza.ru/2008/05/26/256.
9. Victoria Khiterer, "The Jewish Songs of Leonid Utesov," *On the Jewish Street* 2, no. 1 (2012): 17–18.
10. Three different people claimed authorship of the lyrics of the song "Without Podol Kiev Is Impossible." Most likely the author of the lyrics was Grigory Bal'ber (1939–2004). This

underground song was unofficially recorded in the 1970s and was often performed in restaurants and homes in Kyiv. Igor' Efimov, "Zagadka Pesni pro Podol," http://a-pesni.org/dvor/a-podol.php; Kyiv Saint Vladimir Monument (sculptors Vasily Demut-Malinovsky and Peter Clodt), dedicated to the Great Prince of Kyiv Vladimir, built in 1853, became a symbol of Kyiv.

11. Estraikh, "From Yehupets Jargonists to Kiev Modernists," 34; Victoria Khiterer, *Jewish City or Inferno of Russian Israel? A History of the Jews in Kiev Before February 1917* (Academic Studies Press, 2016), 14.
12. Paul Robert Magocsi, *History of Ukraine* (University of Toronto Press, 1996), 504.
13. Cited in Hillel Kazovsky, *The Artists of the Kultur-Lige* (Gesher, 2003), 18.
14. Kazovsky, *The Artists of the Kultur-Lige*, 18.
15. Zvi Y. Gitelman, *Jewish Nationality and Soviet Politics: The Jewish Sections of CPSU, 1917–1930* (Princeton University Press, 1972), 273.
16. Gitelman, *Jewish Nationality and Soviet Politics*, 274.
17. M. O. Rybakov, ed., *Pravda Istorii: Diial'nist' Evreis'koi kul'turno-prosvitnytskoi organizatsii "Kul'turna Liga" u Kyevi (1918–1925)* (Kyi, 2001), 3–12.
18. Rybakov, *Pravda Istorii*, 8.
19. Kazovsky, *The Artists of the Kultur-Lige*, 24.
20. Kazovsky, *The Artists of the Kultur-Lige*, 26; David Shneer, *Yiddish and the Creation of Soviet Jewish Culture. 1918–1930* (Cambridge University Press, 2004), 150.
21. Shneer, *Yiddish and the Creation of Soviet Jewish Culture*, 163.
22. Shneer, *Yiddish and the Creation of Soviet Jewish Culture*, 24.
23. Arno Lustiger, *Stalin and the Jews: The Tragedy of the Jewish Anti-Fascist Committee and the Soviet Jews* (Enigma Books, 2003), 221–44.
24. Moisei Loev, *Ukradennaia Muza: Vospominaniia o Kievskom gosudarstvennom evreiskom teatre imeni Sholom Aleikhema, Kharkov-Kiev-Chernovtsy, 1925–1950* (Dukh i Litera, 2004), 47–82.
25. Loev, *Ukradennaia Muza*, 85–86.
26. State Archive of City Kyiv (DAMK), f. R-1, op. 1, d. 2297, ll. 54–57.
27. DAMK, f. R-1, op. 1, d. 9575.
28. Central State Archive of the Higher Authorities and Government of Ukraine (TsDAVO U), f. 166, op. 4, d. 974, l. 89.
29. TsDAVO U, f. 166, op. 4, d. 974, l. 89.
30. Victoria Khiterer, *Documenty po evreiskoi istorii XVI–XX vekov v kievskikh arkhivakh* (Gesharim Publishing House and Institute of Jewish Studies, 2001), 135–36.
31. Victoria Khiterer, ed., *Dokumenty, sobrannye evreiskoi istoriko-arkheograficheskoi komissiei Vseukrainskoi Akademii Nauk* (Hebrew University of Jerusalem and Gesharim Publishing House, 1999), 6–7.
32. Khiterer, *Dokumenty*, 5.

33. Central State Historical Archive of Ukraine in City Kyiv (TsDIAK U), f. 1423, op. 1, 42 files.
34. Saul Borovoi, *Vospominaniia* (Gesharim, 1993), 186.
35. Khiterer, *Dokumenty*, 9.
36. Abraham Greenbaum, *Evrei v Rossii: Istorikograficheski ocherki 2-aia polovina XIX veka–XX vek.* (Gesharim Publishing House, 1994), 27–28; Veniamin Lukin, "Fond Evreiskogo istoriko-etnograficheskogo obschestva v Tsentral'nom Gosudarstvennom Arkhive Leningrada," in *Istoricheskie sud'by evreev v Rossii i SSSR: nachalo dialoga*, ed. E. Krupnik (Evreiskoe istoricheskoe obshchestvo, 1992), 252.
37. Before the revolution Galant worked as the personal secretary of Baron David Gintsburg, not Brodsky.
38. Spivak confused archaeography—the discipline of publishing old manuscripts—with archaeology.
39. Khiterer, *Dokumenty*, 14.
40. Khiterer, *Dokumenty*, 14.
41. Saul Borovoi, "Vospominaniia ob I. V. Galante," in *Dokumenty*, ed. Khiterer, 18.
42. Borovoi, "Vospominaniia," 20.
43. Gennady Estraikh, *Soviet Yiddish: Language Planning and Linguistic Development* (Clarendon Press, 1999), 68–70, 74, 82.
44. Greenbaum, *Evrei v Rossii*, 38.
45. Khiterer, *Dokumenty*, 10.
46. Khiterer, *Dokumenty*, 10.
47. Khiterer, *Dokumenty*, 10.
48. Greenbaum, *Evrei v Rossii*, 38.
49. Khiterer, *Dokumenty*, 10.
50. Mendele Moykher-Sforim (pseudonym of Sholem Yankev Abramovitsh, 1835–1917), Yiddish writer, one of the forefathers of Yiddish literature in Russia, often called the "grandfather" of Yiddish literature.
51. Borovoi, *Vospominaniia*, 114.
52. Nikolai Senchenko and Irina Sergeeva, "Sud'ba biblioteki," *Vechernii Kiev*, November 27, 1990, 2.
53. The Minsk Institute for Jewish Proletarian Culture was established in 1933. Its predecessor institutions were the Jewish section of the Institute for Belorussian Culture (Inbelkult) founded in 1921 and transformed into the Jewish division of the Belorussian Academy of Sciences in 1928. Elissa Bemporad, *Becoming Soviet Jews: The Bolshevik Experiment in Minsk* (Indiana University Press, 2013), 100–102.
54. Greenbaum, *Evrei v Rossii*, 45.
55. E. I. Melamed, "Likvidatsiia Kievskogo Instituta evreiskoi proletarskoi kul'tury i repressii protiv ego sotrudnikov. Po materialam arkhivno-sledstvennykh del 1930-kh godov," in

Archiv evreiskoi istorii, ed. O. B. Budnitsky, Vol. 10 (Politicheskaia entsiklopediia, 2018), 172.
56. Leonid Fliat, "Liberberg i drugie... K istorii instituta evreiskoi kul'tury (Kiev)," *Novosti Nedeli*, July 15, 1999, 8.
57. Greenbaum, *Evrei v Rossii*, 39.
58. Central State Archives of Supreme Bodies of Power and Government of Ukraine (TsDAVO U), f. 413, op. 1, d. 592, ll. 14–20.
59. Khiterer, *Dokumenty*, 15.
60. Alfred Abraham Greenbaum, *Jewish Scholarship and Scholarly Institutions in Soviet Russia* (Hebrew University of Jerusalem, Centre for Research and Documentation of East European Jewry, 1978), 68.
61. Greenbaum, *Jewish Scholarship*, 46.
62. Gennady Estraikh, *In Harness: Yiddish Writers' Romance with Communism* (Syracuse University Press, 2005), 136.
63. Estraikh, *In Harness*, 136.
64. Iosif Brener, "Semia Liberberg," *My zdes'*, no. 581, March 8–18, 2019, http://www.newswe.com/index.php?go=Pages&in=view&id=5694; Melamed, "Likvidatsiia Kievskogo Instituta evreiskoi proletarskoi kul'tury," 171.
65. Melamed, "Likvidatsiia Kievskogo Instituta evreiskoi proletarskoi kul'tury," 174.
66. Melamed, "Likvidatsiia Kievskogo Instituta evreiskoi proletarskoi kul'tury," 188.
67. "Liberberg Iosif Izraelivich," *Vspomnim vsekh poimenno*, http://eao.memo27reg.org/pamat-1/semletmyziliozidaniempisem.
68. Brener, "Semia Liberberg," *My zdes'*.
69. The Military Collegium of the Supreme Court of the USSR was located at Nikolskaia Street, 23, Moscow, in the so-called shooting house, where 31,000 death sentences were issued. The house is situated 600 meters (less than half a mile) from Red Square. Death sentences were often carried out in the basement of the building. Many members of the Soviet political and military elite were sentenced to death there, including Nikolai Bukharin, Alexei Rykov, Lev Kamenev, Grigory Zinoviev, Marshall Mikhail Tukhachevsky, and many others. Ilia Udovenko, "Rasstrel'nyi dom na Nikol'skoi," *Zhivaia istoria*, http://lhistory.ru/statyi/rasstrelnyj-dom-na-nikolskoj.
70. Nataliia Stavyts'ka, "Likvidatsiia naukovo-doslidnykh ustanov VUAN z doslidzhennia natsional'nykh men'shyn Ukrainy (ii pol. 1920-1930-kh rr.)," *Istoria Ukrainy: Malovidomi imena, podii, facty. Zbirnyk statei*, 34 (Kyiv: Instytut Istorii Ukrainy NAN Ukrainy, 2007), 38–39.
71. Bemporad, *Becoming Soviet Jews*, 200.
72. "Sosis, Israel," *Rossiiskaia evreiskaia entsiklopedia*, 2nd ed. (Moscow, Epos, 2000), Vol. III, 98.
73. Melamed, "Likvidatsiia Kievskogo Instituta evreiskoi proletarskoi kul'tury," 171; Greenbaum, *Evrei v Rossii*, 68.
74. Gennady Estraikh, "Spivak, Elye," *The YIVO Encyclopedia of Jews in Eastern Europe*, https://yivoencyclopedia.org/article.aspx/Spivak_Elye.

75. Gitelman, *Jewish Nationality and Soviet Politics*, 271.
76. Rybakov, *Pravda Istorii*, 8–9.
77. Gitelman, *Jewish Nationality and Soviet Politics*, 301.
78. Mykhailo Kal'nytsky, "Vykorystannia Evreis'kykh gromads'kykh sporud u Kyevi (1920-i–1930-i rr.)," in *Dolia evreis'koi dukhovnoi ta material'noi spadschyny v XX stolitti: Materialy conferentsii 28–30 serpnia 2001 r.* (Dukh i Litera, 2002), 16–17.
79. Kal'nytsky, "Vykorystannia Evreis'kykh gromads'kykh sporud u Kyevi," 16–17.
80. Kal'nytsky, "Vykorystannia Evreis'kykh gromads'kykh sporud u Kyevi," 16–17.
81. Kal'nytsky, "Vykorystannia Evreis'kykh gromads'kykh sporud u Kyevi," 18; Victoria Khiterer, "Konfiskatsiia evreiskikh documental'nyh materialov i evreiskoi sobstvennosti v Ukraine v 1919–1930 gg.," in *Dolia evreis'koi dukhovnoi ta material'noi spadschyny v XX stolitti: Materialy conferentsii 28–30 serpnia 2001 r.* (Dukh i Litera, 2002), 11.
82. Khiterer, "Konfiskatsiia evreiskikh documental'nyh materialov," 13.
83. Naum Korzhavin, *V soblaznakh krovavoi epokhi*, Vol. I (Zakharov, 2007), 99.
84. The People's Commissariat of Internal Affairs (NKVD) was organized in July 1934 and was the successor to the OGPU. In 1933 the political police were called the OGPU.
85. Vasily Grossman, *Forever Flowing* (Harper & Row, 1970), 162.
86. A. B. Zubov, *Istoria Rossii XX vek. Epokha Stalinisma (1923–1953)*, Vol. II (Izdatel'stvo "E," 2016), 190.
87. Grossman, *Forever Flowing*, 162.
88. Bohdan Klid and Alexander J. Motyl, eds., *The Holodomor Reader: A Sourcebook on the Famine of 1932–1933 in Ukraine* (Canadian Institute of Ukrainian Studies Press, 2012), 117.
89. Klid and Motyl, *The Holodomor Reader*, 130.
90. Robert Conquest, *The Harvest of Sorrow: Soviet Collectivization and the Terror-Famine* (Oxford University Press, 1986), 248.
91. Grossman, *Forever Flowing*, 161.
92. Grossman, *Forever Flowing*, 161–63.
93. Grossman, *Forever Flowing*, 162.
94. Korzhavin, *V soblaznakh krovavoi epokhi*, 60.
95. Klid and Motyl, *The Holodomor Reader*, 131.
96. Grossman, *Forever Flowing*, 163.
97. Omelian Rudnytskyi et al., "Demography of a Man-Made Human Catastrophe: The Case of Massive Famine in Ukraine 1932–1933," *Canadian Studies in Population* 42, no. 1–2 (2015): 53; Natalia Levchuk et al., "Vtraty mis'koho i sil's'koho naselennia Ukraïny vnaslidok Holodomoru 1932–1934 rr.: novi otsinky," *Ukraïns'kyi istorychnyi zhurnal*, no. 4 (2015): 84–112.
98. Aleksander Naiman, "Evreiskoe zemledelie na Ukraine v 1930-e gody," *Vestnik Evreiskogo Universiteta v Moskve* 8, no. 1 (1995): 221.
99. Grossman, *Forever Flowing*, 162–63.
100. Grossman, *Forever Flowing*, 162–63.

101. Klid and Motyl, *The Holodomor Reader*, 130–31.
102. Harry Lang, "Sered ievreiv u Kyievi," *Yehupets'* 20 (2011): 187.
103. Klid and Motyl, *The Holodomor Reader*, 131.
104. Klid and Motyl, *The Holodomor Reader*, 131.
105. Klid and Motyl, *The Holodomor Reader*, 132.
106. Klid and Motyl, *The Holodomor Reader*, 135.
107. Klid and Motyl, *The Holodomor Reader*, 131.
108. Korzhavin, *V soblaznakh krovavoi epokhi*, 58.
109. Elena Osokina, *Zoloto dlia industrializatsii: Torgsin* (Rosspen, 2009), 163.
110. Korzhavin, *V soblaznakh krovavoi epokhi*, 58.
111. Korzhavin, *V soblaznakh krovavoi epokhi*, 58.
112. Lang, "Sered ievreiv u Kyievi," 188.
113. Lang, "Sered ievreiv u Kyievi," 188–90.
114. Lang, "Sered ievreiv u Kyievi," 188–90.
115. The correct name of the organization was OGPU.
116. Klid and Motyl, *The Holodomor Reader*, 134.
117. Khiterer, *Jewish City or Inferno of Russian Israel?*
118. Korzhavin, *V soblaznakh krovavoi epokhi*, 95–100.
119. Korzhavin, *V soblaznakh krovavoi epokhi*, 100.
120. Korzhavin, *V soblaznakh krovavoi epokhi*, 100.
121. Korzhavin, *V soblaznakh krovavoi epokhi*, 95.
122. Anatoli (Kuznetsov), *Babi Yar*, 359–60.
123. Anatoli (Kuznetsov), *Babi Yar*, 359–60. Aleksander Shlikhter (1868–1940) was a professional revolutionary and Soviet apparatchik. After the October revolution, Shlikhter was the people's commissar of provisions of the Russian Soviet Socialist Republic. He was the people's commissar of agriculture in the Ukrainian Soviet Socialist Republic in 1927–29 and vice president of the Ukrainian Academy of Sciences in 1931–38. It is notable that Shlikhter, as a representative of the national minorities, was chosen to make a speech about "the wrecking activity of the various nations" at the Thirteenth Congress of the Communist Party of Ukraine.

CHAPTER 2

1. Feliks Levitas, "Babi Yar (1941–1943)," in *Katastrofa ta opir ukrains'kogo evreistva (1941–1944): Narysy z Istorii Kholokostu ta oporu v Ukraini*, ed. Ster Elisavetsky (Institute of Political and Ethnic Studies, National Academy of Sciences of Ukraine, 1999), 88.
2. Victoria Khiterer, "Babi Yar, the Tragedy of Kiev's Jews," *Brandeis Graduate Journal* (2004): 3–4.
3. Khiterer, "Babi Yar, the Tragedy of Kiev's Jews," 3–4.
4. Khiterer, "Babi Yar, the Tragedy of Kiev's Jews," 3–4; A. Anatoli (Kuznetsov), *Babi Yar: A Document in the Form of a Novel; New, Complete Uncensored Version* (Farrar, Straus and

Giroux, 1970), 38; A. Kruglov, A. Umansky, and I. Shchupak, eds., *Kholokost v Ukraine: Reikhskomissariat "Ukraina," Gubernatorstvo "Transnistriia"* (Ukrainskii institut izucheniia kholokosta "Tkuma," 2016), 228–32.

5. Yitzhak Arad, Shmuel Krakowsky, and Shmuel Spector, eds., *The Einsatzgruppen Reports* (Holocaust Library, 1989), 165; Tatiana Evstaf'eva and Vitaliy Nachmanovich, eds., *Babi Yar: chelovek, vlast', istoriia: Dokumenty i materialy v 5 knigakh. Kniga 1: Istoricheskaia topographiia. Khronologiia sobytii* (Kyiv: Vneshtorgizdat Ukrainy, 2004), 102; Karel C. Berkhoff, "Babyn Yar: mistse naimashtabnogo roztrilu evreiv natsystamy v Radians'komu Soiuzi," in *Babyn Yar: masove ubyvstvo i pam'iat' pro ni'ogo. Materialy mizhnarodnoi naukovoi konferentsii 24–25 zhovtnia 2011 r., m. Kyiv*, ed. Vitaliy Nakhmanovich and Mykhailo Tiagly (Ukrains'kyi tsentr vyvchennia istorii Golocostu, 2012), 8–20; Oleksandr Kruglov, "'My povynni buly vykonuvaty brudnu robotu . . .': Znyshchennia evreiv Kyieva voseny 1941 r. U svitli nimets'kykh dokumentiv," in *Babyn Yar: masove ubyvstvo*, 19.
6. Ilya Ehrenburg and Vasily Grossman, eds., *The Black Book: The Ruthless Murder of Jews by German-Fascist Invaders Throughout the Temporarily-Occupied Regions of the Soviet Union and in the Death Camps of Poland During the War of 1941–1945* (Holocaust Library, 1981), 3.
7. F. L. Levitas, "Babi Yar (1941–1943)," 94.
8. Arad, Krakowsky, and Spector, *The Einsatzgruppen Reports*, 165.
9. Evstaf'eva and Nachmanovich, *Babi Yar*, 66, 69–70.
10. Arad, Krakowsky, and Spector, *The Einsatzgruppen Reports*, 173.
11. Karel C. Berkhoff, "Babi Yar: Site of Mass Murder, Ravine and Oblivion," *J. B. and Maurice C. Shapiro Annual Lecture*, February 9, 2011, 5, https://www.ushmm.org/m/pdfs/Publication_OP_2011-02.pdf.
12. Ehrenburg and Grossman, *The Black Book*, 6.
13. Karel C. Berkhoff, *Harvest of Despair: Life and Death in Ukraine Under Nazi Rule* (Belknap Press of Harvard University Press, 2004), 65–66.
14. Berkhoff, *Harvest of Despair*, 66.
15. F. L. Levitas, "Babi Yar (1941–43)," 98.
16. Vitaliy Nachmanovich, "Babyn Yar: The Holocaust and Other Tragedies," in *Babyn Yar: History and Memory*, ed. Vladyslav Hrynevych and Paul Robert Magocsi (Dukh i Litera, 2016), 67.
17. Feliks Levitas, *Babi Yar: Sud'by i pamiat'* (Nash Chas, 2016), 66.
18. Berkhoff, *Harvest of Despair*, 66.
19. A. Anatoli (Kuznetsov), *Babi Yar*, 94.
20. Nachmanovich, "Babyn Yar: The Holocaust and Other Tragedies," 67.
21. Ehrenburg and Grossman, *The Black Book*, 8.
22. Berkhoff, *Harvest of Despair*, 67.
23. Berkhoff, *Harvest of Despair*, 67–68.
24. Ehrenburg and Grossman, *The Black Book*, 8; F. Levitas, *Babi Yar: Sud'by i pamiat'*, 60.

25. Berkhoff, "Babyn Yar," 13.
26. Berkhoff, "Babyn Yar," 13.
27. Nachmanovich, "Babyn Yar: The Holocaust and Other Tragedies," 67–68.
28. Berkhoff, "Babyn Yar," 13.
29. Karel C. Berkhoff, "The Dispersal and Oblivion of the Ashes and Bones of Babi Yar," in *Lesson and Legacies XII: New Directions in Holocaust Research and Education*, ed. Wendy Lower and Lauren Faulkner Rossi (Northwestern University Press, 2017), 256–57.
30. Berkhoff, "Babyn Yar," 13.
31. F. Levitas, "Babi Yar (1941–1943)," 98.
32. Karel C. Berkhoff, "Dina Pronicheva's Story of Surviving the Babi Yar Massacre: German, Jewish, Soviet, Russian, and Ukrainian Records," in *The Shoah in Ukraine: History, Testimony, Memorialization*, ed. Ray Brandon and Wendy Lower (Indiana University Press, 2008), 294; Ehrenburg and Grossman, *The Black Book*, 8–9.
33. Berkhoff, "Babyn Yar," 14.
34. Nachmanovich, "Babyn Yar: The Holocaust and Other Tragedies," 68.
35. F. Levitas, "Babi Yar (1941–1943)," 98.
36. Lucy S. Dawidowicz, ed., *A Holocaust Reader* (Behrman House, 1975), 90.
37. Nachmanovich, "Babyn Yar: The Holocaust and Other Tragedies," 68.
38. Ehrenburg and Grossman, *The Black Book*, 11.
39. Berkhoff, "The Dispersal and Oblivion of the Ashes and Bones of Babi Yar," 257.
40. Berkhoff, "Babyn Yar," 117–56.
41. Kruglov, Umansky, and Shchupak, *Kholokost v Ukraine*, 249.
42. Nachmanovich, "Babyn Yar: The Holocaust and Other Tragedies," 68.
43. F. Levitas, *Babi Yar: Sud'by i pamiat'*, 63.
44. The Nazis were often called fascists in Soviet sources.
45. V. Stepanenko, "Chto proiskhodit v Kieve," *Pravda*, November 29, 1941, cited in F. Levitas, *Babi Yar: Sud'by i pamiat'*, 68.
46. Yehuda Bauer, *A History of the Holocaust*, rev. ed. (Franklin Watts, 2001), 217.
47. Berkhoff, "The Dispersal and Oblivion of the Ashes and Bones of Babi Yar," 258.
48. Konstantin Goreshin, ed., *Niurembergskii Protsess: Sbornik Materialov*, Vol. I, 3rd ed. (Gosudarstvennoe izdatel'stvo iuridicheskoi literatury, 1955), 548.
49. Central State Archive of Public Organizations of Ukraine (TsDAHO U), f. 1, op. 23, d. 4913, ll. 2–3; A. V. Kudrytskyi, ed., *Kyiv: Entsyklopedychnyi dovidnyk* (Golovna redaktsiia Ukrains'koi Radians'koi Entsyklopedii, 1981), 32.
50. TsDAHO U, f. 1, op. 23, d. 4913, ll. 2–3.
51. Sergii Kot, "Uchasnyky pidpillia OUN (m)—zhertvy Babynogo Yaru (1941–1943)," in *Babyn Yar: Masove Ubuistvo i pam'iat' pro n'iogo. Materialy mizhnarodnoi naukovoi konferentsii 24–25 zhovtnia 2011 r. Kyiv*, ed. Vitaliy Nakhmanovich and Mykhailo Tiagly (Komitet "Babi Yar," 2012), 101.

52. F. Levitas, "Babi Yar (1941–43)," 93; Tatiana Evstaf'eva, "Tragedia Babynogo Yaru u 1941–1943 rr." (Za Dokumentamy Galuzevogoderzhavnogo Arkhivu Sluzhby bezpeky Ukrainy)," *Z Arkhiviv VUCHK, GPU, NKVD, KGB* 22/23, no. 1–2 (2004): 358; Yuriy Varshaver (Shcheglov), *Vospominaniia o Viktore Platonoviche Nekrasove*, http://nekrassov-viktor.com/AboutOfVPN/Nekrasov-Sheglov-Yriy.aspx.
53. Arad, Krakowsky, and Spector, *The Einsatzgruppen Reports*, 164–65.
54. Varshaver (Shcheglov), *Vospominaniia o Viktore Platonoviche Nekrasove*.
55. Alexander Kruglov, "Jewish Losses in Ukraine, 1941–1944," in *The Shoah in Ukraine: History, Testimony, Memorialization*, ed. Ray Brandon and Wendy Lower (Indiana University Press, 2008), 274–75.
56. Arad, Krakowsky, and Spector, *The Einsatzgruppen Reports*, 164.
57. Berkhoff, "Babyn Yar," 10.
58. Victoria Khiterer, *Jewish City or Inferno of Russian Israel? A History of the Jews in Kiev Before February 1917* (Academic Studies Press, 2016), 259–89.
59. Arad, Krakowsky, and Spector, *The Einsatzgruppen Reports*, 173.
60. Arad, Krakowsky, and Spector, *The Einsatzgruppen Reports*, 173.
61. Irina Khoroshunova, *Dnevnik Kievlianki*, Part II, https://gordonua.com/specprojects/khoroshunova2.html.
62. A. Anatoli (Kuznetsov), *Babi Yar*, 359–60.
63. Korzhavin, *V soblaznakh krovavoi epokhi*, Vol. I (Zakharov, 2006), 109.
64. Korzhavin, *V soblaznakh krovavoi epokhi*, 108–109.
65. Korzhavin, *V soblaznakh krovavoi epokhi*, 108–109.
66. Korzhavin, *V soblaznakh krovavoi epokhi*, 104.
67. Ilya Ehrenburg and Vasily Grossman, eds., *The Complete Black Book of Russian Jewry*, trans. and ed. David Patterson (Transaction Publishers, 2003), 4.
68. Anatoly Kuznetsov (A. Anatoli), *Babi Yar: roman-dokument* (Radians'kyi pysmennyk, 1991), 156.
69. A. Anatoli (Kuznetsov), *Babi Yar: roman-dokument*, 156.
70. Timothy Snyder, *Black Earth: The Holocaust as History and Warning* (Tim Duggan Books, 2015), 181.
71. Kruglov, Umansky, and Shchupak, *Kholokost v Ukraine*, 241.
72. F. Levitas, *Babi Yar: Sud'by i pamiat'*, 66.
73. F. Levitas, *Babi Yar: Sud'by i pamiat'*, 66.
74. F. Levitas, *Babi Yar: Sud'by i pamiat'*, 66.
75. Oleksandr Melnyk wrote that the pogrom was on either September 30 or October 1, 1941. However, one of the perpetrators, Nikifor Yushkov, testified that he participated in the pogrom and murder of Jews for two days. The Soviet investigation of the pogrom in Podil was in December 1943–January 1944, more than two years after the events. So, some eyewitnesses and perpetrators might not remember the exact date. Oleksandr Melnyk, "Stalinist

Justice as a Site of Memory: Anti-Jewish Violence in Kyiv's Podil District in September 1941 Through the Prism of Soviet Investigative Documents," *Jarhbücher fuer Geschichte Osteuropas* 61 (2013), Heft 2: 226; Kruglov, Umansky, and Shchupak, *Kholokost v Ukraine*, 241.

76. Melnyk, "Stalinist Justice as a Site of Memory," 226.
77. Melnyk, "Stalinist Justice as a Site of Memory," 223.
78. Sectoral State Archive of the Security Services of Ukraine (HDA SBU), f. 5, op. 1, d. 46837, volume I.
79. Melnyk, "Stalinist Justice as a Site of Memory," 232, 244.
80. Melnyk, "Stalinist Justice as a Site of Memory," 241–42.
81. Melnyk, "Stalinist Justice as a Site of Memory," 242.
82. Melnyk, "Stalinist Justice as a Site of Memory," 242.
83. Melnyk, "Stalinist Justice as a Site of Memory," 229.
84. Kruglov, Umansky, and Shchupak, *Kholokost v Ukraine*, 241.
85. Kruglov, Umansky, and Shchupak, *Kholokost v Ukraine*, 241.
86. Melnyk, "Stalinist Justice as a Site of Memory," 236.
87. Victoria Khiterer, "The October 1905 Pogrom in Kiev," *East European Jewish Affairs* 22, no. 2, (1992): 21–37; Melnyk, "Stalinist Justice as a Site of Memory," 242.
88. Seven Jewish corpses were found in two graves during the interrogation.
89. A. Kruglov, ed., *Sbornik dokumentov i materialov ob unichtozhenii natsistami evreev Ukrainy v 1941–1944 godakh* (Institut iudaiki, 2002), 141.
90. Mordechai Altshuler, "The Unique Features of the Holocaust in the Soviet Union," in *Jews and Jewish Life in Russia and the Soviet Union*, ed. Yaacov Ro'i (Frank Cass, 1995), 178.
91. Simon Petliura (1879–1926) was a Ukrainian politician and publicist. He was the supreme commander of the Army of the Ukrainian National Republic (1918–20) and president of the Directory of the Ukrainian National Republic. The soldiers of the Ukrainian National Army, so-called *petliurovtsy*, conducted many bloody pogroms in Ukraine during the civil war in 1918–20. When the Bolsheviks conquered Ukraine, Petliura moved to Warsaw and then to Paris, and he was the head of the government-in-exile of the Ukrainian National Republic. A Jew, Samuel (Sholem) Schwarzbard, assassinated Petliura in Paris in revenge for Jewish pogroms in Ukraine during the civil war.
92. Kruglov, Umansky, and Shchupak, *Kholokost v Ukraine*, 229.
93. TsDAHO U, f. 1, op. 23, d. 121, l. 61.
94. Berkhoff, "Babi Yar: Site of Mass Murder, Ravine of Oblivion," 6.
95. V. Nachmanovich, "Do pytannia pro sklad uchasnykiv karal'nykh aktsii v okupovanomu Kyevi (1941–1943)," in *Druga svitova viina i dolia narodiv Ukrainy: materialy 2-i Vseukrains'koi naukovoi konferentsii, m. Kyiv, 30–31 zhovtnia 2006 r.*, ed. V. Nachmanovich (Zovnishtorgvydav, 2007), 258.
96. Berkhoff, "Dina Pronicheva's Story," 303.
97. Berkhoff, "Babi Yar: Site of Mass Murder, Ravine of Oblivion," 7.

98. Berkhoff, "Dina Pronicheva's Story," 303.
99. Berkhoff, "Dina Pronicheva's Story," 303.
100. Per Anders Rudling, "Terror and Local Collaboration in Occupied Belarus: The Case of the Schutzmannschaft Battalion 118," *Romanian Academy "Nicolae Iorga" History Institute: Historical Yearbook*, Vol. VIII (Bucharest, 2011): 201.
101. Ivan Dereiko, "Ukrains'ki dopomizhni voenizovani formuvannia nimetts'koi armii i politsii v general'niy okruzi Kyiv u 1941–1943 rr.," in *Arkhivy okupatsii 1941–1944*, ed. Nataliia Makovs'ka, Vol. I, 2nd ed. (Kyevo-Mogylians'ka Akademiia, 2008), 797–98.
102. Dereiko, "Ukrains'ki dopomizhni voenizovani formuvannia nimetts'koi armii i politsii v general'niy okruzi Kyiv," 799.
103. Dereiko, "Ukrains'ki dopomizhni voenizovani formuvannia nimetts'koi armii i politsii v general'niy okruzi Kyiv," 799. Jews were held in the concentration camp on Kerosynna Street and two other concentration camps in Kyiv. One was near Kyiv Pechersk Lavra (Kyiv Cave Monastery), where there were 75–80 young Jewish prisoners, and the other on Instytutska Street had 150 Jewish prisoners. The Jewish prisoners were used as forced laborers. All Jewish prisoners of the concentration camp near Lavra were used as agricultural workers and were executed after the end of the agricultural season in fall 1942. The Jewish prisoners from the Instytutska Street camp worked on the reconstruction of the ruined building on the same street and later were transferred to the Syrets concentration camp. Kruglov, Umansky, and Shchupak, *Kholokost v Ukraine*, 249.
104. Melnyk, "Stalinist Justice as a Site of Memory," 224.
105. Paul Robert Magocsi, *A History of Ukraine: The Land and Its Peoples*, 2nd ed. (University of Toronto Press, 2010), 670.
106. Magocsi, *A History of Ukraine*, 671.
107. Magocsi, *A History of Ukraine*, 672.
108. Magocsi, *A History of Ukraine*, 671.
109. Regarding the relations between Nazis and the Organization of Ukrainian Nationalists (OUN), please see Karel C. Berkhoff and Marco Carynnyk, "The Organization of Ukrainian Nationalists and Its Attitude Toward Germans and Jews: Iaroslav Stets'ko's 1941 Zhytiepys," *Harvard Ukrainian Studies* 23, no. 3 (January 1999): 149–84; Per A. Rudling, *The OUN, the UPA and the Holocaust: A Study in the Manufacturing of Historical Myths. The Carl Beck Papers in Russian & East European Studies* (November 2011), no. 2107, 3; Yuri Radchenko, "The Organization of Ukrainian Nationalists (Mel'nyk Faction) and the Holocaust: The Case of Ivan Iuriiv," *Holocaust and Genocide Studies* 31 (111), no. 2 (Fall 2017): 215–39; Yuri Radchenko, "Babyn Yar: A Site of Massacres, (Dis)Remembrance and Instrumentalization," *New Eastern Europe*, October 11, 2016, https://neweasterneurope.eu/2016/10/11/babyn-yar-a-site-of-massacres-dis-remembrance-and-instrumentalisation/.
110. M. Yurkevich, "Organization of Ukrainian Nationalists," *Encyclopedia of Ukraine* (University of Toronto Press, 1993), III, 709.

111. "The Foremost Enemy of Ukraine—the YID!," *Ukrains'ke slovo*, October 2, 1941.
112. "Malen'kyi budynochok," *Ukrains'ke slovo*, October 9, 1941.
113. The All-Union Association for Trade with Foreigners (Torgsin) functioned in the Soviet Union in 1931–36. Torgsin stores sold food to foreigners and Soviet citizens for hard currency, or exchanged food for gold, silver, and precious stones.
114. Karel C. Berkhoff, "The Great Famine in Light of German Invasion and Occupation," *Harvard Ukrainian Studies* 30, no. 1/4 (2008): 166.
115. Berkhoff, "The Great Famine," 166.
116. Berkhoff, "The Great Famine," 167.
117. Berkhoff, "The Great Famine," 167.
118. Tanya Penter, "Pid slidstvom za spivpratsiu: sudove peresliduvannia kolaborantiv u SRSR pislia Drugoi svitovoi viiny ta zlochyniv u Babiemu Iaru," in *Babyn Yar: masove ubyvstvo i pam'iat'pro ni'ogo*, 195–97; Maksym Chornyi, "Babi Yar: Istoriia," https://war-documentary.info/babi-yar/.
119. Kuznetsov, *Babi Yar: roman-dokument*, 157.
120. Per Anders Rudling, "Terror and Local Collaboration in Occupied Belarus," 201–202; Victor Glazkov, "Gibel' Katyni: Taina bez sroka davnosti," *Sputnik: Belarus'*, https://sputnik.by/longrid/20160704/1023934943.html; Sergey "Crasher," "Khatyn': istoria derevni, sozhzhenoi fashistami vo vremia voiny," https://poznamka.ru/belarus/kto-szheg-hatyn.
121. Zvi Arieli, "Ukraina: edinstvo natsii ili spornye geroi?" https://censor.net.ua/blogs/4075/ukraina_edinstvo_natsii_ili_spornye_geroi; Eduard Dolinsky, "Vedomstvo Viatrovicha ustanovilo v Babiem Iare stend pamiati 'palachu' evreev—Ukrainskiy Evreiskii Komitet," *Ukrains'ki Novyny*, October 8, 2016, http://ukranews.com/news/453489-vedomstvo-vyatrovycha-ustanovylo-v-babem-yare-stend-pamyaty-palachu-evreev-ukraynskyy-evreyskyy-komytet/.
122. Eduard Dolinsky, "V Babiem Iaru ustanovili stend pamiati palachu evreev," https://strana.ua/news/35156-babem-yare-ustanovili-stend-pamyati-palachu-evreev.html.
123. A. Kruglov and A. Umansky, *Babi Yar: zhertvy, spasiteli, palachi* (Ukrainskii institute izucheniia Kholokosta "Tkuma," 2019), 30; *The Righteous Among the Nations Database*, https://righteous.yadvashem.org/.
124. Kruglov and Umansky, *Babi Yar: zhertvy, spasiteli, palachi*, 30; Il'ia Levitas, *Pravedniki Babiego Yara*, Fond "Pamiat' Babego Yara," 2001, 6.
125. I. Levitas, *Pravedniki Babiego Yara*, 8–255.
126. I. Levitas, *Pravedniki Babiego Yara*, 8–10.
127. I. Levitas, *Pravedniki Babiego Yara*, 15–16.
128. I. Levitas, *Pravedniki Babiego Yara*, 21–23.
129. I. Levitas, *Pravedniki Babiego Yara*, 27–28.
130. I. Levitas, *Pravedniki Babiego Yara*, 24–25.
131. I. Levitas, *Pravedniki Babiego Yara*, 32–34.

132. Evstaf'eva, "Tragedia Babynogo Yaru u 1941–1943 rr.," 363.
133. Evstaf'eva, "Tragedia Babynogo Yaru," 363.
134. M. A. Glagoleva-Palian, "Vospominaniia ob Aleksandre Aleksandroviche Glagoleve," *Yehupets* 8 (2001): 311–38.
135. "Glagolev Alexei & Glagoleva Tatiana (Hulashevich)," *The Righteous Among the Nations Database.* Yad Vashem, https://righteous.yadvashem.org/?search=Glagolev&searchType=righteous_only&language=en&itemId=4044305&ind=0.
136. Kruglov and Umansky, *Babi Yar: zhertvy, spasiteli, palachi,* 31–32; Il'ia Levitas, *Babi Yar: Spasiteli i spasennye* (Stal', 2005), 325–26.
137. Kruglov and Umansky, *Babi Yar: zhertvy, spasiteli, palachi,* 33.
138. I. Levitas, *Pravedniki Babiego Yara,* 201–202.
139. I. Levitas, *Pravedniki Babiego Yara,* 202.
140. Evstaf'eva, "Tragedia Babynogo Yaru u 1941–1943 rr.," 363.
141. "Tkachenko Natalia," *The Righteous Among the Nations Database.* Yad Vashem, https://righteous.yadvashem.org/?search=Babi%20Yar&searchType=righteous_only&language=en&itemId=4017887&ind=57; I. Levitas, *Pravedniki Babiego Yara,* 216–17.
142. "Tkachenko Natalia," *The Righteous Among the Nations Database.* Yad Vashem, https://righteous.yadvashem.org/?search=Babi%20Yar&searchType=righteous_only&language=en&itemId=4017887&ind=57.
143. "Tkachenko Natalia," *The Righteous Among the Nations Database*; I. Levitas, *Pravedniki Babiego Yara,* 217.
144. I. Levitas, *Pravedniki Babiego Yara,* 217.
145. I. Levitas, *Pravedniki Babiego Yara,* 122–23.
146. I. Levitas, *Pravedniki Babiego Yara,* 215.

CHAPTER 3

1. Karel C. Berkhoff, *Harvest of Despair: Life and Death in Ukraine Under Nazi Rule* (Belknap Press of Harvard University Press, 2004), 59. *Shoah* is the Hebrew term for the Holocaust.
2. Karel Berkhoff et al., *Basic Historical Narrative of the Babi Yar Holocaust Memorial Center,* 205, http://api.babiyar.org/uploads/files/fund/ff5be4721f4ef9d0cee21b34e17e8c05.pdf.
3. Andrej Kotljarchuk, "The Memory of Roma Holocaust in Ukraine: Mass Graves, Memory Work and the Politics of Commemoration," in *Disputed Memories: Emotions and Memory Politics in Central, Eastern and South-Eastern Europe,* ed. Tea Sindbæk Andersen and Barbara Tornqvist-Plewa (Walter de Gruyter, 2016), 162–63.
4. Anatoly Kuznetsov (A. Anatoli), *Babi Yar: roman-dokument* (Radians'kyi pysmennyk, 1991), 154.
5. Vitaliy Nachmanovich, "Babyn Yar: The Holocaust and Other Tragedies," in *Babyn Yar: History and Memory,* ed. Vladyslav Hrynevych and Paul Robert Magocsi (Dukh i Litera, 2016), 96–97.

6. N. Bessonov and N. Demeter, "Struktura tsyganskogo tabora," in *Istoriia tsygan—novyi vzgliad*, ed. N. Bessonov and N. Demeter (Institut antropologii i etnologii RAN, 2000), http://gypsy-life.net/history13.htm.
7. "Godovshchina tragedii Babiego Iara: obrashchenie prezidenta Ukrainy," *V Chas Pick*, September 29, 2019, https://vchaspik.ua/ukraina/468182-godovshchina-tragedii-babego-yara-obrashchenie-prezidenta-ukrainy; "Massovye rasstrely v Bab'em Iare. Archivnye fotografii," *RIA Novosti Ukraina*, September 29, 2016, https://rian.com.ua/photolents/20160929/1017016453.html.
8. Berkhoff et al., *Basic Historical Narrative of the Babi Yar Holocaust Memorial Center*, 212, http://api.babiyar.org/uploads/files/fund/ff5be4721f4ef9d0cee21b34e17e8c05.pdf.
9. The hospital was established by the order of Catherine the Great at Kyrylivs'ky Monastery in 1786, and it is located on Kyrylivs'ky Street, so many sources refer to it as Kyrylivs'ky Hospital.
10. TsDAVO U, f. 4620, op. 3, d. 280, ll. 9–12.
11. Andrii Rukkas, "Tragediia Gorikhovoi dibrovy: Iak natsysty rozstriliuvaly dushevnokhvorykh u Kyievi," *Istorychna Pravda*, October 29, 2020, https://www.istpravda.com.ua/articles/2020/10/29/158369/.
12. Rukkas, "Tragediia Gorikhovoi dibrovy."
13. TsDAVO U, f. 4620, op. 3, d. 280, ll. 9–12.
14. TsDAVO U, f. 4620, op. 3, d. 280, ll. 9–12.
15. Rukkas, "Tragediia Gorikhovoi dibrovy."
16. TsDAVO U, f. 4620, op. 3, d. 280, ll. 9–12.
17. Rukkas, "Tragediia Gorikhovoi dibrovy."
18. Rukkas, "Tragediia Gorikhovoi dibrovy."
19. TsDAVO U, f. 4620, op. 3, d. 280, ll. 9–12; Rukkas, "Tragediia Gorikhovoi dibrovy."
20. Rukkas, "Tragediia Gorikhovoi dibrovy."
21. Rukkas, "Tragediia Gorikhovoi dibrovy."
22. TsDAVO U, f. 4620, op. 3, d. 280, ll. 9–12.
23. TsDAVO U, f. 4620, op. 3, d. 280, ll. 9–12.
24. TsDAVO U, f. 4620, op. 3, d. 280, ll. 9–12; Nachmanovich, "Babyn Yar: The Holocaust and Other Tragedies," 97.
25. TsDAVO U, f. 4620, op. 3, d. 280, ll. 9–12.
26. TsDAVO U, f. 4620, op. 3, d. 280, ll. 9–12.
27. TsDAVO U, f. 4620, op. 3, d. 280, ll. 9–12.
28. TsDAVO U, f. 4620, op. 3, d. 280, ll. 9–12, l. 2.
29. Dmytro Malakov, *Kyiv 1939–1945, Fotoal'bom* (Kyi, 2005), 163.
30. Berkhoff, *Harvest of Despair*, 96.
31. Berkhoff, *Harvest of Despair*, 96.
32. Malakov, *Kyiv 1939–1945*, 166.

33. Berkhoff, *Harvest of Despair*, 98.
34. Irina Khoroshunova, *Dnevnik Kievlianki*, Part II, https://gordonua.com/specprojects/khoroshunova2.html.
35. Berkhoff, *Harvest of Despair*, 96.
36. Nachmanovich, "Babyn Yar: The Holocaust and Other Tragedies," 100.
37. Nachmanovich, "Babyn Yar: The Holocaust and Other Tragedies," 100.
38. Stanislav Aristov, "Next to Babi Yar: The Syrets Concentration Camp and the Evolution of Nazi Terror in Kiev," *Holocaust and Genocide Studies* 29, no. 3 (Winter 2015): 443–44.
39. Ivan Dereiko, "Ukrains'ki dopomizhni voenizovani formuvannia nimetts'koi armii i politsii v general'niy okruzi Kyiv u 1941–1943 rr.," in *Arkhivy okupatsii 1941–1944*, ed. Nataliia Makovs'ka, Vol. I, 2nd ed. (Kyiv: Kyevo-Mogylians'ka Akademiia, 2008), 798.
40. Malakov, *Kyiv 1939–1945*, 170.
41. Malakov, *Kyiv 1939–1945*, 170.
42. Malakov, *Kyiv 1939–1945*, 170.
43. Berkhoff, *Harvest of Despair*, 106.
44. Berkhoff, *Harvest of Despair*, 106.
45. Berkhoff, *Harvest of Despair*, 106.
46. Tatiana Evstaf'eva and Vitalii Nachmanovich, eds., *Babi Yar: chelovek, vlast', istoriia: Dokumenty i materialy v 5 knigakh. Kniga 1: Istoricheskaia topographiia. Khronologiia sobytii* (Vneshtorgizdat Ukrainy, 2004), 99.
47. Dereiko, "Ukrains'ki dopomizhni voenizovani formuvannia," 798–99.
48. Vladislav Hrynevych and Anatoly Pogorelov, "Babyn Yar: Zlochyn bez terminu davnosti," *Istorychna Pravda*, August 30, 2020, https://www.istpravda.com.ua/articles/2020/08/30/158036/.
49. Einsatzgruppe C reported to the chief of the Security Police and Security Service in Berlin about the execution of several thousand Jews in Kyiv after the Babyn Yar massacre. Yitzhak Arad, Shmuel Krakowsky, and Shmuel Spector, eds., *The Einsatzgruppen Reports* (Holocaust Library, 1989), 228, 252, 324.
50. Tatiana Evstaf'eva, "Syretskiy kontsentratsionnyi lager'," in *Babi Yar: chelovek, vlast', istoriia*, 172–173.
51. Aristov, "Next to Babi Yar: The Syrets Concentration Camp," 438.
52. Note of the former prisoners of the Syrets Concentration Camp, D. Budnik, V. Davydov, Z. Trubakov, I. Doliner, V. Kuklia, "In Syrets Concentration Camp," May 20, 1945, in *Babi Yar: chelovek, vlast', istoriia*, 361.
53. "In Syrets Concentration Camp," 361.
54. Evstaf'eva, "Syretskiy kontsentratsionnyi lager'," 176.
55. Aristov, "Next to Babi Yar: The Syrets Concentration Camp," 439.
56. TsDAHO U, f. 7, op. 10, d. 3, ll. 136–39.
57. Berkhoff, *Harvest of Despair*, 99.

58. I. Morozov was arrested by the Germans in May 1942 and sent to the Syrets concentration camp. He collaborated with the Nazis and tortured other prisoners. Morozov was executed in December 1943 by the decision of a Soviet military tribunal. Evstaf'eva, "Syretskiy kontsentratsionnyi lager'," 177.
59. Evstaf'eva, "Syretskiy kontsentratsionnyi lager'," 177.
60. Evstaf'eva, "Syretskiy kontsentratsionnyi lager'," 175–77.
61. Evstaf'eva, "Syretskiy kontsentratsionnyi lager'," 175–77.
62. TsDAHO U, f. 7, op. 10, d. 3, l. 136.
63. Aristov, "Next to Babi Yar: The Syrets Concentration Camp," 443–44.
64. Aristov, "Next to Babi Yar: The Syrets Concentration Camp," 443–44.
65. Evstaf'eva, "Syretskiy kontsentratsionnyi lager'," 177.
66. Aristov, "Next to Babi Yar: The Syrets Concentration Camp," 444.
67. Evstaf'eva, "Syretskiy kontsentratsionnyi lager'," 177.
68. Aristov, "Next to Babi Yar: The Syrets Concentration Camp," 441.
69. Aristov, "Next to Babi Yar: The Syrets Concentration Camp," 441.
70. One pud is 16 kilograms or about 35 pounds.
71. Evstaf'eva, "Syretskiy kontsentratsionnyi lager'," 177.
72. Ilya Ehrenburg and Vasily Grossman, eds., *The Complete Black Book of Russian Jewry*, trans. and ed. David Patterson (Transaction Publishers, 2003), 11.
73. Aristov, "Next to Babi Yar: The Syrets Concentration Camp," 446.
74. Ehrenburg and Grossman, *The Complete Black Book of Russian Jewry*, 11.
75. Evstaf'eva and Nachmanovich, *Babi Yar: chelovek, vlast', istoriia*, 222–321.
76. Evstaf'eva and Nachmanovich, *Babi Yar: chelovek, vlast', istoriia*, 270.
77. Aristov, "Next to Babi Yar: The Syrets Concentration Camp," 447.
78. Evstaf'eva and Nachmanovich, *Babi Yar: chelovek, vlast', istoriia*, 363.
79. Evstaf'eva and Nachmanovich, *Babi Yar: chelovek, vlast', istoriia*, 363.
80. The Soviet interrogation report of Vladimir Davydov on November 9, 1943, states that he was born in 1915 in Kyiv and was Jewish. TsDAVO U, f. 4620, op. 3, d. 243b, l. 13.
81. Ehrenburg and Grossman, *The Complete Black Book of Russian Jewry*, 11–12.
82. *The Black Book* mentions 12 survivors. David Budnik said in his memoirs that 14 people survived the uprising. David Budnik and Yakov Kaper, *Nothing Is Forgotten. Jewish Fates in Kiev 1941–1943*, ed. Erhard Roy Weihn (Hurtung-Gorre Verlag, 1993), 42. Yakov Kaper wrote in his memoir that 18 people survived the uprising, but further in the memoir he mentioned that he actually did not know who survived, because the prisoners ran in different directions in small groups. So, 18 prisoners are perhaps just an estimate. Budnik and Kaper, *Nothing Is Forgotten*, 171.
83. TsDAVO U, f. 4620, op. 3, d. 243b, ll. 1–17. The Soviet interrogation reports of Vladimir Davydov, Semen Berliant, Leonid Ostrovsky, and Yakov Steiuk, November 1943; Budnik and Kaper, *Nothing Is Forgotten*, 118–19.

84. Evstaf'eva and Nachmanovich, *Babi Yar: chelovek, vlast', istoriia*, 364.
85. Evstaf'eva and Nachmanovich, *Babi Yar: chelovek, vlast', istoriia*. Nikita Sergeevich Khrushchev had been the First Secretary of the Central Committee of the Communist Party (Bolsheviks) of Ukraine since 1938. During the war, Khrushchev was a member of the Military Councils of several fronts of the Red Army. Khrushchev came to Kyiv immediately after its liberation with the troops of the First Ukrainian Front.
86. TsDAVO U, f. 4620, op. 3, d. 334, l. 6.
87. Malakov, *Kyiv 1939–1945*, 165.
88. Report about the mass extermination of Soviet POWs in the [concentration] camps of village Darnitsa of Kyiv region, GARF, f. R-7021. op. 65, d. 235, ll. 426–50, http://www.battlefield.ru/mass-murders-of-soviet-pows-in-darnitza.html.
89. Martin J. Blackwell, *Kyiv as Regime City: The Return of Soviet Power After Nazi Occupation* (University of Rochester Press, 2016), 22.
90. Kevin E. Simpson, *Soccer Under the Swastika: Stories of Survival and Resistance During the Holocaust* (Rowman & Littlefield, 2016), 67.
91. Tatiana Evstaf'eva, "Futbol'nye matchi 1942 goda komandy 'Start' v okkupirovannom nemtsami Kieve i sud'by ee igrokov," in *Babyn Yar: masove ubyvstvo i pam'iat' pro ni'ogo. Materialy mizhnarodnoi naukovoi konferentsii 24–25 zhovtnia 2011 r., m. Kyiv.*, ed. Vitaliy Nakhmanovich and Mykhailo Tiagly (Ukrains'kyi tsentr vyvchennia istorii Golocostu, 2012), 34–38; Evgeny Antoniuk, "Mify i pravda o 'Matche smerti.' Chto stalo s futbolistami, pobedivshimi nemtsev?" https://pikabu.ru/story/mifyi_i_pravda_o_matche_smerti_chto_stalo_s_futbolistami_pobedivshimi_nemtsev_6086263.
92. "Flakelf" is an abbreviated combination of the German words *Flak* (*Fliegerabwehrkanone*—air defense artillery) and *elf* (eleven), which was used to denote an association football team.
93. Georgy Kuzmin, "Goriiachee leto sorok vtorogo," *Futbol* 13 (1995), http://www.junik.lv/~dynkiev/dk-1942/futbol_13-1995/futbol_13-1995.htm.
94. Kuzmin, "Goriiachee leto sorok vtorogo."
95. Simpson, *Soccer Under the Swastika*, 79.
96. Kuzmin, "Goriiachee leto sorok vtorogo."
97. Evstafieva, "Futbol'nye matchi 1942 goda," 46.
98. Kuzmin, "Goriachee leto sorok vtorogo."
99. Kuzmin, "Goriachee leto sorok vtorogo."
100. Evstaf'eva, "Futbol'nye matchi 1942 goda," 48–49.
101. Kuzmin, "Goriachee leto sorok vtorogo."
102. Kuzmin, "Goriachee leto sorok vtorogo."
103. Kuzmin, "Goriachee leto sorok vtorogo."
104. Oleg Yasinsky, "'Start'—Flakelf—'match smerti?'" http://www.2000.net.ua/d/48513.
105. Simpson, *Soccer Under the Swastika*, 83.
106. Tatiana Chebrova, "Bolel'shchik s 72-khletnim stazhem akademik Viacheslav Sabaldyr':

'Blagodaria razvedchikam-dinamovtsam byl sorvan fashistskii shturm Stalingrada,'" *Bul'var Gordona* 35 (227), September 1, 2009, https://bulvar.com.ua/gazeta/archive/s35_63236/5608.html.
107. Evstaf'eva, "Futbol'nye matchi 1942 goda," 52.
108. Evstaf'eva, "Futbol'nye matchi 1942 goda," 57.
109. Aksel' Vartanian, "Futbol v gody voiny. Chast' piataia. Mif o matche smerti," *Futbol*, February 16, 2007, https://www.sport-express.ru/newspaper/2007-02-16/16_1/.
110. Nachmanovich, "Babyn Yar: The Holocaust and Other Tragedies," 102.
111. A. K. Kasimenko, ed., *Istoriia Kieva* (Academy of Sciences of the Ukrainian SSR, 1964), Vol. II, 441–77.
112. Ster Elisavetsky, "Izvestnoe i novoe slovo o Tane Markus," *Zerkalo Nedeli*, August 9, 2002, https://zn.ua/SOCIUM/izvestnoe_i_novoe_slovo_o_tane_markus.html.
113. Anonymous, "Geroi Ukrainy Tatiana Markus," *Evreiskiy Mir*, February 14, 2007, http://evreimir.com/14407/.
114. Aleksander Naiman, "Tania Markus—angel mesti," *Evreiskii Obozrevatel'* no. 12 (288), December 2016, https://jew-observer.com/imya/tanya-markus-angel-mesti/.
115. Ster Elisavetsky, "Izvestnoe i novoe slovo o Tane Markus."
116. Eleonora Skliarevskaia, "Ubiistvennaia krasota evreiskoi podpol'shchitsy," https://ujew.com.ua/history/ubijstvennaya-krasota-evrejskoj-podpolshhiczyi.
117. Gennady Mesh, "Ei bylo tol'ko dvadtsat'," *Russkii globus*, no. 3 (April 2002), http://www.russian-globe.com/N3/Markus.htm.
118. Sergii Kot, "Uchasnyky pidpillia OUN(m)—zhertvy Babynogo Yaru," in *Babyn Yar: masove ubyvstvo i pam'iat' pro n'iogo. Materialy mizhnarodnoi naukovoi konferentsii 24–25 zhovtnia 2011 r. Kyiv* (Komitet "Babi Yar," 2012), 103.
119. Kot, "Uchasnyky pidpillia OUN(m)—zhertvy Babynogo Yaru," 106.
120. Kot, "Uchasnyky pidpillia OUN(m)—zhertvy Babynogo Yaru," 106.
121. Kot, "Uchasnyky pidpillia OUN(m)—zhertvy Babynogo Yaru," 111.
122. Kot, "Uchasnyky pidpillia OUN(m)—zhertvy Babynogo Yaru," 111.
123. Nachmanovich, "Babyn Yar: The Holocaust and Other Tragedies," 99.
124. Victoria Yaremenko, "Elena Teliga: Zhenskie istorii Vtoroi mirovoi," *Svoboda FM*, May 6, 2016, http://svoboda.fm/culture/Culture/245446.html?language=ru; "Teliga ne byla rasstreliana v Babiem Yaru," *The Kiev Times*, November 9, 2013, http://thekievtimes.ua/society/271625-teliga-ne-byla-rasstrelyana-v-babem-yaru.html; "Teliga Elena Ivanovna," *Geroi Ukrainy*, http://heroes.profi-forex.org/ru/teliga-olena-ivanivna.
125. Oleksandr Kucheruk, "Mykola Pervach: I vy pochuete shche znovu i znovy poetovu prorochu movu," *Organizatsiia Ukrains'kykh Natsionalistiv*, http://kmoun.info/2016/10/10/oleksandr-kucheruk-mikola-pervach-i-vi-pochuyete-shhe-znovu-i-znovu-poetovu-prorochu-movu/.
126. Kucheruk, "Mykola Pervach."

127. Kucheruk, "Mykola Pervach."
128. Olena Teliga, *Lysty: Spogady*, 2nd ed. (Vydavnytstvo im. O. Teligy, 2004), 228.
129. Kucheruk, "Mykola Pervach."
130. Kuznetsov, *Babi Yar*, 158.
131. Anonymous, "Mucheniki," https://www.babiy-yar.org/mucheniki; Mikhail Odintsov, "Mitropolit Sergii Stragorodsky v evakuatsii," *Nepridumannye rasskazy o voine*, http://www.world-war.ru/mitropolit-sergij-stragorodskij-v-evakuacii/.
132. Nikolai Agafonov, "Golgofa arkhimandrita Aleksandra Vishniakova," *Omilia: Mezhdynarodnyi literaturnyi klub*, https://omiliya.org/content/golgofa-arkhimandrita-aleksandra-vishnyakova.
133. Agafonov, "Golgofa arkhimandrita Aleksandra Vishniakova."
134. Vadim Maksimov and Konstantin Kapkov, *Za sluzhbu i khrabrost: Sviashchenniki—kavalery ordena Sviatogo Georgiia. Neizvestnye stranitsy* (Knizhnyi Mir, 2018), 181.
135. Kirill Frolov, "Archimandrit Aleksandr (Vishniakov)," *Vestnik*, no. 12, September 1, 2002, http://pravoslavye.org.ua/2002/09/k_frolov_arhimandrit_aleksandr_vishnyakov/.
136. Frolov, "Archimandrit Aleksandr (Vishniakov)"; Agafonov, "Golgofa arkhimandrita Aleksandra Vishniakova"; Anonymous, "Mucheniki"; Odintsov, "Mitropolit Sergii Stragorodsky v evakuatsii."
137. TsDAVO U, f. 4620, op. 3, d. 2436, ll. 68–69.
138. TsDAVO U, f. 4620, op. 3, d. 2436, ll. 68–69.
139. Berkhoff et al., *Basic Historical Narrative*, 215.
140. TsDAVO U, f. 4620, op. 3, d. 280, l. 1.
141. Kurt Eberhard was involved in planning and supervising the Babyn Yar massacre. He was captured by US authorities after the end of World War II, in November 1945, and imprisoned in Stuttgart. He committed suicide on September 8, 1947.
142. Malakov, *Kyiv 1939–1945*, 246.
143. Berkhoff, *Harvest of Despair*, 164–86.
144. Kuznetsov, *Babi Yar: A Document in the Form of a Novel*, 161–66, 209–17.
145. Kuznetsov, *Babi Yar: A Document in the Form of a Novel*, 74.
146. Kuznetsov, *Babi Yar: A Document in the Form of a Novel*, 161.
147. Kuznetsov, *Babi Yar: A Document in the Form of a Novel*, 161–62, 211.
148. Kuznetsov, *Babi Yar: A Document in the Form of a Novel*, 163.
149. Kuznetsov, *Babi Yar: A Document in the Form of a Novel*, 211, 347–48.
150. Berkhoff et al., *Basic Historical Narrative*, 227.
151. Berkhoff, *Harvest of Despair*, 169.
152. Berkhoff, *Harvest of Despair*, 171.
153. Kuznetsov, *Babi Yar: A Document in the Form of a Novel*, 221–22.
154. Berkhoff, *Harvest of Despair*, 165.
155. Berkhoff, *Harvest of Despair*, 165.

156. TsDAHO U, f. 1, op. 23, d. 121, l. 6.
157. TsDAHO U, f. 1, op. 23, d. 121, , l. 5.
158. Kuznetsov, *Babi Yar: A Document in the Form of a Novel*, 151.
159. Dmytro Malakov, *Doli kyian (1941–1943)* (Folio, 2017), 116–19.
160. Malakov, *Doli kyian (1941–1943)*, 123.
161. Berkhoff, *Harvest of Despair*, 59–60; Malakov, *Kyiv, 1939–1945*, 349.
162. Malakov, *Doli kyian (1941–1943)*, 129.
163. Blackwell, *Kyiv as Regime City*, 22.
164. Malakov, *Doli kyian (1941–1943)*, 136–42.
165. TsDAVO U, f. 4620, op. 3, d. 2436, l. 11.
166. TsDAVO U, f. 4620, op. 3, d. 2436, l. 11.
167. TsDAVO U, f. 4620, op. 3, d. 2436, l. 11.
168. TSDAVO U, f. 4620, op. 3, d. 243a, l. 30.
169. A. Anatoli (Kuznetsov), *Babi Yar. A Document in the Form of a Novel*, 393.
170. TsDAVO U, f. 4620, op. 3, d. 2436, l. 12.
171. Kasimenko, ed., *Istoriia Kieva*, Vol. II, 499.
172. A. Anatoli (Kuznetsov), *Babi Yar*, 406.
173. TSDAVO U, f. 4620, op. 3, d.243a, ll. 29–30.
174. Kasimenko, *Istoriia Kieva*, Vol. II, 499.
175. Kasimenko, *Istoriia Kieva*, 499.
176. A. Anatoli (Kuznetsov), *Babi Yar*, 419–20.
177. The Righteous Among the Nations Database, https://collections.yadvashem.org/en/righteous/4045085.

CHAPTER 4

1. A. K. Kasimenko, ed., *Istoriia Kieva*, Vol. II (Academy of Arts and Sciences of the Ukrainian SSR, 1964), 499.
2. Martin J. Blackwell, *Kyiv as Regime City: The Return of Soviet Power After Nazi Occupation* (University of Rochester Press, 2016), 22.
3. Kasimenko, *Istoriia Kieva*, 502.
4. Moisei Loev, *Ukradennaia Muza, Vospominaniia o Kievskom gosudarstvennom evreiskom teatre imeni Sholom Aleikhema, Kharkov-Kiev-Chernovtsy, 1925–1950* (Dukh i Litera, 2004), 135. The play *Tevye the Dairyman* was performed in many theaters around the world, and Sholom Aleichem's novel became the basis for the Broadway musical and Hollywood film *Fiddler on the Roof*.
5. Loev, *Ukradennaia Muza*, 135.
6. Loev, *Ukradennaia Muza*, 135–37. The Ukrainian State Jewish Theater was not allowed to return to Kyiv from evacuation in Kazakhstan after the war, on the pretext that the theater building had been destroyed during the war and no other suitable building was available.

Instead, the theater was sent "temporarily" to Chernovtsy and was subsequently closed during the anticosmopolitan campaign in 1950.

7. Loev, *Ukradennaia Muza*, 135; Moyshe (Moisei) Goldblatt (1896–1974), Jewish actor and director of the Ukrainian State Jewish Theater in 1939–50.
8. The American writer John Steinbeck and his friend American photojournalist Robert Capa (Endre Friedmann) traveled to the Soviet Union in 1947 and published a report about their trip in *A Russian Journal*. They visited Moscow, Kyiv, Stalingrad, and Soviet Georgia during their trip.
9. Video interview with Leonid Bodankin and Emilia Osterman recorded by Victoria Khiterer in February 2021.
10. Sergiy Vakulyshin, *(Ne)miy Kyiv: Zbirka statei z kontseptual'nogo kyevoznavstva* (Svit uspikhu, 2014), 93.
11. Solomon M. Schwartz, *The Jews in the Soviet Union* (Arno Press, 1972), 233.
12. Kasimenko, *Istoriia Kieva*, 499.
13. Elena Sokolovsky's memory about her mother-in-law recorded by Victoria Khiterer in November 2015.
14. Arkady Vaksberg, *Stalin Against the Jews*, trans. Antonina W. Bouis (Vintage Books, 1994), 144.
15. Tsentral'nyi Derzhavnyi Arkhiv Hromads'kykh Obiednan' Ukrainy (TsDAHO U), f. 1, op. 63, d. 1363, l. 4.
16. Mordechai Altshuler, "Antisemitism in Ukraine Toward the End of World War II," in *Bitter Legacy: Confronting the Holocaust in the USSR*, ed. Zvi Gitelman (Indiana University Press, 1997), 80.
17. M. Altshuler, "Antisemitism in Ukraine Toward the End of the Second World War," *Jews in Eastern Europe* 3 (1993): 66.
18. TsDAHO U, f. 1, op. 23, d. 2366, ll. 10–11.
19. TsDAHO U, f. 1, op. 23, d. 2366, l. 6.
20. TsDAHO U, f. 1, op. 23, d. 2366, ll. 1–2.
21. TsDAHO U, f. 1, op. 23, d. 2366, ll. 10–11.
22. TsDAHO U, f. 1, op. 23, d. 2366, ll. 10–11.
23. TsDAHO U, f. 1, op. 23, d. 2366, ll. 10–11.
24. TsDAHO U, f. 1, op. 23, d. 2366, l. 21.
25. S. M. Shvarts, *Antisemitism v Sovetskom Soiuze* (Izd-vo im. Chekhova, 1952), 196.
26. TsDAHO U, f. 1, op. 23, d. 2366, ll. 19–20.
27. TsDAHO U, f. 1, op. 23, d. 2366, ll. 19–20.
28. TsDAHO U, f. 1, op. 23, d. 2366, l. 21.
29. TsDAHO U, f. 1, op. 23, d. 2366, ll. 3–4.
30. TsDAHO U, f. 1, op. 23, d. 2366, ll. 3–4.
31. Blackwell, *Kyiv as Regime City*, 166.

32. TsDAHO U, f. 1, op. 23, d. 1363, l. 5.
33. TsDAHO U, f. 1, op. 23, d. 1363, l. 6.
34. TsDAHO U, f. 1, op. 23, d. 1363, l. 6.
35. Shvarts, *Antisemitizm v Sovetskom Soiuze*, 195–96.
36. TsDAHO U, f. 1, op. 23, d. 1363, l. 3.
37. TsDAHO U, f. 1, op. 23, d. 1363, l. 12.
38. TsDAHO U, f. 1, op. 23, d. 1363, l. 12.
39. TsDAHO U, f. 1, op. 23, d. 1363, l. 12. The Union of Russian People was an Imperial Russian nationalist, monarchist, and anti-Semitic organization.
40. TsDAHO U, f. 1, op. 23, d. 1363, l. 12.
41. TsDAHO U, f. 1, op. 23, d. 1363, 28.
42. TsDAHO U, f. 1, op. 23, d. 1363, 10.
43. TsDAHO U, f. 1, op. 41, d. 4, ll. 41–45.
44. TsDAHO U, f. 1, op. 41, d. 4, ll. 41–45.
45. TsDAHO U, f. 1, op. 41, d. 4, ll. 41–45.
46. Blackwell, *Kyiv as Regime City*, 164.
47. Mikhail Mitsel, *Evrei Ukrainy v 1943–1953 gg.: Ocherki dokumentirovannoi istorii* (Dukh i Litera, 2004), 32.
48. TsDAHO U, f. 1, op. 23, d. 4913, ll. 2–3.
49. "Kiev," *Elektronnaia Evreiskaia Entsiklopedia*, http://www.eleven.co.il/?id=12072.
50. Shvarts, *Antisemitism v Sovetskom Soiuze*, 203.
51. W. J. Tompson, *Khrushchev: A Political Life* (Palgrave Macmillan, 1995), 93.
52. L. M. Kaganovich, *Pamyatnye zapiski rabochego, kommunista-bol'shevika, profsoyuznogo, partiinogo i sovetsko-gosudarstvennogo rabotnika* (Vagrius, 1996), 488–89, 492.
53. Tompson, *Khrushchev*, 93.
54. Tompson, *Khrushchev*, 93.
55. G. V. Kostyrchenko, *Tainaia politika Stalina: Vlast' i antisemitism* (Mezhdunarodnye otnosheniia, 2001), 358.
56. Kostyrchenko, *Tainaia politika Stalina*, 361.
57. M. A. Mel'nik, "Golod v Ukraine 1946–1947 gg.," *Derzhavnyi arkhiv Mykolaievskoi oblasti*, http://mk.archives.gov.ua/pubonsite/93-pubgolod4647.html.
58. Mel'nik, "Golod v Ukraine 1946–1947 gg."; T. N. Fedchun, "Golod 1946–1947 godov po documentam gosarchiva," *Letopis' Dondassa*, http://donbass.name/letopis/964-golod-1946-1947gg.-po-dokumentam-gosarkhiva.html.
59. Serhy Yekelchyk, *Stalin's Citizens: Everyday Politics in the Wake of the Total War* (Oxford University Press, 2014), 212.
60. In 1952 the Communist Party Bolsheviks of Ukraine (KP(b)U) was renamed as the Communist Party of Ukraine (KPU).
61. The Central Archives for the History of the Jewish People (CAHJP), RU/1603, l. 78.

62. Mitsel, *Evrei Ukrainy v 1943–1953 gg.*, 27.
63. Yekelchyk, *Stalin's Citizens*, 212.
64. Itsik Kipnis, "Babi Yar," *Golokost i suchasnist'*, http://www.holocaust.kiev.ua/bulletin/vip10/vip10_1.htm.
65. Benjamin Pinkus, *The Jews of the Soviet Union: The History of a National Minority* (Cambridge University Press, 1988), 145.
66. Ronald Grigor Suny, *The Soviet Experiment: Russia, the USSR, and the Successor States* (Oxford University Press, 2010), 396.
67. Pinkus, *The Jews of the Soviet Union*, 146.
68. Blackwell, *Kyiv as Regime City*, 167.
69. Pinkus, *The Jews of the Soviet Union*, 157.
70. Lesia Ukrainka (literary pseudonym of Larysa Petrivna Kosach-Kvitka, 1871–1913) was one of Ukraine's best-known poets and writers.
71. CAHJP, RU/2435, l. 17.
72. David E. Fishman, *The Book Smugglers: Partisans, Poets, and the Race to Save Jewish Treasures from the Nazis* (ForeEdge and the University Press of New England, 2017), 233.
73. Ronald Grigor Suny, ed., *The Structure of Soviet History: Essays and Documents*, 2nd ed. (Oxford University Press, 2014), 286–87.
74. Howard Margol, "The Lithuanian Jewish Museum Rises from the Ashes," http://www.rtrfoundation.org/webart/B&L-VilnaMuseum.pdf.
75. Kostyrchenko, *Tainaia politika Stalina*, 359.
76. Kostyrchenko, *Tainaia politika Stalina*, 359.
77. Kostyrchenko, *Tainaia politika Stalina*, 359.
78. Kostyrchenko, *Tainaia politika Stalina*, 359, 397.
79. Joshua Rubenstein, "Jewish Anti-Fascist Committee," *YIVO Encyclopedia of Jews in Eastern Europe*, http://www.yivoencyclopedia.org/article.aspx/Jewish_Anti-Fascist_Committee; Arno Lustiger, *Stalin and the Jews, Red Book: The Tragedy of the Jewish Anti-Fascist Committee and the Soviet Jews* (Enigma Books, 2003), 241–43.
80. Avraam Grinbaum, *Evreiskaia nauka i nauchnye uchrezhdeniia v Sovetskom Soiuze, 1918–1953* (Gesharim, 1994), 169.
81. E. M. Beregovskaia, "Eshche raz o sud'be M. Ia. Beregovskogo," in M. Beregovsky, *Purim-shpil'. Evreiskie Narodnye muzykal'no-teatral'nye predstavleniia* (Dukh i Litera, 2001), 20.
82. Introduction to the liner notes for the CD *Yiddish Glory: Life and Fate of Soviet Jewish Folk Music During World War II*. The songs were considered lost for a long time. In the 1990s, they were found in the Vernadsky National Library of Ukraine. Anna Shternshis, Pavel Lion, and a group of professional musicians prepared the CD, which contains eighteen songs.
83. CAHJP, RU 1542, l. 2.
84. CAHJP, RU 1542, l. 3.

85. Kostyrchenko, *Tainaia politika Stalina*, 360.
86. Mitsel, *Evrei Ukrainy v 1943–1953 gg.*, 154.
87. Mitsel, *Evrei Ukrainy v 1943–1953 gg.*, 181.
88. Mitsel, *Evrei Ukrainy v 1943–1953 gg.*, 155.
89. Shvarts, *Antisemitism v Sovetskom Soiuze*, 221.
90. Dmitriy Vedeneev and Sergei Shevchenko, "Sredi veshchdokov, vyiavlennykh v 1952 godu po 'Delu Khaina' byli nakhodki, kotorye smogli by ukrasit' almaznyi fond SSSR," *Fakty*, August 3, 2000, https://crime.fakty.ua/107195-sredi-vecshdokov-vyyavlennyh-v-1952-godu-po-quot-delu-haina-quot-byli-nahodki-kotorye-smogli-by-ukrasit-almaznyj-fond-sssr.
91. Juliette Cadiot, "L'affaire Hain, Kyiv, Hiver 1952," *Cahiers du Monde Russe* 59, no. 2–3 (2018): 255–88, https://www.cairn.info/article.php?ID_ARTICLE=CMR_592_0255#xd_co_f=ZTEzOTk5N2UtNDdhMyooODAxLTg3MDctOTI2ZjcıYWY5ZDA3~.
92. Vedeneev and Shevchenko, "Sredi veshchdokov, vyiavlennykh v 1952 godu po 'Delu Khaina.'"
93. Cadiot, "L'affaire Hain, Kyiv, Hiver 1952."
94. Vedeneev and Shevchenko, "Sredi veshchdokov, vyiavlennykh v 1952 godu po 'Delu Khaina.'"
95. Vedeneev and Shevchenko, "Sredi veshchdokov, vyiavlennykh v 1952 godu po 'Delu Khaina.'"
96. Cadiot, "L'affaire Hain, Kyiv, Hiver 1952."
97. Cadiot, "L'affaire Hain, Kyiv, Hiver 1952."
98. Cadiot, "L'affaire Hain, Kyiv, Hiver 1952."
99. Cadiot, "L'affaire Hain, Kyiv, Hiver 1952."
100. Pinkus, *Jews of the Soviet Union*, 177.
101. Pinkus, *Jews of the Soviet Union*, 178.
102. Oskar Rokhlin, "Kyiv: 1945–1955," *Zametki po evreiskoi istorii* 182, no. 2–3 (February–March 2015), https://berkovich-zametki.com/2015/Zametki/Nomer2_3/Rohlin1.php.
103. Rokhlin, "Kyiv: 1945–1955."
104. Rokhlin, "Kyiv: 1945–1955."
105. Jonathan Brent and Vladimir P. Naumov, *Stalin's Last Crime: The Plot Against the Jewish Doctors, 1948–1953* (Harper Perennial, 2003), 253–54.
106. Brent and Naumov, *Stalin's Last Crime*, 257.
107. Mitsel, *Evrei Ukrainy v 1943–1953 gg.*, 261.
108. Mitsel, *Evrei Ukrainy v 1943–1953 gg.*, 261.
109. Mitsel, *Evrei Ukrainy v 1943–1953 gg.*, 261.
110. Mitsel, *Evrei Ukrainy v 1943–1953 gg.*, 261–62.
111. Mitsel, *Evrei Ukrainy v 1943–1953 gg.*, 261–62.
112. Mitsel, *Evrei Ukrainy v 1943–1953 gg.*, 261–62.
113. Mikhail Mitsel', *Obshchiny iudeiskogo ispovedaniia v Ukraine (Kyiv, L'vov: 1945–1981 gody)* (Biblioteka Instituta Iudaiki, 1998), 77–78.
114. CAHJP, RU 1603, l. 74.
115. Mitsel, *Evrei Ukrainy v 1943–1953 gg.*, 263.

116. Brent and Naumov, *Stalin's Last Crime*, 286.
117. Antony Polonsky, *The Jews in Poland and Russia: Volume III: 1914 to 2008* (Littman Library of Jewish Civilization, 2012), 657.
118. Naum Korzhavin, *V soblaznakh krovavoi epokhi*, 2 vols. (Zakharov, 2006), Vol. I, 653.

CHAPTER 5

1. Jeff Mankoff, "Babi Yar and the Struggle for Memory, 1944–2004," *Ab Imperio*, 2 (2004): 396; Arkadi Zeltser, "Tema 'Evrei v Babiem Iaru' v Sovetskom Soiuze v 1941–1945 godakh," in *Babyn Yar: Masove Ubuvstvo i pamiat' pro n'ogo: Materialy mizhnarodnoi naukovoi konferentsii 24–25 zhovtnia 2011 r., m. Kyiv*, ed. Vitaliy Nakhmanovich and Mykhailo Tiagly (Ukrains'kyi tsentr vyvchennia istorii Golocostu, 2012), 84.
2. The Nazis were usually called fascists in Soviet sources.
3. V. Stepanenko, "Chto proiskhodit v Kieve," *Pravda*, November 29, 1941, cited in Feliks Levitas, *Babi Yar: Sud'by i pamiat'* (Nash Chas, 2016), 68.
4. Yehuda Bauer, *A History of the Holocaust*, rev. ed. (Franklin Watts, 2001), 217.
5. Zeltser, "Tema 'Evrei v Babiem Iaru' v Sovetskom Soiuze v 1941–1945 godakh," 86–87.
6. Zeltser, "Tema 'Evrei v Babiem Iaru' v Sovetskom Soiuze v 1941–1945 godakh," 88–89.
7. Itsik Fefer, "Pepel Babiego Yara zhet nashi serdtsa," in *Evreiskii narod v bor'be protiv fashisma. III antifashistskii miting predstavitelei evreiskogo Naroda. III Plenum Evreiskogo antifashistskogo komiteta v SSSR* (Der Emes, 1945), 26–28.
8. Zeltser, "Tema 'Evrei v Babiem Iaru' v Sovetskom Soiuze v 1941–1945 godakh," 88.
9. Itsik Fefer, "Pepel Babiego Yara zhet nashi serdtsa," 27.
10. *Evreiskii narod v bor'be protiv fashisma. III antifashistskii miting predstavitelei evreiskogo Naroda. III Plenum Evreiskogo antifashistskogo komiteta v SSSR* (Der Emes, 1945).
11. Vladyslav Hrynevych, "Babyn Yar After Babyn Yar," in *Babyn Yar: History and Memory*, ed. Vladyslav Hrynevych and Paul Robert Magocsi (University of Toronto Press, 2023), 153.
12. Aleksei Borisov, ed., *Sbornik Materialov Chrezvychainoi Gosudarstvennoi Komissii po ustanovleniiu i rassledovaniiu zlodeianii nemetsko-fashistskikh zakhvatchikov i ikh soobshchnikov*, http://samlib.ru/b/borisow_aleksej_wiktorowich/materialychgk.shtml.
13. Ilia Altman, *Kholokost i evreiskoie soprotivlenie na okkupirovannoi territorrii SSSR* (Fond "Kholokost," 2002), https://jhist.org/shoa/hfond_124.htm.
14. Altman, *Kholokost i evreiskoie soprotivlenie na okkupirovannoi territorrii SSSR*.
15. Altman, *Kholokost i evreiskoie soprotivlenie na okkupirovannoi territorrii SSSR*.
16. Borisov, *Sbornik Materialov Chrezvychainoi Gosudarstvennoi Komissii*.
17. Borisov, *Sbornik Materialov Chrezvychainoi Gosudarstvennoi Komissii*.
18. Tatiana Evstaf'eva, "Babi Yar vo vtoroi polovine XX st.," in *Babi Yar: chelovek, vlast', istoriia. Dokumenty i materialy v 5 knigakh. Kniga 1: Istoricheskaia topografiia. Khronologiia sobytii*, ed. Tatiana Evstaf'eva and Vitalii Nachmanovich (Vneshtorgizdat Ukrainy, 2004), 187.
19. Lev Fridman, "In Search of Mykola Bazhan's Legacy on the Eve of Commemorations of

Babyn Yar," *Odessa Review*, November 9, 2016, http://odessareview.com/search-mykola-bazhans-legacy-eve-commemorations-babyn-yar/.

20. Chana Pollack, "'Cattle Grazed Among the Bones of Our Sacred Martyrs': Covering Babyn Yar Through the Decades," *Forward*, March 11, 2022, https://forward.com/archive/483853/babyn-yar-russia-ukraine-soviets-nazis-wwii-massacre-bombing/.

21. Pollack, "'Cattle Grazed Among the Bones of Our Sacred Martyrs.'"

22. Bill Lawrence, *Six Presidents: Too Many Wars* (Saturday Review Press, 1972), 92–95.

23. W. H. Lawrence, "50,000 Kiev Jews Reported Killed," *New York Times*, November 29, 1943, 3.

24. W. H. Lawrence, "50,000 Kiev Jews Reported Killed," 3.

25. B. Lawrence, *Six Presidents: Too Many Wars*, 92–95.

26. W. H. Lawrence, "50,000 Kiev Jews Reported Killed," 3.

27. W. H. Lawrence, "Little Evidence Supports Story of Nazi Atrocity," *Buffalo Courier-Express*, November 29, 1943, 1.

28. David Shneer, "Is Seeing Believing?" in *The Holocaust: Memories and History*, ed. Victoria Khiterer (Cambridge Scholars Publishing, 2014), 64.

29. Shneer, "Is Seeing Believing?"

30. Bill Downs, "Blood at Babii Yar—Kiev's Atrocity Story," *Newsweek*, December 6, 1943, 22, https://www.billdownscbs.com/2013/07/blood-at-babii-yar-kievs-atrocity-story.html.

31. Martin Dean, *Investigating Babyn Yar: Shadows from the Valley of Death* (Lexington Books, 2024), 32; Vladimir Mislavsky, *Evreiskaia tema v kinematographe Rossiskoi imperii, SSSR, Rossii, SNG and Baltii (1909–2009). Filmo-biograficheskii spravochnik* (OOO "Skorpion," 2013), 176.

32. Hrynevych, "Babyn Yar After Babyn Yar," 150.

33. Hrynevych, "Babyn Yar After Babyn Yar," 150.

34. Dieter Pohl, "Die einheimischen Forschungen und der Mord an Juden in den besetzten Gebieten," in *Täter im Vernichtungskrieg: Der Überfall auf die Sowjetunion und der Völkermord an den Juden*, ed. Wolf Kaiser (Propyläen, 2002), 206.

35. Hrynevych, "Babyn Yar After Babyn Yar," 151.

36. Hrynevych, "Babyn Yar After Babyn Yar," 151–52.

37. L. M. Abramenko, ed., *Kievskiy process: dokumenty ta materialy* (Lybid', 1995), 5, 201.

38. Dean, *Investigating Babyn Yar*, 232.

39. Dean, *Investigating Babyn Yar*, 232.

40. Dean, *Investigating Babyn Yar*, 232.

41. Abramenko, *Kievskiy process*, 145.

42. Abramenko, *Kievskiy process*, 155.

43. Abramenko, *Kievskiy process*, 201.

44. Stanislav Tsalik, "1946: Kak vo vremia 'Kievskogo Niurberga' kaznili nazistov," *BBC News, Ukraina*, January 29, 2016, https://www.bbc.com/ukrainian/ukraine_in_russian/2016/01/160129_ru_s_tsalyk_blog_historian.

45. Jonathan Romney, "The Kiev Trial: Another Chilling War-Crimes Documentary from

Sergei Loznitsa," *British Film Institute*, October 22, 2022, https://www.bfi.org.uk/sight-and-sound/reviews/kiev-trial-another-chilling-war-crimes-documentary-from-sergei-loznitsa.
46. Pavel Polian, "Babi Yar i vozmezdie: sudebnye protsessy and palachami," *Neprikosnovennyi zapas* 149, no. 3 (2023): 54.
47. Hrynevych, "Babyn Yar After Babyn Yar," 166.
48. Polian, "Babi Yar i vozmezdie," 55.
49. Polian, "Babi Yar i vozmezdie," 55.
50. Polian, "Babi Yar i vozmezdie," 51; Karel Berkhoff et al., *Basic Historical Narrative of the Babyn Yar Holocaust Memorial Center* (Kyiv, 2018), 80, https://babynyar.org/storage/main/e0/ce/e0ced2fd93bcb8a9abbdeb5df828416f12fdac9eaf096d2766b54c989e86e48b.pdf.
51. Dean, *Investigating Babyn Yar*, 138.
52. Dean, *Investigating Babyn Yar*, 45, 56–57, 232.
53. Anonymous, "Germany: Case Closed," *Time*, June 18, 1951, https://content.time.com/time/subscriber/article/0,33009,814963,00.html.
54. Polian, "Babi Yar i vozmezdie," 56–57.
55. Ernst Klee, *Das Personenlexikon zum Dritten Reich: Wer war was vor und nach 1945*, 2nd ed. (Fischer-Taschenbuch-Verlag, 2007), 476.
56. Polian, "Babi Yar i vozmezdie," 57.
57. Polian, "Babi Yar i vozmezdie."; Ernst Klee, *Das Personenlexikon zum Dritten Reich*, 89–90; Yad Vashem Archives (YVA), P. 13/190 Benjamin Sagalowitz Archive: Newspaper clippings regarding the Darmstadt Trial against the men of Sonderkommando A-4 who were accused of participating in the mass murder at Babyn Yar and other murders of Jews, 1963–68, https://collections.yadvashem.org/en/documents/3689862.
58. Berkhoff et al., *Basic Historical Narrative of the Babyn Yar Holocaust Memorial Center*, 85–86.
59. Dean, *Investigating Babyn Yar*, 136.
60. "80 Years On: The True Faces of the Babyn Yar Murders Are Being Revealed," BYHMC Press Release, October 5, 2021, https://babynyar.org/en/news/455.
61. Dean, *Investigating Babyn Yar*, 143.
62. Dean, *Investigating Babyn Yar*, 234.
63. Polian, "Babi Yar i vozmezdie," 58–60.
64. Polian, "Babi Yar i vozmezdie," 57–59; David Budnik and Yakov Kaper, *Nothing Is Forgotten: Jewish Fates in Kiev 1941–1943*, ed. Erhard Roy Weihn (Hartung-Gorre Verlag, 1993), 53–54, 184–86.
65. "80 Years On: The True Faces of the Babyn Yar Murders Are Being Revealed."
66. "80 Years On: The True Faces of the Babyn Yar Murders Are Being Revealed."
67. "The Times of Israel" Staff, "Names, Testimonies of Nazis in Babi Yar Massacre Released 80 Years On," *The Times of Israel*, October 6, 2021, https://www.timesofisrael.com/names-testimonies-of-nazis-in-babi-yar-massacre-released-80-years-on/.
68. "80 Years On: The True Faces of the Babyn Yar Murders Are Being Revealed."

69. Paul Blobel received a death sentence and was executed.
70. "80 Years On: The True Faces of the Babyn Yar Murders Are Being Revealed."
71. Obituary of Gertrud von Radetzky, wife of Waldemar von Radetzky, *Deutsch-Baltische Gesselschaft* (German-Baltic Society), e. V, August 1, 2014–January 16, 2016, http://www.deutsch-balten.de/175.html.
72. Extract from the letter of Dr. Gutin, in Efrem Baukh, ed., *Babi Iar* (Moria, 1981), 58. "El Malei Rachamim" is a Jewish prayer for the soul of a person who has died.
73. Vladyslav Hrynevych, "Babyn Yar After Babyn Yar," 114.
74. Mordechai Altshuler, "Antisemitism in Ukraine Toward the End of World War II," in *Bitter Legacy: Confronting the Holocaust in the USSR*, ed. Zvi Gitelman (Indiana University Press, 1997), 80.
75. Itsik Kipnis, "Babi Yar," *Evreiskii mir Ukrainy*, http://www.ju.org.ua/ru/publicism/646.html.
76. Kipnis, "Babi Yar."
77. Kipnis, "Babi Yar."
78. Kipnis, "Babi Yar."
79. Kipnis, "Babi Yar."
80. Kipnis, "Babi Yar," 59–60.
81. Moisei Loev, *Ukradennaia Muza Vospominaniia o Kievskom gosudarstvennom evreiskom teatre imeni Sholom Aleikhema, Kharkov-Kiev-Chernovtsy, 1925–1950* (Dukh i Litera, 2003), 137–38.
82. Loev, *Ukradennaia Muza*; Iryna Meleshkina, *Mandrivni zori v Ukraini: Storinku istorii evreis'kogo teatru* (Dukh i litera, 2019), 244–45.
83. Loev, *Ukradennaia Muza*, 137–38.
84. Joshua Rubenstein and Vladimir P. Naumov, *Stalin's Secret Pogrom: The Postwar Inquisition of the Jewish Anti-Fascist Committee* (Yale University Press, 2001), 1.
85. Yaacov Ro'i, "Nehama Lifshitz: Symbol of the Jewish National Awakening," in *Jewish Culture and Identity in the Soviet Union*, ed. Yaacov Ro'i and Avi Beker (New York University Press, 1992), 172.
86. Ro'i, "Nehama Lifshitz: Symbol of the Jewish National Awakening," 172.
87. Ro'i, "Nehama Lifshitz: Symbol of the Jewish National Awakening," 173.
88. Reprinted with permission from Shike Driz, "Babi Yar," in *We Are Here: Songs of the Holocaust*, ed. Malke Mlotek and Eleanor Gottlieb (Workmen's Circle and Hippocrene Books, 1983), https://yiddishsongs.org/babi-yar/.
89. Ro'i, "Nehama Lifshitz: Symbol of the Jewish National Awakening," 179.
90. Hrynevych, "Babyn Yar After Babyn Yar," 126.
91. Efrem Baukh, ed., *Babi Iar* (Moria, 1981), 95–98.
92. Ilya Ehrenburg and Vasily Grossman, eds., *The Black Book: The Ruthless Murder of Jews by German-Fascist Invaders Throughout the Temporarily-Occupied Regions of the Soviet Union*

and in the Death Camps of Poland During the War of 1941–1945 (Holocaust Publications: Distributed by Schocken Books, 1981).

93. Mikhail Kalnitsky, "Ilya Ehrenburg: Svidetel' Veka," *Kievskie Vedomosti*, http://www.c-cafe.ru/days/bio/28/036_28.php.
94. Kalnitsky, "Ilya Ehrenburg: Svidetel' Veka."
95. Kalnitsky, "Ilya Ehrenburg: Svidetel' Veka."
96. Kalnitsky, "Ilya Ehrenburg: Svidetel' Veka."
97. Maxim D. Shrayer, "Jewish-Russian Poets Bearing Witness to the Shoah, 1941–1946: Textual Evidence and Preliminary Conclusions," in *Studies in Slavic Languages and Literatures*, ed. Stefano Garzonio (ICCEES Congress, Papers and Contributions, 2010), 77.
98. Kalnitsky, "Ilia Erhenburg. Svidetel' Veka."
99. Shrayer, "Jewish-Russian Poets Bearing Witness to the Shoah, 1941–1946," 76.
100. Mordechai Altshuler, Yitzhak Arad, and Shmuel Krakowski, eds., *Sovetskie evrei pishut Il'e Erenburgu* (Yad Vashem, 1993), 56.
101. Vladyslav Hrynevych, "Babyn Yar After Babyn Yar," 109.
102. Solomon M. Schwartz, *The Jews in the Soviet Union* (Syracuse University Press, 1951), 359.
103. Schwartz, *The Jews in the Soviet Union*, 359.
104. Schwartz, *The Jews in the Soviet Union*, 359.
105. Yehoshua A. Gilboa, *The Black Years of Soviet Jewry 1939–1953* (Little, Brown, 1971), 90.
106. Gilboa, *The Black Years of Soviet Jewry*, 91.
107. Joshua Rubenstein, *Tangled Loyalties: The Life and Times of Ilya Ehrenburg* (Basic Books, 1996), 248.
108. Eva Berar, *Burnaia zhizn' Il'i Erenburga* (Novoe literaturnoe obozrenie, 2009), 184.
109. Berar, *Burnaia zhizn' Il'i Erenburga*, 184.
110. Berar, *Burnaia zhizn' Il'i Erenburga*, 184.
111. Ilya Ehrenburg, *The Ninth Wave* (Greenwood Press, 1974), 462.
112. Rubenstein, *Tangled Loyalties*, 248.
113. Berar, *Burnaia zhizn' Il'I Erenburga*, 184.
114. Altshuler, Arad, and Krakovski, *Sovetskie evrei pishut Il'e Erenburgu*.
115. Olga Gershenson, *The Phantom Holocaust: Soviet Cinema and Jewish Catastrophe* (Rutgers University Press, 2013), 46.
116. Gershenson, *The Phantom Holocaust*, 40.
117. Gershenson, *The Phantom Holocaust*, 45; Jeremy Hicks, *First Films of the Holocaust: Soviet Cinema and the Genocide of the Jews, 1938–1946* (University of Pittsburg Press, 2012), 134–56.
118. Gershenson, *The Phantom Holocaust*, 48.
119. Gershenson, *The Phantom Holocaust*, 49.
120. Hicks, *First Films of the Holocaust*, 151.
121. "Ukrainskiy khudozhnik-kosmopolit," article prepared by Odesa Art Museum, *Migdal' Times*, no. 158, https://www.migdal.org.ua/times/158/50533/.

122. "Ukrainskiy khudozhnik-kosmopolit."
123. D. Fedorovs'ky, "Bab'iachyi Yar: V maisterni khudozhnyka Ovchynnikova," *Radians'ke Mystetstvo*, July 30, 1947.
124. "Ukrainskiy khudozhnik-kosmopolit."
125. "Ukrainskiy khudozhnik-kosmopolit."
126. "Ukrainskiy khudozhnik-kosmopolit."
127. Pavel Polian, "Babi Yar v zhivopisi i skul'pture: ot Vasilia Ovchinikova do Vadima Sidura," *Lekhaim*, https://lechaim.ru/events/babiy-yar-v-zhivopisi-i-skulypture-ot-vasiliya-ovchinikova-do-vadima-sidura-2/.
128. Natalia Symonenko, "Babyn Yar in Music," in *Babyn Yar: History and Memory*, ed. Vladyslav Hrynevych and Paul Robert Magocsi (University of Toronto, 2023), 373.
129. Symonenko, "Babyn Yar in Music," 374.
130. Pavel Polian, "Rasstrel'naia nota: Ternistyi put' temy Babiego Yara v Sovetskoi muzyke i poezii," *Novaia Gazeta*, August 16, 2022, https://novayagazeta.ru/articles/2022/08/17/rasstrelnaia-nota-media.
131. Symonenko, "Babyn Yar in Music," 374.
132. Symonenko, "Babyn Yar in Music," 375.
133. Polian, "Rasstrel'naia nota."
134. Symonenko, "Babyn Yar in Music," 375.
135. Symonenko, "Babyn Yar in Music," 375.

CHAPTER 6

1. Zvi Gitelman, "Soviet Reactions to the Holocaust, 1945–1991," in *The Holocaust in the Soviet Union*, ed. Lucjan Dobroszycki and Jeffery S. Gurock (Routledge, 1994), 9–10.
2. Gitelman, "Soviet Reactions to the Holocaust, 1945–1991," 9–10.
3. Arkadi Zeltser, *Unwelcome Memory: Holocaust Monuments in the Soviet Union* (Yad Vashem, the International Institute for Holocaust Research, 2018), 26.
4. Zeltser, *Unwelcome Memory*, 112.
5. The Central State Archive of the Highest Authorities of Ukraine (TsDAVO U), f. 2, op. 7, d. 2103, l. 22.
6. TsDAVO U, f. 2, op.9, d. 6430, l. 154.
7. TsDAVO U, f. 2, op. 7, d. 2103, ll. 22-23; f. 2, op. 9, d. 6430, ll. 147–150.
8. As shown in archival photos and documents, the monument was designed as a pyramid. TsDAVO U, f. 2, op. 9, d. 6430, ll. 147–150, 153.
9. Anonymous, "Pamiatnik pogibshim v Bab'em Yaru," *Pravda*, April 4, 1945, 3.
10. Pavel Polian, *Babi Yar: Refleksiia* (Publishing House "Zebra E," 2022), 560.
11. M. Aizenshtadt, "A denkmol in Babi Yar," *Eynikayt*, July 7, 1945, 2, cited in Polian, *Babi Yar: Refleksiia*, 560.
12. TsDAVO U, f. 2, op. 9, d. 6430, l. 153.

13. Avraam Miletsky, *Naplyvy pamiati* (Philobiblon, 1998), 32.
14. P. Andreev and Iu. Iaralov, "Aleksandr Vlasov," *Sovetskaia Arkhitektura*, 16 (1964): 89–102.
15. TsDAVO U, f. 2, op. 9, d. 6430, l. 153.
16. Amir Weiner, *Making Sense of War: The Second World War and the Fate of the Bolshevik Revolution* (Princeton University Press, 2000), 232.
17. Alexander A. Kruglov, "Jewish Losses in Ukraine, 1941–1944," in *The Shoah in Ukraine: History, Testimony, Memorialization*, ed. Ray Brandon and Wendy Lower (Indiana University Press, 2008), 273.
18. CAHJP, RU 1891.
19. Evstaf'eva, "Babi Yar vo vtoroi polovine XX st.," in *Babi Yar: chelovek, vlast', istoriia: Dokumenty i materialy v 5 knigakh. Kniga 1: Istoricheskaia topographiia: Khronologiia sobytii*, ed. Tatiana Evstaf'eva and Vitalii Nachmanovich (Vneshtorgizdat Ukrainy, 2004), 188.
20. Richard Sheldon, "The Transformations of Babi Yar," in *Soviet Society and Culture: Essays in Honor of Vera S. Dunham*, ed. Terry L. Thompson and Richard Sheldon (Westview Press, 1988), 31.
21. Anatoly Kuznetsov, *Babi Yar: roman-dokument* (Radians'kyi pysmennyk, 1991), 345.
22. Yehoshua A. Gilboa, *The Black Years of Soviet Jewry 1939–1953* (Little, Brown, 1971), 36, 195.
23. CAHJP, RU-1915, 1–2.
24. David Silberklang, "More Than a Memorial: The Evolution of Yad Vashem," *Yad Vashem Quarterly Magazine* (Fall 2003, Special Commemorative ed.): 6–7, https://www.yadvashem.org/sites/default/files/yv_magazine31.pdf.
25. CAHJP, RU-1915, 1–2.
26. Gilboa, *The Black Years of Soviet Jewry 1939–1953*, 36, 195.
27. Karel C. Berkhoff, "The Dispersal and Oblivion of the Ashes and Bones of Babi Yar," in *Lessons and Legacies XII: New Directions in Holocaust Research and Education*, ed. Wendy Lower and Lauren Faulkner Rossi (Northwestern University Press, 2017), 266.
28. Berkhoff, "The Dispersal and Oblivion of the Ashes and Bones of Babi Yar," 266.
29. Victoria Khiterer, "Victor Nekrasov and the Babi Yar Massacre Commemoration," *Forgotten Heritage*, http://lostart.org.ua/en/research/739.html.
30. Miletsky, *Naplyvy pamiati*, 110.
31. Victor Nekrasov, "Pochemu eto ne sdelano?" in *Pamiat' Babiego Iara: Vospominaniia, dokumenty*, ed. Ilia Levitas (Evreiskii Sovet Ukrainy, 2001), 232–33.
32. Nekrasov, "Pochemu eto ne sdelano?," 232–33.
33. Nekrasov, "Pochemu eto ne sdelano?," 267.
34. Nekrasov, "Pochemu eto ne sdelano?," 267.
35. Victoria Khiterer, "Memorialization of the Holocaust in Minsk and Kiev," in *Holocaust Resistance in Europe and America: New Aspects and Dilemmas*, ed. Victoria Khiterer (Cambridge Scholars Publishing, 2017), 111.
36. Sergei Tiktin, "Babi Yar: Aprel' 1961," in *Babi Iar*, ed. Efrem Baukh (Moria, 1981), 138.

37. Alexander Anisimov, *"Kurenivs'kyi Apokalipsis" Kyivs'ka tragediia 13 bereznia 1961 roku u fotografiiakh, dokumentakh, spogadakh* (Fact, 2000), 77.
38. Berkhoff, "The Dispersal and Oblivion of the Ashes and Bones of Babi Yar," 268.
39. Solomon Volkov, *Dialogi s Evgeniem Evtushenko pri uchastii Anny Nel'son* (AST, 2018), 220.
40. Volkov, *Dialogi s Evgeniem Evtushenko pri uchastii Anny Nel'son*, 222–24.
41. William Korey, "A Monument over Babi Yar?," in *The Holocaust in the Soviet Union: Studies and Sources on the Destruction of the Jews in the Nazi-Occupied Territories of the USSR, 1941–1945*, ed. Lucjan Dobroszycki and Jeffery S. Gurock (M. E. Sharpe, 1993), 65–66.
42. Korey, "A Monument over Babi Yar?," 65–66.
43. Arkadii Belkin, "Vokrug stikhotvoreniia 'Babi Yar,'" https://proza.ru/2010/10/11/1615.
44. Oksana Dvornichenko, *Dmitri Shostakovich: Puteshestvie* (Tekst, 2006), 451.
45. Korey, "A Monument over Babi Yar?," 66.
46. Korey, "A Monument over Babi Yar?," 66.
47. Recently the number of Soviet victims of World War II was revised by Russian historians who claim that the Soviet Union lost 27 million people in the Second World War.
48. G. V. Kostyrchenko, *Tainaia politika Khrushcheva: Vlast', intelligentsia, evreiskii vopros* (Mezhdunarodnye otnosheniia, 2012), 352.
49. Kostyrchenko, *Tainaia politika Khrushcheva*, 352–53.
50. Korey, "A Monument over Babi Yar?," 67.
51. Yevgeny Yevtushenko, *The Most Famous Symphony of the 20th Century: Dmitri Shostakovich Symphony #13* (University of Tulsa, 2005).
52. Kuznetsov, *Babi Yar: roman-dokument*, 345.
53. Kuznetsov, *Babi Yar: roman-dokument*, 345.
54. Korey, "A Monument over Babi Yar?," 67–68; G. V. Kostyrchenko, *Tainaia politika: ot Brezhneva do Gorbacheva, Part I: Vlast'—intelligentsia—evreiskii vopros* (Mezhdunarodnye otnosheniia, 2018), 207–208.
55. Yury Shapoval, "The Defection of Anatoly Kuznetsov," *Den'*, January 18, 2005.
56. Korey, "A Monument over Babi Yar?," 68.
57. Mikhail Mitsel, "Zapret na uvekovechivanie pamiati kak sposob zamalchivaniia Kholokosta: praktika KPU v otnoshenii Babiego Yara," *Kholokost i Suchasnist'* 1 (2007): 21.
58. Intourist was the Soviet tour operator, which served as the primary travel agency for foreign tourists.
59. Elie Wiesel, *The Jews of Silence: A Personal Report on Soviet Jewry* (Schocken Books, 2011), 36.
60. Vadim Kipling, "Ushel, ostaviv zhizn' v kamne," *Ekho*, http://exo.net.ua/arkhiv/2423-2013-01-03-09-29-52.
61. Tatiana Evstaf'eva, "K istorii ustanovleniia pamiatnika v Babiem Yaru," *Evreiskii Obozrevatel'* 11, no. 30 (June 2002), http://jewukr.org/observer/jo11_30/p0102_r.html.
62. Evgenii Olenin, "Zabytyi konkurs 65-go goda," http://archive.is/Dja2.
63. Evstaf'eva, "K istorii ustanovleniia pamiatnika v Babiem Yaru."

64. Ada Rybachuk and Volodymyr Mel'nychenko, *Koly ruinuet'sia Svit* ... (Iurinform, 1991), 13.
65. Evstaf'eva, "K istorii ustanovleniia pamiatnika v Babiem Yaru."
66. Olenin, "Zabytyi konkurs 65-go goda."
67. Evstaf'eva, "K istorii ustanovleniia pamiatnika v Babiem Yaru."
68. Amik (Emanuil) Diamant, "Babyn Yar abo Pam'iat' pro te iak nepokirne plem'ia peretvoriuvalosia v narod," *Istpravda*, August 30, 2021, https://www.istpravda.com.ua/articles/2021/08/30/160079/.
69. Diamant, "Babyn Yar abo Pam'iat'."
70. Diamant, "Babyn Yar abo Pam'iat'."
71. Diamant, "Babyn Yar abo Pam'iat'."
72. Zeltser, *Unwelcome Memory*, 101, 159–61.
73. Yohanan Petrovsky-Shtern, "A Paradigm Changing Day: The Twenty-Fifth Anniversary of Babyn Yar and Ukrainian-Jewish Relations," *Harvard Ukrainian Studies* 38, no. 3–4 (2021): 234.
74. Petrovsky-Shtern, "A Paradigm Changing Day," 234.
75. Diamant, "Babyn Yar abo Pam'iat'."
76. Diamant, "Babyn Yar abo Pam'iat'."
77. There were no rabbis in Kyiv because the authorities deprived two Kyiv rabbis of their accreditation in the 1950s. So, the Kyiv Jewish community was ruled by a Religious Board of twenty people.
78. Mikhail Mitsel', *Obshchiny iudeiskogo ispovedaniia v Ukraine (Kyiv, L'vov: 1945–1981 gody)* (Biblioteka Instituta Iudaiki, 1998), 122–23.
79. Mitsel', *Obshchiny iudeiskogo ispovedaniia v Ukraine*, 234.
80. HDA SBU, f. 16, op. 1, d. 957, l. 40.
81. HDA SBU, f. 16, op. 1, d. 957, l. 40.
82. Rybachuk and Mel'nychenko, *Koly ruinuet'sia Svit* ... , 45.
83. Vladimir Potresov, "Vozvrashenie Nekrasova," in Victor Nekrasov, *Zapiski zevaki* (Vagrius, 2003), 21–22.
84. Potresov, "Vozvrashenie Nekrasova," 21–22.
85. Anonymous, "Babi -Yar-I," http://berdichev.org/babi_yar.htm.
86. Victor Nekrasov, "Babi Yar: Otryvok iz knigi *Zapiski zevaki*," *Novoe Russkoe Slovo*, September 7, 1975, https://nekrassov-viktor.com/images/Books/articles-ob-antisemitizme/07_09.1975big.jpg.
87. Vladyslav Hrynevych, "Babyn Yar After Babyn Yar," in *Babyn Yar: History and Memory*, ed. Vladyslav Hrynevych and Paul Robert Magocsi (University of Toronto Press, 2023), 137.
88. Mitsel, "Zapret na uvekovechivanie pamiati kak sposob zamalchivaniia Kholokosta," 14.
89. *Babi Yar, 1941–1991: A Resource Book and Guide*, ed. and compiled by the Staff of the Simon Wiesenthal Center (Simon Wiesenthal Center, 1991), 34.
90. *Babi Yar, 1941–1991: A Resource Book and Guide*, 34.

91. Izrail Kleiner, "Cto mozno sdelat' is dvuch treugol'nikov," in *Babi Iar*, ed. Efrem Baukh (Moria, 1981), 131–32.
92. Kleiner, "Cto mozno sdelat' is dvuch treugol'nikov," 132–33.
93. Kleiner, "Cto mozno sdelat' is dvuch treugol'nikov," 132–33.
94. Kleiner, "Cto mozno sdelat' is dvuch treugol'nikov," 132–33.
95. Kleiner, "Cto mozno sdelat' is dvuch treugol'nikov," 134–35.
96. Hrynevych, "Babyn Yar After Babyn Yar," 132.
97. Hrynevych, "Babyn Yar After Babyn Yar," 132.
98. The Russian State Archive of Contemporary History (RGANI), f. 5, op. 63, d. 29, l. 96, https://liders.rusarchives.ru/andropov/docs/o-merakh-predprinyatykh-po-presecheniyu-sionistskoi-provokatsii-v-babem-yaru.html.
99. Hrynevych, "Babyn Yar After Babyn Yar," 133.
100. Hrynevych, "Babyn Yar After Babyn Yar," 133.
101. RGANI, f. 5, op. 63, d. 29, l. 96.
102. Genrietta Friedman, "29 Sentiabria 1971 . . . ," in *Babi Iar*, ed. Efrem Baukh (Moria, 1981), 140.
103. Anonymous, "2,500 Soviet Jews Mark the Massacre at Babi Yar," *New York Times*, September 30, 1971, 8.
104. Friedman, "29 Sentiabria 1971 . . . ," 140.
105. Hrynevych, "Babyn Yar After Babyn Yar," 135.
106. Petrovsky-Shtern, "A Paradigm Changing Day," 247.
107. Petrovsky-Shtern, "A Paradigm Changing Day," 247.
108. Hrynevych, "Babyn Yar After Babyn Yar," 137.
109. Hrynevych, "Babyn Yar After Babyn Yar," 137.
110. Friedman, "29 Sentiabria 1976 . . . ," 141. There is an incorrect date in the title of the article; the article described the thirty-second anniversary of the Babyn Yar massacre, so the date should be September 29, 1973.
111. Friedman, "29 Sentiabria 1976 . . . ," 141.
112. Friedman, "29 Sentiabria 1976 . . . ," 141.
113. Pollack, "Cattle Grazed Among the Bones of Our Sacred Martyrs: Covering Babyn Yar Through the Decades," *Forward*, March 11, 2022, https://forward.com/archive/483853/babyn-yar-russia-ukraine-soviets-nazis-wwii-massacre-bombing/.
114. HDA SBU, f. 16, op. 1, d. 1097, l. 79.
115. HDA SBU, f. 16, op. 1, d. 1097, l. 79.
116. HDA SBU, f. 16, op. 1, d. 1097, l. 111.
117. HDA SBU, f. 16, op. 1, d. 1097, l. 111.
118. HDA SBU, f. 16, op. 1, d. 1097, l. 112; Iosif Begun, Soviet refusenik, prisoner of conscience, human rights activist, author, and translator.
119. HDA SBU, f. 16, op. 1, d. 1097, l. 112.
120. HDA SBU, f. 16, op. 1, d. 1097, l. 112.

121. HDA SBU, f. 16, op. 1, d. 1097, l. 119.
122. HDA SBU, f. 16, op. 1, d. 1097, l. 112.
123. Extract from the article in *Allgemeine Zeitung*, October 5, 1976, in *Babi Iar*, ed. Efrem Baukh (Moria, 1981), 142.
124. HDA SBU, f. 16, op. 1, d. 1136, 196.
125. HDA SBU, f. 16, op. 1, d. 1136, 196.
126. HDA SBU, f. 16, op. 1, d. 1136, 196.
127. Hrynevych, "Babyn Yar After Babyn Yar," 139.
128. Hrynevych, "Babyn Yar After Babyn Yar," 141.
129. Hrynevych, "Babyn Yar After Babyn Yar," 141.
130. Hrynevych, "Babyn Yar After Babyn Yar," 141.
131. Lucy S. Dawidowicz, "Babi Yar's Legacy," *New York Times*, September 27, 1981, https://www.nytimes.com/1981/09/27/magazine/babi-yar-s-legacy.html.
132. Hrynevych, "Babyn Yar After Babyn Yar," 141.
133. Hrynevych, "Babyn Yar After Babyn Yar," 141.
134. Jessica Rapson, *Topographies of Suffering: Buchenwald, Babi Yar, Lidice* (Berghahn Books, 2017), 114.
135. Hrynevych, "Babyn Yar After Babyn Yar," 141–42.
136. Rapson, *Topographies of Suffering*, 115.
137. Rapson, *Topographies of Suffering*, 114.
138. Rapson, *Topographies of Suffering*, 114–15.
139. Rapson, *Topographies of Suffering*, 117.
140. Rapson, *Topographies of Suffering*, 117.
141. James E. Young, *The Texture of Memory: Holocaust Memorials and Meaning* (Yale University Press, 1993), 295–96.
142. Young, *The Texture of Memory*, 295–96.
143. Archive of the Interregional Public Organization "Federation of Jewish Organizations and Communities—Vaad" (Archive of VAAD), f. 1, op. 1, d. 41, l. 1.
144. Archive of VAAD, f. 1, op. 1, d. 41, l. 1.
145. Archive of VAAD, f. 1, op. 1, d. 41, ll. 1–10.
146. Archive of VAAD, f. 1, op. 1, d. 41, l.10.
147. Archive of VAAD, f. 1, op. 1, d. 41, l.10.
148. TsDAHO U, f. 2, op. 15, d. 1715, l. 74.
149. TsDAHO U, f. 2, op. 15, d. 1715, l. 75.
150. Yuliia Mel'nichuk, "Kogda prishla nastoiashchaia nishcheta odin iz avtorov pamiatnika v Babiem Iaru Viktor Sukhenko dobrovol'no ushel iz zhizni," *Fakty*, July 2, 2003, 5.
151. L. Lysenko, "Skul'ptor Mikhail Lysenko i ego ucheniki," *Arkhitetura, Stroitel'stvo, Dizain*, 2004, http://www.archjournal.ru/rus/04%2049%202007/lisenko.htm.
152. Khiterer, "Memorialization of the Holocaust in Minsk and Kiev," 118–19.

153. Liudmila Lysenko, "Dve monumental'nye istorii," https://kulupa.livejournal.com/328747.html.
154. Lysenko, "Dve monumental'nye istorii."
155. Lysenko, "Dve monumental'nye istorii."
156. Mel'nichuk, "Kogda prishla nastoiashchaia nishcheta," 5.
157. Mel'nichuk, "Kogda prishla nastoiashchaia nishcheta," 5.
158. Mel'nichuk, "Kogda prishla nastoiashchaia nishcheta," 5.
159. Mel'nichuk, "Kogda prishla nastoiashchaia nishcheta," 5.
160. Mel'nichuk, "Kogda prishla nastoiashchaia nishcheta," 5.
161. Mel'nichuk, "Kogda prishla nastoiashchaia nishcheta," 5.
162. Hrynevych, "Babyn Yar After Babyn Yar," 138; Stanislav Tsalyk, "Blok istorika. 1976: Otkrytie pamiatnika v Babiem Yaru," BBC News, *Ukraina*, https://www.bbc.com/ukrainian/ukraine_in_russian/2016/07/160702_ru_s_history_blog_babyn_yar.
163. Hrynevych, "Babyn Yar After Babyn Yar," 138.
164. *Vechernii Kiev* was a popular local newspaper to which many Kyivans subscribed.
165. Mitsel, "Zapret na uvekovechivanie pamiati kak sposob zamalchivaniia Kholokosta," 19.
166. Arn Vergelis, "Der denkmol in Babi Yar vet shteyn ledoyres," *Sovetish Heymland* 6 (1975): 158–64.
167. Miriam Schulz, "We Pledge, as if It Was the Highest Sanctum, to Preserve the Memory: *Sovetish Heymland*, Facets of Holocaust Commemoration in the Soviet Union and the Cold War," in *Growing in the Shadow of Antifascism: Remembering the Holocaust in State-Socialist Eastern Europe*, ed. Kata Bohus, Peter Hallama, and Stephan Stach (Central European University Press, 2022), 262.
168. Probably they were representatives of the Anglo-Jewish Association.
169. Mel'nichuk, "Kogda prishla nastoiashchaia nishcheta," 5.
170. Mel'nichuk, "Kogda prishla nastoiashchaia nishcheta," 5.
171. Mel'nichuk, "Kogda prishla nastoiashchaia nishcheta," 5.
172. Emanuil (Amik) Diamant, "Babii Yar o kotorom Vy nichego (ili pochti nichego) ne znaete, Neizvestnye ili maloizvestnye materialy po istorii Babiego Yara," Diamant-Emanuel-Babiy-Yar-o-kotorom-vi-nichego-ili-pochti-nichego-ne-znaete.pdf.
173. Diamant, "Babii Yar o kotorom Vy nichego."
174. Hrynevych, "Babyn Yar After Babyn Yar," 139.
175. M. Odinets, "Monument u Babiego Yara," *Pravda*, June 23, 1976, p. 6, https://marxism-leninism.info/paper/pravda_1976_175-6649.
176. The article is cited in Archive of VAAD, f. 1, op. 1, d. 41, l. 5.
177. Tsalyk, "Blok istorika: 1976: Otkrytie pamiatnika v Babiem Yaru."
178. Victor Nekrasov, "Vzgliad i nechto," *Lit Mir, elektronnaia biblioteka*, 49, https://www.litmir.me/br/?b=250635&p=49.
179. On November 1, 1978, President Jimmy Carter established the President's Commission

on the Holocaust and charged it with the responsibility to submit a report "with respect to the establishment and maintenance of an appropriate memorial to those who perished in the Holocaust." "The President's Commission on the Holocaust," https://www.ushmm.org/information/about-the-museum/presidents-commission.

180. Mitsel, "Zapret na uvekovechivanie pamiati," 24; Anthony Austin, "U.S. Unit, at Babi Yar, Stunned by Soviet Silence on Jews," *New York Times*, August 4, 1979, 2, https://www.nytimes.com/1979/08/04/archives/us-unit-at-babi-yar-stunned-by-soviet-silence-on-jews-a-contrast-in.html.

181. Obituary, "Edward Sanders Dies at 87; Advisor to President Carter on the Middle East," *Los Angeles Times*, December 8, 2009, https://www.latimes.com/local/obituaries/la-me-edward-sanders8-2009dec08-story.html.

182. Bayard Rustin (1912–1987) was an American political activist, a prominent leader in social movements for civil rights, socialism, nonviolence, and gay rights.

183. Austin, "U.S. Unit, at Babi Yar, Stunned by Soviet Silence on Jews," 2.

184. Mitsel, "Zapret na uvekovechivanie pamiati," 24.

185. Elie Wiesel, *Report to the President, President's Commission on the Holocaust, September 27, 1979* (Reprinted by the United States Holocaust Memorial Museum, 2005), 23, https://www.ushmm.org/m/pdfs/20050707-presidents-commission-holocaust.pdf.

CHAPTER 7

1. Vladyslav Hrynevych, "Babyn Yar After Babyn Yar," in *Babyn Yar: History and Memory*, ed. Vladyslav Hrynevych and Paul Robert Magocsi (Dukh i Litera, 2016), 145–46.
2. Hrynevych, "Babyn Yar After Babyn Yar," 152.
3. Evstaf'eva, "Babi Yar vo vtoroi polovine XX st.," in *Babi Yar: chelovek, vlast', istoriia. Dokumenty i materialy v 5 knigakh. Kniga 1: Istoricheskaia topografiia. Khronologiia sobytii*, ed. Tatiana Evstaf'eva and Vitalii Nachmanovich (Vneshtorgizdat Ukrainy, 2004), 204.
4. Shimon Briman, "Babyn Yar: neizvestnye podozhgli Menoru," *Evreiskii mir*, September 15, 2015, http://evreimir.com/106055/babij-yar-neizvestnye-podozhgli-menoru/; Anonymous, "Klichko potreboval rassledovat' akt vandalism v Babiem Yaru," *Nedelia*, http://nedelya-ua.com/news/klichko-potreboval-rassledovat-akt-vandalizma-v-babem-yaru.
5. John-Paul Himka, "The Reception of the Holocaust in Postcommunist Ukraine," in *Bringing the Dark Past to Light: The Reception of the Holocaust in Postcommunist Europe*, ed. John-Paul Himka and Joanna Beata Michlic (University of Nebraska Press, 2013), 646.
6. Himka, "The Reception of the Holocaust in Postcommunist Ukraine," 646.
7. Victoria Khiterer, "Memorialization of the Holocaust in Minsk and Kyiv," in *Holocaust Resistance in Europe and America: New Aspects and Dilemmas*, ed. Victoria Khiterer (Cambridge Scholars Publishing, 2017), 123.
8. Khiterer, "Memorialization of the Holocaust in Minsk and Kyiv," 123.
9. Himka, "The Reception of the Holocaust in Postcommunist Ukraine," 646.

10. Iurii Vynnychuk, "Nepodilenyi Babyn Yar," *Zbruc*, September 10, 2016, https://zbruc.eu/node/57120.
11. Anonymous, "Diial'nist' gromads'kogo komitetu 'Babyn Yar,' 2003–2013," *Uroky Golokostu: Informatziino-pedagogichnyi buleten' Ukrains'kogo tsentru vyvchennia istorii Golokostu* 1(33), 2013, 7.
12. "Decree on the National Historical Memorial Preserve 'Babyn Yar,'" http://babynyar.gov.ua/en/decree-national-historical-memorial-preserve-babyn-yar.
13. Irina Koval'chuk, "V Babiem Yaru postroiat unikal'nyi memorial'nyi complex," *Segodnia*, June 25, 2013, http://www.segodnya.ua/ukraine/V-Babem-YAru-postroyat-unikalnyy-memorialnyy-kompleks-444135.html.
14. Koval'chuk, "V Babiem Yaru postroiat unikal'nyi memorial'nyi complex."
15. Koval'chuk, "V Babiem Yaru postroiat unikal'nyi memorial'nyi complex."
16. Anonymous, "Diial'nist' gromads'kogo komitetu 'Babyn Yar,' 2003–2013," 8–9.
17. "V Ukraine proidut traurnye meropriiatia k 75-oi godovshchine massovykh rasstrelov v Babiem Yaru," http://112.ua/obshchestvo/ukraina-chtit-pamyat-zhertv-babego-yara-75-ya-godovshhina-tragedii-342236.html.
18. Sam Sokol, "Ukraine Backtracks on Babyn Yar Plans Amid Accusations of Holocaust Revisionism," *Jerusalem Post*, February 8 and 9, 2016, http://www.jpost.com/Diaspora/Ukraine-backtracks-on-Babi-Yar-plans-amid-accusations-of-Holocaust-revisionism-444268.
19. Anonymous, "International Architectural Ideas Competition for Complex Integration of Memorial Area in Kyiv, Ukraine, Babyn Yar, Dorogozhichi Nekropolis," April 4, 2018, http://konkurs.kby.Kyiv.ua/en/best-projects/.
20. Masha Gessen, "The Holocaust Memorial Undone by Another War," *The New Yorker*, April 11, 2022, https://www.newyorker.com/magazine/2022/04/18/the-holocaust-memorial-undone-by-another-war.
21. Josh Cohen, "Ukraine Is Finally Ready to Memorialize Its Holocaust Past," *Atlantic Council*, September 28, 2018, http://www.atlanticcouncil.org/blogs/ukrainealert/ukraine-is-finally-ready-to-memorialize-its-holocaust-past.
22. BYHMC Financial Statement, https://babynyar.org/en/about#about-financial-statement.
23. Gessen, "The Holocaust Memorial Undone by Another War."
24. Babyn Yar Holocaust Memorial Center (BYHMC), http://babiyar.org/en/byhmc/about.
25. Babyn Yar Holocaust Memorial Center (BYHMC).
26. Rona Tausinger, "Babyn Yar: The Story of a Lost Universe," *Israel Hayom*, August 4, 2020, https://www.israelhayom.com/2020/08/04/babi-yar-the-story-of-a-lost-universe/.
27. "United States Holocaust Memorial Museum Expresses Deep Concern About Anti-Romani Violence in Ukraine," Press release of the US Holocaust Memorial Museum, May 14, 2018, https://www.ushmm.org/information/press/press-releases/museum-expresses-deep-concern-about-anti-romani-violence-and-antisemitism-i.
28. Cohen, "Ukraine Is Finally Ready to Memorialize Its Holocaust Past."

29. "Musei 'Babyn Yar': Vidkrytyi Lyst—Zasteredzhennia Ukrains'kykh Istorykiv," *Ukrains'ka Pravda*, March 28, 2017, http://www.istpravda.com.ua/articles/2017/03/28/149652/.
30. H. Boriak et al., *Concept of the Complex Memorialization of Babyn Yar with Extending Borders of the National Historical Memorial Preserve Babyn Yar* (Ministry of Culture of Ukraine; National Academy of Sciences of Ukraine, Institute of the History of Ukraine; National Historical Memorial Preserve Babyn Yar, November 9, 2019), http://resource.history.org.ua/item/0014671.
31. Boriak et al., *Concept of the Complex Memorialization of Babyn Yar*, 10.
32. Boriak et al., *Concept of the Complex Memorialization of Babyn Yar*, 10.
33. Boriak et al., *Concept of the Complex Memorialization of Babyn Yar*, 94.
34. Babyn Yar Holocaust Memorial Center (BYHMC), https://babynyar.org/en.
35. "The Winner Announced of Architectural Competition for the Best Project of Holocaust Memorial Center in Kyiv," September 9, 2019, https://babynyar.org/en/news/55.
36. "Winner Announced of Architectural Competition."
37. "Winner Announced of Architectural Competition."
38. Vladislav Davidzon, "Turning Babyn Yar into Holocaust Disneyland," *Tablet*, May 26, 2020, https://www.tabletmag.com/sections/arts-letters/articles/dau-babyn-yar-khrzhanovsky; Cnaan Liphshiz, "Film Director Panned for Plan to Turn Ukraine Museum into 'Holocaust Disneyland,'" *The Times of Israel*, May 26, 2020, https://www.timesofisrael.com/film-director-panned-for-plan-to-turn-ukraine-museum-into-holocaust-disneyland/.
39. *BYHMC Digest*, October 5–19, 2020.
40. "Two Research Institutes Opened at the Babyn Yar Holocaust Memorial Center," April 30, 2020, https://babynyar.org/en/news/10.
41. "Two Research Institutes Opened."
42. "Historians and Architects of the Babyn Yar Memorial Center Have Established the Sites of the Mass Shootings of 33,771 Jews in Kyiv in Late September 1941," November 16, 2020, https://babynyar.org/en/news/2028.
43. Alan Rosenbaum, "The Sounds of Babyn Yar," *The Jerusalem Post*, October 15, 2020, https://www.jpost.com/jerusalem-report/the-sounds-of-babyn-yar-644608.
44. "Doslidnykty rozshukaly sotni novykh prizvishch zhertv roztriliv u Babynomu Yaru," August 4, 2020, https://gazeta.ua/articles/Kyiv-life/_doslidniki-rozshukali-sotni-novih-prizvisch-zhertv-rozstriliv-u-babinomu-aru/977640?utm_source=yxnews&utm_medium=desktop; About the Names project, https://babynyar.org/en/names/about.
45. "Tsentr 'Babyn Yar' vosstanovit imena bolee treti zhertv pogibshikh v urochishche pod Kyivom," *Gordon*, November 5, 2020, https://gordonua.com/news/culture/centr-babiy-yar-vosstanovit-pamyat-bolee-treti-zhertv-1526105.
46. "Announcing the New Educational Partnership Between the Babyn Yar Holocaust Memorial Center and Centropa," October 13, 2020, https://babynyar.org/en/news/2008/2007.
47. "Announcing the New Educational Partnership."
48. "Babyn Yar Holocaust Memorial Centre Launches 'A Letter to the Righteous' Initiative,"

April 14, 2020, https://babynyar.org/en/news/13/memorialnij-centr-babin-ar-zapuskae-iniciativu-list-pravedniku.

49. "Babyn Yar Holocaust Memorial Centre Launches 'A Letter to the Righteous' Initiative."
50. Jadwiga Rogoża, "Ukraine's Disputes over the 80th Anniversary of the Babyn Yar Massacre," *OSW Commentary*, October 22, 2021, https://www.osw.waw.pl/en/publikacje/osw-commentary/2021-10-22/ukraines-disputes-over-80th-anniversary-babi-yar-massacre.
51. Babyn Yar Holocaust Memorial Center Press Release, "Ukraine Government Announces Official Commemorations Marking 80th Anniversary of Babyn Yar Massacre," June 17, 2021, https://www.prnewswire.com/il/news-releases/ukraine-government-announces-official-commemorations-marking-80th-anniversary-of-babyn-yar-massacre-892527747.html.
52. "Ukraine Government Announces Official Commemorations Marking 80th Anniversary of Babyn Yar Massacre."
53. Laurence Peter, "Babyn Yar: Synagogue Opens at Nazi Massacre Site in Ukraine," *BBC News*, May 14, 2021, https://www.bbc.com/news/world-europe-57114197.
54. Peter, "Babyn Yar: Synagogue Opens at Nazi Massacre Site in Ukraine."
55. Margaryta Chornokondratenko, "Artist Marina Abramovic's 'Crystal Wall of Crying' Commemorates Jews Killed in Babyn Yar Massacre," *Reuters*, October 7, 2021, https://www.reuters.com/world/europe/artist-marina-abramovics-crystal-wall-crying-commemorates-jews-killed-babyn-yar-2021-10-06/.
56. "Kristal'naia stena placha, film Loznitsy i visit trekh prezidentov: programma meropriiatii k 80-i godovshchine tragedii Babiego Iara," *New Voice, Ukraina*, September 21, 2021, https://nv.ua/ukraine/events/babiy-yar-plan-meropriyatiy-v-Kyive-k-80-y-godovshchine-tragedii-novosti-Kyiva-50184681.html.
57. Philissa Cramer, "'Killed in a Fire': Zelensky Gives New Details About His Family's Holocaust History," *The Times of Israel*, March 23, 2022.
58. The Kaddish is a Jewish prayer traditionally recited for the dead.
59. Matt Lebovic, "Using Rare Archival Films, Ukrainian Director Forces Viewers to Face Babyn Yar," *The Times of Israel*, March 28, 2021, https://www.timesofisrael.com/using-rare-archival-films-ukrainian-director-forces-viewers-to-face-babyn-yar/.
60. Rogoża, "Ukraine's Disputes over the 80th Anniversary of the Babyn Yar Massacre."
61. Anonymous, "Ukraine Government Announces Official Commemorations Marking 80th Anniversary of Babyn Yar Massacre," *PR Newswire*, June 17, 2021, https://www.prnewswire.com/news-releases/ukraine-government-announces-official-commemorations-marking-80th-anniversary-of-babyn-yar-massacre-301314772.html.
62. Press Release of the BYHMC, October 2021, https://www.facebook.com/babynyar.memorial.
63. Judah Ari Gross, "Russia Strikes Kyiv TV Tower, Killing 5 and Damaging Babyn Yar Holocaust Site," *The Times of Israel*, March 1, 2022, https://www.timesofisrael.com/russia-strikes-tv-tower-in-heart-of-kyiv-damaging-babi-yar-holocaust-memorial/.

64. David Fishman, "The Shellings in Ukraine and the Jewish Community," *The War in Ukraine: Jewish News*, no. 14, January 19, 2024.
65. Gross, "Russia Strikes Kyiv TV Tower, Killing 5 and Damaging Babyn Yar Holocaust Site."
66. Fishman, "The Shellings in Ukraine and the Jewish Community."
67. "Ukraine President Zelensky's Speech to Israeli Lawmakers. Full Text," *The Times of Israel*, March 20, 2022, https://www.timesofisrael.com/full-text-ukraine-president-zelenskys-speech-to-israeli-lawmakers/.
68. *The Times of Israel* Staff, "Israeli Lawmakers Tear into Zelensky for Holocaust Comparisons in Knesset Speech," *The Times of Israel*, March 20, 2022, https://www.timesofisrael.com/israeli-lawmakers-tear-into-zelensky-for-holocaust-comparisons-in-knesset-speech/.
69. "The Babyn Yar Holocaust Memorial Center Strongly Condemns Russian Aggression Against Ukraine (Statement)," March 1, 2022, https://babynyar.org/en/news/495/memorial-holokostu-babyn-yar-rizko-zasudzhuie-ahresiiu-rosii-proty-ukrainy-zaiava.
70. "Ilya Khrzhanovsky on Russian Aggression Against Ukraine," March 3, 2022, https://www.youtube.com/watch?v=DDN138LT4wk.
71. Anonymous, "Ilia Khzhanovsky ushel s posta khudruka ukrainskogo memorial'nogo tsentra Kholokosta Babi Yar iz-za voiny," *The Insider*, September 4, 2023, https://theins.ru/amp/news/264810.
72. Gessen, "The Holocaust Memorial Undone by Another War."
73. "Memorial 'Babyn Yar' zapustil Martirolog zhertv rosiis'ko-ukrains'koi viyny 'Zakryti Ochi,'" August 16, 2022, https://babynyar.org/en/news/513/Babyn-Yar-Memorial-launched-the-Martyrology-of-the-Russian-Ukrainian-War-Victims-Closed-Eyes.
74. "Russian Ideology Is Aimed at the Destruction of the Ukrainian People: Academics and Prosecutors Discussed how Putin's Propaganda Should Be Put to the International Trial," February 24, 2023, https://babynyar.org/en/news/519/online_conference_on_propaganda.
75. "The 'Babyn Yar' Holocaust Memorial Center Together with the March of Remembrance Organization Celebrated the 82nd Anniversary of the Babyn Yar Tragedy," September 29, 2023, https://babynyar.org/en/news/528/babyn-yar-day-2023.
76. "The 'Babyn Yar' Holocaust Memorial Center Together with the March of Remembrance Organization."
77. "The Dodd Prize," https://doddcenter.humanrights.uconn.edu/the-dodd-prize/.
78. "The Dodd Prize."
79. Hrynevych, "Babyn Yar After Babyn Yar," 218.
80. Vitaliy Nachmanovych, "Babyn Yar: A Place of Memory in Search of a Future," in *Babyn Yar: History and Memory*, ed. Vladyslav Hrynevych and Paul Robert Magocsi (Dukh i Litera, 2016), 416.

CONCLUSION

1. TsDAVO U, f. 2, op. 7, d. 2103, l. 22.

BIBLIOGRAPHY

Abramenko, L. M., ed. *Kievskiy process: dokumenty ta materialy*. Lybid', 1995.

Agafonov, Nikolai. "Golgofa arkhimandrita Aleksandra Vishniakova." *Omilia: Mezhdynarodnyi literaturnyi klub*. https://omiliya.org/content/golgofa-arkhimandrita-aleksandra-vishnyakova.

Aizenshtadt, M. "A denkmol in Babi Yar." *Eynikayt*, July 7, 1945. Cited in Pavel Polian, *Babi Yar: Refleksiia*. Publishing House Zebra E, 2022, 560.

Altman, Ilia. *Kholokost i evreiskoie soprotivlenie na okkupirovannoi territorrii SSSR*. Fond "Kholokost," 2002. https://jhist.org/shoa/hfond_124.htm.

Altshuler, Mordechai. "Antisemitism in Ukraine Toward the End of the Second World War." *Jews in Eastern Europe* 3 (1993): 40–81.

Altshuler, Mordechai. "Antisemitism in Ukraine Toward the End of World War II." In *Bitter Legacy: Confronting the Holocaust in the USSR*, edited by Zvi Gitelman, 77–90. Indiana University Press, 1997.

Altshuler, Mordechai. *Soviet Jewry on the Eve of the Holocaust: A Social and Demographic Profile*. The Center for Research of East European Jewry of the Hebrew University of Jerusalem, Yad Vashem, 1998.

Altshuler, Mordechai. "The Unique Features of the Holocaust in the Soviet Union." In *Jews and Jewish Life in Russia and the Soviet Union*, edited by Yaacov Ro'i, 171–211. Frank Cass, 1995.

Altshuler, Mordechai, Yitzhak Arad, and Shmuel Krakowski, eds. *Sovetskie evrei pishut Il'e Erenburgu*. Yad Vashem, 1993.

Anatoli, A. (pseudonym of Anatoly Kuznetsov). *Babi Yar: A Document in the Form of a Novel. New, Complete Uncensored Version*. Farrar, Straus and Giroux, 1970.

Andreev, P., and Iu. Iaralov. "Aleksandr Vlasov." *Sovetskaia Arkhitektura* 16 (1964): 89–102.

Anisimov, Alexander. *"Kurenivs'kyi Apokalipsis" Kyivs'ka tragediia 13 bereznia 1961 roku u fotografiiakh, dokumentakh, spogadakh*. Fact, 2000.

Anonymous. "Announcing the New Educational Partnership Between the Babyn Yar Holocaust Memorial Center and Centropa." October 13, 2020. https://babynyar.org/en/news/2008/2007.

Anonymous. *Babi Yar, 1941–1991: A Resource Book and Guide*. Edited and compiled by the Staff of the Simon Wiesenthal Center. Simon Wiesenthal Center, 1991.

Anonymous. "The 'Babyn Yar' Holocaust Memorial Center Together with the March of Remembrance Organization Celebrated the 82nd Anniversary of the Babyn Yar Tragedy." September 29, 2023. https://babynyar.org/en/news/528/babyn-yar-day-2023.

Anonymous. Babyn Yar Holocaust Memorial Center. "Ukraine Government Announces

Official Commemorations Marking 80th Anniversary of Babyn Yar Massacre." June 17, 2021. https://www.prnewswire.com/il/news-releases/ukraine-government-announces-official-commemorations-marking-80th-anniversary-of-babyn-yar-massacre-892527747.html.

Anonymous. "Babyn Yar Holocaust Memorial Centre Launches 'A Letter to the Righteous' Initiative." April 14, 2020. https://babynyar.org/en/news/13/memorialnij-centr-babin-ar-zapuskae-iniciativu-list-pravedniku.

Anonymous. "Diial'nist' gromads'kogo komitetu 'Babyn Yar,' 2003–2013." *Uroky Golokostu. Informatziino-pedagogichnyi buleten' Ukrains'kogo tsentru vyvchennia istorii Golokostu* 1(33), 2013.

Anonymous. "Doslidnykty rozshukaly sotni novykh prizvishch zhertv roztriliv u Babynomu Yaru." August 4, 2020. https://gazeta.ua/articles/Kyiv-life/_doslidniki-rozshukali-sotni-novih-prizvisch-zhertv-rozstriliv-u-babinomu-aru/977640?utm_source=yxnews&utm_medium=desktop.

Anonymous. "80 Years On: The True Faces of the Babyn Yar Murders Are Being Revealed." BYHMC Press Release, October 5, 2021. https://babynyar.org/en/news/455.

Anonymous. "Germany: Case Closed." *Time*, June 18, 1951. https://content.time.com/time/subscriber/article/0,33009,814963,00.html.

Anonymous. "Geroi Ukrainy Tatiana Markus." *Evreiskiy Mir*, February 14, 2007. http://evreimir.com/14407/.

Anonymous. "Historians and Architects of the Babyn Yar Memorial Center Have Established the Sites of the Mass Shootings of 33,771 Jews in Kyiv in Late September 1941." November 16, 2020. https://babynyar.org/en/news/2028.

Anonymous. "Ilia Khzhanovsky ushel s posta khudruka ukrainskogo memorial'nogo tsentra Kholokosta Babi Yar iz-za voiny." *The Insider*, September 4, 2023. https://theins.ru/amp/news/264810.

Anonymous. "International Architectural Ideas Competition for Complex Integration of Memorial Area in Kyiv, Ukraine, Babyn Yar, Dorogozhichi Nekropolis." April 4, 2018. http://konkurs.kby.Kyiv.ua/en/best-projects/.

Anonymous. *Jarhbücher fuer Geschichte Osteuropas* 61, 2013.

Anonymous. "Kristal'naia stena placha, film Loznitsy i visit trekh presidentov: programma meropriiatii k 80-i godovshchine tragedii Babiego Iara." *New Voice, Ukraina*, September 21, 2021. https://nv.ua/ukraine/events/babiy-yar-plan-meropriyatiy-v-Kyive-k-80-y-godovshchine-tragedii-novosti-Kyiva-50184681.html.

Anonymous. "Liberberg Iosif Izraelivich." *Vspomnim vsekh poimenno.* http://eao.memo27reg.org/pamat-1/semletmyziliozidaniempisem.

Anonymous. "Massovye rasstrely v Bab'em Iare. Archivnye fotografii." *RIA Novosti Ukraina*, September 29, 2019. https://rian.com.ua/photolents/20160929/1017016453.html.

Anonymous. "Memorial 'Babyn Yar' zapustil Martirolog zhertv rosiis'ko-ukrains'koi viyny 'Zakryti Ochi.'" August 16, 2022. https://babynyar.org/en/news/513/Babyn-Yar-Memorial-launched-the-Martyrology-of-the-Russian-Ukrainian-War-Victims-Closed-Eyes.

Anonymous. "Mucheniki," https://www.babiy-yar.org/mucheniki.
Anonymous. Obituary: "Edward Sanders Dies at 87; Advisor to President Carter on the Middle East." *Los Angeles Times*, December 8, 2009. https://www.latimes.com/local/obituaries/la-me-edward-sanders8-2009dec08-story.html.
Anonymous. Obituary of Gertrud von Radetzky, Wife of Waldemar von Radetzky. *Deutsch-Baltische Gesselschaft* (German-Baltic Society), e. V, 8/1/2014–1/16/2016. http://www.deutsch-balten.de/175.html.
Anonymous. "Pamiatnik pogibshim v Bab'em Yaru." *Pravda*, April 4, 1945.
Anonymous. "The President's Commission on the Holocaust." https://www.ushmm.org/information/about-the-museum/presidents-commission.
Anonymous. "Russian Ideology Is Aimed at the Destruction of the Ukrainian People: Academics and Prosecutors Discussed How Putin's Propaganda Should Be Put to the International Trial." February 24, 2023. https://babynyar.org/en/news/519/online_conference_on_propaganda.
Anonymous. "Teliga Elena Ivanovna." *Geroi Ukrainy*. http://heroes.profi-forex.org/ru/teliga-olena-ivanivna.
Anonymous. "Teliga ne byla rasstreliana v Babiem Yaru." *The Kiev Times*, November 9, 2013. http://thekievtimes.ua/society/271625-teliga-ne-byla-rasstrelyana-v-babem-yaru.html.
Anonymous. *The Times of Israel* Staff. "Israeli Lawmakers Tear into Zelensky for Holocaust Comparisons in Knesset Speech." *The Times of Israel*, March 20, 2022. https://www.timesofisrael.com/israeli-lawmakers-tear-into-zelensky-for-holocaust-comparisons-in-knesset-speech/.
Anonymous. *The Times of Israel* Staff. "Names, Testimonies of Nazis in Babi Yar Massacre Released 80 Years On." *The Times of Israel*, October 6, 2021. https://www.timesofisrael.com/names-testimonies-of-nazis-in-babi-yar-massacre-released-80-years-on/.
Anonymous. "Tsentr 'Babyn Yar' vosstanovit imena bolee treti zhertv pogibshikh v urochishche pod Kyivom." *Gordon*, November 5, 2020. https://gordonua.com/news/culture/centr-babiy-yar-vosstanovit-pamyat-bolee-treti-zhertv-1526105.
Anonymous. "2,500 Soviet Jews Mark the Massacre at Babi Yar." *New York Times*, 8. September 30, 1971.
Anonymous. "Two Research Institutes Opened at the Babyn Yar Holocaust Memorial Center." April 30, 2020. https://babynyar.org/en/news/10.
Anonymous. "Ukrainskiy khudozhnik- kosmopolit." Article prepared by the Odesa Art Museum. *Migdal' Times*, no. 158. https://www.migdal.org.ua/times/158/50533/.
Anonymous. "United States Holocaust Memorial Museum Expresses Deep Concern About Anti-Romani Violence in Ukraine." Press Release of the US Holocaust Memorial Museum, May 14, 2018. https://www.ushmm.org/information/press/press-releases/museum-expresses-deep-concern-about-anti-romani-violence-and-antisemitism-i.
Anonymous. "V Ukraine proidut traurnye meropriiatia k 75-oi godovshchine massovykh rasstrelov v Babiem Yaru." http://112.ua/obshchestvo/ukraina-chtit-pamyat-zhertv-babego-yara-75-ya-godovshhina-tragedii-342236.html.
Antoniuk, Evgeny. "Mify i pravda o 'Matche smerti.' Chto stalo s futbolistami, pobedivshimi

nemtsev?" https://pikabu.ru/story/mifyi_i_pravda_o_matche_smerti_chto_stalo_s_fut bolistami_pobedivshimi_nemtsev_6086263.

Arad, Yitzhak, Mordechai Altshuler, and Shmuel Krakowski, eds. *Sovetskie evrei pishut Il'e Erenburgu*. Yad Vashem, 1993.

Arad, Yitzhak, Shmuel Krakowsky, and Shmuel Spector, eds. *The Einsatzgruppen Reports*. Holocaust Library, 1989.

Arieli, Zvi. "Ukraina: edinstvo natsii ili spornye geroi?" https://censor.net.ua/blogs/4075/ukraina_edinstvo_natsii_ili_spornye_geroi.

Aristov, Stanislav. "Next to Babi Yar: The Syrets Concentration Camp and the Evolution of Nazi Terror in Kiev." *Holocaust and Genocide Studies* 29, no. 3 (Winter 2015): 431–59.

Austin, Anthony. "U.S. Unit, at Babi Yar, Stunned by Soviet Silence on Jews." *New York Times*, August 4, 1979, 2. https://www.nytimes.com/1979/08/04/archives/us-unit-at-babi-yar-stunned-by-soviet-silence-on-jews-a-contrast-in.html.

Bauer, Yehuda. *A History of the Holocaust*, rev. ed. Franklin Watts, 2001.

Baukh, Efrem, ed. *Babi Iar*. Moria, 1981.

Belkin, Arkadii. "Vokrug stikhotvoreniia 'Babi Yar.'" https://proza.ru/2010/10/11/1615.

Bemporad, Elissa. *Becoming Soviet Jews: The Bolshevik Experiment in Minsk*. Indiana University Press, 2013.

Berar, Eva. *Burnaia zhizn' Il'i Erenburga*. Novoe literaturnoe obozrenie, 2009.

Beregovskaia, E. M. "Eshche raz o sud'be M. Ia. Beregovskogo." In M. Beregovsky, *Purimshpil'. Evreiskie Narodnye muzykal'no-teatral'nye predstavleniia*. Dukh i Litera, 2001, 12–27.

Berkhoff, Karel C. "Babi Yar: Site of Mass Murder, Ravine and Oblivion." *J. B. and Maurice C. Shapiro Annual Lecture*. February 9, 2011. https://www.ushmm.org/m/pdfs/Publication_OP_2011-02.pdf.

Berkhoff, Karel C. "Babyn Yar: mistse naimashtabnogo roztrilu evreiv natsystamy v Radians'komu Soiuzi." In *Babyn Yar: masove ubyvstvo i pam'iat'pro ni'ogo. Materialy mizhnarodnoi naukovoi konferentsii 24–25 zhovtnia 2011 r., m. Kyiv*, edited by Vitaliy Nakhmanovich and Mykhailo Tiagly, 8–20. Ukrains'kyi tsentr vyvchennia istorii Golocostu, 2012.

Berkhoff, Karel C., et al. *Basic Historical Narrative of the Babi Yar Holocaust Memorial Center*. http://api.babiyar.org/uploads/files/fund/ff5be4721f4ef9d0cee21b34e17e8c05.pdf.

Berkhoff, Karel C. "Dina Pronicheva's Story of Surviving the Babi Yar Massacre: German, Jewish, Soviet, Russian, and Ukrainian Records." In *The Shoah in Ukraine: History, Testimony, Memorialization*, edited by Ray Brandon and Wendy Lower, 291–317. Indiana University Press, 2008.

Berkhoff, Karel C. "The Dispersal and Oblivion of the Ashes and Bones of Babi Yar." In *Lessons and Legacies XII: New Directions in Holocaust Research and Education*, edited by Wendy Lower and Lauren Faulkner Rossi, 256–76. Northwestern University Press, 2017.

Berkhoff, Karel C. "The Great Famine in Light of German Invasion and Occupation." *Harvard Ukrainian Studies* 30, no. 1–4 (2008): 165–81.

Berkhoff, Karel C. *Harvest of Despair: Life and Death in Ukraine under Nazi Rule.* Belknap Press of Harvard University Press, 2004.

Berkhoff, Karel C., and Marco Carynnyk. "The Organization of Ukrainian Nationalists and Its Attitude Toward Germans and Jews: Iaroslav Stets'ko's 1941 Zhytiepys." *Harvard Ukrainian Studies* 23, no. 3 (January 1999): 149–84.

Bessonov, N., and N. Demeter. "Struktura tsyganskogo tabora." In *Istoriia tsygan—novyi vzgliad*, edited by N. Bessonov and N. Demeter. Institut antropologii i etnologii RAN, 2000. http://gypsy-life.net/history13.htm.

Blackwell, Martin J. *Kyiv as Regime City: The Return of Soviet Power After Nazi Occupation.* University of Rochester Press, 2016.

Boriak, H., et al. *Concept of the Complex Memorialization of Babyn Yar with Extending Borders of the National Historical Memorial Preserve Babyn Yar.* Ministry of Culture of Ukraine; National Academy of Sciences of Ukraine, Institute of the History of Ukraine; National Historical Memorial Preserve Babyn Yar. November 9, 2019. http://resource.history.org.ua/item/0014671.

Borisov, Aleksei, ed. *Sbornik Materialov Chrezvychainoi Gosudarstvennoi Komissii po ustanovleniiu i rassledovaniiu zlodeianii nemetsko-fashistskikh zakhvatchikov i ikh soobshchnikov.* http://samlib.ru/b/borisow_aleksej_wiktorowich/materialychgk.shtml.

Borovoi, Saul. *Vospominaniia.* Gesharim, 1993.

Borovoi, Saul. "Vospominaniia ob I. V. Galante." In *Dokumenty, Sobrannye Evreiskoi Istorikoarkheographicheskoi Komissiei Vseukrainskoi Akademii Nauk*, edited by Victoria Khiterer, 18. Hebrew University of Jerusalem and Gesharim Publishing House, 1999.

Brener, Iosif. "Semia Liberberg." *My zdes'*, no. 581, March 8–18, 2019. http://www.newswe.com/index.php?go=Pages&in=view&id=5694.

Brent, Jonathan, and Vladimir P. Naumov. *Stalin's Last Crime: The Plot Against the Jewish Doctors, 1948–1953.* Harper Perennial, 2003.

Briman, Shimon. "Babyn Yar: neizvestnye podozhgli Menoru." *Evreiskii mir*, September 15, 2015. http://evreimir.com/106055/babij-yar-neizvestnye-podozhgli-menoru/.

Budnik, David, and Yakov Kaper. *Nothing Is Forgotten: Jewish Fates in Kiev 1941–1943*, edited by Erhard Roy Weihn. Hartung-Gorre Verlag, 1993.

Burakovsky, Aleksandr. "Holocaust Remembrance in Ukraine: Memorialization of the Jewish Tragedy at Babi Yar." *Nationalities Papers* 39, no. 3 (2011): 371–89.

Cadiot, Juliette. "L'affaire Hain, Kyiv, Hiver 1952." *Cahiers du Monde Russe*, 59, no. 2-3 (2018): 255–88.

Chebrova, Tatiana. "Bolel'shchik s 72-khletnim stazhem akademik Viacheslav Sabaldyr': 'Blagodaria razvedchikam-dinamovtsam byl sorvan fashistskii shturm Stalingrada.'" *Bul'var Gordona* 35 (227), September 1, 2009. https://bulvar.com.ua/gazeta/archive/s35_63236/5608.html.

Cherepinsky, Jacqueline. "Babi Yar: The Absence of the Babi Yar Massacre from Popular Memory." In *The Holocaust: Memories and History*, edited by Victoria Khiterer, 143–73. Cambridge

Scholars Publishing, 2014.

Chornokondratenko, Margaryta. "Artist Marina Abramovic's 'Crystal Wall of Crying' Commemorates Jews Killed in Babyn Yar Massacre." *Reuters*, October 7, 2021. https://www.reuters.com/world/europe/artist-marina-abramovics-crystal-wall-crying-commemorates-jews-killed-babyn-yar-2021-10-06/.

Chornyi, Maksym. "Babi Yar: Istoriia." https://war-documentary.info/babi-yar/.

Cohen, Josh. "Ukraine Is Finally Ready to Memorialize Its Holocaust Past." *Atlantic Council*, September 28, 2018. http://www.atlanticcouncil.org/blogs/ukrainealert/ukraine-is-finally-ready-to-memorialize-its-holocaust-past.

Conquest, Robert. *The Harvest of Sorrow: Soviet Collectivization and the Terror-Famine*. Oxford University Press, 1986.

Cramer, Philissa. "'Killed in a Fire': Zelensky Gives New Details About His Family's Holocaust History." *The Times of Israel*, March 23, 2022.

"Crasher," Sergey. "Khatyn': istoria derevni, sozhzhenoi fashistami vo vremia voiny." https://poznamka.ru/belarus/kto-szheg-hatyn.

Davidzon, Vladislav. "Turning Babyn Yar into Holocaust Disneyland." *Tablet*, May 26, 2020. https://www.tabletmag.com/sections/arts-letters/articles/dau-babyn-yar-khrzhanovsky.

Dawidowicz, Lucy S. "Babi Yar's Legacy." *New York Times*, September 27, 1981, A. 48. https://www.nytimes.com/1981/09/27/magazine/babi-yar-s-legacy.html.

Dawidowicz, Lucy S., ed. *A Holocaust Reader*. Behrman House, 1975.

Dean, Martin C. *Investigating Babyn Yar: Shadows from the Valley of Death*. Lexington Books, 2024.

Dereiko, Ivan. "Ukrains'ki dopomizhni voenizovani formuvannia nimets'koi armii i politsii v general'niy okruzi Kyiv u 1941–1943 rr." In *Arkhivy okupatsii 1941–1944*, edited by Nataliia Makovs'ka, Vol. I, 2nd ed., 796–803. Kyevo-Mogylians'ka Akademiia, 2008.

Diamant, Amik (Emanuil). "Babyn Yar abo Pam'iat' pro te iak nepokirne plem'ia peretvoriuvalosia v narod." *Istpravda*, August 30, 2021. https://www.istpravda.com.ua/articles/2021/08/30/160079/.

Diamant, Emmanuil (Amik). "Babii Yar o kotorom Vy nichego (ili pochti nichego) ne znaete, Neizvestnye ili maloizvestnye materialy po istorii Babiego Yara." Diamant-Emanuel-Babiy-Yar-o-kotorom-vi-nichego-ili-pochti-nichego-ne-znaete.pdf.

Dolinsky, Eduard. "V Babiem Iaru ustanovili stend pamiati palachu evreev." https://strana.ua/news/35156-babem-yare-ustanovili-stend-pamyati-palachu-evreev.html.

Dolinsky, Eduard. "Vedomstvo Viatrovicha ustanovilo v Babiem Iare stend pamiati 'palachu' evreev—Ukrainskiy Evreiskii Komitet." *Ukrains'ki Novyny*, October 8, 2016. http://ukranews.com/news/453489-vedomstvo-vyatrovycha-ustanovylo-v-babem-yare-stend-pamyaty-palachu-evreev-ukraynskyy-evreyskyy-komytet/.

Downs, Bill. "Blood at Babii Yar—Kiev's Atrocity Story." *Newsweek*, December 6, 1943. https://www.billdownscbs.com/2013/07/blood-at-babii-yar-kievs-atrocity-story.html.

Driz, Shike. "Babi-Yar." https://lullabiesofloss.wordpress.com/2012/12/25/lullabies-and-the

-holocaust/.

Driz, Shike. "Babi-Yar." In *The Last Lullaby: Poetry from the Holocaust*, translated and edited by Aaron Kramer, 60. Syracuse University Press, 1998.

Dvornichenko, Oksana. *Dmitri Shostakovich: Puteshestvie*. Tekst, 2006.

Efimov, Igor'. "Zagadka Pesni pro Podol." http://a-pesni.org/dvor/a-podol.php.

Ehrenburg, Ilya. *The Ninth Wave*. Greenwood Press, 1974.

Ehrenburg, Ilya, and Vasily Grossman, eds. *The Black Book: The Ruthless Murder of Jews by German-Fascist Invaders Throughout the Temporarily-Occupied Regions of the Soviet Union and in the Death Camps of Poland During the War of 1941–1945*. Holocaust Publications. Distributed by Schocken Books, 1981.

Ehrenburg, Ilya, and Vasily Grossman, eds. *The Complete Black Book of Russian Jewry*. Translated by David Patterson. Transaction Publishers, 2003.

Elisavetsky, Ster. "Izvestnoe i novoe slovo o Tane Markus." *Zerkalo Nedeli*, August 9, 2002. https://zn.ua/SOCIUM/izvestnoe_i_novoe_slovo_o_tane_markus.html.

Estraikh, Gennady. "From Yehupets Jargonists to Kiev Modernists: The Rise of a Yiddish Literary Centre, 1880s–1914." *East European Jewish Affairs* 30, no. 1 (2000): 17–38.

Estraikh, Gennady. *In Harness: Yiddish Writers' Romance with Communism*. Syracuse University Press, 2005.

Estraikh, Gennady. *Soviet Yiddish: Language Planning and Linguistic Development*. Clarendon Press, 1999.

Estraikh, Gennady. "Spivak, Elye." *The YIVO Encyclopedia of Jews in Eastern Europe*. https://yivoencyclopedia.org/article.aspx/Spivak_Elye.

Evreiskii narod v bor'be protiv fashisma. III antifashistskii miting predstavitelei evreiskogo Naroda. III Plenum Evreiskogo antifasshistskogo komiteta v SSSR. Der Emes, 1945.

Evstaf'eva, Tatiana. "Babi Yar vo vtoroi polovine XX st." In *Babi Yar: chelovek, vlast', istoriia. Dokumenty i materialy v 5 knigakh. Kniga 1: Istoricheskaia topografiia. Khronologiia sobytii*, edited by Tatiana Evstaf'eva and Vitalii Nachmanovich, 187–206. Vneshtorgizdat Ukrainy, 2004.

Evstaf'eva, Tatiana. "Futbol'nye matchi 1942 goda komandy 'Start' v okkupirovannom nemtsami Kieve i sud'by ee igrokov." In *Babyn Yar: masove ubyvstvo i pam'iat' pro ni'ogo. Materialy mizhnarodnoi naukovoi konferentsii 24–25 zhovtnia 2011 r., m. Kyiv.*, edited by Vitaliy Nakhmanovich and Mykhailo Tiagly, 32–82. Ukrains'kyi tsentr vyvchennia istorii Golocostu, 2012.

Evstaf'eva, Tatiana. "K istorii ustanovleniia pamiatnika v Babiem Yaru." *Evreiskii Obozrevatel'* 11, no. 30 (June 2002). http://jewukr.org/observer/jo11_30/p0102_r.html.

Evstaf'eva, Tatiana. "Syretskiy kontsentratsionnyi lager'." In *Babi Yar: chelovek, vlast', istoriia. Dokumenty i materialy v 5 knigakh. Kniga 1: Istoricheskaia topografiia. Khronologiia sobytii*, edited by Tatiana Evstaf'eva and Vitalii Nachmanovich, 171–86. Vneshtorgizdat Ukrainy, 2004.

Evstaf'eva, Tatiana. "Tragedia Babynogo Yaru u 1941–1943 rr. (Za Dokumentamy Galuzevogoderzhavnogo Arkhivu Sluzhby bezpeky Ukrainy)." *Z Arkhiviv VUCHK, GPU, NKVD, KGB* 22/23, no. 1–2 (2004): 355–86.

Evstaf'eva, Tatiana, and Vitalii Nachmanovich, eds. *Babi Yar: chelovek, vlast', istoriia. Dokumenty i materialy v 5 knigakh. Kniga 1: Istoricheskaia topographiia. Khronologiia sobytii*. Vneshtorgizdat Ukrainy, 2004.

Fedchun, T. N. "Golod 1946–1947 godov po documentam gosarchiva." *Letopis' Dondassa*. http://donbass.name/letopis/964-golod-1946-1947gg.-po-dokumentam-gosarkhiva.html.

Fedorovs'ky, D. "Bab'iachyi Yar. V maisterni khudozhnyka Ovchynnikova." *Radians'ke Mystetstvo*, July 30, 1947.

Fefer, Itsik. "Pepel Babiego Yara zhet nashi serdtsa." In *Evreiskii narod v bor'be protiv fashisma. III antifashistskii miting predstavitelei evreiskogo Naroda. III Plenum Evreiskogo antifasshistskogo komiteta v SSSR*, 26–28. Der Emes, 1945.

Fishman, David E. *The Book Smugglers: Partisans, Poets, and the Race to Save Jewish Treasures from the Nazis*. ForeEdge and the University Press of New England, 2017.

Fishman, David E. "The Shellings in Ukraine and the Jewish Community." *The War in Ukraine: Jewish News*, no. 14, January 19, 2024.

Fliat, Leonid. "Liberberg i drugie . . . K istorii instituta evreiskoi kul'tury (Kyiv)." *Novosti Nedeli*, July 15, 1999.

Fridman, Lev. "In Search of Mykola Bazhan's Legacy on the Eve of Commemorations of Babyn Yar." *Odessa Review*, November 9, 2016. https://odessareview.com/search-mykola-bazhans-legacy-eve-commemorations-babyn-yar/.

Frolov, Kirill. "Archimandrit Aleksandr (Vishniakov)," *Vestnik*, no. 12, September 1, 2002. http://pravoslavye.org.ua/2002/09/k_frolov_arhimandrit_aleksandr_vishnyakov.

Galich, Alexander. "Zasypaia i prosypaias'." https://www.culture.ru/poems/3429/zasypaya-i-prosypayas.

Gershenson, Olga. *The Phantom Holocaust: Soviet Cinema and Jewish Catastrophe*. Rutgers University Press, 2013.

Gessen, Masha. "The Holocaust Memorial Undone by Another War." *The New Yorker*, April 11, 2022. https://www.newyorker.com/magazine/2022/04/18/the-holocaust-memorial-undone-by-another-war.

Gilboa, Yehoshua A. *The Black Years of Soviet Jewry 1939–1953*. Little, Brown, 1971.

Gitelman, Zvi Y. *Jewish Nationality and Soviet Politics: The Jewish Sections of CPSU, 1917–1930*. Princeton University Press, 1972.

Gitelman, Zvi. "Soviet Reactions to the Holocaust, 1945–1991." In *The Holocaust in the Soviet Union*, edited by Lucjan Dobroszycki and Jeffery S. Gurock, 3–28. Routledge, 1994.

Glagoleva-Palian, M. A. "Vospominaniia ob Aleksandre Aleksandroviche Glagoleve." *Yehupets* 8 (2001): 311–38.

Glazkov, Victor. "Gibel' Katyni: Taina bez sroka davnosti." *Sputnik: Belarus'*, https://sputnik.by/longrid/20160704/1023834943.html.

Goreshin, Konstantin, ed. *Niurembergskii Protsess: Sbornik Materialov*, Vol. I, 3rd ed. Gosudarstvennoe izdatel'stvo iuridicheskoi literatury, 1955.

Greenbaum, Abraham. *Evrei v Rossii: Istoriograficheski ocherki 2-aia polovina XIX veka–XX vek*.

Gesharim Publishing House, 1994.

Greenbaum, Alfred Abraham. *Jewish Scholarship and Scholarly Institutions in Soviet Russia, 1918–1953*. Hebrew University of Jerusalem, Centre for Research and Documentation of East European Jewry, 1978.

Grinbaum, Avraam. *Evreiskaia nauka i nauchnye uchrezhdeniia v Sovetskom Soiuze, 1918–1953*. Gesharim, 1994.

Gross, Judah Ari. "Russia Strikes Kyiv TV Tower, Killing 5 and Damaging Babyn Yar Holocaust Site." *The Times of Israel*, March 1, 2022. https://www.timesofisrael.com/russia-strikes-tv-tower-in-heart-of-kyiv-damaging-babi-yar-holocaust-memorial/.

Grossman, Vasily. *Forever Flowing*. Harper & Row, 1970.

Hicks, Jeremy. *First Films of the Holocaust. Soviet Cinema and the Genocide of the Jews, 1938–1946*. University of Pittsburgh Press, 2012.

Himka, John-Paul. "The Reception of the Holocaust in Postcommunist Ukraine." In *Bringing the Dark Past to Light: The Reception of the Holocaust in Postcommunist Europe*, edited by John-Paul Himka and Joanna Beata Michlic, 626–61. University of Nebraska Press, 2013.

Himka, John-Paul, and Joanna Beata Michlic, eds. *Bringing the Dark Past to Light: The Reception of the Holocaust in Postcommunist Europe*. University of Nebraska Press, 2013.

Hrynevych, Vladyslav. "Babyn Yar After Babyn Yar." In *Babyn Yar: History and Memory*, edited by Vladyslav Hrynevych and Paul Robert Magocsi, 145–220. University of Toronto Press, 2023.

Hrynevych, Vladyslav, and Paul Robert Magocsi, eds. *Babyn Yar: History and Memory*. Dukh i Litera, 2016.

Hrynevych, Vladyslav, and Paul Robert Magocsi, eds. *Babyn Yar: History and Memory*. University of Toronto Press, 2023.

Hrynevych, Vladislav, and Anatoly Pogorelov. "Babyn Yar: Zlochyn bez terminu davnosti." *Istorychna Pravda*, August 30, 2020. https://www.istpravda.com.ua/articles/2020/08/30/158036/.

Kaganovich, L. M. *Pamyatnye zapiski rabochego, kommunista-bol'shevika, profsoyuznogo, partiinogo i sovetsko-gosudarstvennogo rabotnika*. Vagrius, 1996.

Kalnitsky, Mikhail. "Ilya Ehrenburg. Svidetel' Veka." *Kievskie Vedomosti*. http://www.c-cafe.ru/days/bio/28/036_28.php.

Kal'nytsky, Mykhailo. "Vykorystannia Evreis'kykh gromads'kykh sporud u Kyevi (1920-i - 1930-i rr.)." In *Dolia evreis'koi dukhovnoi ta material'noi spadschyny v XX stolitti: Materialy konferentsii 28–30 serpnia 2001 r.*, 16–21. Dukh i Litera, 2002.

Karamash, Sergiy. *Babyn yar u tragichnykh podiiakh 1941–1943 rokiv. Istoria i Suchasnist' (istoriko-arkhivne doslidzhennia)*. KMM, 2014.

Kasianov, Georgii. "Sharing the Divided Past: Symbols, Commemorations and Representations at Babyn Yar." *Ukrainian-Jewish Encounter: Cultural Dimensions*, edited by Wolf Moskovich and Alti Rodal, *Jews and Slavs* 25 (2016): 281–91.

Kasimenko, A. K., ed. *Istoriia Kieva*, Vol. II. Academy of Arts and Sciences of the Ukrainian

SSR, 1964.

Kazovsky, Hillel. *The Artists of the Kultur-Lige.* Gesharim Publishing House, 2003.

Khanin, Vladimir. "Jewish Politics in the Post-Communist World: Personality, Ideology and Conflict in Contemporary Ukrainian Jewish Movement." *Journal of Social, Political and Economic Studies* 25, no. 3 (2000): 319–50.

Khanin, Vladimir. "Judaism and Organized Jewish Movement in the Public Square of the USSR/CIS After World War II: The Ukrainian Case." *Jewish Political Studies Review* 11, no. 1–2 (Spring 1999): 75–100.

Khanin, Vladimir. "The Postcommunist Order, Public Opinion and the Jewish Community of Independent Ukraine." *Harvard Ukrainian Studies* 23, no. 1–2 (June 1999): 85–108.

Khiterer, Victoria. "Babi Yar, the Tragedy of Kiev's Jews." *Brandeis Graduate Journal*, 2004. http://www.brandeis.edu/gradjournal.

Khiterer, Victoria. *Documenty po evreiskoi istorii XVI–XX vekov v kievskikh arkhivakh.* Gesharim Publishing House and Institute of Jewish Studies, 2001.

Khiterer, Victoria, ed. *Dokumenty, Sobrannye Evreiskoi Istoriko-arkheographicheskoi Komissiei Vseukrainskoi Akademii Nauk.* Hebrew University of Jerusalem and Gesharim Publishing House, 1999.

Khiterer, Victoria. *Jewish City or Inferno of Russian Israel? A History of the Jews in Kiev Before February 1917.* Academic Studies Press, 2016.

Khiterer, Victoria. "The Jewish Songs of Leonid Utesov." *On the Jewish Street* 2, no. 1 (2012): 1–48.

Khiterer, Victoria. "Konfiskatsiia evreiskikh documental'nyh materialov i evreiskoi sobstvennosti v Ukraine v 1919–1930 gg." In *Dolia evreis'koi dukhovnoi ta material'noi spadchyny v XX stolitti. Materialy conferentsii 28–30 serpnia 2001 r.*, 8–15. Dukh i Litera, 2002.

Khiterer, Victoria. "Memorialization of the Holocaust in Minsk and Kiev." In *Holocaust Resistance in Europe and America: New Aspects and Dilemmas*, edited by Victoria Khiterer, 95–131. Cambridge Scholars Publishing, 2017.

Khiterer, Victoria. "The October 1905 Pogrom in Kiev." *East European Jewish Affairs* 22, no. 2 (1992): 21–37.

Khiterer, Victoria. "Vasilii Shul'gin and the Jewish Question: An Assessment of Shul'gin's Anti-Semitism." *On the Jewish Street* 1, no. 2 (2011): 137–63.

Khiterer, Victoria. "Victor Nekrasov and the Babi Yar Massacre Commemoration." *Forgotten Heritage*. http://lostart.org.ua/en/research/739.html.

Khoroshunova, Irina. *Dnevnik Kievlianki*, Part II. https://gordonua.com/specprojects/khoroshunova2.html.

Khrzhanovsky, Ilya. "On Russian Aggression Against Ukraine." March 3, 2022. https://www.youtube.com/watch?v=DDN138LT4wk.

Kin, Ostap, ed. *Babyn Yar: Ukrainian Poets Respond.* Harvard Ukrainian Research Institute, 2023.

Kipling, Vadim. "Ushel, ostaviv zhizn' v kamne." *Ekho*. http://exo.net.ua/arkhiv/2423-2013-01-03-09-29-52.

Kipnis, Itsik. "Babi Yar." *Evreiskii mir Ukrainy.* http://www.ju.org.ua/ru/publicism/646.html.

Kipnis, Itsik. "Babi Yar." *Golokost i suchasnist'.* http://www.holocaust.kiev.ua/bulletin/vip10/vip10_1.htm.

Klee, Ernst. *Das Personenlexikon zum Dritten Reich: Wer war was vor und nach 1945.* 2nd ed. Fischer-Taschenbuch-Verlag, 2007.

Klid, Bohdan, and Alexander J. Motyl, eds. *The Holodomor Reader: A Sourcebook on the Famine of 1932–1933 in Ukraine.* Canadian Institute of Ukrainian Studies Press, 2012.

Korey, William. "A Monument over Babi Yar?" In *The Holocaust in the Soviet Union: Studies and Sources on the Destruction of the Jews in the Nazi-Occupied Territories of the USSR, 1941–1945,* edited by Lucjan Dobroszycki and Jeffery S. Gurock, 61–74. M. E. Sharpe, 1993.

Korzhavin, Naum. *V soblaznakh krovavoi epokhi,* 2 vols., Vol. I. Zakharov, 2007.

Kostyrchenko, G. V. *Tainaia politika Khrushcheva: Vlast', intelligentsia, evreiskii vopros.* Mezhdunarodnye otnosheniia, 2012.

Kostyrchenko, Gennadii. *Tainaia politika: ot Brezhneva do Gorbacheva.* Part I: *Vlast—intelligentsia—evreiskii vopros.* Mezhdunarodnye otnosheniia, 2018.

Kostyrchenko, G. V. *Tainaia politika Stalina: Vlast' i antisemitism.* Mezhdunarodnye otnosheniia, 2001.

Kot, Sergii. "Uchasnyky pidpillia OUN (m)—zhertvy Babynogo Yaru (1941–1943)." In *Babyn Yar: Masove Ubuistvo i pam'iat' pro n'iogo. Materialy mizhnarodnoi naukovoi konferentsii 24–25 zhovtnia 2011 r. Kyiv,* 101–116. Komitet "Babi Yar," 2012.

Kotljarchuk, Andrej. "The Memory of Roma Holocaust in Ukraine: Mass Graves, Memory Work and the Politics of Commemoration." In *Disputed Memories: Emotions and Memory Politics in Central, Eastern and South-Eastern Europe,* edited by Tea Sindbæk Andersen and Barbara Tornqvist-Plewa, 149–74. Walter de Gruyter, 2016.

Koval'chuk, Irina. "V Babiem Yaru postroiat unikal'nyi memorial'nyi complex." *Segodnia,* June 25, 2013. http://www.segodnya.ua/ukraine/V-Babem-YAru-postroyat-unikalnyy-memorialnyy-kompleks-444135.html.

Kruglov, Alexander A. "Jewish Losses in Ukraine, 1941–1944." In *The Shoah in Ukraine: History, Testimony, Memorialization,* edited by Ray Brandon and Wendy Lower, 272–90. Indiana University Press, 2008.

Kruglov, Alexander A., ed. *Sbornik dokumentov i materialov ob unichtozhenii natsistami evreev Ukrainy v 1941–1944 godakh.* Institut iudaiki, 2002.

Kruglov, Alexander, A. Umansky, and I. Shchupak, eds. *Kholokost v Ukraine: Reikhskomissariat "Ukraina," Gubernatorstvo "Transnistriia."* Ukrainskii institute izucheniia kholokosta "Tkuma," 2016.

Kruglov, A., and A. Umansky. *Babi Yar: zhertvy, spasiteli, palachi.* Ukrainskii institute izucheniia Kholokosta "Tkuma," 2019.

Kruglov, Oleksandr. "'My povynni buly vykonuvaty brudnu robotu . . .': Znyshchennia evreiv Kyieva voseny 1941 r. U svitli nimets'kykh dokumentiv." In *Babyn Yar: masove ubyvstvo i pam'iat'pro ni'ogo. Materialy mizhnarodnoi naukovoi konferentsii 24–25 zhovtnia 2011 r., m. Kyiv*, edited by Vitaliy Nakhmanovich and Mykhailo Tiagly, 117–56. Ukrains'kyi tsentr vyvchennia istorii Golocostu, 2012.

Kucheruk, Oleksandr. "Mykola Pervach: I vy pochuete shche znovu i znovy poetovu prorochu movu." *Organizatsiia Ukrains'kykh Natsionalistiv*. http://kmoun.info/2016/10/10/oleksandr-kucheruk-mikola-pervach-i-vi-pochuyete-shhe-znovu-i-znovu-poetovu-prorochu-movu/.

Kudryts'kyi, A. V., ed. *Kiev: Entsyklopedychnyi Dovidnyk*. Golovna redaktsia Ukrains'koi Radians'koi Entsyklopedii, 1981.

Kuzmin, Georgy. "Goriiachee leto sorok vtorogo . . ." *Futbol* 13 (1995). http://www.junik.lv/~dynkiev/dk-1942/futbol_13-1995/futbol_13-1995.htm.

Kuznetsov, Anatoly (published as A. Anatoli). *Babi Yar: A Document in the Form of a Novel. New, Complete Uncensored Version*. Farrar, Straus and Giroux, 1970.

Kuznetsov, Anatoly. *Babi Yar: roman-dokument*. Radians'kyi pysmennyk, 1991.

Lang, Harry. "Sered ievreiv u Kyevi." *Yehupets'* 20 (2011): 176–90.

Lawrence, Bill. *Six Presidents: Too Many Wars*. Saturday Review Press, 1972.

Lawrence, W. H. "50,000 Kiev Jews Reported Killed." *New York Times*, November 29, 1943, 3.

Lawrence, W. H. "Little Evidence Supports Story of Nazi Atrocity." *Buffalo Courier Express*, November 29, 1943, 1.

Lebovic, Matt. "Using Rare Archival Films, Ukrainian Director Forces Viewers to Face Babyn Yar." *The Times of Israel*, March 28, 2021. https://www.timesofisrael.com/using-rare-archival-films-ukrainian-director-forces-viewers-to-face-babyn-yar/.

Levchuk, Natalia, et al. "Vtraty mis'koho i sil's'koho naselennia Ukraïny vnaslidok Holodomoru 1932–1934 rr.: novi otsinky." *Ukraïns'kyi istorychnyi zhurnal*, no. 4, (2015): 84–112.

Levitas, Feliks. "Babi Yar (1941–1943)." In *Katastrofa ta opir ukrains'kogo evreistva (1941–1944): Narysy z Istorii Kholokostu ta oporu v Ukraini*, edited by Ster Elisavetsky, 88–117. Institute of Political and Ethnic Studies, National Academy of Sciences of Ukraine, 1999.

Levitas, Feliks. *Babi Yar: Sud'by i pamiat'*. Nash Chas, 2016.

Levitas, Il'ia. *Babi Yar: Spasiteli i spasennye*. Stal', 2005.

Levitas, Il'ia. *Pravedniki Babiego Yara*. Fond "Pamiat' Babego Yara," 2001.

Liphshiz, Cnaan. "Film Director Panned for Plan to Turn Ukraine Museum into 'Holocaust Disneyland.'" *The Times of Israel*, May 26, 2020. https://www.timesofisrael.com/film-director-panned-for-plan-to-turn-ukraine-museum-into-holocaust-disneyland/.

Loev, Moisei. *Ukradennaia Muza, Vospominaniia o Kievskom gosudarstvennom evreiskom teatre imeni Sholom Aleikhema, Kharkov-Kiev-Chernovtsy, 1925–1950*. Dukh i Litera, 2004.

Lukin, Veniamin. "Fond Evreiskogo istoriko-etnograficheskogo obschestva v Tsentral'nom Gosudarstvennom Arkhive Leningrada." In *Istoricheskie sud'by evreev v Rossii i SSSR: nachalo dialoga*, edited by E. Krupnik, 245–61. Evreiskoe istoricheskoe obshchestvo, 1992.

Lustiger, Arno. *Stalin and the Jews: Red Book: The Tragedy of the Jewish anti-Fascist Committee and the Soviet Jews*. Enigma Books, 2003.

Lysenko, Liudmila. "Dve monumental'nye istorii." https://kulupa.livejournal.com/328747.html.

Lysenko, Liudmila. "Skul'ptor Mikhail Lysenko i ego ucheniki," *Arkhitetura, Stroitel'stvo, Dizain* (2004). http://www.archjournal.ru/rus/04%2049%202007/lisenko.htm.

Magocsi, Paul Robert. *History of Ukraine*. University of Toronto Press, 1996.

Magocsi, Paul Robert. *A History of Ukraine: The Land and Its Peoples*. 2nd ed. University of Toronto Press, 2010.

Maksimov, Vadim, and Konstantin Kapkov. *Za sluzhbu i khrabrost: Sviashchenniki–kavalery ordena Sviatogo Georgiia. Neizvestnye stranitsy*. Knizhnyy Mir, 2018.

Malakov, Dmytro. *Doli kyian (1941–1943)*. Folio, 2017.

Malakov, Dmytro. *Kyiv 1939–1945: Fotoal'bom*. Kyi, 2005.

Mankoff, Jeff. "Babi Yar and the Struggle for Memory, 1944–2004." *Ab Imperio* 2 (2004): 393–415.

Margol, Howard. "The Lithuanian Jewish Museum Rises from the Ashes." http://www.rtrfoundation.org/webart/B&L-VilnaMuseum.pdf.

Melamed, E. I. "Likvidatsiia Kievskogo Instituta evreiskoi proletarskoi kul'tury i repressii protiv ego sotrudnikov: Po materialam archivno-sledstvennykh del 1930-kh godov." In *Archiv evreiskoi istorii*, edited by O. B. Budnitsky, Vol. 10, 171–95. Politicheskaia entsiklopediia, 2018.

Meleshkina, Iryna. *Mandrivni zori v Ukraini: Storinku istorii evreis'kogo teatru*. Dukh i Litera, 2019.

Mel'nichuk, Yuliia. "Kogda prishla nastoiashchaia nishcheta odin iz avtorov pamiatnika v Babiem Iaru Viktor Sukhenko dobrovol'no ushel iz zhizni." *Fakty*, July 2, 2003.

Mel'nik, M. A. "Golod v Ukraine 1946–1947 gg." *Derzhavnyi arkhiv Mykolaievskoi oblasti*. http://mk.archives.gov.ua/pubonsite/93-pubgolod4647.html.

Melnyk, Oleksandr. "Stalinist Justice as a Site of Memory: Anti-Jewish Violence in Kyiv's Podil District in September 1941 Through the Prism of Soviet Investigative Documents." *Jahrbücher für Geschichte Osteuropas* 61 (2013), H. 2, 223–48.

Mesh, Gennady. "Ei bylo tol'ko dvadtsat'." *Russkii globus* no. 3 (April 2002). http://www.russian-globe.com/N3/Markus.

Miletsky, Avraam. *Naplyvy pamiati*. Philobiblon, 1998.

Mislavsky, Vladimir. *Evreiskaia tema v kinematographe Rossiskoi imperii, SSSR, Rossii, SNG and Baltii (1909–2009): Filmo-biograficheskii spravochnik*. OOO "Skorpion," 2013.

Mitsel', Mikhail. *Evrei Ukrainy v 1943–1953 gg.: Ocherki dokumentirovannoi istorii*. Dukh i Litera, 2004.

Mitsel', Mikhail. *Obshchiny iudeiskogo ispovedaniia v Ukraine (Kiev, L'vov: 1945–1981 gody)*. Biblioteka Instituta Iudaiki, 1998.

Mitsel, Mikhail. "Zapret na uvekovechivanie pamiati kak sposob zamalchivaniia Kholokosta: praktika KPU v otnoshenii Babiego Yara." *Kholokost i Suchasnist'* 1.2 (2007): 9–30.

Nachmanovich, Vitalii. "Do pytannia pro sklad uchasnykiv karal'nykh aktsii v okupovanomu

Kyevi (1941–1943)." In *Druga svitova viina i dolia narodiv Ukrainy: materialy 2-i Vseukrains'koi naukovoi konferentsii, m. Kyiv, 30–31 zhovtnia 2006 r.*, edited by V. Nachmanovich, 227–62. Zovnishtorgvydav, 2007.

Nachmanovich, Vitaliy. "Babyn Yar: The Holocaust and Other Tragedies." In *Babyn Yar: History and Memory*, edited by Vladyslav Hrynevych and Paul Robert Magocsi, 65–106. Dukh i Litera, 2016.

Nachmanovych, Vitaliy. "Babyn Yar: A Place of Memory in Search of a Future." In *Babyn Yar: History and Memory*, edited by Vladyslav Hrynevych and Paul Robert Magocsi, 291–314. Dukh i Litera, 2016.

Naiman, Aleksander. "Evreiskoe zemledelie na Ukraine v 1930-e gody." *Vestnik Evreiskogo Universiteta v Moskve* 8, no. 1 (1995): 217–21.

Naiman, Aleksander. "Tania Markus—angel mesti." *Evreiskii Obozrevatel'* no. 12, December 2016. https://jew-observer.com/imya/tanya-markus-angel-mesti/.

Nakhmanovich, Vitaliy, and Mykhailo Tiagly, eds. *Babyn Yar: masove ubyvstvo i pam'iat'pro ni'ogo. Materialy mizhnarodnoi naukovoi konferentsii 24–25 zhovtnia 2011 r., m. Kyiv*. Ukrains'kyi tsentr vyvchennia istorii Golocostu, 2012.

Nekrasov, Victor. "Babi Yar: Otryvok iz knigi Zapiski zevaki." *Novoe Russkoe Slovo*, September 7, 1975. https://nekrassov-viktor.com/images/Books/articles-ob-antisemitizme/07_09.1975big.jpg.

Nekrasov, Victor. *Iz dal'nikh stranstvii vozvratias', Rim, Parizh, New York, Kamchatka i dale vezde . . .* http://nekrassov-viktor.com/Friends/Praxova-Nanina.aspx.

Nekrasov, Victor. "Pochemu eto ne sdelano?" In *Pamiat' Babiego Iara. Vospominaniia, dokumenty*, edited by Ilia Levitas, 232–33. Evreiskii Sovet Ukrainy, 2001.

Nekrasov, Victor. "Vzgliad i nechto." *Lit Mir, elektronnaia biblioteka*. https://www.litmir.me/br/?b=250635&p=49.

Nekrasov, Victor. *Zapiski zevaki*. Vagrius, 2003.

Odinets, M. "Monument u Babiego Yara." *Pravda*, June 23, 1976, 6. https://marxism-leninism.info/paper/pravda_1976_175-6649.

Odintsov, Mikhail. "Mitropolit Sergii Stragorodsky v evakuatsii." *Nepridumannye rasskazy o voine*. http://www.world-war.ru/mitropolit-sergij-stragorodskij-v-evakuacii/.

Olenin, Evgenii. "Zabytyi konkurs 65-go goda." http://archive.is/Dja2.

Osokina, Elena. *Zoloto dlia industrializatsii: Torgsin*. Rosspen, 2009.

Penter, Tanya. "Pid slidstvom za spivpratsiu: sudove peresliduvannia kolaborantiv u SRSR pislia Drugoi svitovoi viiny ta zlochyniv u Babiemu Iaru." In *Babyn Yar: masove ubyvstvo i pam'iat'pro ni'ogo. Materialy mizhnarodnoi naukovoi konferentsii 24–25 zhovtnia 2011 r., m. Kyiv*, edited by Vitaliy Nakhmanovich and Mykhailo Tiagly, 195–97. Ukrains'kyi tsentr vyvchennia istorii Golocostu, 2012.

Peter, Laurence. "Babyn Yar: Synagogue Opens at Nazi Massacre Site in Ukraine." *BBC News*, May 14, 2021. https://www.bbc.com/news/world-europe-57114197.

Petrovsky-Shtern, Yohanan. "A Paradigm Changing Day: The Twenty-Fifth Anniversary of Babyn Yar and Ukrainian-Jewish Relations." *Harvard Ukrainian Studies* 38, no. 3–4 (2021): 227–58.

Pinkus, Benjamin. *The Jews of the Soviet Union: The History of a National Minority*. Cambridge University Press, 1988.

Pogrebinskaia, E. M. "Istoria evreiskikh nauchnykh uchrezhdenii na Ukraine." In *Ievreis'ki naukovi ustanovi v Ukraini u 20-30-ti roki XX stolittia*, edited by O. V. Zaremba, 9–30. Institut nazional'nykh vidnosen' i politologii, 1997.

Pohl, Dieter. "Die einheimischen Forschungen und der Mord an Juden in den besetzten Gebieten." In *Täter im Vernichtungskrieg: Der Überfall auf die Sowjetunion und der Völkermord an den Juden*, edited by Wolf Kaiser, 204–16. Propyläen, 2002.

Polian, Pavel. "Babi Yar i vozmezdie: sudebnye protsessy nad palachami." *Neprikosnovennyi zapas* 149, no. 3 (2023): 45–60.

Polian, Pavel. *Babi Yar: Refleksiia*. Publishing House Zebra E, 2022.

Polian, Pavel. "Babi Yar v zhivopisi i skul'pture: ot Vasilia Ovchinikova do Vadima Sidura." *Lekhaim*. https://lechaim.ru/events/babiy-yar-v-zhivopisi-i-skulypture-ot-vasiliya-ovchinnikova-do-vadima-sidura-2/.

Polian, Pavel. "Rasstrel'naia nota: Ternistyi put' temy Babiego Yara v Sovetskoi muzyke i poezii." *Novaia Gazeta*, August 16, 2022. https://novayagazeta.ru/articles/2022/08/17/rasstrelnaia-nota-media.

Pollack, Chana. "'Cattle Grazed Among the Bones of Our Sacred Martyrs': Covering Babyn Yar Through the Decades." *Forward*, March 11, 2022. https://forward.com/archive/483853/babyn-yar-russia-ukraine-soviets-nazis-wwii-massacre-bombing/.

Polonsky, Antony. *The Jews in Poland and Russia, Volume III, 1914 to 2008*. Littman Library of Jewish Civilization, 2012.

Potresov, Vladimir. "Vozvrashenie Nekrasova." In Victor Nekrasov, *Zapiski zevaki*. Vagrius, 2003, 5–26.

Radchenko, Yuri. "Babyn Yar: A Site of Massacres, (Dis)Remembrance and Instrumentalization." *New Eastern Europe*, October 11, 2016. https://neweasterneurope.eu/2016/10/11/babyn-yar-a-site-of-massacres-dis-remembrance-and-instrumentalisation/.

Radchenko, Yuri. "The Organization of Ukrainian Nationalists (Mel'nyk Faction) and the Holocaust: The Case of Ivan Iuriiv." *Holocaust and Genocide Studies* 31 (111), no. 2 (Fall 2017): 215–39.

Rapson, Jessica. *Topographies of Suffering: Buchenwald, Babi Yar, Lidice*. Berghahn Books, 2017.

Rogoża, Jadwiga. "Ukraine's Disputes over the 80th Anniversary of the Babyn Yar massacre." *OSW Commentary*, October 22, 2021. https://www.osw.waw.pl/en/publikacje/osw-commentary/2021-10-22/ukraines-disputes-over-80th-anniversary-babi-yar-massacre.

Ro'i, Yaacov. "Nehama Lifshitz: Symbol of the Jewish National Awakening." In *Jewish Culture and Identity in the Soviet Union*, edited by Yaacov Ro'i and Avi Beker, 172–79. New York

University Press, 1992.

Rokhlin, Oskar. "Kyiv: 1945–1955." *Zametki po evreiskoi istorii* 182, no. 2–3 (February–March 2015). https://berkovich-zametki.com/2015/Zametki/Nomer2_3/Rohlin1.php.

Romney, Jonathan. "The Kiev Trial: Another Chilling War-Crimes Documentary from Sergei Loznitsa." *British Film Institute*, October 22, 2022. https://www.bfi.org.uk/sight-and-sound/reviews/kiev-trial-another-chilling-war-crimes-documentary-from-sergei-loznitsa.

Rosenbaum, Alan. "The Sounds of Babyn Yar." *Jerusalem Post*, October 15, 2020. https://www.jpost.com/jerusalem-report/the-sounds-of-babyn-yar-644608.

Rubenstein, Joshua. "Jewish Anti-Fascist Committee." *YIVO Encyclopedia of Jews in Eastern Europe*. http://www.yivoencyclopedia.org/article.aspx/Jewish_Anti-Fascist_Committee.

Rubenstein, Joshua. *Tangled Loyalties: The Life and Times of Ilya Ehrenburg*. Basic Books, 1996.

Rubenstein, Joshua, and Ilya Altman, eds. *The Unknown Black Book: The Holocaust in the German-Occupied Soviet Territories*. Indiana University Press, 2008.

Rubenstein, Joshua, and Vladimir P. Naumov. *Stalin's Secret Pogrom: The Postwar Inquisition of the Jewish Anti-Fascist Committee*. Yale University Press, 2001.

Rudling, Per A. *The OUN, the UPA and the Holocaust: A Study in the Manufacturing of Historical Myths*. The Carl Beck Papers in Russian and East European Studies. November 2011, no. 2107.

Rudling, Per Anders. "Terror and Local Collaboration in Occupied Belarus: The Case of the Schutzmannschaft Battalion 118." *Romanian Academy "Nicolae Iorga" History Institute: Historical Yearbook*, Vol. VIII (Bucharest, 2011): 195–214.

Rudnytskyi, Omelian, et al. "Demography of a Man-Made Human Catastrophe: The Case of Massive Famine in Ukraine 1932–1933." *Canadian Studies in Population* 42, no. 1–2 (2015): 53–80.

Rukkas, Andrii. "Tragediia Gorikhovoi dibrovy: Iak natsysty rozstriliuvaly dushevnokhvorykh u Kyevi." *Istorychna Pravda*, October 29, 2020. https://www.istpravda.com.ua/articles/2020/10/29/158369/.

Rybachuk, Ada, and Volodymyr Mel'nychenko. *Koly ruinuet'sia Svit* . . . Iurinform, 1991.

Rybakov, M. O., ed. *Pravda Istorii: Diial'nist' Evreis'koi kul'turno-prosvitnytskoi organizatsii "Kul'turna Liga" u Kyevi (1918–1925)*. Kyi, 2001.

Schulz, Miriam. "We Pledge, as if It Was the Highest Sanctum, to Preserve the Memory: *Sovetish Heymland*, Facets of Holocaust Commemoration in the Soviet Union and the Cold War." In *Growing in the Shadow of Antifascism: Remembering the Holocaust in State-Socialist Eastern Europe*, edited by Kata Bohus, Peter Hallama, and Stephan Stach. Central European University Press, 2022.

Schwartz, Solomon M. *The Jews in the Soviet Union*. Syracuse University Press, 1951.

Schwartz, Solomon M. *The Jews in the Soviet Union*. Arno Press, 1972.

Senchenko, Nikolai, and Irina Sergeeva. "Sud'ba biblioteki." *Vechernii Kiev*, November 27, 1990, 2.

Shapoval, Yury. "The Defection of Anatoly Kuznetsov." *Den'*, January 18, 2005.

Shcheglov, [Varshaver]. *Vospominaniia o Viktore Platonoviche Nekrasove*. http://nekrassov-viktor.com/AboutOfVPN/Nekrasov-Sheglov-Yriy.aspx.

Sheldon, Richard. "The Transformations of Babi Yar." In *Soviet Society and Culture: Essays in Honor of Vera S. Dunham*, edited by Terry L. Thompson and Richard Sheldon, 125–33. Westview Press, 1988.

Shlaien, Alexander. *Babi Yar.* Abris, 1995.

Shneer, David. "Is Seeing Believing?" In *The Holocaust: Memories and History*, edited by Victoria Khiterer, 64–85. Cambridge Scholars Publishing, 2014.

Shneer, David. *Yiddish and the Creation of Soviet Jewish Culture, 1918–1930*. Cambridge University Press, 2004.

Shrayer, Maxim D., ed. *An Anthology of Jewish-Russian Literature: Two Centuries of Dual Identity in Prose and Poetry*. Vol. I: 1801–1953. M. E. Sharpe, 2007.

Shrayer, Maxim D. "Jewish-Russian Poets Bearing Witness to the Shoah, 1941–1946: Textual Evidence and Preliminary Conclusions." In *Studies in Slavic Languages and Literatures*, edited by Stefano Garzonio, 59–119. ICCEES Congress, Papers and Contributions, 2010.

Shternshis, Anna, and Pavel Lion, and a group of professional musicians. Introduction to the liner notes for the CD *Yiddish Glory: Life and Fate of Soviet Jewish Folk Music During World War II*. The CD contains eighteen songs.

Shvarts, S. M. *Antisemitism v Sovetskom Soiuze*. Izd-vo im. Chekhova, 1952.

Silberklang, David. "More Than a Memorial: The Evolution of Yad Vashem." *Yad Vashem Quarterly Magazine*. Special Commemorative ed. 6–7. Fall 2003. https://www.yadvashem.org/sites/default/files/yv_magazine31.pdf.

Simpson, Kevin E. *Soccer Under the Swastika: Stories of Survival and Resistance During the Holocaust*. Rowman & Littlefield, 2016.

Skliarevskaia, Eleonora. "Ubiistvennaia krasota evreiskoi podpol'shchitsy." https://ujew.com.ua/history/ubijstvennaya-krasota-evrejskoj-podpolshhiczyi.

Snyder, Timothy. *Black Earth: The Holocaust as History and Warning*. Tim Duggan Books, 2015.

Sokol, Sam. "Ukraine Backtracks on Babyn Yar Plans Amid Accusations of Holocaust Revisionism." *Jerusalem Post*, February 8 and 9, 2016. http://www.jpost.com/Diaspora/Ukraine-backtracks-on-Babi-Yar-plans-amid-accusations-of-Holocaust-revisionism-444268.

Stavyts'ka, Nataliia. "Likvidatsiia naukovo-doslidnykh ustanov VUAN z doslidzhennia natsional'nykh men'shyn Ukrainy (ii pol. 1920–1930-kh rr.)." *Istoria Ukrainy: Malovidomi imena, podii, facty. Zbirnyk statei*, 34–43. Instytut Istorii Ukrainy NAN Ukrainy, 2007.

Stepanenko, V. "Chto proiskhodit v Kieve." *Pravda*, November 29, 1941. Cited in Feliks L. Levitas, *Babi Yar: Sud'by i pamiat'*, 68. Kyiv: Nash chas, 2016.

Suny, Ronald Grigor. *The Soviet Experiment: Russia, the USSR, and the Successor States*. Oxford University Press, 2010.

Suny, Ronald Grigor, ed. *The Structure of Soviet History: Essays and Documents*, 2nd ed. Oxford University Press, 2014.

Symonenko, Natalia. "Babyn Yar in Music." In *Babyn Yar: History and Memory*, edited by Vladyslav Hrynevych and Paul Robert Magocsi, 371–90. Toronto: University of Toronto, 2023.

Tausinger, Rona. "Babyn Yar: The Story of a Lost Universe." *Israel Hayom*, August 4, 2020.

https://www.israelhayom.com/2020/08/04/babi-yar-the-story-of-a-lost-universe/.

Teliga, Olena. *Lysty: Spogady*, 2nd ed. Vydavnytstvo im. O. Teligy, 2004.

Tiktin, Sergei. "Babi Yar: Aprel' 1961." In *Babi Iar*, edited by Efrem Baukh, 137–38. Moria, 1981.

Tompson, William J. *Khrushchev: A Political Life*. Palgrave Macmillan, 1995.

Tsalik, Stanislav. "1946: Kak vo vremia 'Kievskogo Niurberga' kaznili nazistov." *BBC News, Ukraina*, January 29, 2016. https://www.bbc.com/ukrainian/ukraine_in_russian/2016/01/160129_ru_s_tsalyk_blog_historian.

Tsalyk, Stanislav. "Blok istorika. 1976: Otkrytie pamiatnika v Babiem Yaru." *BBC News, Ukraina*, https://www.bbc.com/ukrainian/ukraine_in_russian/2016/07/160702_ru_s_history_blog_babyn_yar.

Udovenko, Ilia. "Rasstrel'nyi dom na Nikol'skoi." *Zhivaia istoria*. http://lhistory.ru/statyi/rasstrelnyj-dom-na-nikolskoj.

Vaksberg, Arkady. *Stalin Against the Jews*. Translated by Antonina W. Bouis. Vintage Books, 1994.

Vakulyshin, Sergiy. *(Ne)miy Kyiv: Zbirka statei z kontseptual'nogo kyevoznavstva*. Svit uspikhu, 2014.

Varshaver (Shcheglov), Yuriy. "Vospominanii ao Viktore Platonoviche Nekrasove." http://nekrassov-viktor.com/AboutOfVPN/Nekrasov-Sheglov-Yriy.aspx.

Vartanian, Aksel'. "Futbol v gody voiny: Chast' piataia. Mif o matche smerti." *Futbol*, February 16, 2007. https://www.sport-express.ru/newspaper/2007-02-16/16_1/.

Vedeneev, Dmitriy, and Sergei Shevchenko. "Sredi veshchdokov, vyiavlennykh v 1952 godu po 'Delu Khaina' byli nakhodki, kotorye smogli by ukrasit' almaznyi fond SSSR." *Fakty*, August 3, 2000. https://crime.fakty.ua/107195-sredi-vecshdokov-vyyavlennyh-v-1952-godu-po-quot-delu-haina-quot-byli-nahodki-kotorye-smogli-by-ukrasit-almaznyj-fond-sssr.

Veitsblit, I.I. *Rukh evreis'koi liudnosti na Ukraini periodu 1897–1926 rr.* Kyiv: Proletar, 1930.

Vergelis, Arn. "Der denkmol in Babi Yar vet shteyn ledoyres." *Sovetish Heymland* 6 (1975): 158–64.

Volkov, Solomon. *Dialogi s Evgeniem Evtushenko pri uchastii Anny Nel'son*. Moscow: AST, 2018.

Vynnychuk, Iurii. "Nepodilenyi Babyn Yar." *Zbruc*, September 10, 2016, https://zbruc.eu/node/57120.

Weiner, Amir. *Making Sense of War: The Second World War and the Fate of the Bolshevik Revolution*. Princeton: Princeton University Press, 2000.

Wiesel, Elie. *The Jews of Silence. A Personal Report on Soviet Jewry*. Schocken Books, 2011.

Wiesel, Elie. Report to the President: President's Commission on the Holocaust. September 27, 1979 (Reprinted by the United States Holocaust Memorial Museum, 2005). https://www.ushmm.org/m/pdfs/20050707-presidents-commission-holocaust.pdf.

Yaremenko, Victoria. "Elena Teliga: Zhenskie istorii Vtoroi mirovoi." *Svoboda FM*, May 6, 2016. http://svoboda.fm/culture/Culture/245446.html?language=ru.

Yasinsky, Oleg. "'Start'—Flakelf—'match smerti?'" http://www.2000.net.ua/d/48513.

Yekelchyk, Serhy. *Stalin's Citizens: Everyday Politics in the Wake of the Total War*. Oxford University Press, 2014.

Yevtushenko, Yevgeny. *The Most Famous Symphony of the 20th Century: Dmitri Shostakovich Symphony #13*. Tulsa, OK: University of Tulsa, 2005.

Young, James E. *The Texture of Memory: Holocaust Memorials and Meaning.* Yale University Press, 1993.
Yurkevich, M. "Organization of Ukrainian Nationalists." *Encyclopedia of Ukraine.* University of Toronto Press, 1993, III, 708–10.
Zabarko, Boris, ed. *Holocaust in the Ukraine.* Vallentine Mitchell, 2005.
Zabarko, Boris, ed. *Life in Shadow of Death: Recent Memories About the Holocaust in Ukraine. Testimonies and Documents.* Vol. II. Melitopol' City Printing House, 2019.
Zelensky, Volodymyr. "Godovshchina tragedii Babiego Iara: obrashchenie prezidenta Ukrainy." *V Chas Pick,* September 29, 2019. https://vchaspik.ua/ukraina/468182-godovshchina-tragedii-babego-yara-obrashchenie-prezidenta-ukrainy.
Zelensky, Volodymyr. "Ukraine President Zelensky's Speech to Israeli Lawmakers. Full Text." *The Times of Israel,* March 20, 2022. https://www.timesofisrael.com/full-text-ukraine-president-zelenskys-speech-to-israeli-lawmakers/.
Zeltser, Arkadi. "Tema 'Evrei v Babiem Iaru' v Sovetskom Soiuze v 1941–1945 godakh." In *Babyn Yar: masove ubyvstvo i pam'iat'pro ni'ogo. Materialy mizhnarodnoi naukovoi konferentsii 24–25 zhovtnia 2011 r., m. Kyiv,* edited by Vitaliy Nakhmanovich and Mykhailo Tiagly, 84–89. Ukrains'kyi tsentr vyvchennia istorii Golocostu, 2012.
Zeltser, Arkadi. *Unwelcome Memory: Holocaust Monuments in the Soviet Union.* Yad Vashem, the International Institute for Holocaust Research, 2018.
Zhiganets, Fima. "Gop so smykom, istoria velikoi pesni." https://www.proza.ru/2008/05/26/256.
Zubov, A. B. *Istoria Rossii XX vek. Epokha Stalinisma* (1923–1953), Vol. II. Izdatel'stvo "E," 2016.

ARCHIVES

Archive of the Interregional Public Organization "Federation of Jewish Organizations and Communities—Vaad" (VAAD)
Center for the Studies of History and Culture of East European Jewry Archive
Central Archives for the History of the Jewish People (CAHJP)
Central State CinePhotoPhono Archives of Ukraine (TsDKFFA U)
Central State Archive of Public Organizations of Ukraine (TsDAHO U)
Central State Archives of the Supreme Bodies of Power and Government of Ukraine (TsDAVO U)
Central State Historical Archive of Ukraine in the City Kyiv (TsDIAK U)
Russian State Archive of Contemporary History (RGANI)
State Archive of the Russian Federation (GARF)
Sectoral State Archive of the Security Services of Ukraine (HDA SBU)
State Archive of the City Kyiv (DAMK)
United States Holocaust Memorial Museum (USHMM)
Yad Vashem Archives (YVA)

INDEX

Page numbers in italics indicate figures and maps

Abakumov, Viktor, 114
Abramovic, Marina, 213–14
Afghanistan, 200
Ageev, Aleksander, 61–62
Ageev, Igor, 61–62
Ageeva, Ida, 61–62
Aizenshtadt, M., 156
Aleksandr, Archimandrite, 87–88
Aleksandrov, Georgy, 126
Alexievich, Svetlana, 208
All-Ukrainian Proletarian Writers Organization, 13–14
All-Union Association for Trade with Foreigners. *See* Torgsin stores
Alper, Leo, 143–44
Alper, Osip, 143–44
Altman, Ilya, 6, 125–26
Altshuler, Mordechai, 56
Alyoshin, Pavel F., 128
American Jewish Joint Distribution Committee, 205
Anatoli, A. (Kuznetsov, Anatoly), 6, 166.
Andreev, A. A., 108
Andriivskyi Descent, 101
Andropov, Yuriy, 177
anti-Semitism: 9–10, 18, 60–61, 151; communism and, 26; conversion and, 87; in Holodomor, 35–36; Judeophobia and, 35; Khrushchev and, 164–65, 223; in Kyiv, 2, 51–52, 100–102, 119–21; popular, 35–36, 101, 103, 106–13, 116–18, 122, 126, 130, 144, 152, 153, 200–1, 205, 222, 225; in press, 4, 183; propaganda for, 66, 224; in Soviet Union, 2–3, 7–8, 177; state, 112–16, 225; in Ukraine, 36–38, 47–49, 110–11; World War II and, 7, 97–99, *98*, *99*, 103–6, 121–22; against Yiddish culture, 104–6, 119–20

Aristov, Stanislav, 76
art. *See* Yiddish culture
Auschwitz, 143–44
Austria, 210

Babat, Malvina, *50*
Babat, Polina, *50*
Babi Yar (Levitas), 3
"Babi Yar" (Ehrenburg), 143
"Babi Yar" (Ozerov), 6
"Babi Yar" (Yevtushenko), 162–65, *164*, 223
Babi Yar: A Document in the Form of a Novel (Kuznetsov): legacy of, 165–67, *166*, *168*, 169, 223; scholarship on, 6, 10–11, 36, 49, 90
Babi Yar Memorial Park (Denver, Colorado), 4, 184–186
Babi Yar: Reflection (Polian), 3
"Babi Yar's Legacy" (Dawidowicz), 4
Babochkin, Boris, 146
Babyn Yar: anti-Semitism in, 48–49; *Concept of the Complex Memorialization of Babyn Yar*, 209; Einsatzgruppen massacres and, xv; historiography of, 2–5; Holocaust Memorial Museum, 96, 210–11, 225; Jewish Communal-Cultural Center at, 205; Jewish Heritage Center at, 4; Jews at, *75*, *129*; Khrushchev in, 222, 245n85; Kurenivska tragedy in, 161–62, *162*; memoirs about, 5–7; mud floods in, 161–62, *162*; photos of, *159*; press party at, *127*; public scandals in, 206; Russia in, *216*, 216–17; Soviet Union and, 187–94, *189*, *191*; unauthorized meetings at, 169–75, *170*, *172*, *174*; World War II and, *41*, 126–31, *127*, *129*–*30*; Yiddish culture in, 103, 187; Zionism in, 177–78. *See also specific topics*
Babyn Yar (conference), 4

Babyn Yar: Lessons of History (documentary), 184
Babyn Yar (Karamash), 3
Babyn Yar (painting series), 146–47
Babyn Yar: Context (documentary), 215
Babyn Yar Holocaust Memorial Center (BYHMC): commemoration at, 213–15, *214*, 220, 225–26; establishment of, 5; Nazis in, 136–37; opponents of, 207–13, *212*; Russia and, 225–26; during Russian invasion, *216*, 216–19
"Babyn Yar: In the studio of Artist Ovchinnikov" (Fedorovs'ky), 147
Babyn Yar: Landscape and Memoryscape (encyclopedia), 210–11
Babyn Yar massacre. *See specific topics*
Babyn Yar Monument, 155, *155–56*, 167, *168*, 169
Babyn Yar Museum in, 4–5
Babyn Yar: Ukrainian Poets Respond (Kin), 3
Babyn Yar uprising, 63, 78
Bakhtin, Vladimir, 11
Balakin, Vladimir, 82
Balasnaia, Riva, 140
Bal'ber, Grigory, 229n10
Bandera, Stepan, 59
Baranov, Venedikt, 53–54
Barg, Batya, 185
Batasheva, Genia, 42, 63
Bazhan, Mykola, 127–8, 143
Begun, Yosif, 196
Beilis, Menachem Mendel, 63, 175
Beilis Affair, 35
Beilis Trial, 26, 63
Beliaeva, Evgeniia, 54
Belza, I., 115
Bemporad, Elissa, 24
Berard, Ewa, 144
Berdichevsky, M., 86
Berdychiv concentration camp, 79
Beregovsky, Moisei, 25, 114–15
Berenshtein, I., 186–87
Berezleva, Valentina, 62
Bergelson, David, 12, 14

Berkhoff, Karel, 40, 46; on authority, 159; on Hitler, 73; on Holodomor, 75–76, 90–91; on prisoners of war, 72; in public scandal, 210; Rudling and, 57–58
Berliant, Semen, 78
Bermingham, John, 185
Bialik, Chaim Nachman, 34
Bila Tserkva, 37
Birobidzhan Jewish Autonomous Region, 23–24
The Black Book (Ehrenburg and Grossman), 5, 40, 41–42, 142, 159, 244n82
Black Hundreds, 48
Blackwell, Martin, 79, 108–9
Blazhkov, Ihor, 150
Blinken, Antony, 167, 214–15
Blobel, Paul, 134–36, *135*
Bloch, Eleonora Abramovna, 187–88
Bohatyrchuk, Fedir, 42
Bolsheviks: 12, 25–26, 36; 107, 111; Kuznetsov on, 52; in Russia, 18; in Ukraine, 56, 109–10, 238n91
Bondarenko, Anastasiya, 95
Bondarenko, Ivan, 95
Bondarenko, Mykhailo, 131
Borodiansky-Knysh, Elena, 44, 65
Borodiansky-Knysh, Ludmila, 65
Borovoi, Saul, 18, 20, 21–22
Botvin, A. P., 172, 193
Bozhkova, Tamara, 62
Brezhnev, Leonid, 194, 201
Brodsky, David, 17–18, 19
Brodsky, Isaak, 64, 78, 82
Brodsky, Lazar, 27, 120
Brovarnik, Il'ia, 101
Brovarnik, Ludmila, 101
Buchma, Amvrosii, 145
Budnik, David, 7, 74, 77–78, 134, 136, 244n82
Buffalo Courier-Express (newspaper), *130*
Bukovinian Battalion, 56–58
Bulletin of the Rescue Committee of the Jewish Agency for Palestine, 106
Burakovsky, Aleksandr, 4

Bush, George W., 203
BYHMC. *See* Babyn Yar Holocaust Memorial Center

Cadiot, Juliette, 117
Callsen, Kuno, 135–37
cannibalism, 90–91
Capa, Robert, 99, 249n8
Carter, Jimmy, 264n179
censorship: anti-Semitism and, 23–24; in communism, 163–64, 190–91, *191*; Nekrasov on, 223; in Soviet Union, 13, 32–33, 143, 149–50, 165–66, 229n3; suppression and, 25–28; after World War II, 2
The Central Rada (the Ukrainian Parliament), 12
Charny, Daniel, 14–15
Chebotarev, Fedor, 101
Cheptsov, Aleksandr, 133
Chernobyl'sky, Lev, 82
children: in Holocaust, 42, *50*, 61–63; Jewish State Children's Theater, 15; in Kyiv, 56; memorials for, 203, *204*; militarization of, 15; as prisoners of war, 7; in Ukraine, 63
Chernovtsy, 114
Clinton, Bill, 203
Cold War, 4; anti-Semitism in, 154; nationalism in, 112–13; politics, 198–201; after Stalin, 130; suppression in, 222–23; World War II and, 151. *See also* Soviet Union
Colorado Committee of Concern for Soviet Jewry, 185
"commercial" stores, 30
communism: 60, 67, 79, 82, 121, 200–3, 225; censorship in, 163–64, 190–91, *191*; Jewish Communist Workers' Party, 26; by Khrushchev, 16; politics of, 24–25, 169; in Russia, 67, 201; by Stalin, Joseph, 14; torture and, 81; in Ukraine, 60–61, 111–12, 121, 141–42; Ukrainian Communist Party, 28; after World War II, 108–9; Yiddish culture in, 223. *See also* Cold War; proletarianization process
concentration camps. *See specific topics*

Concept of the Complex Memorialization of Babyn Yar, 209
Conquest, Robert, 30
crime: German-Fascist Crimes Committed on Soviet Territory, 78–79, 101, 125–26, 131–33; Gestapo police, 52; informants and, 64; by Nazis, 78; politics of, 26–28; in Soviet Union, 23–24, 31, 174–75; Textile Affair, 116–18; Ukrainian police, 40–41, 56–58; war crimes trials, 131–37, *132*, *135*
Crystal Wall of Crying (memorial), 213–14

Darnytsia concentration camp, 79
Dashkevich, Raisa, 95
Davydov, Vladimir, 6, 72, 77–78, 128, *129*, 134, 136
Dawidowicz, Lucy S., 4
Dean, Martin C., 3, 132, 211
Degen, Ion, 117
Denver, Colorado, 184–86
Department of Jewish Language, Literature, and Folklore, 16, 25, 114
Der Nister (Pinhas Kahanovitch), 12
Derkach, Praskovya, 52
Desbois, Patrick, 137, 210, 214
détente, 4, 194, 199–201, 224
Diamant, Emanuel (Amik), 169–72, *170*, 195
Dinaburg (Dinur), Ben-Zion, 16–17, 158
Dobrotvor, V., 200
Dobrovol'skaia, Nataliia, 83
Dobrushin, Yeheskel, 12
"Doctor's Plot," 119–21
Dodd, Thomas J., 218–19
Doliner, I., 77
Donskoi, Mark, 145
Dovzhenko, Valerian, 150–51
Downs, Bill, 130–31
Driz, Shyke, 140–41
Dubnov, Simon, 12
Dziuba, Ivan, 173, 178
Dynamo-Kyiv soccer team, 79–82

Eastern Europe, *xv*

Eastern European Holocaust Studies, 212, 218
Eberhard, Kurt, 89–91
Ehrenburg, Ilya, 86, 124; colleagues of, 163; family of, 143–44; Grossman and, 142; reputation of, 142–45, 158; Spivak and, 5–6. *See also The Black Book*
Einikait (Unity), newspaper, 156
Einsatzgruppe C, 40–41, 44–45, 47–49, 134–36, 243n49
Einsatzgruppen massacres, xv, *135*
Eisenstein, Sergei, 146
Elgort, Nesya, 44
Estraikh, Gennady, 23
Europe, 212
European Union, 225
Evsektsiia (the Jewish section of the Communist Party), 19, 26
Evstaf'eva, Tatiana, 7
Extraordinary State Commission for Investigation of German-Fascist Crimes Committed on Soviet Territory (ChGK), 46, 78–79, 101, 125–26, 131

Falikman, Ikhil, 124
The Fall of Paris (Ehrenburg), 142
famine. *See* Holodomor; during the Nazi occupation, 90–91; in 1946–47, 110
fascism: genocide and, 187; German-Fascist Crimes Committed on Soviet Territory, 78–79, 101, 125–26, 131–33; in Germany, 1, 46, 149; Jewish Anti-Fascist Committee, 5–6, 113, 124–25; Jews and, 201; in Kyiv, 7–8, 194–95; in press, 17; Soviet Union and, 158, 173–74; symbols of, 175–76
Fedorchuk, Vitalii, 178–83
Fedorovs'ky, D., 147
Fefer, Itzik, 12, 14, 107, 124–25
Feldman, Dvoira, 37
The First Symphony: In Memory of the Martyrs of Babyn Yar (Klebanov), 149–50
Forverts (Forward), Jewish newspaper, 29, 180
France, 144, 214
Fraser, Kieran, 210
French Revolution, 20–21

Fridman, Mikhail, 207
Friedman, Genrietta, 179
Frolov, Kirill, 88
Fuks, Pavel, 207

Galant, Ilia, 17–20
Galich, Alexander, 1
Gal'perin, Yakov, 85–86
Geilig, M., 115
genocide, 3–4, 67–69, 187, 217
Georgia, 116, 177
Germany: 13, 53, 64, Einsatzgruppe C for, 243n49; German-Fascist Crimes Committed on Soviet Territory, 78–79, 101, 125–26, 131–33; German troops, 74–75, 93–94; Gestapo police, 52, 64, 70–71, 81–83, 85–86; Nuremberg trials, 3; Poland and, 16; police in, 58; propaganda from, 221; Red Army in, 79; slave labor in, 92; Soviet Union and, 45–46, 51–52, 79–81, 173–74; Ukraine and, 43–44, 73–74, 92; in World War II, 58–59. *See also* Nazis
Gershenson, Olga, 145–46
Gershman, Ella, 62
Gerzon, David, 118
Gessen, Masha, 217, 219
Gestapo police, 52, 64, 70–71, 81–83, 85–86
Giller, B., 203, *203*
Gitelman, Zvi, 12–13, 26, 152
Glagolev, Aleksey, 62–63
Glagolev, Alexander, 62–63
Glagolev, Tatyana, 63
Glinberg, Anna, *50*
Goldberg, Lev, 6
Goldblatt, Moisei, 139–40
Goldblatt, Moyshe, 98
Golovatenko, Nadiia, 86
Golovchenko, Ivan, 180–82
Goncharenko, Makar, 80–81
Goodfriend, Isaac, 198
Gorbacheva, N. T., 125
Gorbatov, Boris, 145–46
Gordeichuk, N., 115
Gordon, Dmitry, 215

Gorky, Maxim, 32
Gorodetsky, Solomon, 65
Gozenpud, A., 115
Grabar, Ivan, 103–4
Greenbaum, Abraham, 22–23
Grigorenko, Luker'ia, 65
Grigorenko, Mikhail, 65
Grossman, Vasily, 5, 28–29, 31–32, 142. *See also The Black Book*
Grushko, Moisei, 118
Gubergrits, M. M., 114
Gurevich, Ilya Shlyomovich, 113
Gusev, Vladimir A., 199

Häfner, August, 136
Harvard Ukrainian Research Institute, 3
Harvest of Despair (Berkhoff), 90
Hasidism, 18
Heorhienko, Volodymyr, 184
Herz, Manuel, 213–14
Herzog, Isaac, 203, 214
Hicks, Jeremy, 145–46
Himka, John-Paul, 4
Himmler, Heinrich, 58
"The History of Jews in Russia" (Sosis), 25
History of Ukraine, 152
Hitler, Adolf: authority of, 69; Berkhoff on, 73; on Jews, 48
Hofshtein, David, 12–14, 25, 103, 107, 114, 138–40
Hofshtein, Feige, 140
Holocaust: amnesia, 177; Babyn Yar Holocaust Memorial Museum, 96; Babyn Yar massacre and, 39–45, *41*; children in, 42, *50*, 61–63; denial, 1–2; ideology of, 48; Jewish resistance to, 65–66; Jews in, 2–5, 58–61, 160–61, *195–97*; KGB and, 178, 182–83; legacy of, 107–8, 122–23, 158–61, *159*, 221–26; in mass media, 7–8; memoirs, 165–67, *166*, *168*, 169; monuments, 152–57, *155*; Nazis in, 38, 46–47; in 1945 Babyn Yar Monument Project, 154–58, *155–56*; politics of, 61–64, 192; in press, 7–8; Pronicheva on, 43–44; Red Army in, 216–17; reputation of, 36; Shargorod ghetto in, 7; in Soviet Union, 7–8, 47–49, *50*, 65–66, 150, 152–53; suppression of, 178–79, 184; survivors, 24–25, 166–67; in Ukraine, 169–75, *170*, *172*, *174*, 202–3, *203–4*, 205–8, 212–13; United States and, 184, 198–99, 264n179; United States Holocaust Memorial Museum, 208; Wiesel on, 198–200; World Holocaust Remembrance Center, 61; in Yiddish culture, 5, 137–42, 150–51; Zionism and, 186–87. *See also specific topics*
"The Holocaust Memorial Undone by Another War" (Gessen), 217–18
Holodomor: 14, 35–36, 49, 58–60; Jews and, 28–38, 59–60; Korzhavin on, 35–36; in Kyiv, 28–33, 59–60; Nazis and, 90–91; in press, 32–34; Stalin and, 49
Holovanivsky, Sava, 143
Horbacheva, Nadiia, 72
hostages, 89–90
housing, 100–102
Hrynevych, Vladyslav, 141–42, 176–77

Iaroshetskiy, Iakov, 118
Ignashchenko, Anatoly, 188
Ilichev, Leonid, 163–64
informants, 14, 22–23, 26–28, 64, 81, 86
Institute of Jewish Proletarian Culture, 16, 20–25, 37
Investigating Babyn Yar (Dean), 3
Iorish, Klara, 62
Iskol'skaia, E., 62
Israel: xi–xii, 5, 112, 114, 140, 158, 167, 176–77, 181–82, 205–9, 214; Jewish Agency for, 205; Jewish Question, 108–10, 114; Jews in, 206; politics in, 178–79; press in, 217; Ukraine and, 5, 176–77; United States and, 209–10; World Holocaust Remembrance Center in, 61
Iunost', journal, 6, 165
Ivanitsky, Victor, 17–18
Izraelson, Yakov, 17
Izvestia, newspaper, 123, 196–97

Janssen, Adolf, 136–37
Jews: activism by, 169–75, *170*, *172*, 195–96; American Jewish Joint Distribution Committee, 205; in Auschwitz, 143–44; at Babyn Yar, *75*, *129*; in Babyn Yar massacre, 45–47, 51–56, 69–71, *75*, 94–95, *129*; Colorado Committee of Concern for Soviet Jewry, 185; "commercial" stores for, 30; Department of Jewish Language, Literature, and Folklore, 16, 25; evacuation of, 99–101; fascism and, 201; for Gestapo police, 82–83; Hitler on, 48; in Holocaust, 2–5, 58–61, 160–61, *195–97*; Holodomor and, 28–29, 31–33, 35–38, 59–60; in hospitals, 69–70; housing for, 100–102; Institute of Jewish Proletarian Culture, 16, 20–25, 37; in Israel, 206; Jewish Agency for Israel, 205; Jewish Anti-Fascist Committee, 5–6, 113, 124–25; Jewish Communal-Cultural Center, 205; Jewish Communist Workers' Party, 26; Jewish Council of Ukraine, 4; Jewish folklore, 11; Jewish Heritage Center, 4; Jewish Historical-Archaeographical Commission, 16–120; Jewish Historical-Ethnographical Society, 17; Jewish nationalism, 15–16, 112–14; Jewish pogrom, 103–6, 123–24; Jewish Question, 108–10; Jewish resistance, 65–66; Jewish scholarly institutions in, 16; Jewish schools 15–16; Jewish State Children's Theater, 15; KGB and, 175–81, 184; Minsk Institute for Jewish Proletarian Culture, 21–22, 24–25, 231n53; Mogen Davids for, 175–76, 181; Nazis and, 47–49, *50*, 131–37, *132*, *135*, 142; NKVD against, 63; non-Jews and, 35–36; Palestine for, 13–14; in Poland, 13; politics of, 25–28; in press, 193–94; as prisoners of war, 239n103; in proletarianization process, 20–25; propaganda against, 119–20; property of, 53, 55, 60, 90; protection of, 78; Red Army and, 60, 83, 101–2; Roma and, 86–87, 95, 164–65, 189–90; in Russia, *172*, 172–73; Society for Spreading Enlightenment Among Jews in Russia, 19, 22; in Soviet Union, 11–16, 36–38, 54–55, 74, 106–12, 181–83, 192–93; Stalin and, 113–14, 119–21; as survivors, 5–7, 157–58; testimony of, 177–78; torture of, 55, 66, 76–77; in Ukraine, 18, 31–33, 61–64, 112–16, 137–42, 187–92, 221–26; Ukrainian State Jewish Theater of Sholom Aleichem, 14–15, 98, 248n6; in United Kingdom, 6; after World War I, 39–40; after World War II, *132*, 150–51. *See also specific topics*
John Paul II (pope), 203
Joint State Political Directorate (OGPU), 28–29, 34

Kagan, Avraam, 17
Kaganovich, Lazar, 28, 109–11, 113–14
Kaganovich, Pinkhas, 12
Kalnitsky, Mikhail, 142
Kaper, Yakov, 7, 78, 124, 136, 244n82
Kapkov, Konstantin, 87
Karakis, Iosif, 167, *168*, 169
Karakis, Irma, 169
Karamash, Sergiy, 3
Kasianov, Georgii, 4
Katsav, Moshe, 203
Kerl, Richard, 63
KGB: Holocaust and, 178, 182–83; Jews and, 175–81, 184; operations, 172–73; suppression by, 182–84, 224; Zionism and, 177–182
Khain, Khanan, 116–18
Khan, German, 207
Khanin, Vladimir, 4
Kharkiv, 14, 106, 149, 218
Kharkiv Ukrainian Theater, 98–99, *99*
Khinchin, Iona, 22–23
Khinchina, L., 115
Khiterer, Boris, 101–2
Khiterer, Mikhail, 102
Kholmiansky, A., 186–87
Khoroshunova, Irina, 49, 72
"Khreshchatyk's Parisian" (Yevtushenko), 142

Khreshchatyk Street, 9–10, *10*, *98*
Khrushchev, Nikita: anti-Semitism and, 164–65, 223–24; in Babyn Yar, 78, 222, 245n85; Brezhnev and, 201; leadership of, 16, 78, 103, 107–10, 126–28; limited powers of, 156–57; Stalin and, 110, 151; Thaw, 140, 158, 165, 169, 194
Khrzhanovsky, Ilya, 210, 217
The Kiev Trial (documentary), 133
Kin, Ostap, 3
King, Martin Luther, Jr., 199
Kipnis, Itsik, 112, 114, 138–40, 171
Klebanov, Dmitry, 146, 149–50
Kleiner, Izrail, 175–76
Klitschko, Vitaly, 213
Kochubievsky, Boris, 175
Kogen, Lazar', 82
Kogut, Revekka, 95
Koller, Johann, 63
Konrad, Victor, 76–77
Kopystinsky, E. A., 69, 71
Kordik, Iosef, 80
Korey, William, 163
Korotchenko, D., *103*
Korotkikh, Nikolai, 81
Korzhavin, Naum, 28, 30, 33–36, 51, 122
Kostyrchenko, Gennady, 113–14
Kot, Sergii, 84
Kotljarchuk, Andrej, 68
Kovtun, Petr Mikhailovich, 107
Kozlovskaia, N., 78
Kravchuk, Leonid, 202, 208, 225
Kravets, Alexander, 35
Kreuzner, Engelbert, 137
Krivolapov, Mykhailo, 190–91
Kruglov, Alexander, 45, 48, 53, 63, 157, 211
Kruglov, Iosef, 154–55, *155*
Krushel'nitsky, Marian, 98
Krymsky, Agafangel, 17–18, 21
Kudritsky, Mitrofan, 51
Kukhlia, V., 77
Kultur-Lige (Cultural League), 12–13
Kuperman, Sofia, 102–3
Kurenivska tragedy, 161–62, *162*

Kuznetsov, Anatoly, 6, 10–11, 36, 42–43; on Babyn Yar massacre, 49, 91, 165–67, *166*, *168*, 169; on Bolsheviks, 52; on evacuation, 93–94; family of, 49; on Jewish property, 60, 90; memories of, 162–63; resistance by, 203; on Roma, 68
Kvitko, Leib, 14
Kyiv: anti-Semitism in, 2, 51–52, 100–102, 119–21; Babyn Yar massacre and, 47–49, *50*, 65–66, 137–38, 205–6; Babyn Yar Museum in, 4–5; Black Hundreds Organization, 35; Brodsky Choral Synagogue, 27; Central Club of Jewish Handicraftsmen "Der Shtern," 27; children in, 56; concentration camps in, 71–79, *75*; destruction of, 93–94; entertainment in, *99*; environs, *xvi*; Gestapo police in, 64; history of, 36–38; Holodomor in, 28–33, 59–60, 90–91; hostages in, 89–90; Institute of Jewish Proletarian Culture in, 16, 20–25, 37; Jewish Historical-Archaeographical Commission in, 16–120; Jewish pogrom in, 103–6; Jewish scholarly institutions in, 16; Khreshchatyk Street in, *10*; Kiev Group, 12; liberation of, *98*, 126–31, *127*, *129*, *129–30*; Lukianivka Jewish cemetery, 42; map of, *xv*; mass graves in, 160–61; in memoirs, 6; mentally ill people in, 69–71, 95; Nazis in, 6, 51–58, 67, 79–82, 84–87, 91–92, 94–96, 100–101; New Economic Policy in, 10; non-Jews in, 35–36, 49, 51; Office of Visas and Registration, 177; pogroms, 53–55, 103–105; politics in, 158–59; press in, 264n164; prisoners of war in, 95, *129*; public scandals in, 210; rations in, 30; Red Army in, 53–54, 78, 132–33; religious life in, 25–28; Roma in, 67–69, 95; Russia and, 161–62, *162*; Soviet Union and, 221–26; state anti-Semitism in, 112–18; synagogues in, 27, 32; Theological Seminary, 62–63; Ukrainian police in, 56–58; underground movements in, 82–84; war crimes trials in, *132*; women with venereal diseases in, 88–89; World War II and, 11–16, 154–55. *See also specific topics*

Kyiv Institute for Polish Culture, 24
Kyiv Jewish Theater of the Working Youth, 15
Kyiv Trial, 132–133

La Guardia, Fiorello, 130
Lang, Harry, 29–34
Lawrence, W. H., *130*
Leneman, Leon, 127–28
Leningrad, 177, 184
Levich, Alexander, 203, *203*
Levich, Yakim, 203, *203*
Levin, Alexander, 205
Levitas, Feliks, 3, 45
Levitas, Il'ia, 4
Levitsky, Grigory, 83
Liberberg, Joseph, 20–25, 37
Liberman, Veniamin, 52, 62
Lifshitz, Nehama, 140–42
Lion, Pavel, 251n82
Litavry, 85-86
Litoshchenko, Yevgenia, 40
"Little Evidence Supports Story of Nazi Atrocity" (Lawrence), *130*
Lithuanian Jewish Museum, 113
Litvinenko, Valentina, 65
Loburenko, I. L., 103
Loev, Moisei, 15
Loznitsa, Sergei, 215
"Lullaby to Babyn Yar" (Driz), 140–41
Lutsenko, Sergey, 42
Lysenko, Lyudmila, 188–89
Lysenko, Mykhailo, 187–90, 192, 194

Magocsi, Paul Robert, 58
Maksimov, Vadim, 87
Malakov, Dmytro, 92
Malyshko, Andriy, 100
Manger, Mikhail, 182
Markish, Perets, 14
Markov, Aleksei, 163
Markus, Iosif, 83
Markus, Tatiana, 83–84
Marshak, Samuil, 163
"Martyrology" (project), 218

Match of Death, 79–82
media. *See* press
Melamed, Zinovii, 178
Mel'nichenko, Vladimir, 167, *168*, 169, 171, 173
Melnikov, Nikolai, 103–4
Mel'nikov, L. G., 111
Melnyk, Oleksandr, 53, 58–59, 237n75
memoirs, 5–7, 40, 91, 122. *See also specific memoirs*
memorials. *See specific memorials*
Menorah (monument), 203, *203*, 225
mentally ill people, 69–71, 95
The Merchant of Venice (Shakespeare), 14
Metzger, Yona, 206
MIFLI. *See* Moscow Institute of Philosophy, Literature and History
Mikhasev, T., 40
Mikhoels, Solomon, 139–40
Mikoian, Arseny, 62
Miletsky, Avraam, 160, 167, *168*, 169
Minsk, 113, 142, 153, 193
Minsk Institute for Jewish Proletarian Culture, 21–22, 24–25, 231n53
Minsky, Oleg, 42
Mirkina, Irina, 63
Mirkina, Izabella, 63
Mirror Field (memorial), 211–12, *212*, 219–20
Mitsel, Mikhail, 116
Mizhiritsky, Moishe, 124
Mogen Davids, 175–76, 181
Moldavanka district, 11
Moldova, 209–10
Molotov, Vyacheslav, 45–46, 124, 126
"A Monument at Babyn Yar" (Aizenshtadt), 156
monuments. *See specific monuments*
Morozov, I., 76
Morrison, Edward, 180
Moscow, 6, 15, 23, 161, 163, 175, 177, 181, 186, 193, 196, 200
Moscow Institute of Philosophy, Literature and History (MIFLI), 6
Moscow Opera Theater, 15
Moscow State Jewish Theater (Moscow GOSET), 139

The Most Famous Symphony of the 20th Century (Yevtushenko), *164*
mud flood, 161–62, *162*

Nabaranchuk, Volodymyr, 68
Nachmanovich, Vitalii, 7, 44–45, 57, 68–69, 85, 219
Naimark, Norman, 210
Nakhmanovich, Rafail, 173, 225
"Names" project, 211–12
nationalism: anti-Semitism and, 9–10, 60–61, 151; in Cold War, 112–13; Jewish, 15–16, 112–14; OUN-M, 47, 58–59; politics of, 58–59; propaganda for, 175; in Russia, 35; in Ukraine, 3, 19, 84–87, 95
Nazis: in Babyn Yar massacre, 36, 160–61; in BYHMC, 136–37; collaboration with, 101–2; crime by, 78; destruction by, 93–94; executions by, 44–45, 65–66; in Holocaust, 38, 46–47; hostages of, 89–90; interrogations by, 53–54; Jews and, 47–49, *50*, 131–37, *132*, *135*, 142; in Kyiv, 6, 51–58, 67, 79–82, 84–87, 91–92, 94–96, 100–101; in memoirs, 40; against mentally ill people, 69–71; NKVD and, 47–48; non-Jews for, 52; at Nuremberg trials, 150; in press, 129–30, *130*; with prisoners of war, 71–79, 75, 194–95, 198, 203, 205; propaganda by, 51, 59–60, 104–5, 122; prostitutes for, 88–89; Red Army and, 62; reputation of, 46, 65; resistance against, 82–84, 190; against Roma, 67–69; against Russian Orthodox clergy, 87–88; Soviet Union and, 39–40, 164–66; in Ukraine, 216–17; Ukrainian police and, 43–45; in Ukrainian press, 58–61; in war crimes trials, *135*; World War II and, 1–2, 131–37, *132*, *135*
Nekrasov, Victor, 10, 48, 158–61; on activism, 174–75; on censorship, 223; colleagues of, 173; Diamant and, *170*, 170–71; reputation of, 170; on Soviet Union, 198; on victims, 169
Netherlands, 209–10
New Economic Policy, 10
1945 Babyn Yar Monument Project, 154–58, 155–56
New York City, 180
New York Student Committee for Aid to Soviet Jews, 182
The New York Times, 4, 177
The Ninth Wave (Ehrenburg), 143–44
NKGB. *See* Security Service of Ukraine
NKVD. *See* People's Commissariat of Internal Affairs
Nothing is Forgotten (memoir), 7
Nuremberg trials, 3, 46, 133–34, 150

Odesa, 11, 22, 116, 140, 153, 177, 184
Office of Visas and Registration, Kyiv, 177
"O Freedom" (song), 198–99
OGPU. *See* Joint State Political Directorate
Ohloblyn, Oleksader, 73, 79–80
Oleinikov, A., 120–21
O'Neill, Eugene, 14
Organization of Ukrainian Nationalists (OUN), 47, 58–59, 84–87, 203–4
Orlova, Pelageya, 106
Osokina, Elena, 33–34
Ostrovsky, Leonid, 76–78, 128, *129*
OUN-M. *See* Organization of Ukrainian Nationalists
Ovchinnikov, Elena, 146–48
Ovchinnikov, Vasily, 146–48
Ozerov, Lev, 6, 143, 159

Pale of Settlement, 9, 36
Palestine: Jewish Question, 108–10; for Jews, 13–14; press in, 106; World War II and, 13, 114, 144
Palladin, Aleksandr Vladimirovich, 19–20
Palti, Mania, 63
Paris, 86, 127, 142–44, 187, 198
Paskevich, Yury, 203, *203*
Paton, Evgenii Oskarovich, 116
Pavlov Psychiatric Hospital, 69–71
People's Commissariat of Internal Affairs (NKVD): 46, 56; informants, 14, 22–23, 26–28, 81; against Jews, 63; Nazis and, 47–48; in press, 56–57; prisons, 55; Spivak and, 115

perestroika, 150, 186–87
Pervach, Mykola, 85
Pervomaisky, Leonid, 113
Petelevich, Yuzef Markovich, 105–6
Petliura, Simon, 56, 238n91
Petrenko, Natalia, 78, 125
Petrovsky-Shtern, Yohanan, 172, 178
Pihido, Fedir, 41–42
Pinchuk, Victor, 207
Pinkus, Benjamin, 112–13, 118
Pisar, Samuel, 167, 215
Po'alei-Zion, the Jewish Communist Workers' Party, 26
Podil district, 10–11, 27, 54
Poland: Germany and, 16; Jews in, 13; Russia and, 17; United States and, 33–34
Polevoy, Boris, 126–27
Polian, Pavel, 3, 134, 150–51, 156
Polianker, Grigoriy, 171
Polinovsky, Iosif, 40
politics: Cold War, 198–201; of communism, 24–25, 169; of crime, 26–28; of genocide, 217; of Holocaust, 61–64, 192; in Israel, 178–79; of Jews, 25–28; in Kyiv, 158–59; minorities in, 12; of nationalism, 58–59; racial, 67–69, 86–87; in Russia, 5; in Soviet Union, 18–19; in Ukraine, 175–84
Polonsky, Antony, xi
popular anti-Semitism, 2–4, 7, 35–36, 101, 103, 106–13, 116–18, 122, 126, 130, 144, 152–53, 200–201, 205, 222, 225
The Porajmos (the Romani genocide), 67
Poroshenko, Petro, 207
Prakhov, Nikolai Andrianovich, 93
Pravda, newspaper, 45–46, 104–5, 119, 121, 123–24, 155, 196–97
President's Commission on the Holocaust, 198–200
press: anti-Semitism in, 4, 183; Babyn Yar massacre in, 85, 142–45, 196–99, 255n57; "Doctor's Plot" in, 119–21; genocide in, 3–4; Gestapo police in, 85; Holocaust in, 7–8; Holodomor in, 32–34; in Israel, 217; Jews in, 193–94; in Kyiv, 264n164; mass media, 7–8; monuments in, 156; Nazis in, 129–30, *130*; NKVD in, 56–57; in Palestine, 106; party, *127*; poetry in, 163–65, *164*; propaganda in, 125–26; Red Army in, 159–60; in Russia, 17; slave labor in, 92; in Soviet Union, 118, 123–24; in Ukraine, 58–61, 208–9; in United States, 6, 180; after World War II, 5–7; Yiddish culture in, 15
prisoners of war: children as, 7; escape by, 7; Jews as, 239n103; in Kyiv, 95, *129*; Nazis with, 71–79, *75*, 194–95, 198, 203, 205; Soviet Union, 1, 45, *75*
proletarianization process: in Soviet Union, 13, 20–25; in Ukraine, 20–25, 37
Pronicheva, Dina, 6, 43–44, 57, *132*, 136
propaganda: for anti-Semitism, 66, 224; about Babyn Yar massacre, 123–26; from Germany, 221; by Hitler, 218; against Jews, 119–20; for nationalism, 175; by Nazis, 51, 59–60, 104–5, 122; by NKGB, 106–7; in press, 125–26; by Soviet Union, 1–2, 121, 142, 150–51
prostitutes, 88–89
Putin, Vladimir, 218
Pyr'ev, Ivan, 146

Quitzrau, Helmut, 92

racial politics, 67–69, 86–87
Radetsky, Victor, 62
von Radetzky, Waldemar, 135, 137
Radomski, Paul, 75
Rakhlin, Natan, 149
Rapson, Jessica, 4
Rasch, Otto, 135
rations, 28–30
Red Army: in Germany, 79; in Holocaust, 216–17; Jews and, 60, 83, 101–2; in Kyiv, 53–54, 78, 132–33; Nazis and, 62; in press, 159–60
Red Cross, 73–74
refuseniks, 177, 182, 193
repression, 13–14, 19, 23–25, 28, 34, 36–37, 49, 51, 53, 109, 140, 165, 169, 173, 175, 178, 182, 184, 221, 224

Reznik, Lipe, 14–15
Riasnoi, V., 105
Riga, 132, 153, 171, 175, 177, 181
Righteous Among the Nations, 61, 64, 95, 212, 218
Righteous of Babyn Yar, 61, 64
The Righteous of Babyn Yar (Levitas, I.), 4
riots, 104–5
Rivlin, Reuven, 203
Road of the Doomed (painting), 147–49, *148*
Rodin, Auguste, 187–88
Rogach, Ivan, 59, 61
Ro'i, Yaacov, 140–41
Rokhlin, Oskar, 118
Roma: Jews and, 86–87, 95, 164–65, 189–90; memorials for, 203, *204*; Nazis against, 67–69
The Roma Wagon (monument), 203, *204*
Romm, Mikhail, 146
Rosenfeld, Sholem, 128
Rostov-on-Don, 201
Rozenshtein, Iosif, 103–4
Rubenstein, Joshua, 6, 144
Rubinshtein, Abram Yakovlevich, 62
Rudling, Per Anders, 57–58
Rukkas, Andrii, 70
Russia: Bolsheviks in, 18; communism in, 67, 201; culture of, 37; Jews in, *172*, 172–73; MIFLI, 6; Moscow Opera Theater, 15; nationalism in, 35; Poland and, 17; politics in, 5; press in, 17; Russian Empire, 9, 11–12, 18, 48; Russian Orthodox clergy, 87–88; Society for Spreading Enlightenment Among Jews in Russia, 19, 22; Ukraine and, 11, 16, 52, 207–8, *216*, 216–20; Yiddish culture in, 11–16. *See also* Red Army; Soviet Union
Rustin, Bayard, 198–99, 265n182
Rybachuk, Ada, 167, *168*, 169, 171, 173, 187
Rybinsky, Valery, 17–18

Sabaldyr, Viacheslav, 81–82
Sanders, Edward, 198
Sapir, Rebekka Yakovlevna, 62
Savchenko, Serhii, 107, 131

Savitskiy, Pelageia, 64–65
Savitskiy, Vladimir, 64
Schlesinger, Elyakim, 206
Schulte, Christian, 137
Schwarz, Solomon M., 100–101, 109, 116
Security Service of Ukraine (NKGB), 53, 103, 106–7
September 29 (art), 146–48, *148*
SETMAS (Union of Jewish Working People), 25
Shakespeare, William, 14
Sharansky, Anatoly, 182, 208
Shargorod ghetto, 7
Shcheglov, Yuri (Yuri Varshaver), 48
Shcherbakov, A., 126
Shcherbytsky, Volodymyr, 60, 178, 180–83, 191–92
Schwarz, Solomon M., 100
Shelest, Petro, 169, 178, 191
Shepelevsky, N. A., 88–89
Shevchenko, Taras, 85, 97–98
Shlaien, Alexander, 3, 184, 187
Shlikhter, Alexander, 37, 234n123
Shneer, David, 13–14, 129
Shoah, 67
Sholom Aleichem, 97–100, 140, 248n4
Shostakovich, Dmitri, 163, *164*, 215
Shovenko, Oleh, 217
Shrayer, Maxim, D., 143
Der Shtern (newspaper), 16
Shternshis, Anna, 251n82
Shtetl, 28
Shtif, Nokhem (Naum), 20–21, 25
Shul'gin, Vasilii, 9–10, 229n3
Siberia, 13, 108, 114
Simonov, Konstantin, 144, 146, 163
slave labor, 91–92
Smirnov, Lev, 133–34
Smirnov, Sergei, 159
Smolar, Hirsh, 142
Snegirev, Gelii, 173
Snyder, Timothy, 52
Society for Spreading Enlightenment Among Jews in Russia, 19, 22

Sokolovsky, Elena, 102
Sokolovsky, Tsil'ia, 102
Soloviev, Ivan, 108–9
Sonderkommando 4a, 48, 63
Soroko, Yurii, 178
Sosis, Israel, 24–25
Soviet Jews write to Ilya Ehrenburg (letters collection), 144–45
"Soviet Reactions to the Holocaust" (Gitelman), 152
Sovetish Heymland, journal, 193
"Soviets Seized Cash Sent by U.S. Kin to Starving Russians" (Lang), 34
Soviet Union: anti-Semitism in, 2–3, 7–8, 177; authority in, 67, 106–12; Babyn Yar and, 187–94, *189, 191*; Babyn Yar massacre in, 158–61, *159*, 194–200, *195–97*; censorship in, 32–33, 143, 149–50, 165–66, 229n3; Colorado Committee of Concern for Soviet Jewry, 185; crime in, 23–24, 31, 174–75; culture of, 9–10; death sentences in, 232n69; détente in, 4, 194, 199–201, 224; "Doctor's Plot" in, 119–21; fascism and, 158, 173–74; German-Fascist Crimes Committed on Soviet Territory, 78–79, 101, 125–26, 131–33; Germany and, 45–46, 51–52, 79–81, 173–74; history of, 7, 36–38; Holocaust in, 7–8, 47–49, *50*, 65–66, 150, 152–53; Jews in, 11–16, 36–38, 54–55, 74, 106–12, 181–83, 192–93; Kyiv and, 221–26; Nazis and, 39–40, 164–66; Nekrasov on, 198; perestroika in, 150, 186–87; politics in, 18–19; press in, 118, 123–24; prisoners of war, 1, 45, *75*; proletarianization process in, 13, 20–25; propaganda by, 1–2, 121, 142, 150–51; slave labor in, 91–92; Stalin for, 122; Torgsin stores in, 33–34; Ukraine and, 4, 31–33, 107, 113, 131–37, *132, 135*, 148–49, 234n123; United States and, 200–201; World War II and, 5, 45–46; Yiddish culture in, 193–94, 199–200. *See also* Red Army; Russia
Spektor, Boris, 104
Spivak, Elie, 5–6, 19–20, 25, 114–15

sports, 79–82
Stalin, Joseph: Cold War after, 130; communism by, 14; Holodomor and, 49; and Jews, 104, 113–14, 119–21; Khrushchev and, 110, 151; leadership of, 113; reputation of, 108–9, 144; for Soviet Union, 122; suppression by, 36; in World War II, 39
Stanislavsky, Constantin, 14–15
Starikov, Dmitri, 163
Start, soccer team, 80
state anti-Semitism, 2, 4–5, 7, 100, 111–19, 121–22, 129, 144, 151, 153–54, 157–58, 160, 183, 192, 201–202, 223–225
Steinbeck, John, 249n8
Steinmeier, Frank-Walter, 214
Steiuk, Yakov, 72, 78
Stepanenko, V., 45
The Storm (Ehrenburg), 143–44
Stragorodsky, Sergiy, 87
Stuckert, Carl, 84
Sudoplatov, Pavel, 109
Sukalo, Akulina, 63–64
Sukalo, Berta, 64
Sukalo, Roman, 63–64
Sukhenko, Victor, 187, 190–92, 194
Sukhonin, V., 171–72
suppression: of minorities, 37; by Stalin, 36; of Yiddish culture, 152–53, 174–75
Sverdlovsk, 177
Sviridenko, Ivan Petrovich, 62
Sviridenko, Ludmila, 62
Sviridovsky, Mikhail, 81
Symonenko, Natalie, 150
Syrets concentration camp, 7, 63, 65, 74, 76, 79, 82

"Take Away the Mask" (*Der Shtern*), 15
Tantsiura, Musii, 70
Tartakovskaia, Sara, 139
Tbilisi, 193
Teliga, Olena, 85–86
Teplitskiy, Lev, 118
Terno, Valentin, 60
Tevye the Dairyman, 97–99, *99*, 248n4

Textile Affair, 116–18
Thirteenth Symphony: Babi Yar (Shostakovich), 163, 215
Tkachenko, Aleksandr, 81–82
Tkachenko, Natalia, 64–65
Tolkachev, Zinoviy, 147–48
Topographies of Suffering (Rapson), 4
Torah scrolls, 27
Torgsin stores, 33–34, 240n113
torture: communism and, 81; by German troops, 74–75; of Jews, 55, 66, 76–77; of women, 84
trade, with Ukraine, 33–34
Trill, Viktor, 136
Trubakov, Zakhar, 77, 183
Tsiferblit, Itskhak, 182
Tychina, Pavlo, 134

Ukraine: anti-Semitism in, 36–38, 47–49, 110–11; authority in, 103–6; Bolsheviks in, 56, 109–10, 238n91; children in, 63; civil war in, 12–13, 16–17; communism in, 60–61, 111–12, 121, 141–42; culture of, 189–90; Germany and, 43–44, 73–74, 92; Gestapo police in, 81; history of, 1–2; Holocaust in, 169–75, *170, 172, 174,* 202–3, *203–4,* 205–8, 212–13; Holodomor in, 28–29; independence of, 7, 17, 58–59, 202–3, *203–4,* 205–6; informants in, 14; Israel and, 5, 176–77; Jewish Council of Ukraine, 4; Jewish Question in, 108–10; Jews in, 18, 31–33, 61–64, 112–16, 137–42, 187–92, 221–26; Kharkiv Ukrainian Theater, 98–99, *99;* memoirs from, 91; nationalism in, 3, 19, 84–87, 95; Nazis in, 216–17; NKGB in, 53, 103, 106–7; OGPU in, 28–29, 34; OUN-M in, 47, 58–59; politics in, 175–84; press in, 58–61, 208–9; proletarianization process in, 20–25, 37; Red Cross, 73–74; Russia and, 11, 16, 52, 207–8, *216,* 216–20; Social Security Administration of, 19–20; Soviet Union and, 4, 31–33, 107, 113, 131–37, *132, 135,* 148–49, 234n123; Textile Affair, 116–18; trade with, 33–34; Ukrainian Academy of Sciences, 16–19, 25; Ukrainian Americans, 185–86; Ukrainian Communist Party, 28; Ukrainian police, 40–41, 43–45, 56–58; Ukrainian National Council, 85; Ukrainian Red Cross, 73; Ukrainian State Jewish Theater of Sholom Aleichem, 14–15, 98, 139, 248n6; after World War II, 100–101; World War II and, 9–11, *10,* 100–101, 157. *See also specific topics*
Ukrains'ke slovo, newspaper, 56, 59, 61, 72, 73, 85, 92
Umansky, Andrej, 53, 63, 136, 137
underground movements, 82–87
United Kingdom, 6
United Nations Relief and Rehabilitation Administration, 130
United States: activism in, 265n182; American Jewish Joint Distribution Committee, 205; Babi Yar Memorial Park in, 4; on Babyn Yar massacre, 177–78; Colorado Committee of Concern for Soviet Jewry, 185; Denver in, 184–86; diplomacy, 199–200; Germany and, 214; Holocaust and, 184, 198–99, 264n179; Holocaust Memorial Museum, 208; Israel and, 209–10; Poland and, 33–34; press in, 6, 180; Soviet Union and, 200–201; in World War II, 167; Yiddish culture in, 29
The Unknown Black Book (Altman and Rubenstein), 6
The Unvanquished (film), 145–46
The Unvanquished (Gorbatov), 145–46
Unwelcome Memory (Zeltser), 152–53
Ustinov, Egor, 53–55
Utesov, Leonid, 11, 163

Vainshtein, David, 17–18
Vakhtangov, Evgeniy, 15
Varshaver, Yuri, 48
Vaslits, M., 105
Vecherniy Kiev, newspaper, 118, 183
Vergelis, Arn, 193–94
Verkhovna Rada (Parliament of Ukraine), 202

The Vernadsky Library of the Academy of Sciences of Ukraine, 22
Vershilov, Boris, 14–15
"Vershilovshchina" (*Der Shtern*), 15
Viachkis, Georgy, 81
Vidrodzhennia, newspaper, 60
Vilkis, Efim, 77, 128, *129*
Vilna (Vilnus), 20, 113
Vishniakov. See Aleksandr, Archimandrite
Vitryk, Oleksandr, 187, 190–92, 194
Vlasiuk, Feofan, 78
Vlasov, Aleksandr, 154–57, *155*
Voinovich, Vladimir, 173
Volkov, Solomon, 163
Vons, Ester, 39–40
Vynnychuk, Yuriy, 205

war crimes trials, 131–37, *132*, *135*
Warsaw, 13
"What is going on in Kyiv" (Stepanenko), 45
"Why Isn't This Done?" (Nekrasov), 223
Wiesbreim, Arkadiy, 63–64
Wiesbreim, Lidia, 63–64
Wiesbreim, Raisa, 63–64
Wiesel, Elie, 166, 198–200
Winchevsky, Morris, 21–22
Wise, Stephen S., 34
"Without Podol Kiev Is Impossible" (song), 11
women, 74, 84, 88–89
World War I, 39–40
World War II: anti-Semitism and, 7, 97–99, *98*, *99*, 103–6, 121–22; Babyn Yar and, *41*, 126–31, *127*, *129–30*; Babyn Yar massacre and, 221–26; censorship after, 2; Cold War and, 151; communism after, 108–9; Germany in, 58–59; Jews after, *132*, 150–51; Kyiv and, 11–16, 154–55; Nazis and, 1–2, 131–37, *132*, *135*; NKVD after, 133–34; Nuremberg trials after, 3; Palestine and, 13, 114, 144; popular anti-Semitism after, 153; popular culture after, 11; press after, 5–7; research on, 67; Soviet Union and, 5, 45–46; Stalin in, 39; Ukraine and, 9–11, *10*, 100–101, 157; United States in, 167
Worzberger, Paul, 63
"A Writer Proposes" (Nekrasov), 159–60

Yad Vashem, 61, 66, 95, 158, 212
Yad Vashem Archive, 6
Yahad-In Unum, 214
Yanukovich, Victor, 205
Yasinsky, Oleg, 81
Yegorycheva, Mariya, 63
Yermak, Andriy, 213
Yevtushenko, Yevgeny, 142, 162–65, *164*, 169, 223
Yiddish culture: poetry from, 22, 25, 140–41; in press, 15; in Russia, 11–16; suppression of, 114, 152–53, 174–75; in United States, 29
Yiddish Glory (album), 114, 251n82
Young, James, 186
Yushchenko, Victor, 84, 205
Yushchinsky, Andriusha, 63
Yushkov, Nikifor, 53–54, 237n75
Yusupov, Usman, 109
YIVO (Yiddish Scientific Institute), 20

Zabarko, Boris, 7
Zak, Lev, 69
Zatonsky, Volodymyr, 24
Zavorotna, Liudmila, 68
Zelensky, Volodymyr, 212–18, 225
Zeltser, Arkadi, 152–53
Zhdanov, Andrei, 113
"Zhil — byl na Podole Gop so smykom" (song), 11
Zhitov, I. N., 93
Zhytomyr, 194
Zionism, 25–26, 122, 174; censorship of, 15–16; Holocaust and, 186–87; for KGB, 182; Mogen Davids and, 181
Zmievskaia Balka, 201
Zubov, Andrei, 29
Zuskin, Veniamin, 145

ABOUT THE AUTHOR

DR. VICTORIA KHITERER IS A PROFESSOR OF HISTORY AT MILLERSVILLE University of Pennsylvania. Khiterer was born and grew up in Kyiv, Ukraine. She is the daughter and granddaughter of Holocaust survivors. Khiterer is a founding member of the Academic Council of the Babyn Yar Holocaust Memorial Center in Kyiv. She is the author and editor of eight books and over a hundred articles on Ukrainian, Russian, and Eastern European Jewish history and the Holocaust. Her book *Jewish City or Inferno of Russian Israel? A History of the Jews in Kiev Before February 1917* received the Choice Outstanding Academic Titles Award in 2017.